Off the Road

Off the Road

Twenty Years with Cassady, Kerouac, and Ginsberg

CAROLYN CASSADY

THE OVERLOOK PRESS
Woodstock & New York

This edition first published in the United States in 2008 by
The Overlook Press, Peter Mayer Publishers, Inc.
Woodstock & New York

WOODSTOCK:
One Overlook Drive
Woodstock, NY 12498
www.overlookpress.com
[for individual orders, bulk and special sales, contact our Woodstock office]

NEW YORK:
141 Wooster Street
New York, NY 10012

First edition published in the United States in 1990
by William Morrow and Company, Inc.
Revised edition published in the United Kingdom in 2007
by Black Spring Press Ltd.

The author would like to thank the following for permission to quote
material in this book: Allen Ginsberg, Gregory Corso, Diana Hansen, Anne Murphy,
Gavin Arthur, Ken Kesey, Elsie Sechrist, Hugh Lynn, and Creative Arts Book
Company (for excerpts from As Ever: The Collected Correspondence of Allen
Ginsberg and Neal Cassady, 1977). Thanks also to the University of Texas for
cooperation in the preparation of this volume.

Cataloging-in-Publication Data is available from the Library of Congress

Manufactured in the United States of America
ISBN 978-1-59020-104-6
1 3 5 7 9 8 6 4 2

To Helen and Al Hinkle

*For He shall give His angels
charge over thee to guard thee
in all thy ways.*

PSALMS 91:11

Portrait of Neal Cassady, by Carolyn Cassady, 1951.

In the middle of the journey of our life
I came into myself in a dark wood
where the straight way was lost.

Ah! how hard a thing it is to tell what a wild and rough
and stubborn wood this was,
which in my thought renews the fear!

So bitter is it that scarcely more is death;
but to treat of the good that I there found,
I will relate the other things that I discerned.

Dante, *The Divine Comedy, Inferno*, Canto I

Off the Road

PART ONE

| ONE |

A little past two o'clock on that Saturday afternoon in March, 1947, the phone rang in my hotel sitting room. Bill Tomson's affected tough-guy drawl was unmistakable. 'H'lo, doll, c'n I come up for a minute?' I hesitated; Bill was becoming a nuisance. He had been turning up on campus nearly every day, and I was finding his impromptu appearances increasingly tedious. Out of curiosity I had continued to talk to him, but so far I had failed to find any subject that he would discuss seriously. He confined his conversation to what he thought would impress me – smart retorts, wild bravado and stories of extraordinary exploits, either his own or those of a friend, one Neal Cassady. Neal was a hero, like Othello, whose praises needed singing, and Bill assumed the role of passionate disciple. He told me of daring escapades in cars, brushes with the law, deep intellectual and musical safaris.

Raised in fear and reverence for the prevailing social code of the Thirties and having led a sheltered, restricted existence, I was amazed to learn from Bill that there were men who dared to live like the characters in my books and movies – if, of course, Bill was not exaggerating. In any case, the life he described was remote and unthreatening to me; I wasn't about to fall in love with Bill, and he told me Neal was in New York studying at Columbia University with two friends, Jack Kerouac and Allen Ginsberg, one a famous football player, the other a poet.

Bill looked vaguely like some movie star whose name I'd long forgotten, and this afternoon I could visualize him leaning on the bar in the hotel lobby, a glass of Scotch in one hand, the other twisting knots in the phone cord, a cigarette dangling from his lips, one eye squinting from the smoke and the other from thick black hair that refused to stay back no matter how often he tossed his head.

After a lengthy silence, I responded, 'All right, Bill, but only for a minute; I have a lot of work to do.' When I opened the door at his knock, I discovered he was not alone. Behind him stood another man who strode past me into the room, his eyes cataloguing the contents before he turned to acknowledge Bill's introduction.

'Cari, this is Neal Cassady.' I could only stare, unhinged at seeing the myth materialize. Neal nodded, and in that instant, the sweep of his blue eyes made me feel I had been thoroughly appraised. I cursed Bill's failure to warn me.

The advance publicity on this man had already rendered him unique, but I was not prepared for his appearance – not so much his physical attributes, which were all fairly average, but his suit. Though not an authentic 'zoot', it had that aura, and I'd never been closer to one than the movie-screen gangsters. It gave him a Runyonesque flavour, a dangerous glamour, heightened by his white T-shirt and bare muscular neck.

Neal walked across the room, seeing a phonograph and a stack of LPs under the window. He turned to me, still a statue by the door.

'Bill tells me you have an unusual collection of Lester Young records.' Bewildered, I stammered: 'Who? Lester who? I…uh… no…unusual, yes; I'm afraid I've not heard of him – all I have are leftovers from college – swing mostly – big bands.' I glared at Bill for this further embarrassment. Neal, too, looked at Bill for a second, mystified. Then he smiled, sat down in my rocker and began flipping through the albums.

'No matter. What have we here? Ah, yes, I see, Artie Shaw, good, the Dorseys, Benny Goodman, great, Harry James, Nat King Cole, Stan Kenton, the Duke – a lot of Ellington. Ah, and what is this?' He held up a boxed set by Josh White.

'That's *Southern Exposure*. It's about as radical as we ever got in college. We were impressed by Josh and his black protest songs about their poor housing, Jim Crow trains, etc. It is banned in the south, I hear. When I lived in New York I got to know Josh a little – I sat at a front table in a club and drew him while he played. I found that ploy worked really well if you wanted to meet an artist. But I was surprised and disappointed finding that he didn't want to discuss the subjects of his work. Probably a good thing, really. That can get sticky.'

I knew I was babbling, but Neal sat transfixed, emitting an empathy and dignity that made me feel special, as if my every word were a gem. Beneath his subtle charm I sensed a taut energy that was subdued and restrained, like a drawn bow.

When I stopped and looked down blushing, he smiled more broadly.

'Fascinating. May I play something?' His eyebrows always sloped upwards and inwards at the centre when he asked a question.

'Of course – please.'

As he placed a record carefully on the turntable, I dived to the floor to gather together the pieces of model stage scenery on which I had been working. Bill stopped pacing and sat in the armchair opposite Neal. Ellington's 'Sophisticated Lady' filled the room, and no one spoke. I glanced up at Neal and quickly down again. As he rocked, his eyes fastened on me so intensely, I felt a physical stab. I was sure he sensed my discomfort, but I also felt those eyes like lasers, unwavering until the record ended. Moving to remove it, Neal's manner eased. I stood up and pottered about the room pretending to straighten things.

Further attempts at conversation were awkward, largely due, I supposed, to the false ideas Bill had given Neal and me. I didn't know how I had been described, except probably as 'My girl', but from Neal's answers to my polite questions, I sensed that Bill's tales of derring-do were attributable solely to Neal. When I shifted the credit for these *beaux gestes* to Neal, Bill had even less to commend him, and Neal began to acquire a layer of enchantment.

Neal was scarcely controlling his restlessness, and Bill was beginning to fidget. Neal looked from Bill to me.

'Well now, you two – do you have any plans for this afternoon?' I wistfully surveyed my scenery project, and Neal picked up the cue.

'Couldn't it wait? Just for an hour or so? I'll bet you need some fresh air. Look, why don't you come with me? I just got off the Greyhound and have to get my things from the house where I used to live. Then we could go downtown – or anything you like.' Neal delivered these suggestions rapidly, not pausing for reply, and then moved towards the door, turning to me with a question in his eyes. Bill got up to follow him.

'Come on, Cari, get your coat.' Over and above my conviction that I should stay home and work, to say nothing of my appearance, I had a compelling desire to see more of this man. I got my coat.

| TWO |

The Denver afternoon air was sharp and exhilarating; the late winter sun made us squint from its brightness on the snow, and was more cheering than warm. We caught a bus in the opposite direction from my daily route to the university. Although I didn't know it, so began a long journey in a direction opposite to any I had ever taken and towards an education of an entirely different nature.

I had been raised, the youngest of five children, in a small college town in Michigan, with glorious summers at a northern lake which we continued to visit until World War II. When I was eight we moved to a home near Nashville, Tennessee where my father got a better job. Although frugal, we lacked for no material or educational needs. I attended both an elite prep school and college, and in a few years Dad bought and restored an old plantation. My parents were strict in Victorian values and English customs; physical contact was discouraged after infancy, and approval given without enthusiasm. My father was a biochemist, my mother an ex-English teacher, and we had a library of over two thousand five hundred books. I became a portrait painter and a designer for theatre productions, the two fields I was studying for my MA degree at the University of Denver, where I was also employed as a teaching assistant.

On arrival at Neal's former lodgings he busied himself about the house, collecting and packing his belongings while Bill and I waited in the cluttered parlour. Neal had a disarming way of looking at me whenever he brushed past, yet he said nothing. His glances and the silence were generating an alarming magnetism that was beginning to unsettle me. On one of these passes he handed me a typewritten love poem 'by Neal Cassady'. No judge of poetry, I could see the poem had been written by someone who was. My admiration jumped up a notch.

When Neal finished his packing we walked to the corner to catch a downtown bus. Our first stop was a small, shabby hotel where in a second-floor room strewn with women's clothing and accessories Neal deposited his bags beside an unmade bed. No explanation was forthcoming. We then walked a few blocks to a tiny short-order café, where Bill and I waited on the sidewalk outside while Neal went in. Through the entrance, which gave out a strong smell of onions, I could see Neal having a heated conversation with a pretty teenage girl behind the counter. My curiosity overruled my scruples, and I badgered Bill until he ran out of dodges and blurted, 'She's his wife, LuAnne.'

His *wife*? My heart dropped suddenly, enough to make me realize the strength of the attraction Neal already held for me. Married? I could not reconcile the impression I had been forming of Neal with the restrictions of married life as I knew it, especially at his tender age of just turned 21. Why had Bill never told me an important fact like that? And if married he be, why was he looking at me in a distinctly unmarried manner?

There was no question in my mind now that that was definitely that. Married men were strictly off-limits, and besides, I now faced the other taboo I'd been trying to ignore: Neal was nearly three years younger than I. The afternoon seemed much less sunny.

When Neal rejoined us he made no mention of his encounter and, smiling broadly with those perfect teeth, suggested we go to a music store to listen to records, since, as he put it, 'I've no place for a phonograph of my own.' Bill and I walked as fast as I was able, but Neal skimmed ahead, every now and then wheeling to face us, walking backwards but never breaking stride. He shouted remarks and flashed his grin, his light brown hair ruffling in the wind, then pivoted again to swing down the street, his coat flapping. He was caught up in observing everything and everybody around him, but was unrelenting in his intimate glances at me. Now I avoided his gaze.

When we arrived at a music store, he bustled about piloting us to a glassed-in booth then rushed out again to return with several records – not Lester Young, but selections inspired by my collection, the most cherished in our memories of this day being Benny Goodman's 'Sing, Sing, Sing'.

Neal was utterly fascinating to watch as he listened to music. He was passionately involved with every instrument, every note, every phrase. He shared his delight by insisting that I become as engrossed as he was, repeating nuances I might have missed, calling my attention to an impending riff, while his face glowed in a wide grin and he exulted, 'Ahhhh – hear *that*?' or with eyes closed, 'Listen now, *listen* – hear it? WhoooeeEE!' followed by gleeful giggling and head-shaking as he clapped his hands and bounced his knees to the beat.

We must have been absorbed like this for two hours or more. I supposed he was waiting for LuAnne to get off work, but neither he nor Bill enlightened me. My curiosity leading me astray, I followed along, spellbound.

Once more in the street, Neal halted, furrowed his brow, then brightened again.

'I know – why don't we all have dinner together? I'll see if I can get Al Hinkle and his girl, Lois, to join us; I haven't seen Al yet. We'll meet at the usual place, huh, Bill? How about it, Carolyn?' And before I could respond, Neal had swept down the street, pirouetting to flash that smile and wave.

Bill and I waited at the appointed restaurant until we were too hungry to hold out any longer. While we sipped our final cup of coffee and I began to feel irritated, a tall blond man leaned over our booth and softly murmured, 'Hi.' Bill and I moved over to make room for Al and Lois, and Bill introduced me. Al apologized for not getting the message in time to join us for dinner, and he passed along an excuse for Neal.

'You see ...' Al stopped, embarrassed. 'Since Neal only arrived today, this is the first time he's seen LuAnne for several weeks, so, uh, they were ... delayed when she went back to the hotel to change.' His eyes scanned my face for a reaction and found it blank. 'But,' he hastened on, 'we're all going to get together at your hotel room, Neal said, to celebrate his homecoming.'

My surprise and shyness prevented me from objecting, but I wondered why *my* room? I mentally surveyed the disorder in which we had left it. They were all natives of Denver; didn't any of them have a home?

I hurried Bill through buying Scotch and ice, anxious to straighten up the room ahead of the others. When they arrived, all except Neal had on their party faces. A different man than the one with whom I had been that afternoon. Neal was grumpy, silent and brooding, and dropped heavily into the armchair. Al was obviously glad to have Neal home, and talked glibly to him of his life while Neal had been in New York. But he failed to get Neal to respond in kind.

LuAnne was merry and bubbling. I didn't find her particularly pretty on this night. Her bronze hair was unbecomingly parted in the middle and pulled back to a clip at her neck. I supposed it represented an effort to look older than her 16 years. Her dress was shapeless, her figure unrevealed. Try as I might, I couldn't imagine her the type of girl Neal would actually marry, considering all that I had heard about his intellectual and educational pursuits, combined with his rather formal manners.

LuAnne. Lois and I sat on the floor. LuAnne gushed about how happy she and Neal were, what an ideal marriage they shared. She thrust out her left hand, wiggling her fingers. 'And see? Look at this beautiful diamond solitaire Neal gave me when we got engaged. He is the most wonderful husband. We have so much fun together. Did you know he took me to New York for our honeymoon? It was so exciting, and we met such interesting people like Allen Ginsberg and Jack Kerouac, who are *writers*! Neal wants to be one too, and they will help him.'

'How long has Neal been enrolled at Columbia?' I interjected. LuAnne looked lost for a minute, but then she continued undaunted.

'Gee, I forget. But he came home just to marry me, and then we went back to New York together. He's so sweet.' I could tell she enjoyed saying 'New York'. 'But he has his funny quirks, too. One of them is he *hates* to get his trousers mussed and lose the crease. Can you imagine? Watch. I'll show you.' She bounded up and onto Neal's lap, twining her arms about his neck. Neal growled and shoved her off angrily, but she bounced back to us, delighted with her demonstration.

Although I wasn't doubting LuAnne's story, Neal was not confirming it. He got up and paced about, deep in thought, and stared out of the window in gloomy preoccupation. I wasn't particularly enjoying myself either, and the strange feeling of apprehension that had clung to me much of the day persisted. Al's suggestion that it was time to go came as a relief.

Everyone except Bill filed out and down the hall to the elevator, Neal lagging behind. I was about to close the door when Neal turned back abruptly and, taking a step towards me, raised two fingers in an urgent gesture, then spun around and joined the others. I asked myself what he could possibly mean by that, but now I was more concerned with getting rid of Bill.

When I was at last alone, I changed into my pyjamas and, in an effort to relax, slowly washed my face while reviewing what had been a perplexing day. As I lowered the hideaway bed from the closet, more than ready to climb in, I was startled by a soft knock on the door. My clock read 2a.m. Who on earth? Cautiously, I opened the door a few inches and was face-to-face with Neal, suitcase in hand. He eased past me, dropped his suitcase, and calmly seated himself on the couch, his knees brushing the foot of the bed. I grabbed my robe, squirmed into it and sat on the opposite end of the couch, ardently wishing I had not lowered that bed.

'What is it, Neal? Why have you come back? Where's LuAnne? What are you doing?' I was babbling questions like a child clutching at bubbles. Neal leaned forward, resting his elbows on his knees, and turned a serious face to me, his wide blue eyes filled with woe.

'I'm truly sorry, Carolyn, to drag you into this. The truth is, you see, LuAnne and I are finished. We've been separated for months. I had hoped that today when I returned we could work it out, but it's no use. She threw me out when we got back to the hotel. I've nowhere else to go – and at this late hour –' He leaned back with a gesture of futility. 'It was foolish of me to marry her. She's way too young, but I felt sorry for her – her mother –' He trailed off.

I reviewed the testimonial LuAnne had given that evening and tried to sound sympathetic, while struggling to preserve some detachment.

'I'm sorry, too, Neal. LuAnne led me to believe she was the happiest of married women.'

'Ah yes, I heard her. Well, you know, she was overwhelmed by you. And she wanted so badly to make a good impression. She is inclined to bend the truth now and again. It's a pity.' He sighed.

'So – what will you do now? Doesn't Al or Bill have a couch? And when do you go back to New York?'

'No, they have no room, and well – uh – I can't afford to go back to college now. I'll have to stay in Denver and get a job. But –' he looked at me forlornly, 'if you'll let me, I'll just stay here tonight and find a place to live tomorrow.' I got up and paced the small space that wasn't occupied by the bed.

'Look, Neal, I'd be glad to help you out, but you don't realize the bind I'm in with this hotel as it is. The elevator men – two brothers – hate me because I don't tip them every time they pilot me three floors as do all the old folks. They'd love to catch me breaking the rules and tell the management.'

'It's okay; don't worry. The elevator was closed and the night clerk asleep. I walked up the stairs and didn't see anyone.' I checked the clock. A quarter past two. Now I knew what he'd meant by the two-fingers stunt. But how could he have known LuAnne would throw him out – at 2 o'clock? I'd worry about all that tomorrow; for the time being I'd have to let him stay.

'Yes, I'm afraid it is too risky for you to leave now.' Defeated without benefit of battle, I waved my hand over the couch. 'This is pretty narrow, I'm sorry, and probably too short, but it's…' Neal stood up and walked to the side of the bed.

'Yes – well – I'm awfully tired; I don't sleep well on buses, and what with all the strain with LuAnne…This bed is too wide for one person, don't you think? It seems ridiculous to waste all that perfectly good space – we can both sleep on it and both be comfortable – you *do* agree.' Cool, reasonable, eyes wide open, he looked at me not expecting an answer and proceeded to sit on the bed and untie his shoelaces. I opened my mouth, but Neal smiled up at me in such innocence that any argument would have sounded obscene. Noticing my stricken look, he stood up and held my shoulders like a big brother.

'Now, now. Don't you worry about a thing. I'll be a good boy, I promise.' He laughed as if to prove he had anticipated my preposterous concern. When he had taken off all but his T- shirt and shorts, he flopped on the bed, pulled the covers to his chin, and was asleep before I reached the other side of the bed. I crawled in gingerly and lay stiff and awake most of the night. Occasionally, Neal turned and his arm flopped over me. I didn't know if this were intentional, but I would move his arm away and inch closer to my edge of the bed.

I must have slept some, because I was startled awake by the bright sunlight whitening the lacy curtains and creeping across the flowered carpet. My clock showed five minutes to ten o'clock. Rarely had I been so glad a night was over. As I tiptoed around Neal's side of the bed, I noticed, uncomfortably, how handsome he looked asleep, and I resisted the urge to straighten the covers which he had kicked into tangles around him. I stopped in the dressing room for jeans and a shirt before locking myself in the bathroom. As I climbed into the shower I turned my thoughts to the uncharted day ahead.

When I switched off the shower I heard the radio and knew Neal was up. He was rummaging in his suitcase as I emerged, but turned to acknowledge my 'Good morning' with his radiant smile. After he had showered and shaved, I told him apologetically that we would have to do without breakfast because I was afraid for him to be seen before noon.

'That's perfectly all right,' he said cheerily. 'I quite understand, and anyway, I'd like to stay. That is, if I'm not interfering with your plans?' I told him my intention had been to work on my model set. He listened with care.

'Well now, perhaps I can help you, if you show me what I can do.'

'Why, yes, I think you could, if you're sure you want to.' Somewhat nervously I showed him the design and explained that the play was about insects, a bedewed spider's web the set's prominent feature. I had finished part of the wire structure, and had begun threading it with tiny transparent glass beads.

'Surely I should be able to do that.' Neal reached for the roll of silver wire and the box of beads. 'I've taken up so much of your time, I owe it to you to help.' He smiled again and sat down in the rocker, having understood exactly what had to be done. I collected more materials and sat on the floor. Neal settled down to work. 'Now then, here we are sentenced to remain together for a period of time – all too short, I fear – so you must tell me all about yourself.'

'Oh? Well – what do you want to know? My life has been just ordinary, conventional and lucky – not nearly as exciting, as yours, from what Bill tells me.'

'Bill, ha! All lies, I'm sure. No, no, I insist. Tell me a story.'

The soft breeze sighed in the curtains at the open window, and the sunlight splashed about the room, but I was only half aware of these effects. Neal had achieved such an atmosphere of warm interest in me, I slipped into a state of contentment and wholeness like none I'd ever known. He was spinning his own web around me as surely as he was constructing the spider's.

| THREE |

The peal of the telephone startled me back to reality. I answered, covered the mouthpiece, and turned to Neal.

'It's Bill – downstairs. I'd just as soon he didn't find you here; would you mind if I go down? I'll get rid of him.'

'Why of course. Good for you. Take your time; I'm completely happy.' I grabbed cigarettes and slipped into sandals.

'You don't have to go on stringing those beads forever, you know. I appreciate all you've done already, but there are books and magazines. Please do what you'd like. I'll hurry.'

I found Bill at the bar dismally sucking on a Scotch and looking every bit the rejected lover. Did he know about Neal? I approached warily and took a stool beside him, waving the bartender away. Bill didn't look at me.

'Well, Bill, what is it?'

'Oh, nothing really, I just wanted to see you. Here, come on, have a drink.'

'No thanks; I have too much to do to sit here for no reason. What did you want to see me about?' How he could irritate me.

'Look, Cari, I feel rotten. It seems to me the least you could do is have one measly, lousy, stinkin' li'l drink with me.' His voice began to rise on its way to a bellow, which he knew I detested.

'Okay, Bill, calm down. Let's go sit in a booth then.' I skimmed off the stool and made for a far corner. Bill followed me with two drinks. He bullied me into staying with him for at least half an hour, then suddenly acquiesced to my insistence that I return upstairs.

As I swung open the door to my room, I froze. Bill's ploy was now exposed. LuAnne sat on the edge of the couch, her hands in her lap pulverizing a damp tissue, her face blotchy and glistening. Neal crouched before her, one hand on her knee, the other brushing back hair from her face.

'Now, now, baby –' he was saying, but when I came in he straightened and walked to the window. LuAnne looked up at me with a weak attempt to smile.

I had almost forgotten Neal was married, happily or not, and I had dropped my guard. Throughout the morning he had slipped into our conversation subtle suggestions that he could tell already I was the girl for whom he had been searching, LuAnne a youthful mistake. I had tried to ignore these insinuations, but how easy it is for a romantic to believe a man who insists how 'different' she is. Some men I knew before were bent on marriage, but marriage to me was a lifetime commitment, and none had come close to a 'one and only'.

To my surprise, LuAnne, though still sniffling, turned to me eagerly and, instead of the angry attack I was braced for, proceeded to tell me how glad she was that Neal had found me, that I was exactly what he needed, that she and Neal would never be able to get along, that he was far too smart for her, and on and on. In spite of her emotional state, I doubted her sincerity, recalling her performance of the preceding evening. Besides, I told her (and myself) I had made no commitments to Neal, so I couldn't see what it mattered and where had she gotten the idea that it did? Even appealing to my own vanity left me unwilling to believe LuAnne's act. I felt maternal and sorry for her, patted her and wished her well. Afterwards I admonished Neal to see she was properly taken care of. I bid them both rejoin Bill – and have a triumphant drink? I could see that now Neal had managed to clear the decks for his campaign to conquer me. His wife had given him ample permission.

From that day forward I saw Neal nearly every day. His company was so much more satisfying and stimulating than any other, I voluntarily gave up other engagements and waited for his calls, which never failed to come when expected. When he couldn't be with me, although I didn't ask, he insisted on telling me precisely where he was going, why and for how long. He must have guessed I would never doubt or check. By treating me as though I had the right to know his every move, he created the impression that ours was a more binding relationship than I felt it was. I did remind him he was married and not responsible to me, nor had I the authority to monitor his actions if I cared to, but he paid no attention, pretending I was putting on a noble act.

His attitude affected me deeply, of course. I had never before experienced such solicitude for my inclusion in anyone's life, or such thoughtfulness and diligence in being agreeable. I accepted as the truth everything he told me, mainly because to my knowledge I had never been lied to in any significant matter. Why would he tell me he loved me if he didn't? What was to be gained? In those first months I knew of nothing I had that he lacked, or would lie to acquire; only later did I learn he had reasons I couldn't have guessed. Then, I respected his freedom of choice as I did my own. I didn't want a love that could be commanded or demanded, but only one that couldn't be denied.

Neal's manner was always formal and polite. There was no hint of sensuality, only a restrained affection, as though he considered our relationship on a higher plane. Very soon I learned to stop fearing the kind of siege to which I'd been subjected by men in the past. I believed I was enjoying most of the complete satisfactions described in my nineteenth-century novels, and I loved it. When any anxiety crossed my mind about Neal's apparent lack of passion, I assumed the physical desires would develop naturally as love ripened, just as they seemed to in my novels. Personally, I felt no 'chemistry' physically for Neal, probably because he was so cool, and my brothers' childhood abuse had frozen any chance of such desire being awakened in me. I had buried their actions from my mind and memory, but this had caused me to be pathologically shy with any male; I couldn't look one in the face nor speak to him. To be the centre of attention in any way was agony. In Neal I found a great relief. He made love with his eyes, his words, and an affectionate hug or two.

As an undergraduate I had studied literature, philosophy and psychology along with the arts and Stanislavsky drama, although there was no way I would ever be able to act on stage. I tried to develop my intellect, partially with the hope that I might have a means of attraction other than my body. Since both my parents were educators, and most of their friends also members of university faculties, I had been raised in an environment of lively debates. These discussions were objective mind-fencing, never personal, and no one ever got hurt or angry. It was exciting to follow the arguments through mazes of logic, to seek meaning and clarity of ideas. I found, however, the men I met either resented the mental competition or were bored, only one idea on their minds. Neal, on the other hand, was a man who could lose himself with me in intellectual give-and-take. The mental tapestries we wove were so stimulating, so exhilarating, that I had to admit I far preferred this kind of mutuality to that of sex – I wonder how he knew that about me, and so managed to relieve me of my shyness.

He encouraged me to talk about my past, but for several months he was somewhat sketchy about his own. The scraps I collected were that he had been born when his parents arrived in Salt Lake City, Utah on a trip to Los Angeles. His mother had died when he was ten, and he said he remembered nothing about her. I found that odd. She had been married before she met his barber father, and already had six children. He had one full younger sister, her whereabouts unknown to him.

The chronology of this patchy history confused me, but a grim picture emerged of living off and on with a wino father in skid row, being treated sadistically by his older half-brothers and running away from a Catholic orphanage. To me it was a tale rivalled only by the orphans in stories by Dickens, which naturally added an unrealistic, romantic touch.

'Oh, poor Neal! What a miracle you have managed to rise above and overcome all that horror. I suppose yours is one of those hardship cases that produce strength of character, like Andrew Carnegie and suchlike. Now all you have to do is build a railroad.' Neal laughed, 'Well, maybe, but my godfather was a Monsignor, and I served as an alterboy, too; does that count?'

'What do you intend to do as a career?'

'When I get a degree, I'd like to write. I've already read a lot of books, more than required for college. Jack Kerouac is a great writer, and he has promised to help me.' Few ambitions could have pleased me more.

Limited financially and not requiring alcohol, we didn't spend evenings drinking and/or dancing as had been my previous custom on weekend dates. Neal said he didn't dance, but he loved movies and sports. One early afternoon we sneaked under the tent of the Great Western Rodeo and spent the rest of the day and evening wallowing in my first real taste of the Old Wild West.

I look back in wonder on one sport Neal introduced me to, which he adored and which I would never have gone to in a million years. He was able somehow to use his persuasive talents and get me to join him – and not once but many many times. That was the midget auto races.

At first I agreed to go to show my devotion to him, but soon just being with him sharing his ecstasy became a source of pleasure, in spite of the choking fumes, the stench of gas, grease and oil, and the skull-shattering roar of engines, squealing tyres and bawling crowds. Because he was so eager to share his passion with me, watching his enthusiasm was compensation enough.

As the cars swirled and growled around the track, Neal yelled a running commentary on every sight and sound, including the names and histories of the drivers, their cars, their track records and all the quirks and characteristics of both. As these became more familiar, my pleasure increased. I was happy just standing in the grandstand in the clear, cool night, the lights blazing and the speakers blaring, romantic ballads and country tunes between announcements. Neal hugged me and swayed to the rhythm while singing along with 'Peg o' My Heart', not altogether in tune.

Occasionally we partied with Al, Lois and Bill, who still sullenly shadowed me. His company was even less agreeable now that I had fallen for Neal, and Bill was drinking more. Jim Holmes was the only other of Neal's friends I met, and I was told he made his living gambling on pool and card games. Jim had big sad dark eyes, and was so sweet and quiet I couldn't believe the nature of his livelihood, which to me was tantamount to a gangster's. Most of the time, however, Neal and I were content to be alone together and talk.

| FOUR |

All this time since Neal's return to Denver, he had been writing long intimate letters to Jack and Allen, apparently in an effort to cement their relationships. I knew nothing of this correspondence until long after Neal and I were married. Then I collected and saved the letters from the two men, but I didn't see those from Allen and Jack in Denver until they were published in books, since both Jack and Allen kept careful files of their correspondence. I did not see letters Neal wrote to them at that time either.

Neal's letters were long, wordy, full of philosophy and psychology describing the nature of each of them and himself and how he defined their relationships. To Allen he signed his letters, 'Your other half,' and to Jack, 'Your brother.'

Neal wrote to Allen soon after he had taken up with me, confiding a fatherly concern for LuAnne, 'who due to our separation... has fallen into a complete apathy towards life. Her inability to meet even the most simple obligations. Her life is a constant march of obsessions – almost terrifying.'

Neal was simultaneously courting and straight-arming Allen.

> I need you more than ever, since I've no one else to turn to... Let us find... the great heights of complete oneness.
> ...Let me end on one line in your wonderful letter: 'I will be prepared for you, I think, when we meet, but on other terms than those which I'd formerly conceived and which I tried to force on you.' I find that statement holds true for me as well as you, Allen, whether for better or worse we must see...

Allen seemed suspicious of Neal's exaggerated warmth and, seeking more reassurance and security, accused him of a lack of 'truth' still. Neal reacted typically, both by an attempt at honest appraisal of himself and by being blunt, bringing them down to hard core facts and thereby decreasing the intricate introspection.

> I really don't know how much I can be satisfied to love you, I mean bodily; you know I somehow dislike pricks & men & before you, I had consciously forced myself to be homosexual; now I'm not sure whether with you I was not just forcing myself unconsciously, that is to say, any falsity on my part was all physical, in fact, any disturbance in our affair was because of this. You meant so much to me I now feel I was forcing a desire for you bodily as a compensation to you for all you were giving me. This is a sad state and upsets me for I want to become nearer to you than anyone & still I don't want to be unconsciously insincere by passing over my non-queerness to please you.
>
> ... Relax, man. Think about what I say and try to see yourself moving toward me without any compulsive demands due to lack of assurance that I love you or because of lack of belief that I understand you, etc. Forget all that and in forgetfulness see if there isn't more peace of mind and even more physical satisfaction than in your present subjective longing... I can't promise a damned thing. I know I'm bisexual but prefer women. There's a slimmer line than you think between my attitude toward love and yours; don't be so concerned; it'll fall into line. Beyond that – who knows? Let's try it and see, huh?

Neal was also securing his friendship with Jack, although anxious about how to approach him to ensure his continued approval and brotherly affection. After expressing doubts as to his own qualifications, Neal spelled out elaborate instructions as to the way in which they should write to each other to guarantee sincerity. Once Neal accused Jack of 'just a hint of falseness' in his previous letter, while he himself displayed an affected style in his own 'missives' to Jack.

To Jack Neal described how the problem of keeping LuAnne and me from knowing about each other was but one factor plaguing his peace of mind. He was threatened with eviction from his 'ideal' basement room because his landlady had discovered he brought girls home for the night. He had managed to sweet-talk her into forgiving him for damaged sheets, but then a new and bizarre threat nearly landed him in jail and necessitated a change of lodging anyway.

While Neal was living in New York after LuAnne had left, a former friend in Chicago was stealing cars and money as well as impregnating a minor, all the while using the name Neal Cassady. After Neal's landlady told him that the police had called, and after he had skipped about a bit to avoid them, he found out the charge. He was genuinely frightened by this ironic twist of fate, since he'd 'faced the Police Chief on similar charges before'. So frightened was he, he even told me about this, wishing to establish his innocence with me before he was arrested, if he were to be. Luckily, he was able to clear himself by tracking down enough evidence to show he had been in New York at the time of the crimes.

Neal had written Allen several times outlining his elaborate plans for the summer and coming year: he would meet Allen at Bill Burroughs's Texas ranch, return to Denver so they could both work at Central City during the opera season, saving their money for a year in New York and Europe later. Part of the plan included having a girl live with them, partly for Neal's needs and partly to assist Allen in becoming 'straight' sexually – a hope at that time. This had caused quite a bit of explaining on Neal's part, as Allen had responded in the negative. But by mid-May Neal's letters became fewer, and he gave Allen long intricate excuses: he was rushing about, having the trouble with the police and LuAnne, looking for jobs etc. These conditions did exist, but in addition he had met and was courting me, and was not only disinclined to inform Allen, but found his plans unsettled as a result.

> I haven't written for two reasons: one, I was indecisive whether I would come to Texas for a week or two to meet Bill and Joan or post-pone that until the latter part of August...I fear that whatever commitments have been made to you about procuring a job in Central City may not be fulfiled. As it now stands I shan't be there; I can't say I'm too sorry as I have found a new interest...besides, I suspect Hal Chase was right in his summary of the place as being 'too gooey.'
>
> At any rate, you musn't remain hanging on a limb in Texas. Although I can promise you nothing in the way of

living quarters, work life, even social activity...I still insist that you hurry to Denver so that we can work something out.

I am anxious to see you, also whatever you may bring with you, i.e. tea – I repeat – tea.

The sudden change in Neal's tone and concern must have impressed Allen, although I know not how. After Neal had chatted some more he added casually,

I have met a wonderful girl [his 'new interest']. Her chief quality, I suspect, lies in the same sort of awareness or intuitive sense of understanding which is our (yours and mine) chief forte. She is getting her Masters at DU. For some strange reason she came to Denver last year, abandoning better places, because she could make money at DU. But she's not really as vulgar as she sounds. Her lack of cynicism, artificial sophistication and sterility in her creative make-up will recommend her to you. She is just a bit too straight for my temperament; however, that is the challenge, just as that is the challenge in our affair. Her basic inhibitions are subtle psychological ones tied up indirectly with conventions, mannerisms and taste, whereas mine with you are more internal, fearful and stronger. She knows all about the theater, draws a fine line and is quite popular. Don't feel that I am overawed by her, though I would have a justifiable right in being subjective to that. Somehow, my respect for her seems unimportant. I feel the only reason, really, that she affects me so is the sense of peace which she produces in me when we are together. Secretly, she is the reason I am postponing the trip to Texas until later in the season – wait till you meet her!

Perhaps Neal meant well by comparing his feelings for me with his for Allen, but I seriously doubt if Allen was comforted.

At the same time Neal was frantically hunting work for himself and Allen, as well as lodgings for Allen, who planned to come to Denver in June. Neal began and quit a few jobs, then settled into happy employment driving a jitney for the May Company, transporting shoppers to and from the parking lot. He carefully pointed out to me that he was capable of working at any job and could manage to earn an income at any time until his writing career proved profitable (unlike Jack). Work, nevertheless, was never allowed to interfere with his capacity for living to the full.

In mid-June Allen arrived, and Neal brought him to my room that evening. Eyes alight, smiling broadly, Neal introduced us. Allen was a slim young man, a little shorter than Neal, with a chunk of thick black hair and intense round black eyes encircled by black-rimmed spectacles. The narrowness of his jaw was heightened by a wide, full, curved mouth. His manner was reserved; he nodded at my 'I'm so happy to meet you, Allen.'

'Hullo,' he said softly, his voice deeper than his slight frame would suggest, but there was no change in his expression. Although his owl-like gaze made me self-conscious, I sensed a note of sad kindness in his tone that soon put me at ease, and I was eager to know him better.

Neal turned to me abruptly and all in a rush said, 'Well, now, darling; Allen has just arrived after a very long bus trip, so naturally he is tired. You know I have no room for him at my place and what with hotels so expensive, I assured Allen you would be pleased to let him sleep on your couch – so – we'll just leave his bag here for the moment – because Allen and I have to go out for just a wee while to check on one more possibility, but I'm sure we'll be right back.' He didn't pause for an answer, but kissed me flamboyantly, placed Allen's suitcase beside the couch, and ushered him out.

It was close to eleven when I heard them at the door, giggling and softly talking. I hurried to let them in, my love for Neal once again overcoming my fear of the management. They looked like a pair of leprechauns, grinning gleefully, their eyes sparkling and very pink. I supposed they'd been drinking, though I smelled no alcohol when Neal nuzzled my neck.

Then *both* men began to undress. I gasped, did a bit of a two-step as Neal approached me, my mind racing, but I couldn't think how to object in front of Allen. Neal saw my shocked expression, I was sure, but he said only, 'I'll just use the bathroom a moment; Allen will help you with the bed.'

When Neal came out, Allen went in. I pounced. 'Neal – you don't mean to stay here, too? What have you told Allen – that we're lovers? That we've been sleeping together? How could you?'

Neal wrapped me in his arms and pecked kisses up and down my throat as he talked.

'Now, now, darling, isn't it about time? How much do you think I can take? I've been a good boy, now haven't I ? But you *know* how much I love you. Please, my darling, don't be upset. It will be all right. What can we *do* with Allen here?'

When Allen was tucked in on the couch and the light out, Neal climbed into bed beside me. We lay still until it seemed Allen was asleep, me quivering. I had expected some build-up, some preliminaries, a few kisses and caresses – why, Neal had never touched me except for hugs, a casual kiss or holding my hand. Now he turned to me and pulled down my pyjama bottoms. My thoughts flurried like snowflakes, and my emotions refused to fall into the proper groove for a surrender to passion, so acutely conscious was I of Allen not two feet from the foot of the bed. How often I had visualized our initial blending physically – certainly not this. I prayed Allen was a sound sleeper as Neal threw back the covers and removed his shorts.

The instant he slid between my thighs, spreading them, nerves electrified every muscle in a futile attempt to resist the pain, and a cry escaped me like an uncaged bird. Where was the tenderness Neal had shown until now? Who was this animal raging in lust? Crushed and bewildered, I could only brace myself against him, fighting tears and the threat of screaming. How could he not notice my stiff frigidity? Even after Neal collapsed beside me whispering profound delight as he fell asleep, I felt chiselled from stone, except for the searing pain.

Numb and shaking, I slipped off the bed to seek refuge in the bathroom and bathed my lap with tears. I told myself I would not despair; I wished so fervently to return to my former state of bliss I convinced myself there was an explanation and a cure. Next time would be better; I would be in the mood and prepared. Allen would not be there. For now, I would put it out of my mind. I slept little, still afraid Neal would attack again.

Allen awoke and rose from the couch. He gave me a doleful 'Good morning'. I returned his greeting. He began folding his blanket, looking away.

'It's nice you and Neal are so compatible,' he said. I must have blushed for the first time in years.

'Uh – oh – I'm so sorry, Allen. Did we keep you awake? I – well – I don't know what to say – I'm so embarrassed.'

'That's all right. It's okay. I didn't mean – it's just that I'm glad he makes you so happy.'

What a lamentable tone! I searched his face to see if he were joking. He looked serious enough, even tragic. He must have thought my cries were of ecstasy? Yet how could I tell him the truth? I said nothing, and Allen trudged into the bathroom.

(Many years later, in the Seventies, when Allen and Timothy Leary had performed in Santa Cruz with my son John's backup on guitar, John was driving Allen to San Francisco and me home to Los Gatos. Allen was sitting beside John in front, I in the back. I can't recall now what made Allen think of this, but he was telling John about that night and his having to hear my shrieks of joy.

'JOY?' I cried. 'Is that what you thought? That was agony!'

'OH, I wish I'd known!' Allen fairly yelled.)

Neal awoke and bounded to me. He hugged me with such genuine joy I was able to renew my faith in 'next time'.

Allen stayed in my room reading and writing while Neal was at work and I at school. I grew increasingly fond of Allen. He was open and frank, yet quiet and thoughtful and always kind. He took a sincere interest in my studies, often helping me with papers and assignments. One time in scene design class I had to read a paper I'd written with Allen's help. Still overcome with self-consciousness, it was torture to stand before the class. When I'd finished there was silence, and I inwardly groaned. Dr Bell suddenly waxed lyrical, saying what a remarkably excellent paper that had been, and the class applauded.

One Sunday afternoon when Neal was home, Allen asked if I would draw Neal. He would read to us as I worked. I said I'd try. Allen then said, 'It must be a full figure – nude.' I wasn't as non-chalant about nudity as the fashion soon became, and the demand shocked and embarrassed me.

As usual, my arguments were overruled.

'Think of the Greek statues – or your art class models.' I sensed this wasn't quite the same, but couldn't squirm away without appearing prudish, so I concentrated on drawing and remained detached. Neal stood like a Greek statue, one knee flexed and that hip dropped, but there was a twinkle in his eyes not found with the Greeks, although some had much the same interest as Allen in nude young men.

The drawing took several hours, both men feigning an academic attitude. When I'd finished, Neal dressed quickly. He asked if he could have the sketch, and although I valued it myself, I let him have it. Some years after we were married I asked him what had become of it. He said he had lost it moving about, but one day I found it crushed in the bottom of his closet. I was hurt he hadn't cared for it. He tried to persuade me he had, but Allen and LuAnne had fought over it. I felt no better, but he said, '*You* have *ME!*'

| FIVE |

On one of Neal's days off he and Allen came to the campus. It was a warm day, and we lounged on the terrace in the sun watching the students and comparing colleges we had known. Perhaps it was the unusual setting in which I now saw Neal, but something made me study him in a more objective way. Why was this man the only man I had ever met to whom I was willing to resign my total being and my future? I didn't think I believed in predestination, but somehow I knew positively that our relationship *was* predestined. Maybe it was simply that Neal was the first man with whom I had fallen in love without physical attraction or romance as the dominant factor. A good sign, I decided; I was being rational and intelligent for once, my mind unclouded by desire. Neal appeared even more unique and special. All at once, I felt an inner chill, and I shuddered. Is that what was meant by 'someone just walked over my grave'? On a level much deeper than the mental I was suddenly aware that I had already surrendered my will unconditionally. Almost physically I felt the cogs mesh in the wheel of fate.

Allen had an appealing sensitivity for the feelings of others, so it surprised me to find him sometimes unaware of others in public. The three of us often went to a little side-street café for coffee. There were few other customers, as a rule. It had a short counter, a few small tables and two white booths under the front window. The compact surroundings made us all the more conspicuous, and easily overheard. Allen would talk and laugh loudly, or suddenly burst into uninhibited song, accompanying himself by drumming on the metal tabletop with his fingers, oblivious to the surprise or irritation of fellow diners. I would shrink into the corner of the booth, hoping to disappear in the plastic upholstery. This made me doubly miserable, sure Neal would disapprove of my not accepting his friend on any terms.

It was here in this café that I was first introduced to the world of mind-altering drugs. My former circle of friends had found their escapist pleasures in the seclusion of murky bars, but since Neal's early childhood memories contained a good deal of sorrow in connection with alcohol, this pastime did not appeal to him. He rarely drank anything stronger than beer.

One afternoon, alone in the café, we ordered coffee, and Allen and Neal produced a Benzadrine inhaler. I knew its purpose was to clear the nasal passages; now I would learn the secret powers hidden within this innocent remedy for a stuffy nose. With much ceremony and glee, the two men demonstrated the process of disembowelling the inhaler's plastic casing to get at the two-inch roll of paper saturated with the magic liquid. From this they tore off quarter-inch strips. Each was wadded into a ball and swallowed with the coffee 'to kill the taste'. This tiny amount, they told me, was sufficient for eight hours of transporting delight, mostly mental, although euphoria of mood could also be expected. They were kind enough to warn me that the price of this treat was another eight hours of deadening depression – but I was not to worry; the pleasure of the 'high' was worth it, and Neal would steer me through the rough spots afterwards.

So as 'not to disturb Allen again', Neal had devised a plan. He would rent a hotel room – 'not for what you're thinking,' he assured me. 'All sexual desire and prowess are eliminated when you're on benny. We'll just talk all night. Think of it, darling. You'll see.' Of course I agreed, even though uneasy. Neal and I were so rarely alone now I was happy he wanted to be. Anyway, he could do no wrong. I trusted him implicitly. I swallowed the pellet, drank my coffee and stepped forth into the gathering dusk, ready for anything.

Alone together Neal insisted we undress in order to lie on the bed and be free to talk comfortably. He took off his clothes as matter-of-factly as usual, and since it was not yet dark, I followed suit and hastily slid under the bedclothes. It was a warm evening, and Neal opened the window. 'It really is too hot, isn't it,' and he pulled off the covers. Instinctively, I covered my breasts with my arms.

'Hey, now, what's all this?' he asked gently as he lay next to me. 'A body like yours and you're ashamed of it?'

'In a way, I guess; I've never been fond of it; it so often betrays me.'

'What do you mean "betrays you"?'

'Well, lots of times it gets too fat. Then it keeps sending out messages to men without my permission or approval, and I have to deal with all their false promises. And I suppose a lot of it is from having been brought up in a Victorian home where I never saw another person, not even my sisters, naked. You see, after infancy I never sat on my father's lap, nor do I remember any hugs or kisses.'

I suddenly became aware I was prattling, and Neal was smiling and giggling because he knew that's what the drug did. I stopped talking, embarrassed again, but then had to laugh, feeling freer than I could ever remember, less afraid each moment, and unable to control the rush of a million thoughts so terribly necessary to communicate at once. Neal urged me on, saying, 'You're so expressive,' because I make a lot of faces. I was deep into schooldays memories when I caught myself again. 'No, no, please stop me, Neal; it's your turn. Besides, you've never told me where you went to highschool, here or in New York.'

'We-e-ll, you see, I didn't finish highschool. I quit in the tenth grade. Later I got a certificate of equivalency from the Army.'

'You were in the Army? Where were you during the war?'

'Um – no – you see, not really – actually, I was in jail.'

'Jail? Jail!' I sat up and looked down at him. It was a joke. Jail was as remote to me as the stars. 'What on earth for?'

'All a mistake, really. I was living with this friend and working nights, so I hardly ever saw him. One day I was home sleeping, when big knocks on the door and "Open up; it's the police" woke me. Of course I was naturally scared, but not having done anything, I jumped up and let them in. They asked me a lot of questions about where I worked, where I'd been at a lot of different times, and I'm trying to remember accurately when the other cop, who'd been poking around, opens this closet and starts dragging out all sorts of stuff – radios, tyres, toasters, record players, and I'm standing there staring, awestruck. Naturally, they didn't believe me, so they took me in. They got the other guy, and even though in court he testified to my innocence, they sent me up anyway for "knowledge of stolen goods".'

'That's not fair – that's terrible! Is that really the law? You poor *dear*!'

'Yeah, well, so when the Army sent my draft notice, I had to tell them I was sorry but I had a previous engagement.' This sent us into paroxysms of laughter, as did the picture of all the stolen property suddenly materializing.

When we could stop, I said, 'Well, it's a blessing you missed the war, except for also missing out on GI benefits. Me too, dammit. I thought, along with my friends, that we were so clever as to choose to be an occupational therapist with the Army, because the Navy demanded you do basic training like other officer candidates. We did exactly the same work as the Navy occupational therapists, but we got no benefits after the war.'

Neal paused to kiss me and giggle some more and then said, 'But actually, darling, just to be perfectly honest with you, I should tell you I've been in jail a time or two since. Mostly for dumb stuff like that time. Misunderstandings, you know. Once, I was working on a parking lot in LA, and I used to borrow the boss's car all the time with his blessing. So one night he wasn't there to ask, but I thought nothing of it and borrowed it again. It broke down a few miles outside of town, and I got out and hailed the next car. It was a cop car!'

'You hailed a *cop* car? Oh no!' Overwhelming laughter again interrupted Neal. He had chosen the proper time to tell me these tales. I doubt they would have sounded so funny as a sober confession.

'Of course he didn't believe me, and accused me of stealing the car. When I got to court, here was the same bailiff who had been there three years earlier when I was sent to a Hollywood work camp from which I had escaped and never been caught. Boy, I knew I was in for it now, because I could see he recognized me too. Somehow, however, I got inspired and talked my head off to that judge with such a rational explanation he actually dismissed both charges.'

'Wow, that's hard to believe. So you didn't go to jail that time. But why were you in the Hollywood camp?'

'Oh, yeah, well, that was another case of a borrowed car. And then there was the time I broke my nose, see?' He pushed down the end of his nose which appeared to have no cartilage.

'It's the bane of my existence. I can't breathe properly. It drives me nuts. Anyway, this time I was in a car my buddy used to rent so we could take out girls. All four of us were in the front seat, his girl in his lap. We're coming down this steep hill – I'm driving of course, and I motion to him to take the wheel while I grab my girl. He thinks I'm saying "Watch this now," so he watches me instead of taking the wheel, and I'm kissing up a storm. We ran smack-dab into a telephone pole, split the bumper in two, flattened all the tyres. His girl broke a rib, I broke my nose, and since we couldn't pay the damages, we all went to jail.'

Both of us hooted over this one until we cried and our stomachs hurt. I was having a fine time, I was. I felt so vibrant, brilliant, witty, happy. How fun to lie side-by-side on the cool sheet, giggling, talking, singing, stroking and watching the play of neon outside the open window, the flimsy net curtains billowing into the shadowy room, we two wrapped up only in the world of each other. The occasional mood dives that suddenly hit me were swept away when Neal bounded in with lovely words and caresses to distract and reassure me and bring me back up again.

We cavorted like children in natural physical contact, affectionate and innocent. As the night wore on, the drug-induced hyperactivity took its toll in weariness. Our muscles stiffened, our tempo eased. We drew up the top sheet and lay mumbling cosily, sometimes in quiet thoughts, sometimes dozing, always vividly aware of being together.

Gradually, Neal began tentative, apparently purposeless caresses, a gentle massage at the back of my neck and shoulders relaxed me so completely that by the time I understood his intent, resistance was out of the question. A wisp of remembered pain floated across my mind, but I couldn't grasp it, and soon all thought ceased in willing surrender.

Then again the sudden thrust and violent pounding with virtually no body-to-body contact, my knees behind my ears. Could anyone call this 'making love'? What kind of women had he known? If this is what he liked and they liked, would he ever like it my way? And why, why, why was I so inhibited and knew not how to talk to him about it? When at last he lay still on top of me, I weakly stroked his head, my hopes shattered for an ideal sex life with Neal.

The lover I'd had just before Neal had been perfect. 'So that's what all the noise is about!' I said to myself then. I didn't learn about zones or foreplay, because we didn't need it. 'I'll burst inside you like a screaming rocket,' he'd quoted, and my body responded as it should. (My first time had been rape by a man in New York in 1943, when I'd said, 'Is that all there is?') I didn't even like the other guy in Denver. All this bothered me quite a lot, because I thought love and sex had to go together. I had one without the other each time.

The brightening sky made the window a raw grey rectangle against the darkened room. Chill, damp air brought colder reality to my aching head, heart and nether regions. We got up and slowly dressed in silence, both in our own and very different thoughts. The 'drag' had set in; each movement demanded extra and concentrated effort. Neal was buttoning his shirt sleeves and didn't look at me. Low and breathlessly he said, 'How'd you like to marry me?'

Again my emotions vied with reason. How odd that here after a rending disappointment his proposal produced in me the traditional heart-skip of the girl who finally wins her man. I was consoled that Neal found the experience significant enough to link it in his mind to marriage. (At that time I did not know his underlying reason for wanting me as his wife.)

'How can I answer that when you're already married?' I hadn't seen nor heard of LuAnne since the first times we met. Neal had told me she had gone back to New York, and I had all but forgotten her. No more was said. He put on his jacket and meticulously arranged a straying hair in the mirror. Then, taking my elbow he guided me down the creaking staircase and out into the cold and empty streets of the Denver dawn.

*　　*　　*

Summer was slow to arrive in this high, thin-aired city. The wind from the snow-capped Rockies was harsh, and just as well. I found it difficult enough to keep my head, and the enormous difference between Neal's and my approach to sex was seldom out of my thoughts. I analyzed, probed, rationalized. Obviously, no one could help me, not even Neal, and this was the unkindest cut of all. Although I managed to conceal the extent of my anxiety, it remained a bewildering enigma to me, a cruel irony. But, as I said to myself, when you are married it will work out. I will find a way. WE *will* find a way, for then I will be able to discuss it with him.

Neal behaved as if I had said yes to his proposal. It was all settled. And he demonstrated a new possessiveness. Unaware of my dilemma, he was more affectionate than ever, and we indulged in cosy talks projecting images of our future life. Neal heartily endorsed all my requirements for happiness: the rural home, the books we'd read together, the trips we'd share, the games we'd play, the artists we'd go to see and hear, the family we'd raise in heaven.

Now he concluded it would solve a lot of problems if we lived together. Allen had found a basement room several blocks from my hotel and a job in the shipping department of the May company. So I told the hotel I was moving out, and Neal and I rented a room with kitchen privileges in an old Victorian house in a more remote downtown neighbourhood – far from the campus to pacify my Puritan ethics.

Neal assured me he would ask LuAnne again for an annulment, which should be simple, since she had been underage when they married, and her mother hated Neal. He said she had returned to Denver, so we borrowed a car and picked her up downtown and deposited her at her mother's home.

She promised to arrange for the annulment right away. What a forlorn child she looked that day, so young and bedraggled, sitting in the back seat, her hair in pigtails, no makeup, wearing a rumpled dress, bobby socks and saddle shoes. I was uncomfortable sitting in front beside Neal, her husband. Yet it was all the more evident we were doing the best thing for all concerned, erasing an error to write anew.

| SIX |

Jack Kerouac had written to Neal from New York that he would be going to San Francisco and would stop in Denver to see old friends from Columbia, as well as us. It must have been quite a surprise to Jack, I mused, to arrive and be introduced to the girl Neal intended to marry, when only a few months earlier he had met Neal's new bride.

Jack's brooding good looks and shy, gentle nature were comforting and attractive to me, but I considered him only as a friend of Neal's. He had clear bright blue eyes, emphasized by his black hair and eyelashes. His complexion was a bit darker than Neal's, whose skin was fair and sensitive. Jack and I got along well in our roles as mutual friends of Neal, both of us programmed for monogamy and fidelity where matrimony was concerned. Jack came several times to the campus theatre to watch rehearsals of the two plays in which some madness (and a Hungarian director) had persuaded me to act. I had forbidden Neal from attending these; his opinion mattered too much, and I knew I was no actress. I had submitted because I thought I should have the experience to round out my knowledge of drama – and hoped it would help with my shyness. In the first play, an Ibsen, I was a stiff board, but in the second, Maeterlinck's *The Bluebird*, I played both Light and the little girl, and enjoyed it. No idea why. Of course, I designed the costumes and makeup as well.

Jack was interested in the plays and complimentary (he only saw the *Bluebird* rehearsals), and I was envied for the attention of this handsome stranger from New York. He was shy too, but we warmed to conversations of our impressions of New England – I had gone to college at Bennington in Vermont – and New York, where I had lived too. We compared tastes in movies, books, authors, art, music etc.

We would ride the rackety streetcars, and I was intrigued with his observations of people and scenes along the route, while he made notes in a little five-cent notebook he told me he carried everywhere to capture impressions for his books.

Jack had nothing but high praise for Neal, but he revealed no new facts about him. Nothing was said about Neal's attendance at Columbia, but I did learn neither Allen nor Jack were now enrolled. How different were these three men from the men I had known in college and after. Jack was a year older than I, Allen and Neal nearly three years younger. The classes I taught occasionally as a teaching assistant at Denver University were filled with war veterans all older than I. School and age no longer matched. Every man I had met since World War II had required at least one whole evening to rehash his war trauma before any other topic could be introduced. Here now were men who had little war experiences to relive. Jack didn't talk about his trip on *The Dorchester* as a merchant seaman for many years after I met him. The homelessness of these three was also new to me. Jack had a mother and a part-time home, and Allen had a father and brother, but he didn't live with them. My past acquaintances had families that generated a sustaining tie, whether positive or negative. In the lives of these three, home was not a major factor of past or present, but only of their dreams of the future.

At Jack's request, one evening he, Neal and I went to a roadhouse. There was a juke box, a little space for dancing, and since Neal wouldn't, Jack felt free to ask me to dance, which we did between conversations and beer in the booth. Neal monopolized the jukebox, and bounded about the room charming any other customers who might have had other choices into an acceptance of his. One or another selection would bring him leaping back to Jack to discuss, or they would lose themselves in an excited contrapuntal dialogue about music and musicians. They were as much fun to watch as to hear. Both mimics, they matched words with facial contortions, vocal gymnastics, wild gestures, and every now and then broke up in laughter at each other's antics. Both had infectious laughs, a combination chuckle-giggle with a rumble of deep merriment that travelled from heart to heart.

Dancing with Jack was the only time I felt the slightest doubt about my dedication to Neal, for here was the warm physical attraction that Neal lacked. This realization disturbed me and was difficult to brush away. Jack's manner was tender without being suggestive, although he did betray some tension. As though he had read my thoughts, he said softly in my ear, 'It's too bad, but that's how it is. Neal saw you first.'

Shortly thereafter Jack became involved entirely with his other friends, whose plans did not include Neal, and he left for San Francisco without seeing us again, although Neal may have somehow said good bye.

My confidence in Neal's sincerity was welded by the attentiveness and pride in me that he had displayed when we were with Jack, and I wrote in my weekly letter home that I was engaged to be married. I omitted the fact that the man I loved was already married, but I thought my parents would approve of what was bound to be a long engagement. I knew they would be disappointed nonetheless. They had already chosen my perfect mate, an Englishman – named Nigel, let's say. They never lost hope that I would come to my senses and accept his repeated proposals. I therefore stressed Neal's assets from their point of view: his extensive reading, his intelligence and vast knowledge, his interest in literature and his own literary aspirations as a student at Columbia University, his dignity, attentiveness, sterling character and aversion to alcohol. So? I bent it a little.

Their response was immediate. My nearest brother was a PhD candidate at nearby Boulder, and shortly after the news reached home, he called to ask to meet my intended. I knew he had been assigned to check out Neal and send home a report. My brother came to Denver one evening, and since I could hardly invite him to our room, we met in a cocktail lounge, where Neal nursed a beer while my brother and I gulped Scotch.

Neal was magnificent. He was poised, reserved, intelligent and articulate, and he could speak brilliantly on any subject my brother introduced. Except one: the war. Brother was no exception to the veterans who liked to compare notes about their military experiences. He had been a Lieutenant Commander in the Navy's demolition and bomb-disposal service. A typical military assignment sent this man – six foot three, with platinum hair – to China, where everyone is short with black hair. He called it the 'Rice Paddy Navy', and spent most of his posting in black pyjamas crawling on his stomach. He, like so many, felt a man's service record was indicative of his character.

Neal was prepared. Looking properly remorseful and disgusted, he admitted he had been classified 4F because of his breathing difficulties and colour-blindness. The subject was dropped. Sports redeemed the day. Neal's photographic memory brought up the personal details of every ball player for decades past, the games they played, the scores, their batting averages, etc., and he could do the same for football, basketball, hockey, you name it. I watched in growing admiration and love. No need to get into literature or philosophy or music, Neal's other interests. The report went home that Neal was 'satisfactory'.

For a while Neal and I enjoyed playing house. I was glad to be able to cook again, and delighted there was nothing Neal wouldn't eat with gusto and praise. The room itself was small, the bed occupying most of it, but Neal said, 'What else do we need, hey baby?'

Then Neal's behaviour changed mysteriously. He became moody and distracted, but would admit to no cause. Three incidents occurred in the last month of that fateful summer that should have been sufficient to cure me of my blind faith in Neal's love and open up my eyes to our future, but he had cast his spell too well.

The first incident was a night he didn't come home for dinner or call. I knew of no place to look for him and was not comforted by the realization that if anything happened to him, I would be the last to know. 'That's the price you pay for living in sin,' I told myself. I put his dinner in the fridge, and after some studying went to bed but not to sleep.

Late that night he came into the room with a friend carrying two or three six-packs of beer and a guitar. Of course Neal was aware of my having to rise early and my busy schedule, so I was dumbfounded by this unusual lack of consideration, both for me and the other residents. Did he want us to get thrown out? He kissed me, patted me, and then his whole attention turned to his friend and their funny stories, the beer and guitar.

The second occasion, and far worse, was a long-anticipated excursion to Central City to see the old mining town and the current summer opera. On the bus Neal was in another grey mood and silent. Immediately after we arrived, he took off, leaving me to wait and weep until I could find a ride home hours after the opera, which I couldn't watch for worrying. I also inconvenienced a school friend working there by spending the time sobbing in his room, impervious to his efforts to comfort me. When, long after the opera and the cast party, someone drove me home, I climbed the stairs to our room to find Neal asleep in our bed. At least it was a weekend.

After both occasions I confronted Neal for an explanation, and he gave me such reasonable and innocent excuses, my concern appeared selfish and uncharitable. He insisted repeatedly that his devotion to me was as strong as ever, and since I still couldn't see why he would say so if it weren't true, I accepted his word. It did briefly occur to me that perhaps the encounter with my brother, the discovery of how thorough was my naive trust in him, and my view of the permanence and solidity of our marriage might have given him cold feet. Perfectly natural, I figured.

Nigel had resurfaced and offered to drive me to Los Angeles when my year at DU ended in August. He was also taking two British friends, and he knew I had applied for jobs in Hollywood. Nigel fulfilled all my mental qualifications for a husband: British with Scottish connections (and the entire clan outfit), a secure future as a city planner and many tastes in common with my family. I could understand my parents' dismay that I wouldn't marry such a perfect match. The trouble was he repelled me physically. He was one of those pudgy men, not exactly fat, but with soft flesh and rosy English cheeks. I couldn't bear for him to touch me. And he was so 'square'. I know that sounds daft coming from me, but there are degrees. He irritated me beyond endurance. Still, I was grateful for the ride and a temporary connection with some of the aspects of the culture I'd known. I expected Neal to follow when he had sufficient funds. We would marry when we were both established.

My plan allowed Neal to reveal one of his own. He said he had reconsidered, and had agreed to go with Allen to Texas after all.

'I couldn't very well join you and your lover in LA, now could I, darling? So it works out perfectly, you see. While you're fol-de-rolling with your veddy, veddy British blokes and setting yourself up as the new Edith Head, I'll redeem my commitment to Allen, whom I let down so badly and disgracefully by not keeping my promise at the beginning of the summer – why? Because I fell in love so completely with the most beautiful and hip chick that ever came out of Nashville. It's your fault, really, darling, so you see you must agree because you have a teeny-weeny bit of guilt in this matter.'

Neal was an expert at using laughter to smooth over sticky situations, and I appreciated his need to soften the blow of our enforced separation.

'Besides,' Neal hesitated and danced about a bit, 'Uh, you see, um – Allen is in love with me too'. Neal looked demurely down at his hands.

'Allen? You mean…? My God, Neal. You knew this when you had him sleep in the same room with us? Why, that's positively sadistic! How could *you* be so mean? And now I see the drawing he asked me to make of you in the nude – the reason he wanted it.' I stopped to think. I wasn't at all prepared for this sort of thing. Neal looked at me suddenly with new concern.

'Wait now – you don't imagine – of course you must know – we don't – I mean, we'd never – now, really Carolyn, nothing like that.'

As a matter of fact, I had not yet considered that actual sex might be involved, not having encountered homosexuality before, and Neal certainly wasn't homosexual, so his reassurance was unnecessary.

Now it was Neal's turn to be shocked by my lack of resistance to his going off in the opposite direction. With honesty and resignation, I responded that I would not dispute his choice. He wasn't free to marry me, anyway, so perhaps a separation would prove if our love was strong enough to withstand one. I still believed Neal was the only man for me, but unless he felt the same, coercion would defeat my goal.

Then occurred the third and what I thought the final incident to set me straight about Neal.

My final week at DU was hectic, and to top it off, I had to perform an extra showing of *The Bluebird* for a group of children in a downtown movie theatre on Saturday morning. I was to leave for Los Angeles that afternoon. I had moved out of our room on Friday, and in with a fellow teacher near the campus, where Nigel would pick me up.

I got up and went downtown earlier than necessary to have one last farewell with Neal over breakfast. I tiptoed up the stairs and, hoping to surprise him, gingerly turned the doorknob. He did the surprising. The scene before me stunned me as if I had run into a wall or been hit on the head. There in *our* bed, nude, lay LuAnne, Neal and Allen in that order. Neal raised his head and mumbled something, but I was already stumbling back down the stairs and out into the street.

Somehow I must have performed my role in that sweet, allegorical, interminable children's play, in which I depicted, of all things, Light. If there was anything I needed, it was light. My mind was a blank, except for that scene in the bedroom replaying over and over in neon against my will, while I prayed for illumination. I had no frame of reference, no related experience, real or fictional, to draw on, and I couldn't discuss it with anyone.

On the afternoon of August 22, 1947, as our jolly party sped westwards, Neal and Allen prepared to head east, and 'never the twain...' So, it was over. Another summer romance. Surely, I told myself, it should take nothing more to convince me that I had been seriously misled. I should be grateful I had escaped in time. I could now forget the past six months and the man I'd met and loved: Neal Cassady.

| SEVEN |

Nigel and his friends took me back to the world I had known before Neal. A world that was stable, dependable, ordered. The last scene I had witnessed in Denver faded slowly into a part of my mind reserved for half-remembered nightmares.

Besides myself and Nigel, our party consisted of an engineer from London on assignment to research American highway construction, and the woman director of a Canadian ballet company. Neither had travelled in the United States before, and I found it refreshing to see the country through their eyes. The most impressive feature to the engineer was the food. Coming from war-starved England, he couldn't get enough of steak and eggs.

This carefree excursion provided salve for my wound, but although we laughed a good deal, it didn't lift the stone in my heart. Neal's ghost accompanied me, and I inwardly communicated with him all of my observations as I would have wanted to share them with him had we been together. In Los Angeles, while Nigel and I danced in the Biltmore Hotel ballroom, he pleaded with me again to wake up and see that he and I belonged together. I told him I could sympathize with his feelings, because I felt exactly the same way about someone else. Here was a man offering me everything I had dreamed of in my teens, yet every bit of me yearned for Neal.

After we explored the movie studios, my three British friends continued their tour to Mexico, leaving me to contend with the Hollywood union hall.

Alone again, I did try not to, but I couldn't help sharing it all with Neal, as I had done all summer. I filled my spare and lonely hours writing to him in Texas, just as a friend now, of course, telling myself I had learned not to regard him as a husband. When I was promised the next vacant job at the Western Costume Company, a prerequisite for film company jobs, I went to San Francisco to wait, preferring to live there. I had an older sister in the city with whom I could stay until settled in my own job and residence.

Two letters from Neal awaited me there. They were filled with even more warmth and love than his previous avowals of undying devotion, and were equally convincing in their apologies and remorse. I forgave him instantly and was again whole. The wheel of fate cranked on.

Neal described Bill Burroughs's ranch, where he and Allen were staying, as a 'crazy spot,' a ramshackle affair of wooden shacks on 97 acres, its chief virtues being its isolation, affordability and plenty of space for growing marijuana. The property was in New Waverly, and Bill lived there with Joan Adams and her two small children, one Bill, Jr, the older a girl, Julie, by a former husband or lover. Staying with them also was Herbert Huncke, a friend of Bill's from New York.

Neal wrote that he helped with the chores, had built a fence, repaired the garage, laid a cement floor and dammed a creek. He didn't mention the marijuana again, or that Bill was also a heroin addict. He did say that Joan was a Benzedrine addict, and required at least eight full tubes of it every day. Huncke enjoyed it as well, with or without large quantities of Nembutal. Neal said he had to drive regularly the 60 miles to Houston to collect these and other supplies. Joan rarely slept, if at all, and worked at household or garden chores day and night.

Neal also wrote that Bill spent most of his time testing his accuracy with one or another of his firearms. He would set, or have Neal set, tin cans on the fence to pick off from the porch or the rocking chair behind the window in the front room. Bill also shot at Benzedrine tubes on the mantle with his airgun. He was proud of his marksmanship and gun collection. Caring for and cleaning his armoury occupied much of his time, too. The composite picture of life in New Waverly was as revolting to me as anything could be.

Neal confessed that one purpose of his going to Texas with Allen besides meeting Bill and Joan was to try to return Allen's physical desires, because it meant so much to Allen, but every attempt failed miserably – or hilariously, when a cot collapsed. Allen, disheartened, planned to sign on a ship to earn money. Now that this issue was settled, all Neal could think of, he wrote, was rejoining me and making up for his foolishness in having allowed our separation. He had promised Bill, however, to drive his family and Huncke to New York, but after this, and when he could raise the fare, he would race to San Francisco and me.

Allen missed the first ship he'd signed on, so Neal and Huncke waited with him for another one. Neal reported that after four hours with no luck 'we made tender good-byes and left Allen... reading Henry James and musing on his fate.' Allen finally got a ship bound for Dakar, Senegal, Africa on which he wrote *Dakar Doldrums*, the sequel to *Denver Doldrums* and not the only poems to be salted by tears from that crucible of a summer.

*　　*　　*

I had learned to love the San Francisco bay area while training with the Army as an occupational therapist at Mills College in Oakland. San Francisco was unique in its openness to the air and light, air that smelled as if it had been washed with soap, the pastel apartment buildings and the casual friendly people. Such a contrast to New York, where we had to go to ballparks to see the sky and grass, except in Central Park. I longed to be more like those courageous, defiant folk who dared construct buildings on hills so steep cars parked sideways at a list, and steps, not sidewalks, flanked the pavement. The clear blue of sky and sea brought exhilarating nostalgia for the waters of my beloved Michigan and the moan of protecting foghorns recalled the sound of Lake Michigan lighthouses – times of security and roots.

After a week or two with my sister and her husband, I got a job 'in jewelry' at Joseph Magnin's, and rented a space in a home on Telegraph Hill.

My 'space' consisted of a cot and a chest in a corner of a glassed-in front porch of a quaint house on the cliff overhanging the bay. I took it at once for the magnificent view, the address being renowned, and a popular dwelling place for that reason. My cousin had once been able to get an apartment there. He was a journalist and was sent to report on a man who had drowned in the bath tub. With the man still in the tub, one of the cops and a paramedic had already applied for the apartment, but my cousin offered more money and got it. I had visited him there and vowed to return one day.

My landlady was in her seventies, the widow of a famous painter. She wore her platinum-dyed hair in thick bangs and a pageboy bob. She fluttered long claw-curved bright red fingernails, dressed herself in oriental pyjamas and drank gin all day. At first by the time I got home each night, she would be staggering and often barely avoided catapulting out the windows and into the bay. She would sit in her rocker at the opposite end of the porch from my cot, flailing away at a ukulele to the accompaniment of a radio, set to a jumble of sounds between stations. After learning to sleep through this cacophony, I was frequently awakened by her lounging on her huge tester bed in the main room while conducting a one-sided telephone conversation at the top of her lungs in Cantonese.

Sometimes she would mistake me for her long-lost daughter and weep over me in bed, clutching me to her ample bosom. On other nights she would insist I stay up late and drink mug after mug of tanic acid she called tea – 'like they make in India. Oh, you have finished – here, let me pour more for you.' If I didn't drink it all, I got severely scolded.

For a while I enjoyed her as a character, and I had fun recounting her antics at work, but it began to wear thin. I still loved my prized address and the nightscape I came home to – the glittering lights on the hills of Oakland and Berkeley connected by the jewelled bracelets of the bridges spanning the water.

I had made friends with Lucy, a girl 'in scarves', her counter across from mine. Her husband, George, was a merchant seaman home on leave, and they were both about five feet tall, shorter than I. He took us to dinner every evening after I told him I couldn't cook at my house, or wouldn't because of the landlady. He always paid, and I got home late enough that often the landlady had succumbed to gin and sleep.

When George learned of Neal's imminent arrival and our plan to live together until we could marry, he asked me if we would do him a big favour. During his travels he had collected many Chinese and other treasures that were buried in expensive storage. He asked that if he rented an apartment in which to keep them, would we live in it and look after them. He would soon be gone again for six months, and during that time we need pay no rent, in exchange for taking care of his acquisitions. I was overjoyed. He found a new one-storey complex well off the street in the Richmond district, and rented a two-bedroom apartment with separate entrance, surrounded by shrubs. He furnished all rooms completely, including the kitchen, and adorned it with his beautiful chests, tables, lamps, statuary, pictures. I couldn't believe he'd trust me with all this, but I couldn't wait to show Neal our elegant home. His first.

| EIGHT |

Although it seemed like years, by the time Neal stepped off the bus in San Francisco on October 4, only five weeks had elapsed since we had parted in Denver. The day of his arrival crawled. I took countless cigarette breaks, chewed my cuticles, and was inattentive on my job. One customer to whom I had shown several necklaces threw the last one in my face and huffed, 'Well, you certainly don't want to sell it very badly!' True enough, and the blow jolted me back to my surroundings. When six o'clock finally rolled around, I fumbled into my coat and even passed the door inspection, although I had forgotten to remove the store's gold earrings.

Emerging into the lowering dusk and fog, I braced myself against the raw, wet wind and walked around to the front door. There I found Neal leaning against the marble storefront, appearing almost as I had first seen him. He wore the same suit and T-shirt, and looked handsome, his hair ruffled over his forehead, his face ruddy from the wind. When he saw me, his pinched expression vanished in the breadth of his smile. We were both awkward, and suddenly too shy to embrace. Beside him was the familiar suitcase, roped together, and two cardboard boxes. My belief in his devotion was confirmed when I learned he had ridden all the way from New York on a *bus*; it deepened when he said how careful he had been to keep his coat tucked under him so as not to wrinkle it. The boxes were full of records given to him by a 'gone singer'.

I persuaded him to let me hire a cab. I was impatient to have him alone and to tell him about our new apartment. As I gushed on, he only held my hand and gazed at me, then nuzzled my neck with his cold nose.

After appropriate exclamations of wonder over our new home, he showered and changed while I prepared the setting for the meal I had mentally rehearsed a hundred times. He took on my mood, and surpassed every movie hero I had ever adored.

'Tonight, my darling, I've got a super-special, extra-ordinary, sen-sa-tion-al treat for us. Yessiree, baby, the best is yet to come.' He stood up and struck his Oliver Hardy pose, chin tucked in, elbows flapping, thumbs in his armpits, fingers rippling on either side of his extended chest while rocking on his toes and heels. His eyes twinkled and crinkled, his lips compressed in a smug smile.

'Can your treat wait until I change? I can't possibly relax in this straightjacket of girdle and hose.'

'Why certainly, my dear. You go right ahead and "slip into something more comfortable" as they say, while I make a few *preparations* here, heh, heh, heh.' Now he was Uriah Heep, churning his hands together.

When I'd donned my housecoat, I went to the kitchen to check the waiting dinner plans. I had partially baked the potatoes that morning, made the salad the night before, and the apple pie would be all right cold with the ice cream. The steak and vegetables would take only minutes to cook while the potatoes finished baking. Okay.

I started to cook, but Neal called me back to the living room. He had spread a newspaper on the coffee table covered in dry green mounds of twisted leaves and twigs and tiny seeds.

'Now, my darling, before we eat we must have just a tiny bit of this to make that beautiful meal of yours taste like something you never had.'

We sat side-by-side on the couch while he delicately removed the seeds and put them carefully in a clean ash tray. In his right hand he now cradled a cigarette paper, and with his left he picked up a pinch of leaves and spread it along the paper.

I knew this had to be marijuana, although I'd never seen it before, and felt a little jolt of fear remembering the stories I'd heard as a teenager about 'devil weed'. But this was Neal, who was about to be my husband and would let nothing harm me.

With a flourish, Neal moistened the paper with his tongue and pressed it down the full length of the skinny cigarette, stroking it and gently rolling it back and forth to even out the lumps. His eyes were glittering like some devilish witch doctor as he carefully twisted one end of the paper and just as carefully pinched the other flat. Holding it before him, thumb and forefinger at its centre, he turned to me. With a sombre expression, he held my eyes with his.

'Now darling, listen to me. You must have no fear, hear me? It is completely harmless, I promise you. All those tales you've doubtless heard are entirely false, perpetrated by Anslinger to keep his narcotic squad boys employed. All this does is heighten your sensory perception and awaken you to your own true awareness and speed up your thought processes while giving the impression time has immeasurably slowed. You will see more and see better – colours, patterns – and music! You think you've heard music? You've never heard it until you hear it on tea; you'll hear every note and every instrument simultaneously as you never have before. Oh, ho, ho, ho – just you wait!'

His own description so excited him his attempt to be serious disintegrated into chortles of delight.

'Then, after a while, we'll dig into that delicious meal and you'll taste as you never have before! Pure ambrosia – you'll see.'

Unable to sit still, Neal had hopped up and was striding around the room punctuating his speech with extravagant gestures and rolling his eyes.

'Ah, but to return to your fears, darling –' He crouched beside me on the floor, growing serious again.

'I must emphasize this point: the most important thing for you to remember is that you are always in control. Anything you have to do you can do! Hear me? Remember that. And another thing: you can't tell in advance how you're going to feel – that is, what you'll feel like doing. Sometimes you'll want to talk or maybe not at all. Other times everything sounds funny, and you'll laugh all night. But, as I said, if you have to do something you always can. *And* you can't take it just one time and know how you are on it. You must use it every night at first, say for a week. That way you'll find out your own different moods and responses. Then you won't have to worry about getting paranoid someplace, because you'll know how it affects *you*, see?' I took it all in through the pores.

'Now then, watch closely, m'dear. You can't smoke these like cigarettes.'

He held the 'joint' away from him while he applied a match to the twisted end and waited for the paper to burn off. Then he put the flat end between his lips and drew in short, noisy breaths without closing his mouth, inhaling more deeply on each gasp until his lungs were fully expanded. He held his breath and became red in the face. When he could hold it no longer he exhaled, expelling very little smoke.

'You see? Keep it all in. Now. You noticed I took in as much air as smoke? Too strong otherwise. Burns your throat too much, and you lose some – ooooooooooh, myyyyyy, this is good shit – oops, I beg your pardon, darling. Excellent product, this, yas indeed!'

His eyes had turned quite pink as his gaze wandered upwards.

'Ah, the point is not to waste any, see; get all you get, dig? Now you try. Prepare yourself for the awakening of your latent mind and senses. You never even *knew*, ho, whooooo.'

I did my best to imitate what he had done, but I'd only inhaled my first weak drag when the unexpected searing in my throat made me cough. He patted my back. 'Here, here; never you mind; everybody does that the first time.' He was growling through clenched teeth and held breath, having frantically relieved me of the joint and puffed rapidly to keep it lit. He then nodded urgently and thrust it at me again. This time I managed to get some smoke and hold it in. My first sensation was a sort of cool feeling inside my chest. There was a pungent, earthy tang to the taste and a generally expanding feeling of wholeness throughout my body.

I moved an ashtray closer to him, but he shook his head. 'No need, see? The ashes are just fluff.' He brushed the end of the joint with his little finger and only a small piece of unburned paper floated down. It had gone out, a frequent occurrence. (In later years, I could tell when he had been smoking tea by the quantity of telltale matches in the ashtray.) When I had had another couple of respectable tokes, he decided that was enough for a beginner and we should now eat.

While I finished the cooking, he sorted through the records he had brought with him and put aside some for us to hear after dinner.

When we finished eating and lingered over our coffee and liquor in the candlelight, a question resurfaced in my mind I had been too happy to notice. Now it needed banishing with an answer. Neal lit a cigarette and leaned back in his chair with a satisfied sigh, patting his tummy. I asked, 'Did you see LuAnne in Denver on your way here? Has she gotten the annulment?'

Neal was absorbed by the end of his cigarette. 'Uh...yes, well, of course, darling – we *must* talk about that, but let's do it in the morning. Can we? Right *now*, so's to continue this marvellous homecoming eve and not bring us down, let me help you put these dishes in the sink so we can keep our high and hear music.'

Everything he had said about the tea effects were true so far. The meal did taste better than any I'd had. My favourite part became the extension of time. He put on a record by Ella Fitzgerald. We lay flat on the floor and were silent, simply letting Ella permeate every nerve. The instrumentals by the Duke were like revelations to me, even having heard his music so often, and each selection seemed to last far longer than usual.

'Ah, my love, we are going to have a beautiful life together. I can just see us at eighty sitting on the verandah, rocking in our chairs and never having to say a word – just look at each other, smile, nod. We'll know exactly what the other is thinking telepathically. We will be so in tune, so *one*, we will communicate without words at all, eh?'

I smiled all over and hugged him, saying, 'You must be exhausted, honey, but you've given me such a lovely time tonight. I've missed you so much and am so happy to have you back.'

'For good now, darling. It's you and me, baby, from now on, right?'

He hugged me closer. We stood up and put the records away.

'And now, my love, it's "past the clock", as your father says – and – Ah HA!' He smirked and twirled an imaginary moustache, bringing our laughter back.

Neal kept his word (happy for the excuse) and put me through a week's indoctrination. I approved of the time expansion and second-by-second awareness, as well as the physical feeling of wellbeing, and certainly the heightened senses. I did try, but I could never get over the fear, not of the drug's dangers so much, but of being caught in an illegal act. Eventually, I also began to resent the control of my mind by an external agent, and gave it up. I want to be the boss and make my own choices. In time, when I was seriously studying meditation and heightened concentration, I found I could replicate some of these effects without 'additives'.

| NINE |

The next day Neal wrote to Jack, who was now back in New York.

> My conviction that Carolyn is enough is, I find, correct – so don't worry about your boy Neal; he's found what he wants and in her is attaining greater satisfaction than he'd ever known... I am finding it easier to lead a more productive life, having escaped the fixation on my need to write. I now find I'm relaxed enough to start plugging away at it; this seems to fit my temperament to a greater extent than the old frantic unreasoning drive... Just got a great letter from Allen; he calls me down plenty, and I'm sure he's right. Now don't you agree with him, well, I agree with both of you but not enough to come back to New York until next year. So *that's settled*.

When Neal had left New York for San Francisco, Allen was still at sea, so Neal had left him a letter that Allen found 'harsh'. Neal wrote, 'I suppose I must say good-bye, then. I don't know how.' He didn't say good-bye, and letters were again exchanged, although not as frequently as before. Allen suffered a long time over Neal's rejection in Texas. 'I have protected myself, armored...from grief or too much self-pity, and as a result saw my mind turn more than ever before...into isolation and phony goodness – to the point of retiring from the world, which I have not, yet, to a furnished room to write cold hot poems.'

Allen made one more all-out agonized appeal to Neal to come back to him in a letter that must be classed as a symphony of unrequited love.

Allen did not address me directly for several years. I was sorry to lose his friendship, and who could understand his feelings better than I? An accident of gender was all that put me where he wanted to be. I was genuinely sorry for him, especially since there seemed no ray of hope, and his poignant letters affected me deeply in their Chekhovian pathos.

The night following my reunion with Neal I came home from work to find Neal restless and preoccupied. When I had done the dishes, he didn't get out the tea right away. He lay on the couch devouring a news magazine. I sat on the floor, leaned back against the couch, and lit a cigarette. Neal threw down his magazine, raised himself on one elbow, and put an arm around my shoulders and chest, his head against mine.

'I've got to tell you something, sweetheart. You see, I did stop in Denver, as you know.' He sat up, swung his feet to the floor and began pacing. 'Well, I finally found LuAnne, and, well, the bitch, she's got some dumb reason why she can't, *won't*, get the annulment. She says she won't have the money for another two or three weeks. And since I don't have any...but she did promise she will definitely do it.' He saw I was about to speak, so continued. 'Now, now, don't you fret. What's a couple of weeks when we have our whole life? It won't be long, you'll see, and I'll keep needling her.'

He turned up my face and pecked kisses all over it so that I couldn't reply.

'Now then,' he coaxed, 'let's forget all about her and all her nonsense.' He bounded up to bring out the tea, and the evening's education began. Although I wondered why LuAnne hadn't gotten the annulment long since, feeling as she apparently did, I trusted Neal as usual and felt I was his responsibility, never doubting he was as anxious as I to tie the knot.

Again LuAnne faded from my mind.

San Francisco offered us a cornucopia of exciting activities to share, and Neal always added another dimension to the entertainment. No matter what amusement we indulged in, whether table games at home, movies, plays, lectures, concerts, jazz musicians, the zoo, Chinatown, galleries, or just watching sailboats on the bay, Neal's mind elaborated on the scene before us and expanded the enjoyment, sometimes sweeping and soaring on wings of fancy, like the ever-present gulls, or relating his observations of obscure minutiae to corresponding ideas in life, literature, philosophy and history. After a lecture we attended, he wrote to Jack:

> I saw the great, one and only Thomas Mann day before yesterday. He gave a terrific lecture on 'Nietsche in the Light of Modern Experience.' It was not a simple rehash of stock thought and inept handling of our Frederick, but rather, pushed into the real 'rarified air' of *true* under-standing; not abstract and nonsense and trashy, trite inquiries into his motives...but honest dealment with the problem...

I was interested in the local little theatre, and Neal accompanied me to several plays, a new experience for him. He could hardly sit still, seeming to enter into every actor's role and becoming aware of all the accoutrements on stage. Again he wrote to Jack:

> Of late I've become more aware of the theater as a release. I love to do take-offs on everybody...Chaplin, Barrymore, etc. I feel the urge to jump up and act out, stage, direct, costume and photograph an entire Class-B movie; all this in a hurried, confused dialogue and pantomime which is mixed in with frantic rushing from one side of the room to the opposite as I progress with the epic. Scene after scene rolls out; one coming out of another, and soon I'm portraying everybody from the scriptwriter to the tem-peramental star, from the leader who arranges and conducts the music for the soundtrack to the stage hands who dash in and out with the sets.

As usual, Neal was high on tea and had Dizzy Gillespie's 'Salt Peanuts' be-bopping at full blast. Intermittently, at record changes or scene shifts, he would bolt to the refrigerator, grab an open quart of beer and pour great glugs down his throat with trickles down his chin and bare chest, eager to unfold his thrilling saga. During one of these breaks, I continued the letter:

> Jack, Neal is now gorging himself with the aforementioned Class B movie. This time, he is sprawling on the couch, as usual nude, gazing cross-eyed into space, wheezing, 'I

retreat – I retreat!' – to Tibet, that is, accompanying each
'retreat' by flailing the arms and legs alternately about.
He becomes annoyed with me now...

Dear Jack – this fiend, Carolyn, has just swiped my typewriter for 30 seconds, while I explained *The Razor's Edge*
in its entirety.

Such were the glorious and fulfilling days of our first two months.
The sex had not improved to the extent I had hoped, but I resigned
myself to that one flaw in an otherwise perfect life. Besides, around
the first part of November, Neal got a job. It was with a service
station chain that had a 'revolutionary' approach and high-powered
promotion. Their idea was for five men to hit a car at once and see
how fast they could service it, including washing the insides of the
windows and vacuuming the floors. This was the kind of challenge
Neal responded to, even if he disapproved of their methods. Soon
Neal had memorized the massive journals of sales procedures and
required attitudes and was out-smiling the other employees as only
he could. He impressed the bosses and got more frequent raises in
pay than anyone else, which did not make him popular with his co-
workers. As a customer, when we'd got a car, I found their methods
startling to say the least, even frightening when one wasn't expecting
the mass onslaught.

Monday was my day off, and on December 1 I was at home. Neal
got home early, and we were cosily relaxing over a game of chess when
the doorbell rang. I answered it and was confronted by two girls
standing on the stoop. It took a moment for me to recognize one of
them as LuAnne and the other as Lois, Al Hinkle's Denver girlfriend.

This LuAnne was not the little girl in pigtails I had last seen. Here
was a beautiful, sophisticated young woman, well groomed and
chic, her shiny bronze hair a mass of loose curls to her shoulders.
Her hazel eyes were shadowed by thick black lashes, her complexion
waxen-smooth, her wet red lips curved in a stunning smile over
perfect teeth, all framed in a huge white fox-fur collar. She was
breathtaking.

'Lu*Anne*! and Lois – do come in. Why, what a surprise. Neal,
look who's here?' The girls teetered on their high heels over our
thick carpet. Neal only stared at LuAnne as she walked towards
him, her hand outstretched.

'Well, Neal – aren't you going to say hello? How have you been?'

'Of course.' Neal rose from the couch but ignored her hand. 'You're looking well. What are you doing in San Francisco?' he added in dull tones.

'Here – let me take your coats; do sit down,' I said. As I went to the hall closet, LuAnne sat on the couch, away from Neal.

'Well, I really don't know yet; we've only been here a few days. We drove out with Greg – you remember him, don't you? Ever since you left he has been nagging me to marry him. Of course, I don't want to do *that*, but I did accept a ride to San Francisco, provided, I said, I could bring Lois along as a chaperone.' She giggled at her own joke, her eyes twinkling as she teased Neal. The more she laughed and chattered, the surlier Neal became, it now being crystal clear where her new look had originated.

'You will stay to dinner, won't you?' I asked. 'It's been so long since I've seen you.' She accepted and offered to help.

'No no, no need. You must tell Neal all the news from Denver.' I was glad I had something to do and didn't need to watch the cat with the mouse.

During the meal, LuAnne's manner was festive and charming in spite of Neal's continued glowering and brusque retorts. She was evidently enjoying some revenge, and I had to agree Neal deserved it. She played her cards well and got just what she wanted. Neal was angry on all counts, including a few that were unknown to me at that time. I was more amused than anything by LuAnne's performance, and, in spite of her new glamour, I felt no threat to our solid and secure marriage – for in my mind Neal and I were already married. The only burning question that remained was whether she had obtained the annulment. I thought Greg might just have lent her the money to support his suit.

When Neal returned from seeing LuAnne and Lois to his car, he said she had not, and it was to this that I attributed (wrongly) his now open fury. A few days later he wrote to Jack:

> On December 1st LuAnne arrived here. She was quite changed, affected a more sophisticated air, came on hep and moved with improved poise. After some preliminary skirmishing, we reverted back to an old naturalness of relationship and it was with great difficulty that I finally managed to extract the commitment of desire to gain an

annulment from her. The process of becoming legally free rests now on money. After the 5th I'll have some and forward it to her mother in Denver to start the divorce.

I think, dear Jack, we've underestimated money. I predict a lucrative year for me, since I'm goin' to make money one object of this year's struggle.

| TEN |

Soon Christmas loomed, and I had gifts to buy, wrap and mail to my extensive family. I had grown up with wonderful Dickensian Christmases, and this holiday represented all that was most sentimental to me.

Gifts began arriving for us as well, postmarked from all over the country and beyond. Along with colourful packages came boxes of traditional food: home-smoked country ham from Tennessee, cheese from Canada, my mother's English plum pudding from a secret family recipe, and the huge box of international cookies baked by my sister who had lived in Germany – some of them even retaining their original shapes in spite of the efforts of the U.S. mail to reduce them all to crumbs.

Neal was dumbfounded by such a display of family affection and tradition, especially since each member included a gift for him. Even though no one imagined we lived together under the same roof, he had been accepted as a family member when I had announced our engagement.

In Neal's efforts to become top candidate for promotion again at work, he had burned himself out. His ardour waned. In spite of his vow to Jack to make money a priority, he was lax, and his attendance lagged. He had another problem of which I was blissfully ignorant then, and it would have stunned me to learn that contributing in large measure to his state of mind and exhaustion was LuAnne. I had not presumed that sex was what Neal meant by the 'naturalness' of their former relationship. She toyed with him and flaunted her lovers and their gifts. It was an effective campaign; she managed to plunge him into agonies of desire and jealousy, since Neal believed 'once his, always his', and after all she *was* still his wife.

The Christmas display at home and these tortures with LuAnne stirred Neal's ambivalence again, the tension erupting in maddening hives on his body. He had not written to Allen for six weeks, but on December 30 he summed up his condition in a private letter he kept from me.

> On December 1st LuAnne came to town and since then has been a constant thorn; she is with an old beau and a girl friend, and together they all live in a downtown hotel. Since she doesn't work (although the other two do) and does nothing, even read, she has much time to come by my station in his car, call on me at home in the morning while Carolyn is away and before I go to work; in short, my efforts toward an annulment have been little rewarded. However, now that I've at least (during several emotional scenes) made it plain to her that all is finished, she has again promised to have her mother gain our legal separation...I am moving by myself again, because Carolyn has practically gotten married to me in the eyes of her family, and unless I break quickly, things may become drastic.

The puzzle I never solved was why Neal gave me no hint of this attitude towards our marriage at that time. I had no reason then to suspect he didn't really want something that he had so strenuously promoted. Neal's pain physically and resulting despondency caused him new doubts even about writing as a career. He discussed it with Jack on paper:

> There is something in me that wants to come out, something of my own that must be said. Yet, perhaps, words are not the way for me...I have found myself looking to others for the answer to my soul, whereas I know this is slowly gained (if at all) by delving into my own self only. I am not too sure that the roots of the impulse to write go deep enough, are necessary enough for me to create on paper. If, however, I find writing a must (as you've seemed to) then I know I must build my life around this necessity; even my most indifferent and trivial hours must become an expression of this impulse and a testimony to it.
>
> I have always held that when one writes, one should forget all rules, literary styles and other such pretensions as large words, lordly clauses and other phrases as such –

rolling the words around in the mouth as one would wine, and proper or not, putting on paper that which he saw and experienced and loved and lost; what his passing thoughts were and his sorrows and desires, and these things should be said with careful avoidance of common phrases, trite usage of hackney words and the like. One must combine Wolfe and Flaubert – and Dickens. Art is good when it springs from necessity. This kind of origin is the guarantee of its value; there is no other.

Jack was then working on his first novel, *The Town and the City*, writing in an academic and traditional style, much influenced by Thomas Wolfe (why Neal mentioned this author no doubt). This letter of Neal's, as well as later ones true to these observations, affected Jack profoundly, as his later works and he himself have testified. To me it was an example of his remarkable mind and wisdom overlooked by commentators on his work.

Because I was kept in the dark regarding LuAnne, I attributed Neal's allergy solely to overwork. He had told me briefly about LuAnne and Lois coming occasionally to the station and his anger at her for delaying the annulment, yet his physical reaction was too severe a consequence to have been caused by that, so I urged him to leave that job and seek one less demanding. After resigning, he did improve some, but the acquisition of his first very own car may have played some part in it (the money not going to LuAnne's mother). He summed up his present condition to Jack.

> I crushed my hand, but it's OK. I took my pills so my hives are OK. I settled LuAnne and Carolyn (inadequately) so that's OK. I guess I'm OK. Twenty years ago General Motors, Chevrolet Division, made a car with a 4-cylinder motor. I now own a copy of same. The paint job is original, the motor's original, the upholstery's original, the wheel's original; in fact, the only thing that didn't come with the car when it left the factory in Flint, Michigan is the license plates. Price? – Gulp – 225 dollars. How much have I paid? 100 dollars. Come to think of it, I'm not OK; I'm broke and in debt up to my ears.

Neal answered an appealing ad for a job selling encyclopedias. The man in charge turned out to be a Charles Adams character with a name too symbolic to be believed – Sinsir. He was very short and round, with greying sparse reddish hair. He looked a combination of old Fuzziwig and Uriah Heep, always grinning, bouncing and rubbing his hands together. He had a chauffeur who was a near-double for Lon Chaney, only more so: tall, heavy-set, dark and ugly, and not too bright. He made up for what he lacked mentally by faithful obedience to his master. These two were the sum total of the 'Book Company'.

Sinsir knew a good thing when he saw Neal, and soon outshone him in con games. He infected Neal with his own enthusiasm for the ease with which they were to amass a fortune.

One of his favourite sadistic tricks was to get out of his car at a busy thoroughfare, step off the curb and, pretending to be spastic, make his contorted way across the street, bringing all the traffic, including heavy trucks, to a screeching standstill, the drivers' faces filled with pity. After a few minutes, he would repeat the 'joke' on the way back, where he and his sidekick would convulse in laughter. I happened to be along on one of those days. I didn't think it at all funny, nor did Neal.

Sinsir's persuasive persistence tended to hypnotize or terrorize poor families, and before they knew it they had borrowed or signed away their grocery or rent money for a set of books they probably couldn't read. Sinsir wasn't aware of Neal's deep compassion for his fellow man, and it didn't take long before Neal became so disgusted and appalled by these two that he quit, Sinsir accusing Neal of owing him money. He hated losing Neal, and only stopped calling when we moved away.

| ELEVEN |

These months of my greatest happiness were about to come to an end. I missed a menstrual period. My feelings gyrated from one extreme to the other. I expected to have a family with Neal, but not yet, not before we were married. More important at that time was the shame I knew I would bring my family. I went to a doctor without telling Neal, hoping against hope. The doctor said, 'Congratulations.' I knew Neal would be no more overjoyed than I, but I also knew he would stand by me and we would work it out together. I told him one night at dinner, and he did very well in almost convincing me

I had not misjudged him. When he told me the next day he thought he had found a way to 'take care of it', I was crushed. (We must keep in mind the difference between my mindset in 1948 and now.)

That morning Neal drove me down Market Street and dropped me off at a tall office building. I had the name of a doctor Neal had found and, trembling, I took the elevator to his office. Much of this visit was shrouded in confusion about my reason for being there. I remember little except the doctor's anger and disapproval of my expectations of him. Dazed, I hurriedly left him and waited in the cold rain for Neal to drive up. I was in tears, and Neal was kind again, but I was in a state of shock, miserable and apprehensive.

'Sh-sh-sh, now, darling, don't cry,' Neal coaxed, sweeping me up in his arms. 'It's just that it worried me, you understand – no job, no money. We're not ready to have a baby yet, now are we? You don't want one now, do you? There's so much more we have to do together before we start a family. I was only trying to think of us and what's best for our baby. Forgive me, love – I'm sorry it was so messed up – shh. You know we love each other, right, darling?' He lifted my chin and kissed my wet cheeks. Although he had uttered all the stock phrases, I believed him again and felt relieved, pushing aside the question of why he hadn't discussed the idea with me first.

This new and unforeseen development made Christmas not the joyous celebration I had hoped for. We did our best, and appreciated all and sundry nonetheless.

For Neal's birthday on February 8, I looked forward to cooking him a special dinner and making as much of it as our finances allowed. I had learned already he took special dates seriously, almost religiously, and some sort of ritual to mark them appealed to him, perhaps because he had never experienced such celebrations when growing up.

Although it was a Sunday, I had to work helping with inventory, and when I emerged from the store into the twilight Neal wasn't parked in the loading zone as usual. He had never been late before. I searched the streets looking for his car without success, and then settled to wait by the side door, wrapping my coat tightly around me against the wind and gusting fog. Funny, he hadn't phoned me, so I assumed he'd had a flat or something. After another fifteen or twenty minutes, I was chilled and walked up to Geary Street to get a street-car, uneasiness and fear beginning to creep up on me.

I had always enjoyed the ride out to the avenues on the big open streetcars, and this evening as we clicked along the tracks and clanged at the crossroads, I tried to relax with a cigarette in the fresh damp air. I reassured myself by supposing that maybe Neal was planning a surprise himself for his birthday.

It was not yet quite dark when I walked across Geary and down the block of 24th Avenue to our apartment. Then I saw the car by the curb. He was home? I figured there must have been something wrong with the car. I quickened my pace. Just as I turned into our walk, from the corner of my eye I saw a movement in the back seat of the car. I swung around and looked in. Neal was lying on the seat. What on earth? Was he hurt? I yanked open the door. 'Darling! What is it? Why...'

'Go away!' he barked in a tone I had never heard before – gruff, hostile, chilling. Stunned, I backed away as though hit, only then seeing the silver revolver in his left hand. I panicked, flung the door shut and ran up the walk and steps into the apartment. I was shaking violently now. I paced rapidly around the rooms in an effort to control my pounding heart. Neal with a gun! He had always told me he felt as I did about them. Violence of any kind sickened me and him, but firearms terrified me. I had only seen one pistol up close in my life; my father forbade any sort of gun in our home. How and where could Neal have found one? More important – why? I didn't know where to begin to unravel the nightmare, nor what to do next. I sat on the edge of the big chair, desperately trying to calm myself and think constructively.

The front door slowly opened, and Neal came in, the pistol dangling in his hand, his face pale and drawn. He slumped down on the chest beside my chair and held the gun butt towards me. 'Here, you do it, *please*, Carolyn, You do it for me. Help me. I've tried all day. I'm a coward. I can't do it.'

I had already sprung from my chair as though it were on fire and he was handing me a rattlesnake. 'Neal, Neal – what is the matter?' I managed to croak weakly from the other side of the room. '*Why*, Neal, oh why?' Actually, I now began to fear for his sanity.

Neal dropped the gun in the chair, rocked back and forth, his head in his hands, but didn't answer. I summoned all my courage and went to pick up the gun to put it up on a high shelf of the bookcase by the door.

'Where on earth did you get that?'

'It's Al's.' Neal leaned back heavily against the wall.

'Al's? Al Hinkle's?' Was Al a member of the cast of this bizarre show?

'What would Al want with a gun?' Crazier and crazier.

'I don't know. I found it in his glove compartment and took it one day.'

So we were back to the beginning, but he wasn't answering the right questions. Although I was still trembling, and my mouth was dry, my teeth chattering, I took off my coat and hung it up. What to do? Get Al. Maybe he could explain, and I would feel better with another man around. I dialled his number in Oakland and he answered, thank God! My tone of voice in saying 'It's Neal' was all he needed. 'I'll be right over,' he said, and hung up. I sat down on the couch and rested my head on the back. Neal stood by the window, calmer now. I waited for him to speak. At length he did, without turning around.

'Please, Carolyn, forgive me. I'm sorry I frightened you; I didn't mean to. I didn't think. Don't worry; I'm all right now. I haven't lost my mind yet, although I thought I had for a while.' Then he came to me and kneeled with his head in my lap. I stroked his hair but didn't know what to say. I was still disturbed, not only from the incident but from seeing this new strange Neal.

When we heard running footsteps on the walk, Neal jumped up to open the door and greet Al, putting on a jovial voice in an effort to clear the heavy air. 'Come right in, old buddy. Ahem, just having a little family crisis here, you know, heh, heh; nothing to be concerned about, really.'

It was a feeble effort, and Al looked past him to me, searching my face and then Neal's again. I pointed to the gun. 'Is that thing yours, Al?' Al reached up and took the gun down from the shelf.

'So that's what happened to it. I forgot to lock my car, and I was sure someone had stolen it. Wow.' He began emptying the chambers.

'I can't imagine you owning a gun. Why would you ever want one?'

'Oh, I dunno; I just saw it in the pawnshop window, and it was so cheap I bought it. Guess it's a leftover from my cowboy hero days.'

Al put the gun down on the carved Chinese chest by the door and turned his attention to Neal, who had sat down. I went over and picked up the gun, somehow fascinated, as though it were a dead snake. I handled it cautiously, trying to fathom the horror it held for me. When I barely grazed the trigger and it released, I dropped it, more frightened than ever, remembering Neal's finger crooked around that trigger the whole time he had held it.

Al could tell Neal was uncomfortable, so he talked in his quiet way about other things and suggested a game of chess. His presence and his homilies did much to soothe me, and he seemed to be having a healthy effect on Neal as well. So I left them and went to change my clothes and get dinner, hoping to bring us back to normality. I didn't quite know how to make this a birthday celebration now. I had only bought him cigarettes and socks. Well, I'd play it by ear and try to choose an appropriate time to present them.

Neal never gave me an explanation, and I was afraid to demand one. I would simply have to be patient and as loving as possible until he felt like unburdening himself.

It was to Jack, five months later, that he did so, or tried to, without my knowledge. He had not answered any of Jack's letters during that time, because, he said, 'describing my tortures by mail would result in my becoming too overbalanced or too distastefully, incoherently mad.' Having failed several times to relate his 'ache and distorted vision of flesh and latest most terrified stupidities' to Jack, he listed chronological events that 'are strangely, entirely removed from my being – almost as if I were telling of another person ... I've nearly gone crazy this last half year or so, so please try to understand that fact (tho you know not the cause) and do be good and forgive me.'

He told Jack that after he had quit the service station job, he was so out of his head, so saturated with grief, he would tear across bus intersections in the car right through red lights, hoping to get hit. He made an effort to write about his suicide attempt, but he said words were of no use.

> I don't feel I need new words to merely translate my private knowledge – I need it to preach a new Psychology, a new Philosophy, a new morality – what a task – how can I expect to speak in a letter? This madness has been unlike any I've ever known, *entirely* different – I feel as if I've never had any life before – I do childish things – I think in new distorted, over-balanced levels, I burn with agony – I sense a loss of most all wisdom I ever had. When I see a girl, I tremble, I spit – I'm lost.

In the days following his birthday, Neal was quiet and sweet, but always distracted and never happy. Even the tea didn't seem to elicit the usual euphoria. He read and wrote, and I let him be, trying to adjust my moods to his, ready whenever he would care to confide in me. Perhaps, I thought, he was simply subject to fits of depression. He had told me of several earlier attempts at suicide when younger, each having ended, as did this one, in self-disgust.

The truth of his birthday was mercifully withheld from me for 12 years until Al and LuAnne filled in the missing pieces of the puzzle of that day. Neal had driven to Oakland, hopeful that 'sensible Al' would lift his depression, but he couldn't find him. Seeing the gun when absentmindedly fiddling with Al's car glove compartment for any clue to his whereabouts, he decided on more desperate action. He took the gun.

LuAnne's taunts were driving him wild, and he drove to her hotel and woke her, demanding at gunpoint that she go with him to Denver. She lured him into bed but failed to change his resolve. She said he forced her to get in the car, drove to a wild section of the beach and raped her. (I am keeping an open mind here.) When he let her crawl back into the car he drove her back to the hotel and ordered her to change and pack. He would pick her up at noon and drive her to Denver. She changed and packed, all right, but then fled to her fiancé's apartment, knowing that Neal did not know the address.

| TWELVE |

On the last day of February, Neal had an idea that considerably brightened his mood. He would drive to Denver himself, make LuAnne's mother start the annulment, and at the same time pick up the books and other belongings I had had to leave behind. He would only be gone a week. The idea seemed a bit rash and expensive to me, but I toned down my objections at the welcome sight of his return to high spirits. He assured me it would cost 'nothing', and we spent a happy tea-enhanced evening for the first time in a month.

The next morning Neal dropped me off at work and sped away. It was our first separation in San Francisco, and that evening, alone with my thoughts, I tried to foresee the future. I even allowed myself to doubt whether this time Neal would come back. My own spirits sagged. Never had I felt so isolated and so immune to human aid. No man, I was sure, could ever understand the helplessness felt by an unmarried pregnant girl in those times. It didn't seem fair. And I was luckier than many; I had a man, or so I believed, but it was hard not to resent him somewhat, if only because he, like everyone else, was so safe, so free. His guilt need never be known; mine would be visible for all to see. Only death is so grimly inevitable and irreversible.

Why had it happened to me? I did not really approve of premarital cohabitation if it could be avoided, which in our case I hadn't thought possible – or sensible. I felt that sin, like everything else, had to be judged in the light of common sense. My only regret was the pregnancy, and not much common sense had gone into that. My naive or stupid romanticism had left contraception mainly to the man, though I couldn't justify that position, especially since I had not been overcome with passion for Neal. I did wonder why it had not happened to LuAnne – although it did instantly when she remarried – or to me previously. These facts added a modicum of weight to my idealized notion that Neal and I had been married in the eyes of heaven.

I debated with myself whether to tell my parents. At first I had not done so, thinking some miracle might cause me to miscarry naturally, and they would never have to know. But now I remembered how shattered they had been when my sister had quit college and eloped, thinking they wouldn't understand. I had watched their suffering, as well as the tearful reunion a year later, and I decided now to give them another chance to 'understand'. Some emotional support from my mother would make my plight far more bearable.

I wrote to her and anxiously awaited her consolation. It did not come. Instead, at the week's end, a letter arrived, flooded with disillusionment, pain and rending accusations of my wanton character and irresponsible selfishness. I had dishonoured all my family – and where was Neal now? I spent a damp and dismal night.

Neal did come back, just as he had said, but he found a pitiful *hausfrau* waiting for him. Now recovered himself, he set about altering the state of my mind, first by a frantic bubbling description of his trip: 'Thirty-three hours, baby – just think of that! It's 2894 miles, y'know. I really had that old clunker mesmerized – hee hee hee, yeaahh. You should seen me going over the Donner Pass – ho, ho! Of course, I had no chains, you understand, so I just barrelled right up that mountain full throttle, and it was snowing hard. Right on top – now get this – on top, see, there were these two snowploughs. They'd stopped to yell at each other – out there in the dark and snow – here was another human be'en – they stopped opposite each other –' Neal was drawing diagrams with his fingers on the table and fell into an Okie accent. 'I couldn't slow down, of course, or I'd never get up my momentum again, so I just whooshed right in between them before they even knowed what passed 'em – hee hee hee – and imagine their faces!

'Then just over the top the damn car quits. There I was – no anti-freeze, you realize – I sat there seven hours – *seven hours*, mind you – freezing my ass off. It was eight degrees below zero, my love. Imagine that! Finally, when I thought my wish to die had come true, a bus came along – they'd opened the road behind me, and I *made* him give me a push so I could coast down the other side of the mountain. He had to, you know – couldn't leave another human in that cold. He'da had it on his conscience always.

'Anyway – on the way down, my windshield wiper broke, see, and I had to stick my head out the window the rest of the way, the windshield being thick with snow and it being dark an' all. Well, when I got to Denver the whole side of my head was froze, and I still can't hear too well out of that ear, but, by golly, I made it, hey? I never let up for an instant – never hit the brakes the whole way down the mountain. Yesssirreee – *thirty-three hours*!'

'Oh, Neal,' I wailed. 'You could have frozen to death!'

'Not me, baby. Indestructible Cass, they used to call me, and we know it's true now, don't we? What with all that nonsense a while back, eh? But listen to *this*: I even made it back in thirty-*six* hours – how about that?' He lunged across the table and planted a big kiss on my mouth, his eyes sparkling as of old.

'Um – were you successful in your mission?' I hated to bring him down, but this was the crucial part to me.

'Why, of course, darling, it's all arranged. LuAnne will go back, get the annulment, and let us know the minute we're free.'

'Ah, well then, thank you, dearest Neal. And thank God you're back safe and almost sound.'

Neal now decided to consider Al's testimony to the joys of working for the Southern Pacific Railroad. One Sunday afternoon Al drove us down the peninsula to Campbell to meet his uncle, a conductor.

His uncle encouraged Neal, spelling out the advantages of railroad life, many of which Al had already touched upon.

As a beginner, a man worked off the 'extra board', so-called because either his runs were non-scheduled or he was filling in for a man who was off. You signed on at the bottom of the list and worked up as men and trains were matched and eliminated. The drawback of the extra board was the need to be near a phone at all times. (What a boon cellphones would have been in those days!) If you missed a call, you went to the bottom of the list again. The advantages were more hours' work and more pay than if you had a regular run. Summer work was busiest because of the perishable, truck-farm produce from the Salinas and Santa Clara valleys. If a man caught a 'local', a freight train serving these areas, he might have to do the same job for a week or two – called a 'hold-down', Although Watsonville was the southern limit of the Coast Division, temporary extra trains might be needed as far down the coast as San Luis Obispo, Bakersfield, Indio, Pixley, towns on the Southern Division. These hold-downs could last indefinitely.

When your name reached the top of the list, you were obliged to take whatever job was next in line. This added a certain amount of suspense and adventure – a perfect set-up for Neal. No boss looking over your shoulder, nothing carved in stone, no set routines. You could get someone to fill in if need be and not lose your place, but Neal never missed a call; the crew-clerks loved him.

As a beginner, after your student trips for two weeks, you were required to start working on freight trains, but when you had accumulated enough years of seniority, you could become a passenger brakeman and then a conductor, and eventually you could earn enough seniority to keep a regular job of your choice, either freight or passenger.

In the first few years, younger men were likely to be cut off in the slack winter season, but most men either got other jobs or saved money to tide them over. The job was for life; you couldn't be fired, unless you grossly broke some rule. Even felons were hired. Alcohol was forbidden, but most of the old guys were alcoholics. You could choose to work or not, and if sufficient notice was given you could take off and keep your seniority as long as you worked 60 days in a year. You got paid for just the days you worked. If you had the money, this allowed for travel, study or any other activity you could afford. You weren't supposed to work other jobs, but many, like Neal, did.

It sounded almost too good to be true, varied and exciting, if somewhat hazardous and uncertain at the start. Tailor-made for Neal. The base pay was average, and the train men's union was ineffectual. Nevertheless, if a man was willing to work hard and often, he could make a good living during the busy season, and as his seniority piled up and more jobs became available the money was better than any other job Neal could have qualified for.

Neal was eager to try it, and Al's uncle put in a good word for him, as he had done for Al. The following week Neal completed the necessary examinations and, although colour-blind, passed that test. Luckily, the old physician used an old-fashioned test using bits of yarn Neal could distinguish or guess right. It was a huge relief, even though Neal had memorized every page of a Japanese colour-blind book, and I had had to test him daily for days.

When I asked him if he wasn't worried about signal lights, he answered, 'Well, dummy, everyone knows the top one is red and the bottom one green, even if they look the opposite to me. I know what they mean.' He still had to wait two more weeks until he could do his student trips, for which he would not be paid.

At my own job, I began the game of announcing my wedding plans. No one knew I was pregnant, and I gave my notice. I worked at being the glowing, happily expectant bride-to-be, and sometimes even convinced myself. It was going to be a far cry from my family's early vision of my sweeping down our plantation's spiral staircase in ice-blue satin!

On Saturday March 27, 1948 I bid farewell to my co-workers with no reluctance – except missing the paycheck. I was confident, as usual, that security would be a simple matter; Neal would soon be working regularly, and as a babe in the financial wood, I considered our small savings more than adequate. We had no rent or utilities to pay, so food and household supplies were all we faced. We ate nutritiously (my father was a biochemist, so I learned early), we only drank the occasional beer, and neither of us craved sweet foods.

Neal and I spent a carefree weekend as of old, enjoying 'the City' (as everyone called San Francisco) and Golden Gate Park. We went to hear Flip Phillips in concert one night, Prez Prado another.

I slept late on Monday morning, and when I awoke Neal was already up and gone. Mystified, I padded to the kitchen and found a sweet note saying he had 'errands' to do but would return soon. 'Soon' turned out to be late in the afternoon, and as time went by I had to rebuff threatening memories of his birthday.

He finally came bursting in the door in a frenzy. LuAnne's mother, he declared, had arranged for the annulment, and LuAnne had agreed to go with him to Denver to sign the papers – tomorrow! Neal was his old best self once more. I voiced the usual anxieties and warnings, but this was the kind of thing that made life worthwhile for him; a challenging drive with a couple of deadlines and no end of obstacles. I was unaware he and LuAnne were still making love, so her presence didn't worry me. And now she was putting it out that she'd become engaged to a seaman. If that were true and not just another ploy to get to Neal, I naively thought that endorsed both their fidelity. (It took me a long time and a lot of examples to learn that 'whatcha don't know don't hurtcha'.) My confidence in Neal's love remained undiminished, and I was sure he cared as I did for the future of our child.

After all the standard loving, reassuring words, he roared off the following morning in the old Packard he had bought in January, for which he had promised to pay $1195, yet had paid only $200 while having driven it already 14,000 miles. It couldn't hold up much longer. I couldn't help worrying about that, remembering his last trip.

Forty-eight hours later Neal returned, held up this time by a minor accident on the way back to San Francisco, or so he said. He let himself in and came to sit on the bed. I awoke and grabbed him, relieved, surprised and thankful. He was free at last, and we already had our marriage licence. LuAnne, he said, had stayed in Denver, a revelation that completed my happiness.

'So get up, you – we gotta have a big celebration breakfast!' Over it, he reached for my hand and looked into my eyes. 'So now, my one and only, you and I will blast down to the courthouse first thing tomorrow morning and get hitched at last – wot, baby, eh? You'n me forever, as I said, hey?' He lifted my hand and planted a big egg-yolky kiss on it as I smiled, nodded and reached for the coffee pot to stem my tears.

| THIRTEEN |

At the jewelry counter I had struck up a friendship with an elderly lady who collected and sold antique jewelry. She had often shown me fabulous, exotic pieces and was herself a living image of fabulous exotica. She was heavily made up, wore a lot of the jewelry, dressed in rare bright fabrics, and always wore fur somewhere as well as big feathered hats.

She begged me to let her provide my wedding rings. I was thrilled.

My theatrical background appreciated the unique and colourful. I had called her as she'd ordered when Neal was away, and although it was short notice, she responded warmly and instructed me to meet her at the side entrance of The White House, a department store on Post Street, at ten the morning of our wedding, where she would bring the rings.

So the rings were settled; now I had to figure out what to wear. The only dress I owned besides my two 'basic blacks' required for work but hardly suitable for my wedding, was a light green wool my mother had made me for Christmas. With it she'd made a light-weight navy blue wool coat lined with the dress material. Little did my mother suspect she was making my wedding dress. It was particularly fortuitous, because the loose coat helped conceal my bulging front. So now the clothes were settled, too.

Only eager to marry, I had not thought about the date. I was born in April and already a fool, so what could be more appropriate than for me to marry on April Fool's day? The future would reveal it more appropriate.

I woke early the next morning, made myself as pretty as possible, and left before Neal, agreeing to meet him at the City Hall at eleven. When he had gone job-hunting I had bought him the second suit he ever owned and had added white shirts and various ties for his birthday, so he was all set as to his wedding gear. The Denver trip had finished off the Packard, however, and he had allowed it to be repossessed, so we were dependent on public transport.

It was a cold, grey morning with clouds and fog chasing each other between the hills and buildings. I rode the streetcar and walked the couple of blocks to stand outside the store in the biting wind, regretting my habit of always being too early. To kill time and to get warm, I went across the street to Woolworth's. Just inside the doors was a display of fake diamonds – 'newly discovered stones that defied comparison' with the real McCoy. I looked them over, smugly pleased I didn't have to wear the traditional 'solitaire'. I had always preferred coloured stones to diamonds by themselves, and I was happy my benefactress dealt only in stones that were antique, colourful and unique.

When I was warmer I crossed back to our appointed meeting place. It was already 10.15, and I began to think my friend had been bluffing, when suddenly I saw her hurrying along the opposite side of the street, grasping her flowered hat and veil, her head bent against the wind that ruffled her fox-fur collar. I nearly called to her, but checked the impulse as she bustled directly into Woolworth's. Could she have forgotten where she told me to meet her? Should I follow? Before I could decide, she emerged and stepped into the traffic and made her way to me. She blossomed into a broad, store-bought smile and opened her purse to paw through its generous womb, bringing out a small box in her gloved hand. She pressed it into mine and held on.

'My very best wishes, my dear,' she oozed the standard words warmly. 'I hope you'll be very happy. He's a lucky man. I'm so pleased you let me share in this happy occasion. I hope you'll both like the rings.' I was impatient to see them, so I disengaged my hand and tore off the wrapping. I lifted the lid of the box and could utter only a weak, 'Oh.' With the utmost effort I cracked my face into a smile. Words of gratitude came haltingly, and with a distinctly hollow ring. Here was a set of rings straight from the display I had just scorned in Woolworth's. I was bewildered, crushed and wanted to cry. Even I could have done much better myself – even Neal could have. I thanked God *he* hadn't presented me with this trash; I'd have had to wear them forever.

She waved good bye, and it was now so late I had to hail a cab or be late meeting Neal. The fare was money I hated to spend. I sat in the cab and looked at the pathetic, molded silvery rings and tried to figure why she had bothered, or why offer some of hers to begin with. Mostly I wondered what I'd done to deserve this – I was sentimental about symbols the way Neal was about dates. Then I had to laugh – my wedding day was becoming more and more a grotesque parody of my youthful dreams and expectations.

My joy was revived when I saw Neal waiting at the curb smiling his beautiful smile. This was all that really mattered. And from behind his back he flipped out his hand and thrust at me a little gold flower box. So totally unexpected was this gesture, I could only gape and stammer in gratitude. His thoughtful mark of affection more than made up for the disappointment of the rings.

I pinned the three fresh gardenias on my coat – they smelled deliciously – as we walked swiftly across the plaza to the huge grey building and into its echoing corridors. We had to wait in the anteroom of the judge's office until he was free. We sat on the worn black leather couch, and I showed Neal the rings, giving him the wedding one while I put the engagement solitaire on my finger. Then I took it off again and asked him to do it. In our nervous condition and with the ridiculous rings we got those irrepressible giggles one only gets at times of great solemnity.

Eventually, we were told by a bored underling that the judge would see us in his chambers. A little plaque on the door read 'Judge Clayton Golden'. In the small room, which was almost completely filled with a large desk and chair, our unrehearsed and varied emotions were amplified by the awkward accommodation. We grew eager to get the ceremony over, instead of gazing into each other's eyes and savouring the significance of the words as we – or I – had planned. Judge Golden was cool, bored and automatic. 'I now pronounce you man and wife'. I wanted to correct him to say 'husband and wife', but resisted the impulse. 'That will be ten dollars.'

Neal turned to me with such a blank look I nearly broke into laughter again. Panic prevented it. I came to with a snap to fumble in my purse until I found my wallet, from which I withdrew the only bill in it – luckily a tenner. I felt as though I had just bought a husband, but it was cheap at that, considering my need.

Once outside again Neal and I let loose our relief and amusement at the absurdities of this wedding and howled with laughter as we ran down the steps into the plaza and out into the now bright April sunlight, scattering pigeons and dodging startled passers-by. 'No wonder his name is Golden,' Neal yelled. Many years later this judge was impeached for overcharging, and Neal was profoundly satisfied that justice had been done.

'We can't just go home,' Neal said when we reached the street. 'What'll we do to retrieve the situation? If that judge hadn't fleeced us, I'd ask my wife to join me in a glass of champagne and an elegant luncheon.'

'What do you mean, "us"? It was *my* ten dollars.'

'Now dear, let's not get petty. All for one and one for all from now on. Isn't that right, my girl? Of course. Well, now, let's see what we have left.' He poked through his pockets as I got out my coin purse, and we pooled our resources. 'Hey, that's a heap! Ahem, my dear Mrs Cassady, would you do me the honour of joining me for lunch at that there quaint little diner yonder?' He added every Chaplinesque flourish he could remember, oblivious to the passers-by, and I couldn't have been happier.

The diner was tiny, grimy and crowded, but we squeezed around a table and did our best to create some romance, lighting the candle in spite of the brilliant daylight all around. Neal turned on all his charm, held my hand throughout the meal, and gave me all his attention. I sniffed my gardenias and glowed. The champagne turned out to be a bottle of beer apiece, but it was spiked with spirits of joy.

As we walked out, Neal spied a small grocery store. 'Aha, I think we have just enough left over after our carfare for a six-pack, by gum. We'll have a celebration yet – a proper wedding day to remember.'

| FOURTEEN |

At last I was Mrs Neal L. Cassady. Although I had been using the name for quite a while, it was an enormous relief to have it made true. The day after the wedding Neal began his railroad student trips. This meant working a daily local freight for five days, followed by five nights, and finishing with a long run to Santa Barbara and back in order to 'make his date'. It was from this date his seniority would be calculated. He found the work something of a strain at first, but on the whole it agreed with his temperament. He was a fast learner, and, as usual, he distinguished himself and became a favourite with the older 'heads'. His diploma came in the form of an official pocket watch, iron-toed laced-up low boots, a retractable key chain for switch keys, and a big freight lantern. He displayed all this to me with as much pride as any cub scout showing his mother his badges.

Neal was ready for work, but the work wasn't ready for him. The season had not yet begun enough for new men to be called. For two weeks following his training, he tried locals in Watsonville with no luck, and he returned home disgusted, announcing he'd do what Jack and Allen had done and go to sea.

'But Neal,' I wailed, 'You'd be gone for months – the baby born without you here?'

'I know, I know, darling. It sounds awful to me, too, but we can't live without an income. And it will only be until the railroad picks up; I'll send you all my pay. What else can I do?' This last question had a ring of desperation, and I backed down. Two days later Neal was a fully-fledged Ordinary Seaman. I said, 'Not so "ordinary" to me.' He had papers, an ID card with his name and new title, and a funny picture of him grinning, taken on the boardwalk under souvenir banners of San Francisco. Two more days and he had signed on a ship bound for Arabia. It might as well have been Mars. I felt the rug being pulled from under me, but I said nothing.

Fate intervened again. On May 15th, Al telephoned to say he was going to the Southern Division, where there were definite jobs. Neal decided to join him, keeping his seaman status in reserve. Once more he was propelled into hyperactivity and good spirits at the chance to be on the move again. The fact that Bakersfield, his destination, had the highest temperatures in the state was of no consequence to him – yet. He also was relieved not to go to sea, because, unlike me, he had never sought water, either for swimming or boating.

The bad news arrived the week after Neal left. George, our bene-factor, who had split with Lucy, had returned and announced he was getting married again. His bride-to-be already had an apartment, so he would immediately move the furniture there. He learned Neal was away and, so that I wouldn't have to move out until Neal returned, said he'd pay the rent until July 15. He left us the leather-look fold-out couch, our bed and one chest of drawers. My foolish pride wouldn't let me tell him how broke we were, or that Neal wouldn't be paid for at least another two weeks. I was down to my last five dollars.

It was an unusually hot May for San Francisco, and after George left I sat and surveyed the bright, white, echoing apartment no longer so richly arrayed. After dark, stark overhead lights replaced the sun and lamps, and in the kitchen only the stove and a few dishes remained, but I had nothing but water to cook, and nothing to cook that in. I recalled my sister telling me that once when she tried playing with Communism she had existed on peanut butter and lettuce, so I followed her lead, adding milk for the child. With no refrigerator I could buy only small amounts at a time, and often had to do without. In a mockery of my plight, a newlywed couple moved next door and invited me in to see their Bermuda honeymoon slides. I was forced to sit amid the warm, rich surroundings and the aroma of the dinner they had just finished.

My pregnancy went into its sixth month, and I had no clothes that fitted. I found some flowered cotton curtain material and sewed by hand a gathered skirt. This and one of Neal's white shirts comprised my entire maternity wardrobe. The heat was getting to me, so I stayed up late at night when it was cooler and napped naked in the afternoon. As the money dwindled, I searched our belongings for something to sell. A used-record store apologetically bought our entire prized collection for $2.50. Tearfully, I kept out a few Billie Holidays and mambos, too sentimental to part with them.

Then I hunted through the closet, where the only garment of any value appeared to be my fur coat from college days, a mink-dyed muskrat. I had heard that often fur department suppliers made jackets or other smaller fur items from full-length coats. I tramped the hot streets of San Francisco in the blazing sun, wearing my curtain skirt and too-big white shirt, to be brushed off with sneers at fur departments of elegant stores. I was finally so weary of carrying it that I thrust it at one of those remake people who didn't want it either but gave me 25 cents. I accepted it for carfare; I wasn't about to lug that hot fur all the way home again.

Looking back, I am amazed I was walking on such thin ice, but I didn't feel that way at the time. I was proud to be 'enduring' for 'us'. I was sustained, too, by the almost daily loving letters from Neal, which described an ordeal far more severe than mine, a gruelling routine in even more intense heat. After a month, Neal was not released as he had expected, but instead was sent to Pixley to work a potato local, and I couldn't even find that town on the map. He wrote, 'Daily routine: Up at 8.30a.m., work from 9 to 7p.m. Sleep in the outfit car here – eat in a café across the street, read, write, think and smoke.' His paycheck had been delayed for no known reason.

My situation was becoming really critical when Al Hinkle suddenly appeared at the door – bearing Neal's first check. I hugged him hard and brushed back the tears of relief. He gave me his handkerchief, smiling.

'You see, Carolyn, I have more seniority than Neal, so I've been called back to the Coast Division, which is picking up now. Neal was really lucky, though, to get so much work already. He'll be paid well when it's finished.'

As Neal's peace of mind improved, knowing I now had some money, he wrote to Allen from Pixley, and Allen answered:

> The great event was your letter – we had assumed you were in jail or something – of course, I had fantasized you dead, more or less, and even suspected suicide some months back. Myself, this spring has been one of madness, much like yours... What finally pulled me out – to name an external cause – was Jack's novel. It is very great, beyond my wildest expectation. I never knew.

Neal also wrote to Jack summarizing the major events of his last six months and relating his tortures, if not their cause, adding, 'I make no attempt to answer your letters; I'm insisting on a copy – with autograph – of the great, perfect and loving tome of yours.'

Upon Neal's exultant deliverance from Pixley at the end of June, we set out to find another apartment. Our days of luxury were over, and most apartments were too expensive. We took the first one we found for $50 a month, in a converted old house high atop a hill overlooking Castro Street, just off Divisadero, aptly named Alpine Terrace.

Steep concrete steps rose up from the street to the front door, from which you looked down on the tops of telephone poles far below. Our apartment was higher still on the second floor at the back, and fortunately for my acrophobia, close against the hillside that continued to rise. Had we been less hurried, we would have noticed it was at least six blocks uphill from the nearest market or laundromat.

But once again, love made all things possible, and I was eager to build a nest for Neal and our child. I was happy and secure once more, and set to work decorating painted muslin for drapes, enamelled orange crates for book cases, tatami mats and peasant designs on the kitchen cabinets. The kitchen was a sort of added porch at the back, and the bedroom had been created from a bigger room in which a new plasterboard wall had been constructed on three sides, so you had to walk around it in a hall thus made to get to the main room. But it had the basics we needed for now.

Now that Neal was working steadily, I learned to adjust to the railroad's unusual demands. We didn't mind the irregular hours – I liked having him home some daytimes, but the drawback was being tied to the telephone. If he went out at all, he would have to keep calling the crew-clerk to try to estimate his next run, not easy to predict. Sometimes it was hours, other times days. The job was now familiar, and stimulating to Neal's restless nature, offering enough variety, action and suspense, as well as periods of quiet riding on the train in which to write and think. It occasionally offered a bonus in vegetables scattered off boxcars – manna from heaven – even if it was hard at times for me to dispose of eleven heads of lettuce before they spoiled.

Neal loved the characters and the whole new language. He had me holding my sides with his imitations of both, such as his descriptions of a 'tagman' on a local job: 'We picked up the switchlist, see, and this guy'd say, "Wall, Neal, let's get two behind three off one, then double to four to set out the east cars, spot the express reefer, pull five and kick seven down the lead. Then it'll be a tray, deuce, four, another deuce, five aces and a tray, hand the head car and come to 15 to shove that rail, then set the crummy off the limey, and we'll cross over, tie eight..."' Neal would get me giggling so hard he'd have to stop. Then he would translate slowly, but still too fast for me to remember past the telling.

His *joie de vivre* was restored in full force, and he wrote to Jack: 'For the first time in more than three years, my soul has faltered in its black, purposeful dash to sick ruin. It's not a cycle...for God has once again touched my seed – it blooms, I blossom.'

Giddy descriptions were revived with details of all the simultaneous creative projects he would accomplish, including 'working seriously on a sort of thing about a man digging – oh well, if I finish it I'll talk about it...'

I was now free of a daily job, and with the apartment liveable I felt the urge to paint again. I bought supplies and began a 'formal' portrait of Neal despite the cramped quarters and poor light. I suggested to Neal that since he could do all the impossible artistic stunts he had described to Jack, he should try painting. To my surprise he went about it with painstaking precision, painting stiff, abstract designs, rigid and tight, flat colour bordered by flat outlines. I had expected him to splash about freely, but no way could I get him to loosen up.

I suppose this must reveal something about him, but it is too deep for me. The same restraint showed in a letter to Jack. After writing, 'Carolyn is doing a tremendous portrait of me – 4 ft by 5 ft [he always exaggerated sizes]. It'll take her 6 months, I'm sure,' he admitted,

> I feel somewhat forced in writing to you and thereby stunted in growth with you…I ask directly, can you think of a way to make me speak more freely to you, and, in doing so, improve my direct, simple style of writing? Any suggestions of this literary question will be gratefully received. Thank you, Mr. Rilke. I want to be a cowboy, a ranch hombre. I'll grow a beard like Gabby Hayes.

Whether this remark started it I can't recall, but Jack wrote to Neal about his ambition to buy a ranch for all of us to share, and Neal answered with enthusiasm:

> Your ranching idea is beautiful! If you…want a man who will make $350–$400 a month on the railroad every year from May to January – and his wife and child and his knowledge of ranch work and his love for you and your mother – then take me. Seriously, now Jack, stop and think of it – it's easy really to do. I know your mother (you must bring her) and Carolyn would get on together famously – and to build a ranch, a great spread, together, would be better than renting rooms for $50 the rest of our lives – we had better start right now – we always put off too much – start now – bring your buddies – we'll have 7–8 bedrooms – your mother (Bless her) and Carolyn (Bless her) are exactly alike – Carolyn's a great worker, an interior decorator – I'm convinced it's easy – and I'll get the money. A home – to go and come to – to grow old in – to make into a great place – you'll never do it if you don't do it now – please think!

To me Neal said, 'Listen, Carolyn, I figure it should take us about two years to achieve the actuality of living in our Shakespearean house. After this month and next, we should have all our bills and the baby things paid off. Then, starting in September, we should be able to save $100 every month. The baby shouldn't cost too much the first six months, should it? So by the first of the year, we oughta have $500, if we really scrimp, eh? Then when I get cut off in January, I'll go to sea till May and get something over $200 per – or, if not, I can get $25 a week unemployment here – maybe I could get another job under an alias.' He saw my scowl. 'No? Well, okay, anyway we'll see how it looks in January.'

In subsequent letters to Jack, Neal rhapsodized further about this idea. He sent for every pamphlet offered by every bureau he could find to learn more about ranches, water rights and land permits. His dedication to the cause and ardent vision of our bucolic life deepened my sense of peace and security. I had reservations about the kind of communal living he envisioned as he added more and more 'guests' and 'ranch hands' to the residents, but I encouraged him for all I was worth and joined him in games of pennypinching.

For once Neal didn't buy another car even; instead he bought a bicycle and rode the long length of Market Street to the depot no matter the weather, the hour, or his state of fatigue.

| FIFTEEN |

The baby had been scheduled for August, but August came and went. I was hot, heavy and ready. Neal was all I could wish for in attentiveness and help, and projected an intense interest in the coming event with genuine pleasure. Earlier he had written to Jack:

> My dear, sweet, great little wife – my perfect Carolyn – is now 7 months along and will present me with a child I shall keep, raise and glory in – needless to say, dear Jack – if my baby is a boy, I shall name him after you – and Allen. If it is a girl, I can't, for a name like Jacqueline is unbearable to think of.

On August 20 Neal wrote to Allen: 'If it is a boy I shall name it Allen Jack Cassady. I anticipate him always signing his name thus: Allen J. Cassady. If my child is a female I have decided to name her: Cathleen JoAnne Cassady.'

Late in the evening of September 6 my time arrived. Neal contacted a railroad friend who drove us to the San Francisco Hospital. Neal was not allowed in with me. I was deposited on a gurney in a huge high-ceilinged dark and cold hall like an enormous tunnel. I could make out two other women down the hall, also parked against the brick wall in the dark.

During the agony of my labour a young doctor came to see me, and I asked him about anaesthetics.

'Not this week,' he said smugly. 'We're trying it without any. Besides, we think women should have this experience,' 'we' obviously meaning men. For my first child I would have appreciated Neal being present. He was not allowed in then, nor during the eight days I was interned, because they had had a case of childbed fever.

Cathleen JoAnne Cassady was born on September 7 at 12.29a.m. I am sure of the time, because it was those 29 minutes that required me to stay an extra day – the longest eight days in living memory. I couldn't breastfeed Cathy adequately, and they wouldn't supplement her milk. I could hear her crying in the nursery, but the nurses blamed me and kept scolding me. Her attempts made my nipples sore and bleeding, but no help was offered.

The other eleven ward-mates furnished some entertainment, and Neal sent flowers and a lovely card. Still, some anxiety assailed me as to his activities. I hadn't thought to grab a book on my way to the hospital; it would have been a nice vacation if I had: I never had enough time to read.

Once home with Cathy, Neal was completely immersed in his daughter and wanted to be a part of everything concerning her. He made formula, changed diapers, took the wash to the laundromat, bathed her and studied Dr Spock as thoroughly as he had Proust or Dostoyevsky. While he fed her a bottle, I beamed at the sight of that tiny pink form, no longer than his forearm, nestled against his bare muscular chest. He was beside himself with delight in her, repeating often, 'I never knew; I never knew.' He wrote to Jack: 'I can't tell you the blubbering glee I've been gurgling since Cathleen's arrival (and before)...She's a month old today, has gone out into the world 3 times...and is thriving in general. She is now 21 inches long and weighs 8lbs, 8ozs. I love her like mad.' Later he wrote, 'I cannot learn sadness from you, Jack; my capacity for it is lost...(I think sadness is gone forever for me...Ah, how sad.)...I used to be truly indefatigable. Sex drove me...now, I like music and am sterile. Maybe my girl, Cathy Jo, will continue to make me content and strong.'

Allen responded to the announcement with a note that cheered me, too:

Congratulations on your little child. How does it feel to be a father? (I mean it, even if it sounds simple.) It certainly feels fine to be a grandfather. If you send me some details surrounding the psychic atmosphere of her birth, I'll write you a triumphal ode...I've put little Cathy in my will... I'm seeing my lawyers tomorrow. She will inherit zillions of dollars when I die. P.S. Blessings on my daughter-in-law for a change, and on you, too, son.

Neal's happiness was sustained further by two great expectations: one was my job in Hollywood. I had received word that the position for which I had been waiting was now available. I had almost forgotten about it, and the timing couldn't be worse. Neal's second source of hope for better times was that he had now been assigned to a regular freight run and could get off the extra board and the telephone vigil. His hours were set as well as his pay, giving us much more freedom and the ability to plan. He elaborated to Allen:

> Carolyn is going to Hollywood...She is thrilled at this chance she's tried so hard to get to crash Hollywood. She begins at $1.11 an hour, then $1.34 an hr. & if she makes good as a costume designer – $500–$1,000 a week. So, my dear boy – if several things break right for me – (1) if the full-crew law is retained in the Nov. elections, (2) Carolyn makes Hollywood money, then you are my guest forever...if this comes to pass, you are to live entirely on my money...except – in November elections the people are to favor or disfavor amendment number 3 – the full-crew law. The roads have tried for years to break this law which states that for every 25 cars there must be one brakeman – obviously, if the...law is broken – I'll lose my job.

At the time I was not aware of how dependent our whole future was on these two eventualities. I did not know of Neal's letter to Allen, and I had written to Western Costume that I had exchanged a career for a family. Neal never let on how disappointed he must have been. Nor was his second hope fulfiled. The power of the Southern Pacific swayed public opinion against the full-crew law, and Neal was laid off. There was no hope for work before the following spring or summer. Neal's spirits plunged again towards despair, and he begged Jack and Allen to come to him. Even Al Hinkle was laid off, and for the next two months he and Neal spent more time together and less time at home.

They sometimes brought other brakemen home – once or twice a young greenhorn named Ardo. He looked at Al and Neal as a couple of Casey Joneses, and they sounded a great deal more experienced while in his company. One Thursday afternoon Al and Neal came in alone and acted strangely self-conscious and nervous. They went into the bedroom mumbling and whispering. After a while, Al came out and sat on the edge of the couch, fidgeting with his cigarette package.

'Uh, I've got a – uh – surprise for you,' he stammered, not looking at me.

'Have you, Al? What is it?'

'I'm getting married.' He looked up at me and smiled.

'Married? Why, Al – to whom? Why haven't I met her? You haven't told me you have a steady girl.'

'I don't – haven't had – that is, I just met her day before yesterday.' This was more surprising still; Al was such a stable, traditional type.

'Whoof – this is the quickest case of "love at first sight" I've ever heard! When do you plan to marry?'

'Saturday morning, actually – in a church.' His eyes – and mine – widened.

Neal emerged from the bathroom during this exchange. 'Yeah, well, what the hell – why does she insist on a church wedding anyway? Come on, Al, let's see if we can't think of something to speed her up.' Neal's tone was nasty. I couldn't imagine why, nor what business it was of his. But he hurried Al out, Al calling back, 'I'll try and get her to come back with us later.'

It was late afternoon when they returned with Helen. I was more mystified than ever when I saw her. I would have bet money Al would choose only a sweet young pretty thing (as I'd heard him tell of in his past).

Here was a woman of indeterminate age – although Al said she was 22, rather solid of figure, an earth-mother type, I thought. Her face looked tired now, her dark brown eyes round and her expression as puzzled as mine. Perhaps I was not what she would have expected Neal to marry either. She had rich, thick brown wavy hair pulled back in a bun, and wore a tailored brown tweed suit that concealed her figure and did not add to an impression of youth. She was nervous, seemed to feel awkward, and responded rather grumpily to my polite inquiries. Why wasn't she glowing? I had to assume she had so much on her mind, she would have preferred not to sit making smalltalk with Neal's wife, especially since she had taken an instant dislike to Neal. Her eyes appealed silently to Al, and he got up to lead her out.

The next day Neal dashed in and out, preoccupied, evasive and jumpy, answering any concern I voiced with the excuse he was helping Al get ready for the following morning's ordeal. Late in the afternoon he bounded into the apartment, grinning broadly, eyes shining and rubbing his hands. Cathy was napping in her crib in the bedroom, so his whisper was more a hiss.

'Come with me, baby; I've got a surprise for you! Come on, now; I'll show you, just wait till you see!' He appeared ready to burst. Now what? I stopped folding diapers and followed him down the inside and outside steps to the street. At the bottom, I asked, 'Where are you taking me? I'm not dressed – Cathy –'

'Nowhere, baby; we're *here*. Right here, my dear. Now – look at *that*, wouldja!' He waved his free arm in a broad gesture towards a shiny, brand new, two-tone metallic maroon and grey car. Noting my blank expression, he leaped into action, tearing open the door on the driver's side. (He had parked it on the wrong side of the street.) 'Just look at this, honey, see? The floor is sunk below the door frame; it's a step-down living – I mean *driving* – room. How about that? And look at that dash – like an airplane, eh? See? Radio – oh and baby, it drives like a dream, smooth as silk. Just wait till you ride in it. Come on, I'll take you for a spin.'

Each word fell on me like a demolition ball, crushing all my hopes. Neal started to take my elbow to lead me around the car, but I wrenched free and bolted up the steps and into the apartment. He ran after me and found me on the couch, my head in my hands. He sat beside me and put his arm around my shoulders. He spoke softly but urgently.

'Now, now, Carolyn, look here. You don't understand. Al and Helen are getting married tomorrow, right? They have to have a honeymoon but have no car. Now then, Jack wants to come out, but he hasn't the money to get here. So, see, old Cass to everybody's rescue. We'll kill two birds with one basket, so to speak. I'll just whip over to New York to get Jack, break in the new car, and at the same time Al and Helen get their honeymoon, see? But the best part is Helen is loaded. She is paying all our expenses! It's a free ride, don't you see?'

'What have all those people to do with us – with me and Cathy? Did Helen pay for the car, too?'

'Why, I bought it, naturally, my dear – well, the down payment of course. It's for you – you and Cathy, so you can take her to the doctor and the store in a safe car, and –'

'You mean to tell me you took our savings? Our ranch money?' I leaped up and stared back at him. He got up to pace, the strain beginning to show on his face.

'Well, our savings, yes, but look, I can make that much back in two months easy when I'm back at work on the railroad again next spring. The monthly payments are practically nothing. It'll be a cinch, honest, baby. You know we need a car with the baby and all, and this one won't be breaking down all the time. Soon as I get back, I promise you I'll get another job until they call me back. It's *all right*, Carolyn, you'll see.'

He made it sound so logical, but it couldn't be. Here we were, living in a cardboard dump with orange-crate bookcases, yet we had a brand new car, no savings, no income, a new baby, and he was talking about driving clear across the country.

'I see. So all the rush about the wedding is just to get Helen and her money to finance *your* trip.'

'Well, ye – no, not entirely. It just works out neatly that way. And I promised Jack –'

I started to cry. 'I seem to remember you promised me a thing or two, like loving and caring for. What about our honeymoon? Oh no, we had to save our money for a home.' I bit my lip and slapped at the tears. Neal tried to come to me, but I dodged him and tried to collect myself. More calmly, I said, 'When do you leave?' He paused and lit a cigarette.

'Right after the wedding – uh –'

'You mean *tomorrow*?' Panic struck. He was serious. This was really happening. He was going to leave us stranded. 'But Neal! What about us? How will we live with no money?'

'Now, honey, don't you worry. I've thought of that, of course. I have everything arranged, so don't fret. Ardo is going to look after you while I'm gone. He'll bring groceries; just give him a list. He'll take the wash, too, see? There is nothing to worry about. I'll pay him back when I'm working. It's all okay, and I'm only going to be gone a week – two at the most.'

'You really mean to tell me it's more important to you to use our money for a car and to keep a promise to Jack, not to your family?'

'It isn't that, Good God. It's just a short trip. Don't I deserve any vacation after I've worked so damn hard?'

I spun around like a wounded animal and snarled, 'What about me? What have I been doing? Can you even imagine what it's been like for me?' Tears made my voice shrill. Neal's face looked pained, but he said nothing, looking at the floor. In a moment he walked to the closet and began hunting for his suitcase. This concrete evidence was too much for me. I dropped on the couch again and wailed.

'Oh Neal, Neal, please don't leave us!'

'Carolyn. I am not *leaving* you. I'll be right back.' He began to sort his clothes.

My fear turned to fury. Something snapped inside me; I felt it. I have never forgotten that feeling of a physical rip. In my mind? My heart? All the discipline of my early training to keep control, bite the bullet, never hurt anyone, never express anything rude or hateful. All that gave way like a bursting dam. I yelled at him: 'How can you? How *can* you do this? I really thought you had a heart. How could you lie about loving me? And Cathy? Use me? Make me bear your child – all you do is take advantage of people. You'll just walk out with all our money? Leave a *baby*? Oh oh OH – you bastard, you lousy *bastard*. You don't care for us one bit. *MY* car! HA. What a riot *that* is! You are finally showing your true colours – you've a heart of stone if you have one at all. You are nothing but a *gutter-snipe* after all. How *stupid* I've been to ever have believed anything you ever said. I had warnings – how could I be so dumb as to ever trust you again. Well, I've got my due now. To think how much I loved you, my God, what a fool, fool fool!!'

All control was gone; I was shrieking, bawling, sobbing, shaking, and sick with self-disgust and fear. When Neal turned to face me, my degradation was complete, for he was crying, too, his face contorted in pain.

Quietly he said, 'I have feelings, too, you know.' He actually said that. How insane it all was. I threw myself on the couch in total despair and sobbed on. Of course, Cathy woke up crying. How could I move? Why must I? I had to. I dragged myself to Cathy and automatically attended to her needs, the sight of her tiny helpless form eliciting a fresh deluge of tears.

As I came back from the kitchen with Cathy on my shoulder, Neal approached us, one hand held out, the other gripping his suitcase, tragic concern on his face. I backed away and spat out. 'Just go, if you're really going. Get out, now! I never want to see you again, not ever!' Cathy began to scream again. All I wanted was for Neal to stay. All I knew to do was to tell him to go. For the first time, I was afraid of life. Yet every word and action was aimed at driving him further away. Neal dropped his hand but looked lovingly at us. 'Ha, don't look like you *care*; you can't fool me again.'

I listened to Neal's departing steps, the closing door, the stairs, the closing outside door, the front steps, the engine starting, and the roar of the departing car. The breaking cord. Gone. Really gone. I am all alone.

My ears were ringing and my body and mind drained. I held Cathy like a doll, feeding her, her tiny eyes scanning my face coolly, her feeble fingers probing my wet face. Without her, what would have happened? Her needs caused me to keep going through the paces, but I didn't know how or what to think. Of course, without Cathy I'd have been free. I'd have never gone back to Neal, I'd have gone to work and moved away. How simple. Yet here this tiny creature could make me so helpless and enslaved. At least it never occurred to me to resent her for it.

| SIXTEEN |

The next morning the phone startled me awake, and it was a second or two before the horror returned. I leaped at the phone to keep it from waking Cathy, and softly said, 'Hello?'

'Now darling, keep calm and listen to me. I feel terrible, I understand how you feel. I see now, and I'm sorry. I do love you; you know I do – and Cathy Jo. Please don't fret. Honest, baby, I'll be right back. I can hardly wait. I'll hurry.' How I loved his voice and ached to have him back. How I hated him. I must be strong, I thought, and not allow myself to be deceived again. Don't listen to him or your heart.

'Where are you?' was all I could safely say.

'Just outside of town. I just had to stop and call you. Everybody's waiting in the car, but I had to talk to you. I love you. Please don't fret – promise me?'

'Outside of town? Then what do you mean by "right back?"' For one wild instant I thought he meant he couldn't do it.

'Just as quick as I can make it, baby. You know me; I'll drive my greatest. I'll really hurry. With this new car it'll be like no time. You'll see. I'll be back before you know it.'

'Oh, *shut up*!' I interrupted, realizing he was still on his way and simply salving his conscience, hoping for my blessing so he could enjoy himself more. 'I never want you to come back. Don't you dare come back here, *ever*!' I slammed down the receiver, venom turned to self-pity, and the sobs took over again.

Cathy woke and began to scream. 'Stop it!' I yelled, and then the guilt and shock at my outburst sobered me. I picked up Cathy and we wailed together.

With Christmas only a couple of weeks away, every day's mail brought packages – my family's abundant offerings again, and this time Cathy as well as Neal were included. It was the final irony. I took off the mailing wrappers but left on the pretty coloured papers and ribbons and put the presents on top of the low bookshelves in an ever-growing array. My marriage over, I had no desire to open them or read their cheery sentiments.

In a few days, Ardo appeared. My emotions towards him were mixed. I resented his existence because he represented the loss of Neal. At the same time I was relieved to open the door and see him, balancing boxes of supplies, for he was my only tie with life. Neal must have given him a well-considered list, and Ardo had not stinted on quality or abundance. I was far from gracious. I thought him a fool and told him so. He adored Neal, and I did my best to disillusion him, as I had been disillusioned. He must have thought Neal all the wiser for having left such a shrew.

'Can't you see he's using you, too, Ardo?' I asked scornfully. 'He'll never pay you back. How can he? Who knows if he'll ever even *come* back?'

'Oh yes he will,' Ardo avowed fervently. 'He's been wonderful to me. He wouldn't lie to me. He's helped me so much at work. I know he'll keep his promise.'

'Ha!' I battered at his staunch faith. 'You and everyone else. Sure, he's just great when he wants something from you. Boy, can he be everything you want and say all you want to hear. Don't *I* know! But you'll see, just as I have. How can you believe a man who deserts his wife and baby?'

'He didn't desert you. He's just gonna be gone a week or two.' Trust shone in Ardo's pale blue, pink-rimmed eyes. He looked such a babe in the woods. I had to soften a little, torn between the need to preserve Ardo's help and the desire to vent my pain and humiliation. I managed to thank him weakly.

As Christmas Day drew near, I knew I'd have to tell my sister, Jane. I couldn't think how. Such a shame, such misjudgement to confess. I had been so proud of Neal, so sure. But she'd have to know; we were expected there for Christmas dinner.

By the time we left her apartment Christmas night, my sister's staunch English stoicism and enduring optimism had helped pacify my anxieties, and as I walked outside to her husband's car, I could see a little of the sprawling city lights and realized there was something outside myself that was not entirely hostile. But when I entered my own dark, close rooms permeated with memories of Neal, weakness and fear threatened again. The task looked too great. No motivation came even to try.

I sat in the big Chinese chair and gave Cathy her bottle, the room lit through the single window only by reflection from the night sky and city lights. Through my tears, the shiny papers and Christmas trimmings on the still-unopened gifts made gay, glittering prisms of colour before my eyes. If only we could pass out of life right now, Cathy and I, I thought. If only time would stop and tomorrow never come.

But morning came, along with the need to cope. Ardo, too, came around, like the days of the week, his being Saturday. I continued to be cool as he reopened my wound and tried to convince me Neal was faithful and true.

One day Ardo triumphantly waved a postcard before me. 'Look, see? I told you so. I got this card from Neal. He does think about us, and he will come back!'

I took the card. A desert scene. It read, 'Great car. Doing 800 miles a day. Made it here in two. All's well, see you soon.' Then I saw the postmark: Denver. A new flash of pain, another surge of shock and realization. Denver equalled LuAnne. So that was what it was all about. I threw the card at Ardo and smashed all his cheery hopes of changing my view of Neal.

Little by little the events that had puzzled me the past year knitted themselves together. Neal's moods, his restlessness, the suicide attempt, his frequent absences and trips. I buried my face in my hands. He had not really ever loved me, only LuAnne. Angered with shame at my blind, trusting stupidity, I laughed in derision at myself and succumbed again to self-pity and tears.

When I caught sight of Ardo's face, hanging dumb and uncomprehending, some pity went out to him as well. He must have thought me quite insane as well as hateful. Although he had provided new ammunition to use against Neal, it was too painful.

'Never mind me, Ardo. I'll explain later. I'm sorry. Now please go.'

This was no doubt the softest tone he had heard, and he was only too glad to comply.

Soon after this, distraction suddenly occurred. My landlady decided to raise the rent in defiance of rent control, and showed frightening signs of insanity. She threatened the young mother on the first floor that she would throw her baby down the front steps if she didn't stop crying. I knew I must move quickly, and a neighbour girl said she would move with me. We rented a second-floor flat a few blocks from Mission Dolores and one block from a small park. The girl had stayed with Cathy while I hunted for a home, but soon after we moved in, she moved on.

My few items of furniture looked bleak in the one huge room, which had high, Gothic undraped windows with a panoramic view of the city and the distant bay, at night a carpet of jewels. I was once again facing life, like Portia, alone. Ardo still did his duty, and was my only contact with the outside world, except for an occasional conversation with my sister. She had lent me money for rent and informed me about welfare. This meant riding miles and miles, and transferring from streetcars to buses three times carrying Cathy, and having to wait hours to be seen. After days of these journeys, this ray of hope was extinguished mysteriously. The Welfare Department's only solution was for me to put Cathy in an 'infant shelter' while I went to work. That I could not do. Years later, when appealing again to this agency, I asked them to check back and explain why my previous request had been refused. The astonishing notation read, 'No apparent need.'

Neal had telephoned me several times on his trip. The first was from Washington DC, and I had immediately let him know I knew about LuAnne. 'LuAnne who?' he asked. My insistence that we were through didn't faze him, and he continued to phone and talk as if we were both desperate to be together again – as if he were away on a business trip. When I'd hang up, I'd weep all over again. Once he called to say he wanted to send me $18, so I had to give him my new address. His delay in returning had been necessitated, he said, because he had to help Jack move his mother from North Carolina to New York, and it was a good thing he had arrived when he had. Helen had been left in Tucson, but Al was still with him. Why, I couldn't make out, but one thing I didn't want to hear were the details of that trip.

Some time in the last week of January, Neal was at the door, all smiles and effervescence, ready for a grand reunion. Arming myself with superhuman determination, I presented only frost and indifference, while my whole being reached out for him. He looked so good to me. But my pride seemed more important. I did my best to pretend I was capable of managing by myself and not at all frightened – what an empty bluff.

'Now then, darling.' He spoke as though I had welcomed him with open arms, but as he looked around the grey apartment he was not deceived, and his cheer dampened. 'Well, so this is the new place? Um – yes.' He poked his head into the unheated bathroom with its ancient fixtures and bare linoleum floor and then strode over to lean down and coo at Cathy asleep in her crib. 'How is she?'

'She's as well as can be expected with no money, no father and no future,' I retorted acidly.

'Now, now, darling, that's no way to talk. The past is past, and I'm back to take over.' He came to sit beside me on the fold-out couch. I knew I must avoid his touch, so I jumped up and walked to the daybed opposite.

'Just go back to LuAnne, Neal. I don't want to start it all over again.'

'LuAnne? Not a bit of it, my dear. I don't know anything about her or where she is. It's you and me, baby. You know that. I'll get a job right away and get you and Cathy out of here. Everything will be all right. Trust me, darling. Come on now, you and me, remember?'

'Oh, I remember all right. No, Neal, it's no use. I can never trust you again. The spell is broken. My faith is gone. Better to stop now that a break has been made and recover sooner. All I've gone through alone while you were gone – Cathy will never know you or what she lost.' My voice began to shake. 'Please go now, and quickly.'

'Go where? I have no place to go.'

'Oh, Neal, come off it.' Anger aborted the tears. 'I'm sure LuAnne is with you. And where's Jack? The whole excuse for this great sacrifice. Where's the great man that means so much more to you than your family?'

'I left him downtown so I could see you alone.'

'Sure, with LuAnne. Just go, will you? Leave me alone.'

'Okay, okay. I'll call you.' He saw I wouldn't bend, and strode to the door. I watched him run down the walk and heard the car zoom away, and with it another part of myself. I lit a cigarette and flopped face-down on the bed. Somehow, in spite of my resolve, I didn't feel quite so desolate. At least he was back and reachable. I wanted him to find a way to make me believe him. But how could he completely erase what he'd just done? I couldn't allow myself to be made a fool of, and why wasn't what he had done enough? Why wasn't I like other women who would get hurt or betrayed once and that was that? Turn it off, I told myself; go on to someone else, pride and honour intact, lesson learned. Why couldn't I change that image that he was my perfect husband, my only husband?

Cathy began her hunger whimper, so I got up and put her bottle on the stove to warm. The sun had set, and as the sky turned to deeper blue the city lights began to blink on like eastern fireflies. The uncovered windows were high enough to let in ample light. I hated the glare of the lamps in the empty room, when all that panorama was like a stage set and gave the illusion of exaggerating my confinement. I changed Cathy in the dusk, and sat watching the show of deepening darkness and polychrome lights while she drank her milk, her little warm body against my stomach. With my free hand, I dropped the needle on the turntable beside the bed and let 'Lady Day' say it for me.

> No good man
> Ever since the world began
> There's been other fools like me
> Born to be…in luuve with a no good maayan.

| SEVENTEEN |

When I awoke in the morning, I turned the record over as usual. 'Good morning, heartache. Here we go again…' This morning was, however, a little brighter than the last dozen. There was *something* to expect, good or bad. With this anticipation, I took an interest in straightening and cleaning what I could. Around noon the telephone rang. It was Neal, bright and perky.

'Good morning, my sweet. Now listen to me, look here. I mean to say, dammit, we have to figure this thing out, now don't we, Carolyn? After all, Cathy has to be cared for properly. I understand, of course, your feelings and all that, but nevertheless, something has to be done. I have to get a job and, you see, darling, I haven't any money, naturally, you understand. And neither has Jack, though he's wired his mother and will have some soon. But we can't stay here. Now just purely for economics, my dear, you do and feel just as you like. I won't bother you at all. Anything you say, but we'll just have to have a place to stay until I can get enough money, you do understand.'

I couldn't help thinking it was rather stupid and counter-productive of me to be so harsh when we needed his support so badly and he was willing to give it. What other solution was there? The Welfare had turned me down. My pride still rebelled, and I stalled. 'Where's LuAnne?' was all I could think of to ask.

'Now darling, I *told* you – I don't know where she is. How should I know?' Neal's voice was edging towards anger. He didn't *like* lying again and again. I was only guessing and trying not to be dumb again – but what if he were telling the truth?

'Well,' I said, 'I suppose I have no choice. As long as you clearly understand it is strictly a business arrangement and only until we can make another. Surely Jack had some plan when he sent for you?'

'Yes, yes, of course, darling. We'll talk about that.' He had gotten his way again, so he couldn't have been more agreeable. 'He won't be in the way, you'll see. And I've got all the Sunday papers right here. We'll start job hunting this very day. I'll go see Ardo first. Then we'll be over. Bye, sweet. I love you.' I hung up the phone, torn in two again, happy and afraid.

Around five o'clock Neal and Jack bounded in, loaded down with bags of groceries courtesy of Ardo. Neal danced around the small kitchen tossing cans to Jack and hoping to ease all our embarrassment with constant chatter.

'You know, Jack, it's strange, but you and I have never played catch, so I could show you my magnificent arm. Seventy yards I used to throw the old pigskin, yessirr, and I never measured the distance with a baseball. I developed this special hop, you see, and I'd astound my buddies with the distance I could peg a rock – too small an area here to demonstrate properly.' A can crashed against the wall. 'Oops, too bad – like most southpaws, I'm slightly erratic in accuracy.' Jack chuckled and tossed back, imitating an exaggerated football action. Without wanting to bring them down too much, I tried to shush them for Cathy's sake, and realized I had not considered all of us living in one room.

Jack and I were more awkward and shy on this second encounter.

Not knowing all he knew about the trip and LuAnne, or what Neal had told him about me, I felt humiliated and at a loss. Jack was embarrassed to be considered the cause of my pain and poverty, and couldn't defend himself without incriminating Neal. Aware of each other's position only made communication more difficult.

The first evening as I did the dishes the two men sat in the built-in booth in the kitchen and tried to be jolly. It was an uphill effort. What could we talk about? I was being the wronged woman, and they only knew painful secrets. Luckily, they were both tired and content to retire early. I had the daybed and offered them the double couch, but Jack preferred his sleeping bag on the floor.

The following day Neal accepted another sales job, this time selling a new line of aluminum cookware. He came home with a huge carton of all sorts of brand-new pots and pans and pressure cookers with piles of pamphlets, recipes and instructions.

'Hey, honey, whoooeey! Lookee hyar what I got.' He staggered in and dropped the carton on the couch. 'Now you and Jack just sit over theah, and I'll show you the greatest breakthrough in the annals of cooking in this century, yas, yas indeedy.' Off he went into a W.C. Fields patent-medicine routine with each pan, exaggerating all the features and adding a few of his own invention until Jack and I were both laughing out loud. When Neal saw he had induced some defrosting on my part, he dropped the pan, climbed and stumbled over all the stuff on the floor and pounced beside me, gurgling, giggling, hugging and kissing me, as I pretended to resist. Then, giddy, he sprang back to his demonstration with renewed glee.

We all knew this job was completely out of character for Neal, seriously selling cookware, being invited to dinner parties to demonstrate, yet with Neal I could never be too sure what he could or couldn't do. Jack opened the quiz when Neal showed signs of running down.

'What are you *doing*, man?' He was still chuckling. 'Where did you get all that stuff? You didn't steal it, did you?'

'My good man, ahem, how can you ask such a thing? Even *think* such a thing?'

'But Neal,' I cut in, 'not selling again. Have you forgotten Sinsir? Do you get a salary or only a commission? Is it door-to-door? What will you wear? How can you...?'

'Tch, tch. Just you relax and leave it to Daddy here. I've been briefed and checked out, and see here, the booklet tells you all about these wonderful little beauties. Nothin' to it. And besides, my dear, *you're* supposed to use them and tell me how great they are, see? See? Your old daddy has already brought home, if not the bacon itself, at least something to cook it in when he does. Not bad, eh?' He walked around in a circle – Oliver Hardy again – beaming at us.

This time my instincts proved accurate. The first two or three days Neal got up early and, taking Jack along, set out with gusto. A few rejections and slammed doors were all that was needed to discourage him. He began to sleep later or sit around reading the papers, never quite getting out. One day the supervisor called, and Neal simply told him he was through. The man came to pick up the pans, which I had gathered into some sort of order.

It was difficult for all of us to be confined to that room, with a baby sleeping most of the time. Neal and Jack soon mustered the nerve to go out 'to dig jazz', and I reverted to the feelings of a neglected wife, though this time I could hardly justify or express them.

At the end of the first week, the jig was up. The telephone rang, and when I answered LuAnne's sweet voice asked for Neal. I handed him the phone and went into the kitchen, tears streaming into the sink as I washed diapers.

Neal was so angry his face turned red, his jaw set and he snapped only a word or two into the receiver, growling under his breath,

'That stupid bitch,' as he slammed down the phone. He marched into the kitchen and started with, 'Now, honey, don't go thinking…'

'Just go. Just go! Don't say another word to me…ever!' I wrung the diapers with a vengeance.

Neal paced around the living room, swearing to himself. Jack had gone out and now returned to walk right into the hornet's nest. When I was unable to answer his 'Hello', he went to Neal for enlightenment. I could hear Neal's explosive answers and curses at LuAnne. Jack, too, was angry with her. She had made a date with him and then right before his eyes climbed into a Cadillac with an older man.

'She pretended not to see me, but I know she did. You're right. She's nothin' but a whore.'

It gave me some slight satisfaction to hear them malign her, yet I knew it was because they *cared*. And she was free to take 'em or leave 'em. I envied her the more.

Whatever Jack's reason for coming to San Francisco, if he had ever had one beyond Neal's plans for him, it didn't materialize. When his mother sent the money, he decided to use it to return to New York. First he bought a loaf of bread and some cold cuts and made a huge stack of sandwiches to take on the bus. When Neal drove him to the station, my instructions were for them both to keep going.

I went back to figuring out how I had gotten here and how I could possibly have become involved in such a sordid mess. Where had I gone wrong? Yet why wasn't I more afraid and worried? Why did I still feel life and living were important? Women had committed suicide for less, and I had no such inclination. My feelings seemed programmed by the stoical family behind me. 'Just do what you have to do and get on with it. No whingeing.' But I was now cut off from that family. I could never tell them all this, and for some time I had avoided any reference to trouble in my weekly letters home.

The following week I looked out the window and saw Neal walking rapidly up the path, grim determination on his face. He burst in and danced around holding his left wrist with his right hand, bending up and down in pain. He was hurt. One can't kick a man when he's down, I told myself, feeling genuine sympathy.

'What is it, Neal? What's happened?'

'Now look, Carolyn, I'm coming back here and I'm staying.' (He only called women by their given names in times of extreme emphasis or stress, perhaps because he talked in his sleep.) 'I'm through with

LuAnne forever, that bitch, absolutely and completely. Do you hear me?' He continued to sway, breathing hard, grasping his wrist.

I finally got him to stand still long enough to look at his left hand. It was swollen from the wrist down, and the thumb was strangely bent. 'It looks broken, Neal. How on earth did you do that?'

'LuAnne – I hit her, stupid broad.'

'You hit her? Neal! Oh no, how could you? Where is she? How is she?' This was more serious than I could have imagined.

'That thick-skulled bitch – *she's* just *dandy*. Nobody could hurt that hard head.' (Later I learned his hand had glanced off her head and hit the door jamb.) He repressed further swearing in expressions of disgust, once again prancing about. 'But look, don't you think I should see a doctor or something?'

'Yes, yes, of course. Come on, I'll drive you to Mission Emergency. I'll get the lady downstairs to listen for Cathy.' I had not driven 'my' car yet, and Neal forgot his pain while instructing me. A wave of sorrow hit me when I noticed its very used and lived-in condition.

I parked opposite the emergency entrance, and Neal went in alone. Once more, warm reassurance washed over me. This must really signify the end of their relationship, if he could stoop so low as to actually hit a woman. Soon he was running back towards the car. I called, 'What did they say?'

'Nothing yet. I have to wait. Listen, love, have you got a nickel? I'll call LuAnne and tell her to put my things together so I can pick them up. Thanks.' He grabbed the coin I offered and ran back into the building.

My moment of rapture was brief. A cab pulled up and out of it sprang LuAnne, consternation on her brow, as they say. She ran towards the entrance, and out of the shadows Neal appeared. LuAnne held his hand and clucked, and by their nodding heads and fervent looks I knew I had been deceived again. Neal walked back into the hospital where Cathy had been born.

LuAnne turned and, seeing me, waved and crossed the parking lot. I forced a smile, and we greeted each other like long-lost sisters.

'How's your head, LuAnne? How terrible for you; I can't believe Neal would do such a thing!' She laughed and leaned on the car door.

'Oh, I'm all right. How have you been? I think it was rotten of Neal to go off and leave you like that, and I told him so. Right at Christmas time, too.'

'Why don't you get in?' I motioned to the passenger seat, although I felt I should move over myself. After all, it was more her car than mine, now that she had been riding in it all over the country. She went around and got in, just as Neal came running over to the car.

'They've taken x-rays, and I have to wait to get a cast put on. Why don't you wait for me at the apartment? I'll call you when I'm ready.' He then disappeared into the hospital again.

LuAnne agreed. 'That would be nice. I haven't seen the baby yet, and I want to very much.' Just like my closest friend.

'Would you like to drive?'

'No, no, you go right ahead.' She settled back in her seat and took out a cigarette. It was dark now, and I had to get her to show me the light switch. I felt altogether crumby.

We tiptoed into the bare room, and I lit one dim lamp by the couch. I checked Cathy, and LuAnne cooed over my shoulder. When we returned to sit opposite each other, the dim light from the windows behind me fell on her face, and the lamp accented the red-gold of her hair, falling in careless burnished ringlets on her shoulders. It may have been because I felt so dowdy, but I had never seen a more luscious girl. She grew prettier in my eyes as we talked. As an artist, I was far more conscious of her beauty than she was, and it affected me with both aesthetic pleasure and personal pain. I knew I would never be able to compete with her physically.

She began relating a series of tales about the many times Neal had disappointed her, each revelation piercing me acutely. In a way, I welcomed the punishment, hoping *something* would be bad enough to cure my attachment to him. Throughout her narrative she omitted any reference to physical abuse.

After an hour or more, the telephone rang at my elbow, and I grasped it quickly, trained to think of Cathy. It was the hospital. Neal was ready to leave, and I said I'd be right there. LuAnne said, 'Let him wait,' and she spent another half hour finishing her recriminations. When she felt he had waited long enough, we drove back to the hospital. She probably expected he'd be storming up and down in another rage, but instead he was sitting bent over on the curb, his head leaning on his arm. My heart went out to him, but I sat still. LuAnne ran over and touched his shoulder. He groggily lifted his head and then staggered to his feet, holding on to her to make his way to the car and collapse in the back seat.

'God, I'm sick,' he muttered. 'Been throwing up for hours.' LuAnne whispered to me, 'Ha! Serves him right.' Gently I started the car and drove to the apartment.

I knew how wretched Neal could be when nauseated, and I had all I could do not to smother him with solicitude in that grotesque cast. It took both LuAnne and me to get him up the stairs and in a position to lie on the daybed. I covered him with a blanket, asking him if there was anything he wanted. He shook his head and was soon asleep. I offered LuAnne some coffee, and we sat down to another chapter of confession and condemnation. I naturally expected Neal to nap some and then accompany her to her hotel. He certainly wouldn't expect to stay with me now, and I was thoroughly tired of the emotional ping-pong.

LuAnne put down her cup and stood up. 'Well, I must be going now – thank you; so nice to see you again.'

'Oh? I'll wake Neal.'

'No, no, don't do that. He's better off as he is.'

'But he can't stay here, you know. He'll have to go with you. You can drive him…'

'Ha! I don't want him back! I can't anyway; my fiancé is due back in San Francisco any time now. It would never do for him to find Neal in my room!' She laughed at the image she created. So she deceives him too.

'How will you get home at this hour? I don't think I should leave…' For a second I was afraid she'd take the car.

'No, no; don't worry. There are plenty of cabs about on Dolores.'

As I walked her to the stairs, I asked, 'Will you live in San Francisco when you're married?' Please say no.

'Yes, I expect so. I met him when I was here before with Lois, and we've been writing to each other while I was in Denver. He asked me to meet him here and marry him. That's the only reason I went with Neal, to get a ride out here.' I didn't add, 'By way of New York.'

Back in the shadowy room, I looked down at the sleeping Neal, wondering if I should wake him to undress. How helpless he looked, and how incapable of inflicting such pain on others. At least I should be convinced now that he could never be trusted. Sighing, I opened the couch and climbed on it, turning out the lamp. The high ceiling flickered rainbow colours from the city lights. Although it wasn't right, he was here, the apartment was full, and we were a family again, even if dysfunctional.

The next morning my defences returned, but I could put off punishing him until his health improved, and this gave me some relief. He felt rotten, his head splitting, his hand throbbing. Codeine disagreed with him, aspirin would only inflame his empty stomach, and the thought of food nauseated him anew. He was punishing himself enough.

'You seem well enough to go back to LuAnne now,' I ventured, pretending I knew nothing of her affairs and to get our relationship on its proper footing. He answered me as though I were an irksome child who insisted on playing the same game too long. He, too, was depressed, not only by the physical discomfort, but by the whole sorry mess. Now that he was injured, he couldn't work. This meant Ardo couldn't be repaid, the car would be repossessed, LuAnne was rapidly getting out of his reach, and a wife and child were dependent on his support. I didn't overlook the opportunity to point out the lesson. 'Well, Neal, I hope it was all worth it to you.'

| EIGHTEEN |

No solution seemed possible other than for Neal to look after Cathy while I went to work. He assured me he could handle it, anything to be able to stay. The day after his injury he felt well enough to take the car and leave it on a side-street. He was two payments behind, and the finance company didn't have his address. It was all a mystery of economics to me, but I was more than conscious of the terrible waste that impulsive trip had created in so many quarters.

So out came the green dress again, and I began a survey of doctors' offices. I had practically lived with medicine all my young life, since my Dad's office was in a medical school where he taught biochemistry; in that hospital I had been a receptionist for many clinics, studied medical illustration, and later served as an occupational therapist during the war, so I was familiar with medical terminology.

The very first afternoon of my search I was lucky. I was hired by an Hungarian radiologist in his mid-fifties. When he asked if I could begin at once, he also tactfully inquired if I'd like an advance on my salary. My wedding outfit had evidently lost its appeal.

Neal was sombre and subdued. One day as I came home I looked up at our window and was startled by an apparition of a man with a bald head. Neal had shaved off his hair. I knew he often grew a beard, as he had begun to again now, because his skin was so sensitive he hated shaving, but he had always been fussy about his hair. Now he gave me no reason for this act, and it made me uneasy. He said he just stayed in the apartment and read, except for taking Cathy in her carriage – a first purchase – to the nearby park. I didn't know then that LuAnne often came to visit, and also accompanied him to the park. Good thing Cathy could not yet talk.

Since I was nursing my disillusionment, we didn't have animated discussions as of previous good times, and we hadn't money enough for entertainment or babysitters. We would sit behind our magazines and books or discuss Cathy. With her, he was still conscientious and loving.

On March 15 he wrote to Allen:

> I'm lonely and restless...Action in the sense of continuity of purpose is now quite impossible. I lead a shallow simpleton life, little agreements of mind and emotion escape my endeavors. Long or involved speech, coherence or logic, literate leadership or conversation all quite beyond me. I'm listless without reason; I sit as would Rodin's statue were his left hand dangling. (*The Thinker*'s brow is false.) I sigh with looking out the window over the city – to the east – and north horizons, clouds, the street below me. I'm as far west as one can go; at a sloppy ebb-tide. I'm free of LuAnne, my friends are my friends, but I have a child.
>
> My life's blood she is, lovely and perfect – she wakes at this very moment. I stop to kiss her. So, I live in the child as long as possible, that's my stand. After that the world, you, saxophones and hardened struggle to succeed. You see, it's all very simple. I will take care of Cathy as long as Carolyn will allow me, which may be, I hope, forever. When she severs relations, I will lead other lives; until that time – Cathleen Joanne Cassady is my charge.

With my regular salary, our first goal was a new home. This time I found a house nestled under the brink of Russian Hill and near all the parts of San Francisco that constituted its essence for me: Aquatic Park, North Beach, Fisherman's Wharf, Telegraph Hill,

Chinatown. In the opposite direction was Nob Hill with the Mark Hopkins and Fairmont Hotels – not that I could go there any more, but they held memories of spendthrift wartime revelries.

The house, built on three levels, was on a short quiet street only a block long. At the end was a long house that had originally been a stable. Our house had the only patch of grass and garden behind it. A small market was half a block away on the corner of Union and Hyde, and the cablecar clanged its musical bell up and down Hyde Street and took me to and from work. The ride was more like one in an amusement park than a means of transportation to work. What a delightful way to begin and end each day.

The change to a decent home, partly furnished and with even more 'possibilities' than the last ones, improved my relationship with Neal, who also became more settled, less morose, and began writing again in spite of the handicap of the cast on his dominant hand, which was changed six times and now had a traction pin. I couldn't allow myself to be as happy as I had been before his trip; my wariness persisted, along with the false pride that I then considered honourable and necessary. I yearned for the old closeness, but I didn't know how to achieve it, given those conditions and conditioning.

Osteomyelitis infected the bones of Neal's thumb, presumably caused by the contamination of washing diapers. He required daily injections of penicillin, and to save expense I convinced the doctor I was capable of administering the shots. Many was the time I regretted that request. Neal was not only fussy and defensive, his buttocks were so lean and taut it was difficult for me and painful for him, his sensitive skin provoking oaths and yelps.

In April, our wedding anniversary and my twenty-sixth birthday came and went with hardly notable commemoration – except from my boss, whose attentions and gifts I'd been staunchly refusing (a stance that was totally incomprehensible to Neal). For these two milestones, courtesy required I accept the doctor's offerings of perfume, brooches, earrings and scarves. In addition, I accepted his ornate, embroidered Chinese smoking jacket for Neal, who loved it. He wore it solo; it reached about an inch below his bottom, and he strutted about, pretending his cigarette was a cigar, and harumphing like Major Hoople, the cartoon character.

My boss took me to symphony concerts while Neal babysat. He also bought a red Buick convertible that he called 'your car' whenever he drove me around. Once I had a delivery of x-rays to make, and I detoured home to let Neal drive it for that trip across the Golden Gate to Marin County. He was over the moon. But my lack of cooperation with the doctor's amorous advances eventually made him unreasonably picky and demanding of my work. So when Neal declared he had been idle as long as he could stand it and wished to go to work, I was overjoyed to give my notice. (I had to give back the jacket, too.) Still no call-back from the railroad, so Neal found a job recapping truck tyres, hard work in blistering heat, but he grabbed the gauntlet as usual. He described it to Jack: 'The cast weighs heavy. Sweating makes the thumb gooey, and it sticks to the plaster-of-p. I do impossible tasks; my job is so difficult, it saps everything from strong, two-fisted men, yet with one hand I throw the heavy truck tyres in a real frenzy of accomplishment. I'm amazed.'

I was not as much amazed as anxious about his stamina and endurance. He was beset with physical problems other than his thumb now. In another somewhat overblown letter to Jack, he explained:

Jazz-hound C. has a sore butt. His wife gives daily injections of penicillin for his thumb, which produces hives, for he's allergic. He must take 60,000 units of Fleming's juice within a month. He must take one tablet every four hours for this month to combat the allergy produced from this juice. He must take codein-aspirin to relieve the pain in the thumb, to which he is allergic. He must have surgery on his leg for an inflamed cyst. He must rise next Monday at six a.m. to get his teeth cleaned. He must see foot doctor twice a week for treatment. He must take cough syrup each night. He must blow and snort constantly to clear his nose, which has collapsed under the bridge where an operation some years ago weakened it. He must lose his thumb on his throwing arm next month.

Sun. p.m.: Sitting on a sore ass in my kitchen with the ball game, gurgling daughter, grass-watering wife, full belly from two-dollar steak…Reading a new book, *Escape From Reality*, by Norman Taylor is fairly interesting and deals with all forms of junk, snuff, coke, tea…Just started reading *Dr. Faustus* by T. Mann. Despite the reviews, I find it the best thing I've ever read by him, except possibly *Magic Mountain* (which I read when young and it influenced me a lot.) Strange to discover his latest work starts much as mine. My terrific darling beautiful daughter can

now stand alone for 30 seconds at a time. She weighs
22 lbs. and is 29 inches long. I've just figured out she is
31¼% English, 27½% Irish, 25% German, 8¾% Dutch,
7½% Scotch, 100% wonderful.

My security was returning day by day. Neal assured me continually
there was no way he would or could see LuAnne any more, and that
spring she had married. Neal told Jack, 'LuAnne has married Ray
Murphy, who has sharpened a sword and is dashing about town
trying to find me so he can cut my throat.' I hoped such a violent
husband would watch LuAnne with the same passionate possessiveness. But he was away at sea a lot.

In May, Allen wrote, 'Are you too occupied to write or don't you
want to for some reason concerning your relationship with us in
New York?...The golden day has arrived for Jack, and he has sold
his book...' Allen also said of Jack, 'He is not mad at you; as a
matter of fact, 5 of the 15 sandwiches he denied you in Frisco went
bad before he could eat them.'

After signing the contract for *The Town and the City*, Jack had
gone to Denver to see his friends again. He was disappointed to find
most of them out of town, and he wrote to Neal for comfort, advice
and amusement. Neal could now compile the many unmailed letters
he had begun since Jack had left San Francisco.

> Your book sold! I sit here thinking of my elation and how
> best to let you know. I come up with but one word: Glad.
> Glad, Glad, Glad. Gee – I'm Glad. Try Five-Points in
> Denver for bop, the Rossonian Hotel, and a couple of
> places across the street on Welton between 26th and 27th
> Streets. There may be a spot or two downtown or on the
> north side...Other than that I just look for good juke-
> boxes. Strangely, last night had big dream about Slim
> Gaillard. Perhaps you might remember the mixed feelings
> of admiration and inability to be close to him I felt. I was
> unable to tell him how dumb I felt not to be coherent about
> my admiration. That's how the dream ended, with me just
> sitting there watching his face and wishing I could speak.
>
> God, just heard that great George Shearing, remember
> God Shearing, Jack? God Shearing and Devil Gaillard.
> That's us, Jack, a mixture of George and Slim. The images
> we struck of George, a sightless God; of Slim, an all-
> seeing Being.

Allen wrote more news of a less ecstatic nature. Bill Burroughs had been arrested and faced a jail sentence for possession of narcotics and guns. 'If he gets out, he will have to leave Texas and LA, as it is hot there for him.' Allen himself was allowing friends to use his apartment as a base of operations for 'various schemes' of an illegal nature. He had planned to sublet his apartment to them and to use the money to visit Bill, but Bill's arrest, he said, 'casts a shade on that'. He complained, 'I can't seem to put my foot down.' His letter ended,

> What are you doing? When will your heart weary of its own indignity and despotism and lack of creation? Why are you not in N.Y.? Can you do anything away from us? Can you feel anybody as you can feel us, even though in N.Y. you did your worst to surround yourself with a sensate fog of blind activity? Are you learning something new? Wherever you are now? If you wonder the motive for these questions, don't undercut it with suspicion of sexual motives of mine. I have none now and was not dominated by them when you were last in N.Y. I am writing a set of psalms…

In the end, Allen became involved in the bust of the tenants, and avoided imprisonment only by arranging to be confined to a psychiatric hospital instead.

This shock was sobering to us, and we heard no more from Allen for nearly a year. Neal wrote dolefully to Jack, 'Bill on the border, Allen in an institution, Huncke in jail, Jack in Denver, Neal in lands end. The horizon here is the sea. I lay me down on the brink, the West end.' Although elated by the sale of Jack's first book, Neal summed up, 'Two things throw reality into sharp relief: your successful sale and Allen's commitment. The whole bugaboo of external forces I've evaded so purposefully for 3 years is brought close once again.' These forces were bigger than both of them. Jack and Allen, and somehow the security Neal had gained from these friends seemed threatened. It gave him pause to think, and his renewed resolve seemed insignificant by comparison. 'May as well say it; started a book – again – 4 pages…' His title: *The First Third*.

| NINETEEN |

Neal was not called back to the railroad at all in 1949, and his present salary was less than we had planned on, so I agreed to return to work. I found a job with two doctors who shared an office: a man who was a surgeon and a woman who was a general practitioner. I had been employed a mere two weeks when I learned I was pregnant again. It was an even greater shock this time, because I had been extremely conscientious in following the doctor's directions for birth control, and I rarely succumbed to Neal's demands. I just could not be pregnant!

This time Neal acted happy, perhaps trying to make up somewhat for the first time, or perhaps because he found such a source of joy in Cathy. I felt trapped, half-wanting another child of his and afraid of being more dependent on him while resisting him. All these pregnancies without any joy in the conception.

The surgeon felt my condition would be a detriment to his practice, but the woman did not. She therefore left him and opened her own office on the floor above. With both Neal and me working, we had to hire a babysitter, and found a warm Mexican woman named Mrs Davis. She mothered us all and improved our existence with her boundless cheer and frequent treats of Mexican delicacies. Although Neal's job was exhausting and dirty, mine was easy. The doctor's office overlooked Union Square, and as I counted pills or typed reports I could watch people and the pigeons below. I could still ride the cablecar too. My defences relaxed, and again I saw a chance our marriage might recover. By now I should have learned to fear the calm more than the storm.

As usually happened, Neal began to miss excitement and diversity, so when Jack wrote at a loose end and undecided about where to go from Denver, Neal frantically answered him, pleading with him to come to him:

> I am so excited as I punch out this plea to you...I am *not* going to work for at least two weeks. You see, the thumb, after three more weeks in the cast, failed to respond to treatment, and last Thursday they decided to cut it off – just the first joint. So, Mon. a.m. I get operated on. Carolyn will be working all day, including Saturday, and we will have the house to ourselves. We can play music,

talk, etc. etc. and in the evenings bop, mad nigger joints, etc…I want to have a perfect two weeks vacation with you…I rush to mail this. I only repeat: think of all the reasons for coming here, then multiply by ten and think of our joy, and then…get 'On the Road.'

Jack didn't answer. Instead, a few nights later there was a knock at the door. We had already gone to bed, but Neal got up – in the altogether as usual, only he grabbed his jeans to hold before him, and opened the front door to find Jack standing on the porch. Jack broke up in laughter, saying, 'My God, man – what if it had been someone else?' They giggled and whispered as Neal conducted Jack downstairs. The old familiar fear crept over me. I imagined a drawbridge being drawn up between me and Neal, enclosing them in their castle of delights and leaving me sitting wistfully on the opposite bank, filling the moat with tears. My fears grew as I heard their exuberant reunion, Neal becoming more forgetful of the sleepers upstairs.

Neal was true to the promises he had made to Jack in his letter, and the two of them exulted in each other like a couple of schoolboys playing hooky. We had let Mrs Davis go for two weeks, and I was worried about Cathy being properly cared for in this atmosphere. I would come home from work and get their dinner, after which they would jump up from the table and rush out into the night. My supersensitivity made our few encounters strained, and the more I behaved like the disapproving parent, the more they treated me like the mother to be lied to and evaded.

Early in the first week Neal tried to break the pattern, annoyed by my constant sulk. 'Why don't you come with us, then?'

'Who'd stay with Cathy?' I asked, icily.

'What do other people do?' Neal retorted, somewhat impatiently. 'Get Louise next door or Mrs Davis again.'

I was afraid to go, but I could hardly maintain my injured air if I didn't. The next Saturday night Mrs Davis came over, and I agreed to join them. My doubts were more than justified. I was a fifth wheel, like a bratty little sister big brother has to take along with his friends. Neal talked over my head to Jack about people and places they had in common and I did not.

The first half of the evening was spent racing around the Fillmore area, populated chiefly by blacks. Every few minutes, Neal would jerk the car to a stop, leap out, whip into a cigar store, bar or door-way and bound back to propel us forward into the traffic until the next stop. It finally dawned on me he was hunting tea, and after an hour or so, it seemed he had 'scored' a connection.

Neal parked the car in a tree-lined residential street where we waited and waited and waited some more. So far, I was not amused and wondered if this was a real example of the jolly times I thought I'd been missing. A sad, far cry from our threesome two years before in Denver. After at least another hour, Neal deduced he had been duped and with much swearing abandoned the vigil.

The rest of the evening was also spent largely waiting around. In a Tenderloin district hotel Jack and I attempted to make conver-sation with a stripper friend of LuAnne's while she made coffee for us on a flat-iron suspended upside down on a coat hanger over the metal waste basket. Then while Neal pursued other leads Jack and I sat in a grimy nightclub having to watch the performances of pathetic strippers. I was thoroughly embarrassed, but not as much as when Neal came back and openly flirted with a vocalist on the stage directly above out table. I demanded he take me home, and he was more than happy to oblige, and went out in front of me to the car. Once I got out at our door, he gunned the engine and roared off. I tried to control my tears until Mrs Davis's son arrived to collect her, I'd paid her and wished her good night. The men stayed out all night.

There was no further mention of my participation in their revelries, and a wall was thrown up between us. Once I overheard Jack ask Neal what the matter was between us, but Neal was unable to explain it properly. He sometimes made attempts to find out exactly why I was behaving so, and to soothe me, but the fact that he couldn't see it for himself only made me worse. I was vaguely aware that this was not all his fault, but I couldn't think how else to behave and preserve my pride and righteous indignation. I wanted him to undo, erase what he had done. That wasn't possible, obviously, and forgiveness was a concept I had yet to learn.

A small thing turned out to be the last straw. One evening I was bathing Cathy surrounded in the tub by her water toys and bubbles, her baby skin rosy, the bathroom warm with steam. Neal and Jack came home, and with them was Jack's French friend Henri Cru. They brought him to the bathroom door and introduced me. Henri knew nothing of our tensions, of course. He beamed at us, 'Ahhh, *tres jolie*! My, my, what a charming domestic scene – *oui*, oui – how very delightful!' He bowed and backed away, following Jack down the steps to the kitchen. It was too much for me. I dissolved into tears, bitterly resenting that my life was not as Henri thought and as I so desperately wished. I was tucking Cathy into her crib when they all came laughing up the stairs to leave again. Jack and Henri went singing out the front door, and Neal came to kiss Cathy goodnight. In his frivolous mood he showered me with empty, pretty endearments, not even *noticing* my wet face. I pushed him away fiercely and unleashed the only weapon I had – again.

'Get out! Just go – *get out*.' My teeth set.

He looked puzzled but said, 'All right, dear, I'm going,' and he fled.

I lay in bed agonizing, yet with some hope revived by the prospect of some kind of a showdown. Sleepless, I waited and waited for Neal's return. Near morning I heard them tiptoe in. I said nothing until Jack had used the bathroom and climbed his stairs to the attic. I sat up and stopped Neal from getting into bed.

'Neal. I told you to go, and I meant it. What do you think I'm made of? Do you expect me to sit here night after night with nobody and work day after day just being your housekeeper and babysitter? Well, I've had all I can take. You don't want my kind of life – go live the one you do. You don't want a wife and family. Get that precious friend of yours and go – go live the life you want – someplace else. GO. NOW.' I turned on my stomach and buried my face in the pillow.

Hopelessly, Neal silently put his clothes back on. Wasn't he going to argue? Reassure me again, as he always did? Now what was I to do? He went up to tell Jack, and I watched in dismay as he packed his old suitcase, everything in me crying out for some way to stop him. Would he say nothing? He would in a day or two, surely – he'd think of some way to solve this. This outburst would make him stop and consider the price he was paying for his fun. I had had to make some sort of impression.

Then they were gone. The house was deathly still. It had taken so little time. I thought of his unhealed hand, of Cathy, of the new one growing inside me. What had I done?

The alarm rang, and I had to go to work. I would have to leave Cathy next door. Responsibility mapped my course. Unconscious of my surroundings, I automatically rode the cablecar and opened the office, my mind locked in a frantic quest for an answer. I had made a terrible mistake this time. Neal must know it was just a fit of temper; he could have talked me back again. If only Jack hadn't been there, I could have talked to Neal. But if Jack hadn't been there, there'd have been no problem. It wasn't Jack's fault. It was Neal's – and mine. Where were they now? Maybe Neal would call me; he had called the last time, but then he had been the one to choose to go. This time I had forced the separation. He must know I didn't mean it.

The doctor would be on hospital rounds all morning, and I had the afternoon off. Besides the two patients coming in for injections, all I had to do was answer the phone and make appointments. I couldn't sit still. Automatically, I straightened instruments and pillows. I heard the reception door open. No one was expected yet. It was only a drug salesman.

'The doctor isn't in, and anyway, she buys from a wholesale house.' He must have heard this before, and it didn't discourage him. I heard the elevator door open and close, and something inside me jolted as never before, as though I had been electrified. I raced to the door to the hall in the private office, where I had heard footsteps outside. As I wrenched open the door, I saw the elevator close, and at my feet was an envelope. Damn fool, why didn't I run to the elevator instead of picking it up? Conditioned restraint again. Shaking, I shut the door and sat down in the doctor's chair. Inside the envelope were three dollars and a page torn from a 1947 desk calendar. In a neat, pencilled hand was written

> Carolyn, am leaving today. Won't ever bother you again. Won't come back in a month to make you start all over again – shudder shudder! Here are a few dollars that I can give you. You won't receive any more until Sept. The things of mine still at the house do what you want with. I am going to Denver, Detroit and New York City and won't ever come back to Frisco. Incidentally, I'm *not* going to see LuAnne – don't know where she is. Written by Helen Hinkle. Neal.

I read the note several times, sifting it for grains of hope. First, he didn't have to write me at all – or send any money. And why tell me where he's going? And what difference would it make now if he did see LuAnne? Maybe he was in no hurry. I ran to the window in my office and scrutinized all the shifting forms below me in Union Square, my desperation mounting. So close. I had almost seen him again, almost prevented this – a second sooner. If he'd only call. Not likely now. Hysteria threatened. That wouldn't help. Think. Where would he go now? Helen would know, but where did she live? Al had left her, too, and I didn't have their number. I had seen neither of them since I first met her. Blast.

I stared dumbly at the leaden sky before me, the soaring gulls as aimless as my futile thoughts, swooping and swirling, resting, dipping, getting nowhere. I was dementedly pushing and pulling back the desk drawer as though I had a nervous tick. Catching myself, I looked down when the drawer was open and noticed the piles of pill samples. This was where I kept all the amphetamines. I had to get through the rest of the morning, I reasoned, nothing mattered anyway, and if I had to live, I might as well make the best of it. Maybe some of these could wind up the clockwork inside me. I chose a variety that sounded balanced with tranquillizers and feeling dramatic, got a cup of water and swallowed two, putting the rest – and the other samples – in my purse.

Louise opened her door to me, holding Cathy, her son on the floor at her feet. 'Come in and stay a minute. Have some coffee.' I shook my head and took Cathy from her. Louise went on, 'Imagine Neal's leaving so early in the morning like that.' Had I told her? What? I supposed in my grief I had said something to try to make it real to myself. She continued, 'Good riddance, if you ask me; it's the best thing that could happen; you shouldn't have put up with him this long. You'll be a lot better off in the end.'

I had heard all this before, and my heart yelled, 'I'm not asking you. It's not the best thing. I will *not* be better off. I love him.' I actually only nodded. I backed out the door with Cathy and mumbled my thanks. I liked Louise, and knew she was not being gossipy but genuinely sympathetic. I also knew the whole world would agree with her. Why couldn't I?

| TWENTY |

The silence in my house was almost suffocating. I got out the pills and gulped down a couple more, ran around opening the windows, turned on the radio and, yammering away, got Cathy ready for bed. I changed into jeans and a shirt and braced myself to face the lonely weekend. I know, I know; he was gone a lot, but there was always some evidence of his presence.

Just as I started down the stairs, I was startled by a knock at the front door, so I backed up and went to open it. At first I didn't recognize Helen, and we stared at one another in nervous silence. She broke through by getting to the point of her visit.

'I'm sorry about Neal, Carolyn. I had to come over and see if there is anything I can do.' I backed away from the door, motioning her to come in.

'How very nice of you, Helen. I was about to make some coffee. Come on downstairs.' I led the way, touched by her concern but somehow even more distressed. Her mission seemed to indicate there was no hope, and I had considered it too early to give up. I put the coffee on the stove while Helen made approving remarks about the funny house. As she settled herself on the couch, I sat facing her at the table, almost afraid to ask. 'When did they leave?'

'They just did. Did you get the note?'

'Yes.' I had to get up and turn down the coffee, glad of the chance to hide my feelings. *Just* left! So he didn't call this time. This time when I would have begged him to come back. But I musn't let Helen know; she was probably another woman who thought me a fool for putting up with him. Probably in her eyes, too, it was all his fault.

'I got so mad at him, Carolyn. How can he just take off and leave a wife and child? How can anyone be so irresponsible? God!'

'How did they happen to come to your place?'

'You see, Carolyn – his *reason* was – it certainly wasn't *my* company – they had no car.' I had folded the couch so the back was up, and Helen settled herself against it and lit a cigarette. I enjoyed listening to her. She spoke with slow intensity, strongly emphasizing certain words with a straightforward quality to her low, mellow voice, and now I hungered for details.

'You had a car?' I handed her a cup of coffee and put milk and sugar on the table next to her.

'No, Lorraine did. She's the girl that introduced me to Al. She used to live next door, and Neal knew she had a car. He and Jack had been riding around all day with Bill Tomson, but he had to go home for dinner.'

'This was last night?' I asked.

'Yes, that's right. There was this tapping on the door, and much to my surprise, it's Neal. Of course he did this little song and dance at the door about his friend Jack, and how they're leaving and going to New York. I didn't know anything about your situation until the next morning. Of course, I think he knew I like Jack, so he asked if they could take a shower. Then Neal asked about Lorraine's car, so I called her.

'They wanted to go hear this fabulous combo on Howard Street, and asked if I wanted to go, too, so I thought – what the hell; it might be fun. Then we couldn't start the car, so we all pushed into the main street, whereupon the gallant gentlemen – ha ha – hid in the back seat! while I pushed and Lorraine steered. It was hilariously funny, actually – looking back – *hiding*!'

'Why did they do that?'

'They reasoned they would get no one to push them with two men…'

'Oh, I get it. They needed a *car* to push…'

'Yeah. That's right, but here I am pushing this car – *up*hill – in the wrong direction, and, sure enough, it worked. We finally got to this club – grimy, filled with negroes and weird winos, and there was this wild negro sax player Neal liked. Neal would stand right in front of the bell of the horn, and the guy would blow right at Neal. Neal is jumping and swaying, half the time with his eyes closed, nodding, smiling to every note.

'We were perched on little stools pretty close, and there was this other guy with wild spears of black hair sticking out all over his head, and he sang "Close Your Eyes". He was something – wow – just great!' Helen paused, remembering and smiling.

'So pretty soon you can smell tea, you know, all over the place. Now this negro with the hair – he had *terrible* scars all over his arms and face, whew – but he was singing to *me*. I realized it suddenly with some embarrassment. But Neal came over and grinned and jumped around and asked, "Don't you dig it? Don't you *dig* it?" And I said, "Don't be ridiculous," and acted like I didn't. But of course I *did*, but I didn't want to get lured into anything like *that*! It was sort of unnerving. The *potential*, wow! But actually, it was really a sort of sharing, and I didn't feel quite so dumpy and dumb, you know?'

She thought about it again. 'Funny how that guy hangs in my mind. Well, we were there several hours. It was dark when we started, so it was probably about ten o'clock then, and after a while Neal says they're going to take a quick run over to Oakland.'

I couldn't help interrupting her, laughing. 'Yeah, that's Neal. "*Quick run*" – clear across the bay. I suppose it was to get more tea?'

'Probably. I don't know. There was a lot of arguing, and for some reason he really wanted us to go too. It smelled to me like one of Neal's plots and "fraught with danger". Neal and Jack got into the car, wild with negroes, and left. So here we are again, Lorraine and I having to push her car. We finally found a guy to help, and we were going to meet Neal at Jackson's Nook when they got back. I've been there lots of times. It's an after-hours club, you know, and the musicians come over there to go on playing after their club has closed. I'd no real expectations of seeing Neal again that night, but, sure enough, in about three more hours they showed up with the same musicians. We stayed until dawn drinking coffee.

'When we got home I just asked Lorraine if I could stay with her and gave Neal and Jack the keys to my apartment. Just before noon today, I went back, and they were up, so I fixed them something to eat. It was only then I noticed their bags, so they really did mean to go to New York. When Neal asked me to write the note to you, I was yelling at him for leaving you, and Jack kept defending him, saying you kicked him out. Tell me, was his hand really so bad he couldn't have written that note?'

'I guess he could have, but it would have been a mess. He's left-handed, you see. He's been typing everything for quite a while.'

'It struck me as an odd thing, and it made me feel kind of in league with him. I felt awful. I wanted to say, "Write it yourself."'

'Or Jack could have.'

'Yeah, right. Why me?'

'That's Neal. Part of his way of getting around people by getting them involved and on his side.'

'Well, I felt terrible writing it – being the *instrument*.'

'Of course, I don't blame you. It is my own fault. I did insist they go. But it was – I was trying to get Neal's attention, you know. I think that's what I was after. I don't know. Life was intolerable the way it was.'

Listening to Helen, I was struck by how casually and comfortably she joined Neal and Jack for a night out with no feeling of disapproval or of being threatened. Why had I been unable to join them as simply as she? The facts she revealed proved that Neal had truly gone, and with him hope. Glad not to be alone, I urged Helen to continue to distract me.

'Tell me about you and Al. I've always wondered about the wedding and how you happened to marry him on such short acquaintance – if you don't mind?'

'No, no. Yes, it's funny, but I just knew he was the one. Something clicked. I guess it sounds crazy.'

'Not to me. That's what happened with me and Neal. There was nothing to consider; I just knew.'

'Yeah, that's it.' She sighed sadly. 'I understand. But the afternoon Al brought Neal over, God – there he was, bopping and beeping, hitting the car, jumping all around. I was *terrified* of him. I told Al afterwards – very seriously, you know, that I thought that guy must smoke *marijuana*!' We fell into gales of laughter.

'Ah me. Well, it was a mad two days. I can't even remember the order. I had to see a doctor. He gave me a diaphragm, which kept popping out all over the bathroom floor. Bad omen, I figured. Neal had planned some big jam session for after the wedding, but I told Al I had already invited my friends from work to have a drink with us at the Fairmont, so that's what we did, and that was the first time I'd met Bill Tomson and his wife Helen – at the wedding.'

'I haven't seen them yet. Neal said they'd come out here. What's she like?'

'Very pretty little blonde. Quiet. I didn't get to talk to her.'

It was now time for Cathy's dinner, and I got it ready, changed her and sat her in the high chair. 'Uh – gosh, Helen, there's still so much I want to ask you. Could you stay and eat with me? It's only hamburger, I'm afraid, but there's plenty.'

'Why yes, thank you. I'd like to. I've nothing to do, and that apartment is so depressing. But it is cheap, and Al wasn't called back to the railroad this summer, so we were scrimping. Of course, when he left me to go off with Jim Holmes, he called to tell me about the nice big apartment they had out in the avenues, and here I sit. Harrumph.' Jim was the friend of Al and Neal I mentioned who earned his living gambling at cards and pool. A sweet, modest guy with a limp.

'Why did Al leave? Neal didn't give me any details.'

'It was getting impossible with Jim living there for weeks and weeks. I just couldn't stand him, and he always seemed to be between us.

We weren't a couple. I understand how you felt when Jack was here – same sort of thing, I suppose. It made Al furious when I was inhospitable to his friend. Al thought of him as so harmless, which he was – but weird. We had a hidabed that I made up for him, but he insisted on sleeping in the bathtub – ridiculous things like that – said he didn't want to impose. Then he'd sit on the toilet for literally hours.'

I was glad Helen could talk about it and laugh. I wondered if the day would come when I could look back and laugh. This was my first experience of seeing Neal through someone else's eyes, and learning about his life when he was away from me. Not quite the same as when he told me about it. I couldn't resist the chance. Maybe I'd hear something that would finally break my chain.

After we ate our meal, I shared my pills with Helen, and we never let up. I mechanically tended to Cathy right on through the night and the next day.

'Tell me about your honeymoon, Helen, if you can call it that.'

'Well, the trip *to* Tuscon was sheer *hell*. I'm still in my wedding clothes, you understand. My girdle is killing me, and Neal, well, you know Neal's *driving*. I was petrified. And of course the radio was on *full* blast, Neal beating on the dashboard and yelling. God, it was horrible. And he absolutely *refused* to stop at a service station for me to go to the the john even. God, how I hated that man! I had on sight, and he returned it. He said awful things to me, insulted me, nasty remarks. Went out of his way to be crude, I thought.'

'Neal? That is really odd. I've never heard him being mean personally to anyone. Certainly not a stranger or a friend's wife. Maybe it was because you're the only woman who didn't respond to him – you think? You saw right through him. He couldn't con *you*. I suppose he couldn't tolerate that.'

'Maybe. I don't know, but it was sure not my idea of a *honeymoon* trip. But you know? He picked up a woman and a child on the way. The child was epileptic or something, and Neal was simply *fantastic*! I've never seen *anyone* be that nice. He was so *considerate* and *concerned*, I just could not believe it was the same *man*. Other times, of course, he picked up all *sorts* of hitchhikers to get them to buy gas. I had to sit on Al's lap.

'Well, I lasted until Tucson, and then I had just had it. I insisted I had to have a bath and Al must get us a hotel room. So that's what we did, and Al and I talked, and I told him I was less than enchanted with our honeymoon, and wanted out. Al said he'd have to go with Neal because he'd agreed to before the wedding and had contributed money –'

I was puzzled. 'I thought the reason for the hurried wedding had been that Neal thought you had money, and if he drove you, you'd finance his trip – that's what he told me, anyway.'

'Ha, he may have thought that, but I *didn't* have very much money, because I was at the end of my six-months' leave and was just about to go back to work. And I certainly wouldn't have put money into *his* pocket! So Al said, okay, I could either wait for him back in San Francisco or go on to New Orleans and wait for him there, which is what he wanted. He had given me Burroughs's address. So when Neal arrived at our hotel, I was still in bed. Neal rushed in and said, "Let's go!" but Al explained, "She's not coming." Neal's mouth dropped in disbelief. He recovered quickly and said, 'Well, whaddya gonna do?' and Al said he'd be right down. Then Al begged me to proceed to New Orleans and get in touch with Burroughs.'

'Did anybody tell you about him?'

'No, oh no! Just a good, *good* friend of Neal's who had a house. I knew nothing about his past or that he was an addict, and Joan, too.'

We both laughed, and for a moment mused on the contrast between Helen's conventional Lutheran upbringing and the new kind of life she had unknowingly let herself in for by marrying Al, just as I had not foreseen my life with Neal.

'Of course, it goes without saying that Al and Neal were going to be back in...'

'Oh, yes, I know – in *no* time at all. Neal's favourite line: "I'll be right back!"'

'Yeah, right. Five days at the *outside*. So here I was. I decided I would go on to New Orleans, mostly because I just *couldn't* go back to San Francisco and try to explain this to my friends. So, it's Christmas Eve, and I'm on a *train*. This was a real *tragedy* to me. Or I thought it should have been, because for us it had always been such a big *family* thing. We always opened our gifts on Christmas Eve, and it seemed such a twist of fate to be on a train, going – you know – where?'

'*And* a new bride.'

'Ha, Yeah. But you know, I kept thinking it's not all that *bad*. Funny. Well, I arrived in New Orleans and took a hotel room. I'd been in New Orleans before, so it wasn't a strange place to me. I wired Al at Jack's mother's to tell him where I was, and I told the hotel people I expected a call any minute. But the days went by and no call, and Al didn't show.

'Finally the hotel staff told me it was the weekend of the Sugar Bowl and all rooms would have to be given up. So one of the bellhops tells me, "Now I know a little place down the street where I can get you a room," so off we go down this little alley. We came to a door, and he rang a bell. We went inside, and here was this great old mysterious entryway, huge and empty except for tapestries and so forth hanging about, and there was another bell to ring. Finally a woman showed up, real weird, with beads, long skirt...'

'Like a "cat house"?'

'That's *it*. It *was*. A whorehouse, and I'm shown a room, a bare, pristine room off another courtyard that was full of weeds, old broken-down cars and so forth. One of my first discoveries was a huge jar of *Vaseline* sitting on the mantel – and two cigarette butts, one with lipstick on it, but I still didn't want to believe what all this looked like. Actually, it wasn't until the middle of the night when the bells kept ringing and people were coming and going that it finally dawned on me...'

'Oh, you were *smart*! I had the very same experience but in a big brownstone in New York – cigarette, Vaseline, and I didn't cotton on at all. Had to be told.'

'Anyway, funds are getting really low at this point, and I wasn't even eating much, so after a week I had to wire San Francisco for more money.

'I'm still expecting Al at any minute. I decided I'd better call Burroughs and maybe find out something. He invited me to lunch. On the phone, he sounded like an ancient, ancient old man. He took me to this evil-looking dark place – Chinese, I think.'

'Probably where he got his opium – morphine?' I laughed.

'No doubt. And we had lunch, and he talked on and on and on about – prefabricated *housing*! He talked a good hour – through the entire meal. I was dying to ask some questions about if he'd heard anything from Jack or Al, but he was really eloquent when he was talking about something impersonal. At the end he said, "Well, why don't you come out to my place?" Just very casually. So I took one of my bags – I owed the brothel $10, so had to leave the other bag there – and Bill and I took the ferry over to Algiers.

'It was a long walk to the house, which was L-shaped with a veranda all along it. I met Joan. The thing that struck me most about them was how laid back they were. They gave me a room between the children's room and Bill's study, which was where he slept. Mine was kind of a charming room – louvred shutters, a faded oriental rug on the floor, a rough-hewn, garden settee made from whole branches, a fireplace and a high iron bed – really sort of charming.'

'You said Bill slept in his study. Where did Joan sleep?'

'She didn't much, as far as I could tell. In the front sort of entry-parlour there was a couch, and over in a corner a table Bill had built "to last a thousand years". Weird. It was quite some time before I was aware of their sleeping arrangements, or lack of them.

'Now that I had a little money, I made myself as scarce as possible and went into New Orleans every day, going to shows, museums, walking around. I never ate with them. Every day I was to pick up a tube of Benzedrine for Joan, though I never knew why. Often I saw the empty tubes in rows on the mantel; Bill sat there and shot them off with his airgun.

'Anyway, one time his druggist told me I could have a dozen if I wished, since he was sure I wouldn't misuse them. I said, "*Misuse* them? How is that possible?" He told me, and I said, "No, *one* is just fine." When I got back and told Joan this, she just about crapped. That was the only time I ever saw her get really excited about anything.

'Really, it was all just so crazy. Bill had this cat thing. He had six or seven cats, and each night he tied them with string – tying up their feet – and *bathed* them. You'd hear these terrible shrieks, and it was so *insane*, but they acted as though it were perfectly natural.

'Then there was the lizard tree – this grotesque, ugly tree that was literally *covered* in lizards. It was one of Joan's duties to rake the lizards off the tree every night. I don't know why she didn't try poison. I'd step out on the veranda after dark, and she'd be raking away in the moonlight.

'I thought everybody was absolutely insane, as if there were some kind of logic they knew about that I was unaware of, and I didn't want to ask more questions. Bill would stay in the bathroom for hours, and there was always a funny odour afterwards and bits of rubber tubing, teaspoons and so forth lying around.

'Joan and Bill had great rollicking discussions. They had brilliant minds and talked about all sorts of subjects, though never anything personal. Bill always wore a shoulder holster, which he was very proud of, and once in a while he'd have a hip holster thing, too, and he loved to get out in the yard and show you his gun and his marksmanship.'

'Yeah, Neal told me about that when he was there.'

'Funny, too, Bill was always alluding to the sinister, criminal elements over in New Orleans whenever he went to the racetrack. It was so ludicrous to see him – spindly, studious-type in a suit, tie, hat, and a shoulder holster. It was like a kid playing games. You couldn't really take him seriously, even when he was just talking about guns.

'Then there were the kids. Julie was about six or seven, and the little boy not quite a year, I think, still in diapers, when he wore them. They were allowed to go to the toilet whenever and wherever they pleased, but particularly in their room. It had been child-proofed – that is, linoleum and so forth – and every night Joan had to go in there with Lysol and scrub it down. Bill teased the little girl terribly. It wasn't that he was mean; you knew there was something between them – something deep. All he'd have to say was, "Here comes Old Bull," and she'd just scream and have a fit. The whole relationship was so strange. She had great horrid scars up her arms, because she chewed them at night.'

I was mesmerized by her stories and frozen in my chair, listening. I did get up and make more coffee, dish out the pills, see to Cathy, but only with half my mind. There seemed no end.

'The little boy was perfectly bea-u-ti-ful. He and Julie could bring anything at all into their room. There were a lot of neighbour kids in and out, too, and there'd be buckets of mud, horse turds, anything the kids could drag in. Anything they wanted to do in that room they did.

'But one thing I'll always be grateful to Bill for was that he intro-duced me to Céline. *Death on the Installment Plan.* When he first handed it to me I thought, "God – what? A mystery story?" That's what really kept me alive; it really helped.'

'Oh yes – I love that book too.'

'Periodically, of course, I would try again to reach Al, without success, so I asked Bill if he would try to reach Jack's mother, because he knew her. I had hated to ask him, though, because he kept up this running criticism of Neal and how he had better not think he was "going to come down here and con me". Of course he knew nothing about Al.

'I also told Bill how I suspected Neal smoked marijuana. Here he had been raising something like twenty-five acres of the stuff. He said marijuana wasn't that *bad* – heroin was the one to be careful of, something he used every day. Ah well, ignorance is bliss.'

'How often did Bill get a fix?'

'About three times a day. Sometimes only twice. I remember there were times when he'd just sit and dream, but I never knew why.

'And then one day they all drove up. There was Al, looking about the same, and Jack too. They filed in one by one, and Bill and Joan looked at each other, and then in walks Neal through the back kitchen and, taking LuAnne's arm, says, "This is my wife, LuAnne." I look at this girl. *Wife?* You know I'd just met you before the trip. Well, there was some greeting and moving around, and one of the first things Jack said was they were hungry, and he knew a wonderful recipe for Crepe Suzettes.'

'Ha ha, that's the first thing he said when he first came to my place. I can't remember if he really cooked them, however. Must be his opener as a guest.'

'Anyway, Al and I went into my bedroom to talk. I can't remember what I said – less than I would have liked, I'm sure. And before we were able to say more than a few words, LuAnne comes in and asks if she can watch us screw.'

'Aye-yi-yi,' I recoiled.

'*Yeah*, yuk. She sat down on the settee, and like, well, "Let's have at it you two." Of course it was the *last* thing in the *world* I wanted to do, much less in *public*. She looked like a child, too – long tumbling hair, unkempt... Then one time I went out to the car to talk to LuAnne about something, and we're sitting in the car when Neal jumped in and started beating the *hell* out of her. I yelled at him to quit: "*Stop it* – Neal!" And she looked at me and said, "No, it's all right; I like it." Well, that just about did it for me.

'Another time we spent an evening in New Orleans on some sort of surreptitious business, I suppose to do with drugs, although I didn't get it then. And I can remember being in the back seat with Bill. He had a cane that was a sword. He pressed a button, and a sword jumped out. Honestly!

'It had taken Bill quite some time to realize I wasn't one of them. I think he got a kick out of my thinking them all quite respectable, and they tried to sort of live up to the image, for which I was grateful in a way. Near the end of the visit, I'd babysit the two children, and Bill and Joan went to the first movie they'd ever seen together. He was grateful I hadn't taken advantage or lived off them, or tried to con them in any way, and he even offered to rebuild the chicken coop, so Al and I could stay. I was tempted for a minute, finances being what they were, but Al said, "Thank you, no." He knew about the drugs, of course.

'Still, I wanted to stay in New Orleans; I really liked it there. And I wasn't about to get in a car again with Neal. So we found a small apartment, and Al got a job to tide us over until he was called back to the railroad. The next week I called Joan, partly to thank her and partly to keep up the contact. She told me Bill had been arrested on a narcotics charge. Boy, were we glad we hadn't stayed with them!'

Helen and I aired all our grievances against our men, and men in general, a great cleansing in a way, though not constructive in developing a positive attitude. Mostly we cemented our conviction that both of us were put-upon and innocent victims. It still seems a miracle that Helen should appear and share such understanding and agreement at that crucial time.

When the second day rolled around and we concluded it was Monday, I woke up to the fact I had to go to work. By now we had decided that Helen would move in with me, an arrangement of mutual benefit. She could save her rent, and in return save me hiring a babysitter, which I couldn't afford without Neal's salary. Obviously, neither Neal nor I had shown much sense of responsibility in our emotional reactions, but it would seem that God – whatever that meant – was still watching over fools.

Helen probably saved my sanity as well as my livelihood. She was marvellous with Cathy and a sympathetic companion, her great sense of humour preventing us from becoming completely depressed or desperate. We wouldn't have said we were happy, and we continued to grumble about our fate, but somehow we usually ended up laughing when the melodrama threatened to become farce.

Still, we made no effort to find constructive new life patterns, and we didn't care to consider the future. We marked time, got through one day at a time, and played cards, content to be addicted – an excellent escape mechanism for three months. Cathy had her first birthday a month after her father left. Neal didn't fail to mark the date by sending me money, but no word of comfort, hope or regret.

Al returned late in the fall from his travels with Jim, and asked Helen to come back to him and return with him to Denver, where he planned to start school. She agreed, but promised to stay with me until my baby was born in January.

And so the second Christmas of my marriage was one step worse than the first, except that Al, Bill Tomson and the two Helens came to my house, all reunited, all dressed up, and full of new plans for the future, while my outlook was a cipher – a lonelier year looming ahead.

Until the end of that year, Neal had sent money whenever he could, small though the amounts were. Now there were no more envelopes with the familiar, cherished scrawl, and I assumed with a heavy heart he was determined to make this the final break. I couldn't possibly concede anything like that with his child stirring within me.

Al went to Denver, and Helen and I returned to our double solitaire and pinochle, although now a door appeared before each of us – hers open, mine shut.

| TWENTY-ONE |

Soon after the dawning of 1950 I answered the phone to hear a low, brash eastern voice say cheerily, 'Hi, Carolyn? This is Diana Hansen in New York. I suppose Neal told you he lives with me? How are you? How's Cathy?' I pulled the telephone to the couch and sat down. My heart had stopped or was lodged somewhere it didn't belong. 'No,' was all I could mutter, but Diana gushed on as though we were old friends.

'Well, as you know by now, I'm sure you and Neal were never right for each other, and since you've kicked him out, never to darken your door again – ha ha – you're absolutely right, of course, and I know how glad you are to be free. So you see, we want to ask a favour from you. That is, Neal asked me to ask you to divorce him. It seems I'm pregnant, and I know you'll understand that we want to get married as soon as possible. Give the little brat a name and all that, you know.'

A cold mass formed in my solar plexus. I had never thought of this possibility, never. No one else could have his children. How could this be? All my strength was needed to push sound into words. 'Why doesn't Neal ask me himself?'

'No reason. He just asked me to. I was going to call you anyway. You and I have a lot to talk about. I've been dying to call you for ages. I hope I have a girl. If I do, I'll name her Jennifer. What do you think? Isn't that a darling name? You know, we have this great apartment, Carolyn. You'd love it. I've decorated it all up like the Village with travel posters, you know? Neal's writing his book, and he's been so good at staying at it. I'm afraid I spoil him terribly. I just wait on him hand and foot, and he never goes out, just likes staying here at home with me. His friends come over a lot, though. I have to admit I don't care much for his friends. Awfully low-brow, you know what I mean – except Jack. I like Jack, and then Allen of course. That's how we met, through Allen, at a party. But the other people who hang around aren't good for Neal. They sponge, and we've barely enough money for ourselves. I work; I'm a model. I love to work…'

And on and on and on. Through it all, the only words that stuck were, 'I'm pregnant.' 'Please, God,' I prayed, 'make this not true.'

'Well, whaddya say, Carolyn? You'll get the divorce, won't you? We'll pay for it, but how long do you think it will take?'

'I'll only do it if Neal asks me himself.' I hung up. That was the bitterest pill I have ever had to swallow, and it never dissolved. In a day or two, I received a typewritten letter, signed by Neal but obviously dictated by Diana. It hurt and disgusted me that he would allow her to do this, but it was his nature to give everyone what they wanted of him.

In martyred agony, I hired a lawyer, but we had a problem finding grounds. Not that there weren't plenty, but rather there were too many of a nature we didn't care to air in public. Helen agreed to serve as my witness. The legal wheels were set in motion.

On Thursday, January 26, I was alone in the office and the doctor was on her rounds, when I was made aware my time had come. I paged the doctor, who told me to go straight to the hospital, a much nicer one than where Cathy had been born. I still felt fine, so I completed my work and took the cablecar home. I had a cup of coffee with Helen, packed my bag and phoned for a cab.

The maternity ward was overflowing, so I was parked on a gurney in the hall and given a caudal anaesthetic, but Jami hardly gave me time to enjoy it. An hour and a half later she arrived, entering the world in a storeroom. She lay screaming on a counter until a nurse remembered to take her away, her damp hair standing out from her head in long black spikes, which, with her eyes swollen from the drops, gave her a decidedly oriental look. Consequently, when later in the afternoon a strange man entered my room and sympathized at length for my having had a 'mongoloid' baby, I had no reason to doubt him, and I simply sighed. 'What next?' When I asked the doctor what to do about it, he went into mild shock and corrected the error. Wrong room; wrong Mrs Cassady, but I wondered if he had taken a good look at Jami.

This time I was home in three days, and Helen left the next to join Al. I was to consider this time off from work as my two weeks' vacation. It was no vacation. Cathy was only 17 months old, and the new sitter I hired had to be paid exactly the sum I earned. My employer came up with an angelic plan. In my house she installed a telephone extension of her office phone, so I could stay home half a day and split my pay with the sitter, who agreed to work part-time.

The divorce suit was filed a month to the day after Jami's birth. Diana wrote me a letter a day after she had first called; her letters were always written on yellow lined paper in a large childish hand. Twice a week at least she phoned, spending twenty-five dollars to tell me how broke she was. Nearly every other afternoon I would type letters in reply, generally contradicting her opinions of Neal and arguing furiously at her arbitrary pronouncements about me and her illogical conclusions. I should have just ignored her and not answered or argued, but of course my real reason for not doing so was so that I could get to Neal somehow. This way I could at least let him know of my remorse and try to win his approval again. At the time I wasn't fully conscious of this motive, and as I was constantly bombarded with the fact of Diana's pregnancy, I tried to be convinced my connection with Neal was really over.

Despite Diana's impatience, my day in court didn't arrive until late June. The court had appointed a lawyer to represent Neal, a man none of us had seen until the case came up. I was overwhelmed by the large, dark, musty varnished courtroom. I'd only seen formal courtrooms like this in the movies. We drew a woman judge who was renowned in San Francisco, and I felt intimidated. My lawyer was timid herself, and barely spoke above a whisper.

Although my complaints against Neal had been so watered down I hardly recognized him, the judge became furious. Gasping, she burst out, 'Wait, wait. I'm going to postpone this hearing until we can find that young man! I want to have a talk with him. How can he be so irresponsible? Two small children!'

From my witness box, I flung a horror-stricken look at my lawyer, shaking my head. She got up and said, 'Please, your honour, we'd prefer to settle this now.' The judge turned to Neal's lawyer and asked, 'Where is Mr Cassady?'

The lawyer stood up and declared, 'He's in Mexico getting married.'

I stared at my lawyer; she stared at me, Helen's chin dropped, and the courtroom fell silent. The judge recovered, actually groaned, banged her gavel and said, 'Interlocutory decree granted.' I was granted $100 a month child support and $1 alimony – the legal reasoning behind the latter quite escaped me. Many years later, this venerable upholder of justice slipped in the courthouse corridor and broke a hip. As in the case of Judge Golden, Neal felt a higher form of justice was on his side.

So that was that. Except for the year to wait before it was a done deal. Here was another painful blow I dealt my family, the first divorce. After their response to my premarital pregnancy, I had been evasive about my married life, but would be unable to keep this from them, even had I wanted to.

Diana was now nearly five months along. I hadn't forgotten what it felt like, and I tried to do unto her as I would want to be done to. I, too, had been careless, knowing Neal was already married. I felt my bitterness towards Diana was justified because she had known he had other children to care for. Later, I could face the probability that he had been as persuasive with her as he had been with me, convincing her she was the 'only' and the 'right' woman for him. So here we both were, suffering unnecessarily when convention had been established precisely to spare humanity this pain.

Because of the required year before a divorce was final, I couldn't see that my getting one was much help, and neither did Diana. She sent Neal to Mexico to get a 'quickie'. I wondered where she was getting the money for these divorces, since I got daily reports of her dire lack of funds. Now I could see Neal would have seen this as a splendid opportunity to obtain a sizeable stock of marijuana, and my guess was corroborated in a letter he later wrote to Jack, describing his trip and his search for their old 'connection', promising he would pick up 'Elitch's Gardens' (a park in Denver where they used to go to smoke and now a code name for tea) in New Victoria.

When Neal's railroad call-back telegram arrived, he hastened back to New York and I was allowed a blessed respite from Diana's bombardment. Even with no papers to prove it, Neal convinced her he had obtained a divorce, and they were bigamously married in New Jersey on July 10. Two hours later Neal was on a train to 'St. Louis and the West; Carolyn & the babies my impending hope,' he wrote to Jack.

Immediately after Neal left her, Diana was writing to me again, this time with her version of the wedding and adding, 'I am ashamed of myself for my worries while Neal was away. I shouldn't be such a baby.' She explained that Neal couldn't find a job in New York to cover 'the Mexican business', and that was the only reason he was returning to the railroad. She gave me another penny-by-penny account of her financial status, 'none of your concern as long as you get your $101.'

Logic being one of my standbys, and determined to preserve some privacy concerning my own husband and my own affairs, every word of Diana's letters seemed uncannily devised to drive me mad. 'I expect Neal will visit you and the kids this weekend,' she wrote. 'I don't know what arrangements you'll want to make about his seeing Cathy and Jami, but please be nice to him. He does love them and they *are* his children, too. I also think *you*'ll find him a good person. See you all in a month or so I hope.'

Seeing her was the very last thing I wanted. From my reaction to her letters, I was positive I would not be able to control my exasperation, and it appeared as if bludgeoning was the only way to get through to her – if then.

Neal arrived on my doorstep the afternoon of July 14. There's no use denying my heart leaped at the sight of him, but I did my best not to show it, and backed away from his proffered embrace, the embrace for which I had been yearning for so many months. I put my finger on my lips; the girls were sleeping. He walked slowly and softly around the house, gazing reverently at everything, touching things – like a man returned from the dead. I attempted some trivial smalltalk he ignored. Barely audibly, he said, 'Oh, darling, you can't know how great it is to be *home*.'

'Uh huh, I'm sure, Neal. But you can cool all that. It's a bit late for such sentiments. Of course, you are entitled to see your children if you want to. You won't recognize Cathy, and you've never seen Jami.' I dug in my heels against the rising impulse to tell him about their growth. 'Help yourself to coffee, if you'd like some; I'll get them up from their naps.'

Neal took no notice of my reactions, persevering in his own game, and, as this history too often recounts, winning me over again into believing in his sincerity. When Cathy clung to me and shyly looked at him, he continued his reverent approach. He held out his arms for Jami, and as he held her to him and rocked her, he reached out and stroked Cathy's hair, smiling at her and talking softly until she came and stood before him. During all this he tried to catch my eyes with his soulful look, but I busied myself around the kitchen and wouldn't look at the little scene of dreams.

After kissing both girls and putting them gently in the new playpen, he blocked my path and followed me if I dodged him, building the tension between us. It was a game we both knew well. It took little time for his request to move back in.

'Certainly not, Neal, not a chance. You were the one who wanted the divorce, not me. You've swapped this family for another, so let's quit while we're ahead. You've really gone too far this time; I've had enough. And I've a good start on my independence. I certainly don't want to "start all over again", shudder, shudder.' I tried to put conviction into my words; it was the wisest course, but why wouldn't my feelings correspond? If only they would turn against him, too, how simple this would be.

I didn't let Neal move in, but he was around most of the time when not at work, insisting he had the 'right to get his hundred dollars' worth', as Diana had said. I had been lonely after Helen left, and Neal made me feel pretty and desirable again. He was wooing me once more, and all the old charm, devotion, helpfulness, kindness and consideration for which I had loved him in the beginning was pouring over me once more. I thoroughly enjoyed being sought after, but by this time I had enough practice to affect indifference so as to prolong my renewed confidence and security. I insisted he maintain the divorced status, partly for punishment and partly for protection from my own desires. Fortunately, in his case no physical passion was involved or I'd have been a gonner for sure.

June 20 ended the year of waiting for the divorce to become final, but my lawyer had not contacted me nor sent any papers, so the final decree was never filed. We were still married.

| TWENTY-TWO |

The doctor for whom I was working had been experimenting with psychotherapy, and when one of her patients committed suicide she was so remorseful she decided to give it up and share an office with a psychiatrist. The new office was too distant and impractical for me to continue my half-day arrangement, but to compensate me she suggested I go on disability insurance for a while. She would verify my illness as postpartum depression which, she said, if I wasn't having I should be. With Neal's regular child support, I would be earning almost as much as if I had been working.

Happily I returned to the role of homemaker and mother, if not wife. Now I would be able to begin work on the correspondence course in illustration that my parents had bought for me. I dived into the first assignment, determined to find a way to support myself at home and to show Neal the seriousness of my intention to be independent.

Diana managed to afford a vacation, but without pay, to fly to California to spend the time with Neal. She hadn't enough time to use his railroad passes. Neal had been living in the train men's dorms in Watsonville, but now he rented a small apartment for Diana's visit.

In those two weeks, Neal came to see us between trains in San Francisco. The Saturday afternoon Diana was to fly back to New York she telephoned and asked if she could stop by and see us before going to Oakland for her flight. She *still* didn't get it.

'No, Diana, definitely not. You somehow have to get it through your head I do not want to meet you, now or ever. The less I hear of or from you, the better I'll like it. If it is beyond your understanding, simply take my word for it and leave me alone!'

'But Carolyn, here I am in California. I don't know when I'll be back. I want to see Russell Street and the house I've heard so much about – and Cathy and Jami.'

'Dear God,' I groaned to myself before going over it all again. Finally Diana said wistfully, 'Well, okay.' My sigh of relief was premature. At about six in the evening, she called from Oakland Airport and said she had missed her plane. Damn her, I thought, she's done it on purpose – or, more likely, made that up.

'What am I going to do, Carolyn? I haven't any money for a room. There isn't another plane until tomorrow afternoon. I'll just *have* to stay with you now, Carolyn.' Wail wail.

Because she was pregnant, somehow I couldn't refuse her, which she had probably figured from the start. She hadn't money for a room, but plenty for a cab across the bay to my door. She gushed all over me and everything in the house, having even brought *gifts* for all of us, proving she had intended to see us all along. I was seething and sullen, but she took no notice, just jabbered on and on about Neal as though we were all in some delicious conspiracy together. She had managed to arrive at an hour when the girls were not yet in bed, so I had to listen to her appalling baby-talk and the insufferable presumption that she had some natural right to make judgements and recommendations concerning them.

During her monologue, I learned why Neal had been attracted to her. She came on as a sophisticated, aggressive New York model, and had told him she was of an old New England family that owned lots of property in upstate New York which she would inherit. When she had sent me photos of herself modelling maternity clothes, I thought there was something wrong with the scale, but as she sat before me I saw she was taller than Neal – close to six feet with size 12 shoes, coarse features, puffy red lips, straight black hair with bangs and bulging black eyes. My revulsion at her appearance was compounded by her huge distended abdomen, full with Neal's child.

Diana also revealed she wasn't as sweet and ever-agreeable as she had led me to believe. She admitted now that she had once thrown a bowl of soup in Neal's face, and he had hit her so hard he broke his thumb again. She thought all this was terribly funny, and laughed loud and long.

I put the girls to bed as soon as I could, moving Cathy's crib into the living room at the front of the house where Jami already slept in the buggy. I showed Diana Cathy's room behind my bedroom, and told her she could sleep on the daybed. I got out sheets, a pillow and blankets, and showed her where the bathroom was on the other side of my bedroom. I said how tired I was and that I wished to retire; she could read if she liked, or whatever. Good night.

Gloomy and disgusted with myself and with her, I climbed into my own bed and tossed. What good was it being angry at someone if it didn't penetrate? Just harming myself. Luckily, however, I was wide awake when first light appeared, or I might not have heard the soft knock on the front door. I opened it to Neal. I knew immediately that he thought Diana was already in New York. I was about to get some satisfaction from this fiasco after all. I couldn't help smiling as he bustled past me and down to the kitchen. I followed and sat down, waiting to pounce until he had puttered around, lively and elated, making coffee, another plan cooking in his mind.

'I have a surprise for *you*, Neal, my dear.' He looked at me warily, not knowing whether to be pleased or suspicious. But I'm no good at cat and mouse. 'Diana's upstairs. She *claims* to have missed her plane.' Suddenly my anger returned. I fired off a list of his recent atrocities, and bore down heavily on how mortifying Diana was to me, especially at this moment. Given Neal's latest campaign to win me over, Diana's presence was disagreeable to him as well. She had caught him red-handed, a rare occurrence that he couldn't tolerate nor forgive, even though it was because she had trusted him that she had come to me. Had she caught her plane, I assumed he would be writing her love letters.

Stirrings above our heads told us Diana was awake and would have heard us talking. Neal looked grim as he went up to her room and closed the door. I heard him cursing her and became apprehensive. I couldn't help feeling sorry for her now. Although I didn't understand her, Neal apparently meant everything to her as he had to me. There she was, pregnant, alone and leaving him behind, and there he was rejecting her. She had asked for punishment by seeing us together here, and could picture the whole setting at this side of the country in her lonely room at the other. By the sound of her sobs and Neal's stony voice, I assumed Neal's usual compassion had been switched off. Perhaps he thought a swift break would be easier on her in the end.

He should have known better. When Diana returned to New York and wrote to Neal, she sounded as if the scene had no significance:

> I dropped a note to Carolyn last week thanking her for putting me up Sat. night, apologizing for my 'breakdown' & asking her about what kind of diapers best & the meaning of all those 'pads' in the essentials list. She hasn't

answered, so I guess she wants to discontinue the communication...As for Sun A.M. we don't have to discuss it because I think I understood. It was just so painful and unpleasant, and I, for one, was completely worn out from the battle with the airlines...By the way, 'Jennifer Jo' it will be...the name I know you know is a little tribute to Cathy, whom I am quite in love with...I'd rather have a little boy & Cathy the big sister. She's so full of silent real conversation and understands so much and is so brave when she doesn't...If Carolyn doesn't want her, I'll bid.

I couldn't believe her act. Meanwhile, Neal redoubled his efforts to be nice to me and to try to persuade me he was through with her, but I still refused to let him move in. He returned to the apartment in Watsonville for the rest of the summer. I didn't learn until later, when LuAnne told me, that he had lured her into moving in with him while her husband was at sea, but they couldn't get along without jealous scenes, so she gave it up. In September from there Neal wrote to Jack:

I am going to my death. It seems to happen every autumn, more particularly each September of late. The realization of the things that go to make up one's death is such a personal thing, with so heavy a pressure on the intelligence, that it becomes unbearable agony to put word to paper. Each one with their privacy contained in mind has within their reach a seed of death which becomes the thing to be aware of and its use is not to be escaped.

Neal soon gave up his Watsonville apartment and rented one in San Francisco on Divisadero Street, asking Diana to send him a radio and anything of his that was left in New York. Diana now had another idea I detested.

'The Divisadero St. move for you sounds just right, provided you don't get too lonely...Would the apt. be any place for you, me and the baby to stay till we find our own apt.?'

I imagined Neal repeating the Denver performance with LuAnne, as well as Diana's sickening chumminess if we were all in the same town. I told her just that, and she wrote to Neal in seeming innocence.

Gee whiz, despite it all, I really hadn't worried about that – just assumed...we'd just lead a peaceful life without emotional turmoil...Would you really try to have an affair with Carolyn? Or try to instigate some 3-part plan? I shouldn't think you would – too damned destructive for all of us…My darling, let's be nice old bourgeois, with salt shakers on the table & a Chevrolet station wagon in the garage…P.S. By the way, can you send me the baby stuff C's been gathering up? Tell C to quit hoping I won't move to SF if I want to…that my marriage to you is some temporary fly-by-night business…

Now that I was maintaining my independent attitude, however, Neal and I had some good times together. I tried telling myself we would never get back together, but I was happy only when he was around and showing an interest in me and the girls. To fortify my position, I accepted dates with friends of Louise, even though I had no conversation to offer, immersed as I was in Neal and simply staying alive. This at least afforded me a glimpse of the world and the arty bars of North Beach, like Vesuvio's. I even got to know the wonderful artist, Wolo, who had decorated the place, inside and out, with colourful, fanciful cartoon-like paintings. Vesuvio's was a quiet laid-back little bar where men played chess and guitar, and you could have a drink and a conversation without having to yell over loud so-called music. Wolo's parties were anything but quiet, but they were certainly arty.

I also learned how men view divorcees, even though I wasn't really one. To Neal these dates *sounded* a good threat, and served to keep him jealous, worried and attentive.

By mid-October, Neal persuaded me that the cost of his apartment was extravagant and foolish to sap that money from our minimal funds. I gave it a lot of thought, but in the end it was so reasonable I gave in and let him move back to Russell Street, but only if he still accepted that it was a business arrangement; we were friends but not lovers, and he would have to sleep on the couch. I now felt strong enough to enforce these conditions. I don't know what reason he gave Diana for this move, other than the expense, but her answer was surprisingly calm. 'Your letter today about no nice Divisadero St. was so tender – also your voice on the phone. To hell with Divisadero. It was between "Hate and Wallow" wasn't it? Let's not jump to any big plan…'

Neal had already been hatching a 'big plan'. After having softened up Diana, he sprang it. He told her he would give each of us a 'test period': six months of living with me and then from January to June living with her in New York, to allow her 'to prove she was the better wife'. Talk about having your cake and eating it, too. What a preposterous idea; how many men have it that good? In other words, he'd figured on staying with me while working on the railroad, then having his fun in New York during the winter cut-off months, all very tidy, but he didn't fool me. Diana didn't like it at all, and the telephone pealed when she got his letter. From then on her correspondence doubled.

My belief that Neal was the only man for me had still not altered, try as I might to deny it, and I found it too easy to slip back into a married feeling with him. Yes, I certainly understood Diana's panic. I also knew her attacks on me narrowed her chances of winning Neal back. He never liked hearing criticism or gossip, and rarely indulged in either himself. I would never acknowledge that Diana had an equal claim, and at that time her ability to compromise with other wives and children was impossible for me to understand.

| TWENTY-THREE |

Neal soon settled in, and returned to writing his autobiography and long letters to Jack. He bought a tape recorder because, he explained in a letter, both he and Jack 'understood the power of voices. I know what voices mean, and since I was so stymied in writing…and finally decided…I had to write from the beginning in words…and you write me about voices…your letter so vital to me because it showed…I wasn't alone in my mental world.'

Neal was encouraged and excited by their letters, and wanted Jack to buy a similar machine so they could swap tapes. He also wrote to Jack, 'I wish Allen would write.'

Eventually Allen did write, recounting his ineptitude at two jobs he had recently tried. 'Truly the real world is my downfall,' he lamented, and ended, 'Hear little from Diana; she seems worried about future, etc., as well she might. So you're back with Carolyn, eh? Well, you old scapegrace you. Why don't you all get married a la Mohammedan customs. Jesus, what the hell are *you* all after in each other?'

When Neal was called to San Luis Obispo, a town on the Southern Division where Al Hinkle was already working, I was relieved of some of the verbiage from Diana. I tried to gain some perspective with no pressure from either of them. Aiding me was a visit from a friend of my brother's, Bud, who came to San Francisco on a month's business trip and looked me up. It was perfect timing. He took me on expense-account carousing in all the beloved places I had remembered from wartime visits with my roommate while we were training in occupational therapy in Oakland.

Louise, still eager for me to find a replacement for Neal, found some friend my size who loaned me a couple of substitutes for my old green dress. Poor Louise: Bud, although only a few years older than I, already had a wife and five children, but his attention worked to my advantage; Neal's response was passionate jealousy – more than after the other one-time dates, because I let Bud sleep on the couch many nights when we'd get home late. Cathy also liked Bud, and when Neal returned he was infuriated by her chatter about 'Bood' as I pointed out how good it was for the girls to have a man around.

While Neal was away, I also tried to re-evaluate and re-analyze my requirements for a husband, all in the spirit of his 'trial period'. While he was still in San Luis, I wrote him a long dissertation, beginning: 'First, know that I love you and all I want in life is to be your wife and the mother of your children... but I want all that this implies. Foremost it means I want you as a husband and father with all that implies.' My chief concern was the discrepancy between his words and his actions, and I spilled plenty of words on the futility of deception and pretense.

> I do not consider you as a husband and father or that you consider me as a wife when two other women can still draw responses of influence or emotion from you as a result of past experiences with them... I realize that when you returned to me, you did not profess that this was a solution in the way it must be for me. Our sex problem has suddenly struck me, too. I know I fail as a 'wife' there, but know that it is because I don't feel I am considered one otherwise... I feel sure that were the other conditions corrected, I could remedy my failure there – with your help. Recently, however, I saw how out of proportion this phase of your life has become... Frankly, I'm frightened of and for you again... I think one of your major difficulties is this whole attitude of 'let it ride; it

will work out.' You should see by now such is rarely the case…at any rate, I am no longer willing to bypass or let ride. If you won't cooperate, then my only choice, my only 'or else' is to do as I said: work toward freezing my love for you and gaining total independence. But the big moves must come from you.

How smugly righteous was I. It was something of a surprise to me when Neal answered my letter not in his usual, reassuring, loving rhetoric, but in a rare sober mood, taking his cue from my accusation that he wasn't being 'honest'.

Dear Carolyn: There are so many things not ever to be understood; certain specific differences between us which are really unimportant, but which, under the stress each of our respective personalities put on our minds cannot be reconciled emotionally. The particular flaws I present your mind with are now stretched from original vices to abstract notions of me, which thru so many modifications are no longer true…

Love has nothing to do with it, for all processes are by nature intellectualizations about abstracts which are conveyed by words whose meanings are lost to the mind…For the first time in years I am returning to an intellectual snobbery, altho, of course, I have no right to, being incoherent as ever and more unable to be understood by any-one on questions of life. Perhaps this is because I'm here with Al and Helen and realize, once again and more fully that neither you nor Diana can see how essentially I am far in the lead of any one of us. This means nothing. Especially in the light of the horrible position I've gotten us all into, but, still, I…cannot help being governed by the things I know…

This means circumstances are now so developed that no matter how we each suffer, there is nothing left but to go through with it (the plan.) Not in any sense of 'truth' am I writing; there is none actually that can be recognized, and 'truth' is a matter of the understanding process only – read Spengler, Vol. I.

Now is a period of interruption. The present is such an iron-clad pressure on the soul that being so weakened by lazy coasting, I can now do nothing but barely summon the strength to keep the process going…however, in my case, no one is sure that I ever had the lost strength. It's worse than that. I know the strength that was there is gone forever, because it was an illusion. This calls for strict measures.

The effort to gain peace has passed, then, into an obnoxious struggle to show people something. This I cannot do; it's not there, no matter how I attempt to manufacture. So let things be; help everyone with kindness, help them to win out, since that's what they want, but, for yourself (me) suffer your peculiar hurts in silence and hope for nothing – except to be able to not regret too much and to forget. N.

Insofar as I could follow Neal's thought (and I have included this rather tedious letter to convey some idea of how Neal's mind worked in order to offset somewhat the usual assessment only of his actions) this letter did little to reassure or guide me, and it made me vaguely anxious and confused in a new way. I was no longer certain I wanted that rarity Neal regarded as the honest truth. I had always believed I could work with the truth, but what I meant by 'fact' is not simple to define. What I wanted was for Neal's extravagant declarations of 'love' to be genuine, as mine were, and for 'love' to be guaranteed, a predictable condition of a definable quality. I felt capable of this, and wondered why Neal did not. That kind of marriage was all I'd ever known, but in time I learned how extremely rare it is, although still possible.

One night soon after this exchange, Neal had to 'make a run' to San Francisco. He arrived when Bud and I were sharing a home-cooked dinner for a change, and I made Neal stay away until Bud had left, partly to show Neal it was still my life, and that I wouldn't be taken for granted, and partly because I felt too gauche in handling his meeting Bud. The fire of Neal's jealousy gave him the eloquence and persuasion that his letter lacked, and he dispelled my fears again, as he always had.

On November 7, 1950 Diana's child was born. A boy. I considered fate cruel in delivering her a son, and I underwent another episode of despair and humiliation. Diana wrote daily to Neal from the hospital, even though he didn't answer until she had gone to her mother's, and then to tell her when he would arrive for the promised visit. Her observations continued to infuriate me: 'Give C the enclosed brass safety-pin to wear as her badge of membership in the "Cassady Mothers Auxillary". It's a leftover from the bracelet and belt kit, and I find it makes a neat scarf pin. I have one for me, too.'

Good God, I thought, has she such a thick hide she could be serious? I was even more irked that she wanted to send announcements of the birth to all of Neal's half-brothers and sisters, and asked how to reach his father as well. She succeeded where even Neal had failed, and we received a nice grandfatherly note from Neal's father congratulating Neal's 'new wife'. The poor man was unaware there were two of us, and that he already had two grandchildren. Trust Diana.

While Neal was away in San Luis, I forwarded his mail, and with his permission read the letters from Jack and Allen beforehand. One day a letter arrived from Allen, dated 'Saturday eve, Nov. 18', carrying stunning news:

> I got home today from Jack's wedding…which took place last night at 6 followed by a big party at Cannastra's pad which his wife had leased and Jack is now master of…He has been strangely out of town the last several months, in retirement and brooding on T alone, and when he rejoined N.Y. society he seemed to me to be more settled in reality, more sober. He talked in a more disillusioned way – not making a fetish of it as I do – but like a post 20s survivor, F. Scott Fitzgerald after the party of ego was over. All of a sudden appears on the horizon this J. in C.'s pad, making a vulturish shrine of it (on the pretext that they had been great lovers)…so…I start moving in on her…in the hope of sleeping with her and ultimately taking over pad with her, also under impression she has money, which she hasn't. But when time comes, I'm…impatient with her sentimentalized version of self, not wanting anything but 'friendship' with menfolk, wanting to be alone and keep shrine and have big parties.
>
> Next thing I know Jack ran into her, two weeks ago, slept and stayed on, decided to marry, and did yesterday. This is just a very sketchy account…The main things I see is this increased wariness and caution in life of Jack, and this mad marriage, they hardly know each other. But maybe it will work out for the rest of his life. I think he hopes for permanence.
>
> …Anyway, I say…we all should have beautiful intelligent wise women for wives who will know us and vice

versa as well as we know ourselves (one another.) I say let
the home be the center of emotional and spiritual life.

When I get married, I want everybody I know to be
there and watch, including all regiments of family, in a
synagogue where will be great, groaning choirs of weepers,
sacraments, everybody in flower and dress clothes, slightly
awed by the presence of eternal vows, chastened by
tradition and individuality of marriage. Then I can go
home to mad pad and have real crazy party with people
jumping out of windows after. And women folk and
menfolk separated for last good byes and vows of eternal
fidelity.

'Amen,' I said. Allen and I were not as at odds in our views as I had
imagined, although the revelation that Allen thought of a marriage
with a woman was a bit of a surprise.

It was a great shock to Neal and me to learn Jack had married.
Quite apart from Allen's optimistic if dubious endorsement, it didn't
strike either of us as a good move. Knowing the depth of Jack's
emotions, his convictions about women, and his sympathy with
Catholic dogma, we found this action really difficult to fathom, and
we felt an ominous wave of apprehension.

It was too late for advice or laments, so we did not dwell on our
doubts but tried to bolster some faith that Jack had taken this step
in an avalanche of intuition. It wasn't easy to think of 'our' Jack as
married to a girl we'd never heard of. I'm sure it hurt Neal and
bowled him over for a time, since all his plans had been securely
aimed at the coming months of travel alone with Jack.

Two weeks passed before Neal could bring himself to write to
Jack, and then he did so in an unusual superficial way. The envelope
was addressed in a self-conscious, giddy manner, and the letter was
delayed for reasons never discovered. It was addressed: 'Dear Jack;
for the first time truly a man of marriage and family.' There followed
several pages of intricate dream recounting in which Jack figured,
and a lengthy description of a man he had met that looked exactly
like Bill Burroughs. Finally, Neal got around to the subject of Jack's
new status:

I'm sure happy to hear you got married, naturally I was
as surprised as all git-out but I knew you had to do it
sometime. When a man approaches 30 (ugh) without being

well on the way to have little kiddilies, it begins to become
a teensy bit too late and soon all he can do is write books.
It'd be fine, then, if you're 'impregnated on the 18th?' is
right and there is abuilding in the mixer a miniature K,
with big ears and a bigger thingajigger.

Neal passed along some advice to the 'wonderful girl you picked
out of the whole big city to not get into the silly habit of worry'. But
he also added, 'Beyond this bunk, tho, Jack, with all your fooleries,
you can never escape your serious and overconcerned nature nor the
destiny of your blood and your inclination to the Home...and all
the times you've spoken about, and otherwise revealed, to me the
hankering for a family.'

A clear example of Neal's humane instincts overcoming his thinly
veiled doubts and dismay.

Included in all of Neal's letters to Jack and Allen was the constant
request for tea. And in this letter, too, he made such a request,
promising to reveal all about Jack to his wife in exchange for a 'joint
of honest weed (or the price of same)'.

| TWENTY-FOUR |

Neal's crisis with me and Diana finally came to a head. I don't know
whether it was caused by the stimulus of Bud's visit, which had
shown me to Neal in a different light, Jack's marriage or by the
letters Neal and I had been exchanging, but Neal said he was tired
of the game. He was sure he wanted to make his permanent home
with me and the girls.

True to form, Neal didn't come right out with it to Diana, but
began the let-down by telling her he didn't have enough money to
send her all of the December allotment. When I objected, he insisted
that Diana had plenty of resources because she was living at
home, and her family wouldn't let her starve. He considered more
important the sudden critical necessity for Cathy to have her tonsils
removed.

At first, Diana was understandably furious, and brought to bear
all the classic, sad and regretful accusations of the wronged woman
– all of which I knew by heart. Then came the letter in the opposite

mode: 'I want so much for you to want me…I want you to feel that I'm the one for you…It just can't happen…I know that if you do not want me as a wife, no one ever will…'

I understood that what Diana was expressing was genuine, and I never overcame my wonder that Neal could convince so many of us, including Allen, of that same level of devotion.

Neal wrote Diana a kind letter, sent her what money he could, and she in turn believed she had a chance. She tried another tack by complimenting me while at the same time revealing derogatory remarks Neal was supposed to have made, giving me grounds to be angry with him. Neal and I both recognized the drowning man's grasping at straws, and honestly pitied her.

She abandoned her vow not to talk about the baby. Every day she sent a description of his every move, internal as well as external, with details sufficient to demonstrate her travails, her courage and her son's captivating appeal. Diana never quite grasped Neal's dedication to making everyone happy – to 'let them win out'. This blind spot required him to go through a gauntlet of unpleasant actions to keep the peace. He often sought relief and compensation for these grim duties in correspondence with Jack.

Although Neal had mailed Jack a response to his marriage on December 7, we received a letter from Jack written on the fourteenth which indicated he hadn't received Neal's. We blamed the frivolity of Neal's envelope. Jack wrote that he was eagerly waiting for Neal's reply and thought it might have been lost among Christmas rush mail. He sounded really happy, praised his wife, couldn't wait for us to meet her. He wrote he had finished *On the Road* and was missing us. He had just heard of Diana's son and looked forward to Neal's coming to see him, when they'd have a big party. He specified before Christmas, so he must have thought Neal and I weren't together and knew nothing of the big decision, but it pleased me, of course, that Neal chose to spend Christmas with us. I knew Diana would be spending one much like my first after my first child, but at least she had a family around her.

The Hinkles shared Christmas Eve with us, because Al was leaving for Denver on Christmas Day. Helen was pregnant and was to stay with us until her baby was born, since she had made all the birth arrangements in San Francisco. This year, of course, there were no presents from my family for Neal; we were supposedly divorced, but

Neal witnessed their solidarity with me and the grandchildren in spite of my transgressions.

The advent of Christmas seemed to help Diana accept the inevitable, although she was far from giving up altogether. She wrote countless pages about her present tragic condition, her mother's tragic illness, her tragic financial situation and 'I'm worried about the job-hunting, because a lot of my old, old hysterical neurotic symptoms have returned, and I get dizzy and faint when I go outside.' After two or three more pages about the baby, she ended, 'Not much to say. I suppose sooner or later we'd better do something legal about dissolving the marriage.' I had been much surprised to learn that the law against bigamy is completely ignored unless one of the wives makes a scene. This made the annulment simpler.

Neal, feeling as though he had made some sort of order out of chaos, sprang back into action. Writing an exuberant letter to Jack on December 30, '1950's last gasp,' he promised he would leave on January 3 for New York, but would have to 'boom' on the way in order to make some money. He had received a letter from his father who was in jail, and Neal planned to detour to Denver to be there when his dad was released. 'I plan for him to live with Carolyn and me. Car and money fallen thru completely, so have Diana and I, so has U.S.A.' He set forth an elaborate plan for Jack and wife to come back to San Francisco with him. 'Carolyn thinks you're it, and all the old nonsense is finished...' Once again, he listed the assets of living with us – 'got everything you'll ever need or want.'

And, once more, the 'best laid plans' went awry. Our finances were such that Neal felt he couldn't leave for New York on the third after all. I noted the difference in his attitude from what it had been in 1948. He found there was a shortage of switchmen in Oakland, and he could hire on until spring.

At the end of February, Neal figured he could take a 'business leave' and wrote again to Jack, outlining in minute detail the new set of plans, insisting that Jack and Joan immediately begin their preparations for returning with him – chief among these being for Jack to find or save the money to buy a truck. Neal had found another '43 Packard Coupe, and I needed a car now to take Cathy to nursery school, Neal insisted.

> Not tomorrow, you hear, you lazy lout, but right now
> YOU GET A JOB!...Pick out the toughest tasks and do
> penance, grovel in the daily horror necessary for the lousy
> few bucks. I am sick. I shudder at the thought...however
> best you can, make it so by my birthday. Amethyst for
> sincerity, Violet for modesty – that's February; Boy Scouts
> founded 1910. Cassady born 1926, that's the 8th...

After defining the exact time Neal would leave and precisely reach each city en route, exactly how each day would be spent in New York, including his helping Jack choose a truck and helping them pack, Neal told them there was a chance they could rent a house next door to us or, if not, they could stay in our attic until more suitable accommodation could be found.

> Carolyn insists that J. become pregnant, to have kids, of
> course and catch up (impossible) with us, but to also live
> next door and we can swap them, tossing the little
> wigglies over the backyard fence...got Joan's fine letter to
> me. Tell her Carolyn feels the same about Pickup, Kickup
> and Shackup.

No sooner were these new plans dispatched than there was a sudden lull in switchmen jobs, and Neal decided to take his leave now so as not to miss any work or income. He took everyone completely by surprise in New York. Diana's daily communications had resumed, and by now she was making veiled threats and frequent allusions to her 'unbalanced condition', and I was apprehensive. As soon as Neal left, I sat down and wrote him a long letter, hoping it would be there when he arrived in New York.

> Don't you ever go away again! I looked back and saw
> your silhouette against the train light...you striding across
> the tracks carrying that big suitcase, and I could hardly
> push on the gas to leave. You looked so little and lonely,
> and it made no sense all of a sudden – I have awful
> superstitions that now you've changed to doing the right
> thing, your so-far-so-good luck will change, too. Just when
> everything is about to be all right...and since D is so
> cold, she might be capable now of carrying out her threat
> – I almost wrote to Jack to ask him to go with you when
> you see her. She called this AM, and tho I didn't talk to
> her, since I wouldn't accept the charges, I felt she wasn't

in quite that state yet, altho now maybe she's madder. I wanted to talk to her, but I realized she could buy her crib and more for the phone bills. I wrote her an airmail special to show her how fast it works and that 21 cents is better than $21. So I hope they won't harm you...

When you get back, we'll show you how much we love you...

There's so much to be done, and the second quarter century must be as rich as the first was wanton...I'm going around in a fog today and feel tired, but I'll get over it...

Neal wrote me a postcard on the way, and after he had seen Diana he whisked away all my anxieties regarding her.

Dear Wife, my only one. Writing a quickie to you while bouncing along on commute from Tarrytown to NYC. I have just left Diana after 48 hours of talk and tears. I am pleased, happy, amazed, proud, over-joyed and impatient to report to you that everything, yes every little thing is completely perfect and absolutely OK – i.e., we have come to an understanding...Actually, she made all the final decisions; to gratify her is simple enuf as it consists of fantasy words...The long trek home to you and my loved children commences on Sun. the 21st.

Neal told me that a great weight had been lifted, and explained that Diana and I were different personalities, so that she really was satisfied and knew she didn't want him because they were so unsuited. This, of course, in contradiction to what she'd been affirming for so long, and I didn't believe a word, only wished it were true.

We both want different things and feel no respect for the other's ideals or desires, i.e...she thinks my writing a joke, or at best a poor hobby. That's OK, you and I feel much the same but somehow are serious about it, huh?

Approaching NYC and night of talk with Allen and Jack and Holmes novel (GO) and other readings, etc. I am whole, happy and for the first time rushing unreservedly to my one and only family, my sweet Carolyn, I love you...PS. Jack and Joan not coming with me. May follow in a month...

It was strange to feel so differently about this trip of Neal's to New York than any of the previous ones. Although I knew he would enjoy it, I considered it primarily an errand of mercy with my blessings. There were many things I wanted to accomplish before his return, but my energy seemed drained, and I felt only like resting and putting off. I credited it to the relief from the strain I'd been under for so long. Then the light dawned, and I had to write to Neal the awful, incredible truth, half thinking he should reconsider his desires again.

In my letter, however, I found myself writing about everything else I could think of – the girls and coy descriptions of my problems with the car. I took the opportunity to put in a section aimed at Jack, explanations and apologies I'd never be able to speak in person, hoping Neal would pass it on, and ending with 'I hope it can be cleared up, and I guess it will through you...he is your only acquaintance who took me seriously and made me feel truly married to you and not just the current "bed with a girl in it".'

But I couldn't dodge the subject forever. I wavered but finally plunged: 'well, damn, now then, hold tight. I still haven't had a period...I just can't accept it; it really burns me up, and believe me, dear, I'm going to do everything I can...after all our precautions – *it cannot BE*.'

I had even gotten an infection because I wouldn't risk taking out the diaphragm. (When the doctor scolded me, I had to tell him that Diana had had Neal's sperm tested, and the little devils lived for at least 36 hours.) What's a girl to do? I was very bitter, and I ranted on about society and its laws, the Catholic church, the peddlers of contraceptives that don't work, and the doctors that guarantee they will. I proposed to demand an abortion from my former employer with the okay from her psychiatrist associate, because of my previous post-partum depression, etc. etc. 'Must I look for this every year?' Before I finished the letter I called the doctor. 'Well, I talked to her. She says it must be fate in my case and that something wonderful must be about to happen to me – (how did she know?) but no abortion.'

Although I didn't see how she figured any of that, nor how we could manage, I thanked God Neal had decided to stay with us. But I wrote, 'I still think you need a lighter dose of family...but don't let me spoil your vacation any longer.'

This gave Neal more inspiration for magnanimous and reassuring words.

the wonderful absolute joy I know and feel at thoughts of next quarter century with you (rich not wanton)...I've learned how to treat possessions...WORRY ABOUT NOTHING – including the third child...you come first, first, first in everything – kids next – perfect just to watch you, work for you, and I'm *not* hung on lazy kicks any more!! I've yet got the secret of perpetual energy...I'm in there with you at last. Trust.

I was glad to do so. How could I not? For the first time since our wedding I felt comfortable, safe and loved again by the only man I wanted. I echoed Neal's words, 'I'm at last ready for you...and life.'

| TWENTY-FIVE |

Spring of 1951 came, and with it the feeling of fresh beginnings and new hope. On our third wedding anniversary, Neal buttressed my aspirations for a new start by writing me a silly poem, but one which showed his understanding and awareness of my feelings. He placed it beside my plate at dinner along with a piece of coloured glass.

To my April Fool's magnificent Ass
So beauteous, though over full, as is your heart
With misery. I here make present a sliver of cut stained glass
Which unable to shave your behind's blubber
Might yet pierce your reservoir of hurt
Enough to make our third anniversary
A day of insight crystal clear
Combined with knowledge thru the ear
So that when this Sabbath sun descends
There'll be an understanding which portends
Henceforth a bliss that never ends
But shows up for joke the fear
That dread neurotic minds hold dear
To all the while make careful file
Of everybody's dreary food
On which they feed of selfish acts
Only to find it does no good
For conscience never has forgot
The pacts made three years ago this day
When each to the other did say those eternal vows
That cost ten bucks
To get from you my legal – shucks. No paper.

Grinning, he watched me read, while I blushed here and there. 'You think Ginsey would be proud of me? Hey?'

With superhuman wizardry Neal had vanquished my jealousy towards LuAnne and Diana, and there remained only the residue of resentment Diana kept alive by her 'daily double', as Neal called her daily letters and frequent phone calls. I took charge of the battle with her in order to protect my home, I thought, and although Neal maintained our harmony, his conscience nagged him badly. On this anniversary he also wrote a postcard to Jack, with 'April Fool' on the date line and no signature.

> I've tried to write and can't. I love you and love you, but am so bothered by other things that each letter I begin ends at first paragraph. I can send you those if you wish. I even have funny little things torn from magazines for you. This card to let you know I'm alive...First 10 torturous sheets of double-space done on novel. Life hard with no tea to swallow or money for anything...C and D having tremendous long distance roaring match this very minute, been yelling in frustrated rage for half hour. I'm sick to my stomach with sorrow...

Diana kept holding out unfounded hopes to us she'd leave us alone, and she'd changed the baby's name from Neal to Curtis, although she insisted on hyphenating 'Cassady' onto the end of her own for a while longer. She was also trying to get to Neal through Allen, which I understood, as well as her need to talk about him. Allen wrote us:

> I saw Diana 3 times for lunch and she is quite upset since all is in confusion, not so much amatorily (I think she's cured) but financially. You are a martyr to that plaything, and Diana said wife Carolyn is due again. You can have my policeman's badge, like in the Charlie Chaplin picture. Congratulations: I hope you may have the pleasure of a boy-child now. And Jack said 2 nights ago, 'he went back to the woman who wanted him the most.' Ideal image of you in my mind has replaced reality. But I send love to the reality. Allen o' the woods.

(I was sure Diana wanted him as much as I.)

So determined were Neal and I to succeed this time, we turned to the only known source of aid. We investigated the facilities for psychological therapy, and began regular sessions at the Langley-Porter

Clinic. Our encounters were erratic, and frequent changes of therapists did little to give us confidence, and no new insights were forthcoming. Neal and I free-associated all the time to each other anyway, and they never made comments. Since Neal often, but not always, got high before a session, I thought they'd missed an opportunity for some research. Dreams were never mentioned, yet Neal remembered his vividly and wrote pages of them to Jack, so that Jack began paying more attention to his own. He began writing them to Neal, who interpreted them as best he could.

Neal may have agreed to this crutch simply to humour me or to show he was willing to *do* something towards our marriage, or it may have been because Allen had pressed him so long to try psychoanalysis. Neal and I both thought we knew enough about psychology as well as marriage already, but perhaps only intellectually. Neal had once written to Allen,

> Scientific psychology has worked out for itself a complete system of images in which it moves with entire conviction. The individual pronouncements of every individual psychologist proves on examination to be merely a variation of this system, conformable to the style of their world science of the day... like everything else that is no longer becoming but become, it has put a mechanism in the place of an organism.

Then Neal became less communicative, whether it was because he was talked out and discouraged with results, or whether it was the tea, as he maintained. He wrote to Jack,

> My mind is utterly blank; can't think of a thing to say. It's really a form of exhaustion brought on by the steady use of t, which with its enormous number of images, contents the brain with just thoughts terrifying tho they now are – so no can write. My brain waves on this stuff must form a very pretty picture: i.e. I feel I have most surely squared the circle tho so jazzed are the jagged lines as they return to the starting point, it makes me tired.

When Allen had written his dismal letter about Jack's marriage, Neal had answered with a lengthy analysis of some possible reasons for Jack's action, and high on the list was the use of the particular batch of marijuana both Jack and Neal had been using at the time:

'because I've noticed that anyone who uses it has a tendency to think the same strange thoughts as do others who use it...' He deduced that by its constant use Jack had seen himself as never before, 'brooding alone on Richmond Hill'. Neal compared Jack's feelings to his own while on tea, and dealt with how impossible it became to make one's thoughts understood to others, 'because all that comes out of one is a caricature of what one is thinking... yet you meant it to be a caricature.' I thought this may have been part of the problem with the psychotherapists.

In analysing Jack's reasons for marriage and in re-evaluating his own, Neal did a good deal of thinking on the subject, and answered Allen's confusion:

> reasons *for* marriage mean less than you believe, Allen...
> A marriage such as I am inclined to believe Jack's is, and
> I know mine were, is a combination of willed blindness,
> a perverted sense of wanting to help the girl and just plain
> what-the-hell... it all depends on the attitude of each
> partner toward the other, as that attitude has been
> conditioned by the various actions and ideas that have
> influenced each person's personality. The many compro-
> mises even tho not begrudged intellectually, push the limits
> of love, and soon each person affects a static compre-
> hension of the other, and there is no changing the view
> point. If one is convinced of the other's integrity, all is
> usually OK, but if this is gone, there is no hope... I could
> go on indefinitely from experience. The conflicting ideas
> of the partners are the crux which combined with the
> emotional habits of each make for the strain that, once
> ruptured, needs an external responsibility to save the
> marriage, like church, family, pride, children or some
> such absolute. My God!, I sound like *The Ladies Home
> Journal* or worse, and never having done this before, give
> that excuse.

This analysis was, of course, of interest to me. It sounded more like Neal's marriages and not a lot to do with Jack's. He had not married Edie, his first wife, for life in the conventional terms, and this one he may have considered so, but not much thought had gone before.

Perhaps this involved diagnosis was an attempt at justification inspired by the sterility of the psychology interviews, but whatever had made Neal's brain work overtime and pour forth so much analysis, his mood was more content; our 'static comprehension' of each other was breaking up somewhat, our 'viewpoints' seeing some change – at least on the surface.

To Jack he wrote,

> Carolyn and I have never gotten along so well; her whole attitude has completely changed, at last. No shit, she is really nice as hell all the time now, I can hardly understand it...I gave Cathy a sip...(a SIP! whole GLASS!) [I typed in] of beer...the depraved action shocked her into a prompt scream of horror, but since we no longer bother to dicker or work up any emotional sweat, she gave up quickly and at the next pass of my chair, she stopped and with a kiss ruined all the thought of this paragraph, and my viperous ideas were nipped temporarily...

For some reason, Neal and Jack had found it difficult to talk during Neal's brief visit to New York, and now Jack's involvement with a new wife made any communication more awkward. With fewer personal anecdotes, Neal occasionally wrote descriptive episodes of past experiences for practice, enjoying the 'Proust-like recollections'. Jack applauded lavishly every word Neal wrote, and went overboard about a long letter in which Neal described an affair with two girls he'd known in his late teens. Jack hailed the letter as a literary masterpiece. Allen was usually less expansive in his praise, preferring to look at a work as literature and comply with Neal's request for constructive criticism, but about this story they both agreed. Allen wrote,

> I finally got your long letter of Dec. 17 the story by stealing it from Jack's desk when he was out. He was afraid I'd lose it. He said to me when he'd read it, 'Neal is a collosus risen to destroy Denver!' I read it with great wonder, stopping and laughing out loud every few paragraphs, so much clarity and grace and vigor seemed to shine in the writing...even now it's hard to say (or feel at the typewriter) how much I am impressed and astonished at the magnitude of the work you have done in the Joan Story, which seems to me an almost pure masterpiece. It's easier to speak of the flaws, which I will do...

For pages and pages Allen did so, giving examples from poetry and literature and including suggestions of style.

At that time Allen was also acting as literary agent for Bill Burroughs.

> Am having trouble publishing Bill's book (still not finished as he decided to write more of shit). But Doubleday already says 'no respectable publisher will put this out' or 'self-respecting' it was...But Jack Kerouac, however, on the ball, had last week finished *On the Road*, writ in 20 days on one sheet of paper yards and yards long, that he got from Cannastra's Apt. once...Jack needs, however, an ending. Write him a serious self-prophetic letter foretelling your fortune in fate, so he can have courage to finish his paean in a proper apotheosis or grinding of brakes. He is afraid to foretell tragedy, or humorable comedy or gray dawn or rosy sunrise, needs help to understand last true longings of your soul, yet, though he surely knows. Truly, what is too foolish to be said is sung.

Neal answered with his own view of *On the Road* and a scheme for Jack's future works:

> Great news that Jack's finished *OTR*; I trust in his writing but fear for it because theme of *On the Road* is too trivial for him, as his dissatisfaction shows. He must either forget it or enlarge it into a mighty thing that merely uses what he's written as a Book 1, since what he's done doesn't lend itself to stuffing. He should create another and another work (like Proust) and then we'll have the great American Novel. I think he would profit by starting a book 2 with the recollections of his early life as they were sent to me and then blend that into his prophetic *DR SAX*. Of course, I'm sure I don't know what I'm talking about, but I do worry for him and want him happy.

Then Neal foretold his 'future in fate' for the ending:

> Tell Jack I become ulcerated old color-blind RR conductor who never writes anything good and dies a painful lingering death from prostate gland trouble (cancer from excessive masturbation) at 45. Unless I get sent to San Quentin for rape of teenager and drown after slipping into slimy cesspool that workgang is unclogging. Of course,

I might fall under freight train, but that's too good, since Carolyn would get around 40 to 50 thousand settlement from RR...one thing sure, I'll keep withering away emotionally at about the same rate as have last 3 years...I'm afraid – I've irrevocably slipped, however, and in my mediocrity have become precisely what Jack long ago feared was my fate: I am blank and getting more so.

How close this came to the actual events history confirms. I just wish I'd paid more attention at the time.

Neal kept on writing, but continued to sweat over his inadequacies, although he told Allen, 're Joan letter; can do same anytime, not now, tho.'

Through the summer his paramount concern was how to persuade Jack to come live with us. Each letter, postcard or even telegrams extolled the advantages of our life and what it could offer Jack. I had furnished half the attic for a den for Neal; the orange crates now supported a large piece of plywood I enamelled heavily in dark green to create a desk, which I placed under the window that overlooked the street with left-over curtains from Alpine Terrace. On the desk was the dictionary, my old portable radio, my college typewriter and a lamp. Beside the desk on the floor was a box spring and mattress for a bed, and before it a fluffy rug. It was cosy and private, and more livable than on Jack's former visit.

Neal not only sung the praises of these improvements as well as of all the things to do in San Francisco, but 'Carolyn loves you, be like mama without you having any need to cater to her, and coffee, gobs of expensive coffee, and clothes washed free, and your portrait painted...' He praised the Dexedrine samples I could get, the wonderful kids, free clinic or analysis, nearby tennis courts, fields for other sports and unlimited freedom to follow his fancy,

> for you don't know what livin' is till you dig old man C's brand at 29 Russell.
> ...Carolyn and I, at last, are a smooth running little team, tho we sputter and snort a bit, are compatible as hell. Naturally, in the back of your mind must be the remembrance of the rough receptions you've had in the past, in fact, less than 2 years ago, but you must concede it was not as difficult for you as a murder or suicide might have made such a brief visit. Carolyn wants to try and

make it up to you. We could try by way of a few group orgies or whatever, although this might be sensibly postponed until after Oct. because she's as big as our house and the bed is only four feet across...You understand that if you don't come here now it will curse my new son forever since you won't be here to be his Godfather, and because you will have deserted him, I would be forced not to name him John Allen Cassady, as is my present intent.

The exuberance of this letter was partly aimed at cheering up Jack and by way of sympathy, for Jack and Joan had separated. Now it was an even more appropriate time for Jack to come; the railroad was actually advertising in the papers for brakemen, a rare necessity.

But Jack did not come. He suddenly got severe phlebitis and was taken to the hospital. I felt I could write to him myself now, although I was still inhibited and could think of little to say except to sympathize with his illness and his separation from Joan, as well as regret his inability to join us. 'I need your help in making life worth living for Neal; I can't seem to make it so by myself. Can you convalesce with us? Neal's mind truly a blank – (he said, "Verify it").'

By now Neal had earned enough seniority to work passenger trains, and he was able to buy our dreamed-of stationwagon and his saxophone. The stationwagon was fine, but the saxophone turned out to be a bitter disappointment, since it was a C-melody and as he wrote to Jack,

the C-melody is so unpopular I can't find an instruction book, and there is almost no music written for it. Looks like I'm stuck with another white elephant...Early AM: Just got back from daily passenger run...I'm a big passenger brakie now with a pretty monkey suit that looks like a tux from the rear...and can't think of much more to say to entice you to cover the long trail to the end of the world for no good reason...except that it's too hot in NY or Mex & too European in France and too trite in Great Neck and too early for Siberia or Africa. Incidentally, when all is lost, you and I will go to Morocco and build a railroad for thousand a month. All we do is ride while African coolies dump ballast over the roadbed.
Am dying to read ON THE ROAD so you better have it published quick or have spare ms. And if you don't come because of intellectual reasons or because you just

feel you can't make it, I will understand just as I think I
do about poor J. and if I pine and die away as she will
without you; just meant to be. N

His passenger work was less tiring and more sociable, and now I
had white shirts to iron and black shoes to polish. He still could not
hold down a regular run, but he enjoyed the greater suspense of
never knowing whether he'd be called for passenger or freight. He had
only begun to get used to the new conditions when the trainmen went
on strike. The switchmen struck in sympathy, but Neal leaped into
the breach and hired on again as a switchman in Oakland, now gone
even longer hours. He was condemned as a scab in San Francisco,
but that didn't bother him as much as not supporting his family.

| TWENTY-SIX |

September of 1951 brought the kind of coastal weather we anticipated in the fall and spring: dazzling blue skies with sun and
wind effecting a perfect balance in warmth and refreshment. On the
Sunday afternoon of the eighth, I collected Helen and her nine-
month-old son, Mark – now living on the outskirts of town – and
with my two girls drove down to Aquatic Park at the foot of
Russian Hill. We sat in the sand and blissfully dangled our legs in
the icy water, while the youngsters got considerably wetter. Behind
us the bright green grass of the sloping lawn tempted lovers,
musclemen and the elderly to bask like so many lizards and look out
over the bay, flecked with sailboats and whitecaps. I felt unusually
peaceful and content.

After two or three hours of this harmony, I drove Helen home,
having some difficulty on the long ride, my tummy interfering with
the steering wheel. Helen's flat was a converted upper storey of an old
Victorian home. In spite of Al's railroad priority, they still didn't
have a telephone, and depended on the people in the flat below.
Since Helen didn't drive, I had been to see her several times, but it
was not until this afternoon I noticed the name on the bell below
hers. It was a long Polish name, unpronounceable for me, but I
looked at it today long and hard, thinking nothing of it in particular.
It wasn't until many years later I learned the ways of angels.

Around 2a.m. I was awakened by the by-now-familiar signs of impending birth. The baby was not due for another month, according to the doctors, but there was no doubt it was on its way. I thought it most considerate to spare me the last hot month, but at the moment the timing was poor: Neal was across the bay in Oakland, Louise had moved to the Peninsula, and Helen had no phone or car. I not only needed transport but a babysitter as well.

Suddenly into my mind came the image of the Polish name on the bell of Helen's neighbour. Breathlessly, I ran downstairs for the phone book. I couldn't have given the name to an operator, nor was I sure of the spelling, but I found the only one that looked similar, and it was on the right street! The phone rang and rang, my panic rising with every buzz. It was finally answered, and relief and apologies muddled my request to wake Helen and call her to the phone. She came, and luckier still Al was home, and as usual they lost no time in responding cheerfully to my distress, even though it meant packing up their own infant too.

While I waited for them I couldn't get over the coincidence leading to this happy solution, and I knew of no other word then to explain it. Still, it gave me a queer, undefinable feeling. When Helen and her baby were settled at my house, Al drove me to the hospital – the same one in which I'd had Jami. This time there was no time for the heavenly caudal anaesthetic, but my joy overcame the pain when I dared ask the sex of the baby. The nurse answered, 'It's a boy' in a tone of 'what else?'. Exactly how I felt; it had to be. Now I was even; I had given Neal a boy. Peacefully, I drifted off to sleep.

Neal had arrived home that morning to find Helen and Al in our bed. When he learned I had delivered a boy at 5.10a.m., he rejoiced then slept for an hour before coming to see me. When he got back home he sat down at once and wrote to Jack: 'My boy is full term and healthy, tho seems a month early. He is amazing looking with *absolutely* White Platinum Blond hair, like Jean Harlow's was, only more striking with it growing over his ears already. I have, of course, already named him after you and Allen: John Allen Cassady, J.A.C.'

Yes, John's hair was like mine. When they first put him into my arms, I looked down at this calm open face, not all pink and wrinkly like most newborns, a picture of peace, 'my little angel'.

(In his later years other people often remarked, 'John is such an angel.')

Neal brought the girls to the window – children not allowed on the maternity ward – whenever he was home in the daytime. He had found his younger sister, Shirley, to stay with them while he worked.

For the first six or eight weeks after I brought John home he continued to be an angelic baby. He took over the buggy, Jami moved to the crib, and Cathy to the daybed. Then one day John wasn't there. That is, he was there physically, and all his bodily functions worked as they should, and he indicated those needs as usual, but that was all. It took me a few days of his being totally unresponsive otherwise to wonder why his individual personality (could it be his mind?) was absent. When I was sure I was not mistaken, I called the paediatrician, finding it extremely difficult to explain my question. He calmed my fears by saying he'd heard of this happening occasionally, and the babies all snapped out of it in time.

Sure enough. In about another week John did. There he was again, cooing and gurgling, bright awareness and movements returned. We puzzled over this occurrence, but were not to find a reasonable explanation for another two years.

The prospect of a son growing up for whom Neal should furnish a model and an example only heightened his feelings of inadequacy, but while John was still an infant and Neal still young and idealistic, these fears were forestalled, and he revelled in the child, writing Allen, 'children, children, the pox of freedom and demander of money that siphons off luxury, but an enormous sponge to absorb your love and a bottomless pleasure pit into which I throw myself...'

His anxieties concerning Diana and her son could not be postponed so easily. She wrote less often but continually, pleading for more money and ruing the day they'd met. She even wrote a ten-page letter to the San Francisco DA, including pictures of herself and Curt. When we responded to a command appearance by the DA, we nervous and afraid, he merely fiddled with her letter and sighed and said, 'That woman should see a psychiatrist.' He dismissed us with no further comment. Another big relief.

On the night I went into the hospital, Neal had been reading the Oakland paper, and one squib sent him wildly searching for all the other papers hoping for more details, for he could hardly believe what he read:

An American tourist trying to imitate William Tell killed his wife while attempting to shoot a glass of Champagne from her head with a pistol, police said today. Police arrested William Seward Burroughs, 37, of St. Louis, Mo. last night after his wife, Joan, 27, died in a hospital of a bullet wound in her forehead received an hour earlier.

Bill! – the perfect marksman! How could this have happened? Two days later we got a letter from Allen from Galveston, Texas. He had gone there with his friend, Claude, after a rapid business trip to Mexico where he had visited Bill and Joan. Allen read of the tragedy in the Texas paper, but he added some observations of his own:

Claude and Joan played games of chance with drunken driving, egging each other on suicidally at times, while we were there…My imagination of the scene and psyches in Mexico is too limited to comprehend the past misery and absurdity and sense of drama that must exist in Bill's mind now…or whatever he feels.

Although later Bill claimed a faulty gun as the cause, Allen's comments made us wonder if there was some desperation in Joan that might have played a part. She could so easily have willed – consciously or unconsciously – to die and moved her head ever so slightly. Well, we didn't want to think about that. I was always proud of Bill that he, himself, never suggested such a thing. The perfect gentleman.

In early January, 1952, the event Neal had anticipated and promoted for so long finally came about: Jack arrived. We had all thought and talked of it so much, the actualization was somewhat awkward for a short time. Neal bounded about showing Jack in rapid succession the wonders he'd described in his letters, overdoing the joyous clowning until Jack was reduced to laughter. Jack and I were even more self-conscious and strange this time, never looking directly at each other without remembering the former times. I didn't know if it was Neal who influenced Jack or the other way around, and Jack probably thought I believed him to be the tempter. A little of both perhaps. Since Neal had told Jack I had 'changed completely', I tried hard to justify this claim. When Neal was with us we were more relaxed; Jack would talk to Neal and include me, and his looks and tone indicated his sympathy and understanding.

He avoided being alone with me, however, staying in his attic or walking around the surrounding city.

Jack and Joan had broken completely and bitterly. 'You see,' he explained, 'she was an only child, raised by women – her mother and aunts. They all hated men and taught her to, too. They were dedicated to revenge and used me to vent their anger – it's true; I'm convinced they did it on purpose.' I wasn't so sure of this. 'I caught her with this Puerto Rican a couple of times, see, and now she's pregnant and says it's my child – *HA* – it ain't *my* child!' He seemed sick at heart but certain, and Joan's betrayal hurt him deeply, especially since she was his second attempt at marriage. I felt truly sorry for him and wondered why his judgement in choosing wives was so poor. I had only heard him speak sympathetically about women in general, and quite sentimentally about marriage and family life.

He was immediately at ease with children, sharing an empathy at their level and communicating naturally without being maudlin. I never got the impression that my girls were a nuisance to him; rather, he sought their company, listened intently to Cathy's prattle, and told her lively stories. He was unaccustomed to small babies, how-ever, and didn't know what to do with them. On hearing him say something to this effect, Neal scooped up John from his crib and thrust him at Jack.

'No, man, here – babies are to *hold*, see? Just feel that – you've never known – see? You gotta *hold* 'em.' Surprised and awkward, Jack still chuckled at this sudden outburst of Neal's and tried to comply. John reared his head back to study the strange face a moment, then sank against Jack's chest. Jack did his best – patted John hesitantly, but he obviously felt he held a bag of eggs, and was relieved when I took John from him. Neal all the while was raving about the advantages of tiny babies over older children.

The attic worked well for Jack. He settled in and carefully arranged the few precious books and papers he needed to make him feel at home and ready to work. The only uncomfortable feature was that access to and from his lair through the high-up door to his stairs was in our bedroom. It surprised me to find him so old-fashioned and modest about his personal physical needs, but he used the bathroom only when no one was around, and made arrangements elsewhere whenever possible. We all tried to cater to his embarrassment, though it was somewhat difficult with small children, and I had to be careful to be fully clothed at all times.

Jack's arrival now turned out to be the worst time for hiring as a brakeman, but after a few weeks Neal managed to get him a job in the baggage room at the depot. This eased things a bit; Jack was forever fearful he was imposing. With a job he not only had money but independence.

Neal's work was slowing down, so they had more time together. I was therefore offered greater opportunities to demonstrate my 'change' by being cheerful and uncomplaining, particularly when they went out for most of a night. Although they tried to show more awareness of my feelings, and talked reassuringly, I can't say I was inwardly any more content than formerly – much less 'completely changed'. Their behaviour appeared to be irreversible, so I searched for attitudes I might have overlooked with my fixed notions regarding the institution of marriage.

Unrelated men living in the household was not new to me; my father often took in associates or students. Still, his family came first, and each time Jack or Neal went gaily out the door as of old, or they shut themselves up in the attic, I could not overcome relapsing into the feelings I had had before. It took a lot of effort for me not to express these feelings, and a physical reaction soon erupted when matters took an extreme turn.

Neal worked the night before his birthday, arriving home about four o'clock n the morning, so I knew he'd want to sleep the next day. I woke early and planned the day ahead, looking forward to another opportunity to wrap socks, T-shirts, underwear and cigarettes into 'prezzies', to baking the cake and the trip to the store for ice cream. With Cathy now four and Jami three, they would enjoy the excitement of a birthday more, and especially since it was their first for 'Poppie'. Jack's presence, too, would make this birthday more festive and more special for Neal.

When John's secret sounds took on a tone of discontent, I swung out of bed and into my robe, swooped him up before he cried, collected the girls (already trained to whisper), and we all tiptoed downstairs without waking Neal. When he joined us around noon, I made him a huge brunch, and he opened his gifts with the usual effusive gratitude as if we'd given him a gold Cadillac. We spent a jolly afternoon together, drinking coffee, reading the paper and playing with the children, being peaceful and glowing – like marriage was meant to be, I thought.

There was only one small flaw at first. During the day, the left side of my face became increasingly sore and stiff. I assumed it was a tooth problem, and when I put the children down for naps, I took some aspirin but said nothing to Neal. Dinner was to be somewhat later than usual owing to the late brunch, but also because Jack had not returned home. I couldn't believe he'd forgotten the occasion, so Neal and I had a beer. When we could postpone dinner no longer, I served the steak, baked potato, vegetables and salad followed by ice cream and the cake. Jollity prevailed, Neal revelling in the attention and the infrequent special food.

After we'd read to the girls and tucked them into bed, my face was so painful and numb I told Neal about it. He insisted I call my doctor friend, even though it was long after office hours and a Friday night.

'You have Bell's Palsy,' the doctor said, 'and you must do something about it immediately if you're going to recover. It didn't used to be curable, but it is now if you catch it in time. I'll call in a prescription for the pain and the hospital – oh dear, I'm afraid you'll have to wait until Monday now, but then you must get to physical therapy for treatment.' As he went on a picture flashed into my mind. It was the face of the woman who taught my sister violin. Now I understood why her face had been askew – one eye glaring and unblinking, her mouth way up one side of her cheek so she drooled when she spoke. I shuddered at that frightening prospect.

'How did I get this?' I asked the doctor.

'We're not sure what causes it,' he replied. 'Soldiers sometimes get it if exposed to cold on one side, and there's new evidence it can be caused by emotional strain or tension.' I said, 'Oh' and 'Thank you,' and said I'd call him on Monday. I was annoyed, afraid and confused, but there was no doubt in my mind it had not been caused by one-sided exposure to cold.

Neal expressed anxiety and sympathy, and insisted on going out for the Codeine right away. When he returned he made me go to bed, and he did, too, holding me close and comforting me. His warmth and the pills put me to sleep feeling happier than I had in years.

| TWENTY-SEVEN |

The shriek of the telephone didn't scare me; we were used to it because of the railroad calls at all hours. Neal had perfected an automatic leap that quelled it quickly before it woke the children, even though it was in the front hall and about ten feet from our bed. I couldn't help hearing what he said. He sounded excited and alarmed, so I turned on the light to be more alert.

'Yeah, Jack, sure – you're where? Oh my God, man, whaja do? No, never mind; I'll be right there.' In one bound Neal was back and pulling on his jeans. 'Jack's in jail. Sounds drunk. Gotta go get him out.'

'In *jail*?' I hated that word and all it implied. 'Whatever for?'

'Don't know yet.' Neal slapped his belt-end through the buckle loop and bent to the mirror to pat his hair. In one continuous sweep he leaned down to kiss me, scooped the car keys from the dresser, and was out the front door. As he left, a chill draught struck my bare shoulders. I turned out the lamp, and the darkness rushed in. I was uneasy and stared out at the dark.

The rest of the night I spent in restlessness and increasing pain. Neal did not return, and before I realized it further sleep was impossible. I heard the girls begin padding about their room, and John's squeaks and coos emanating from the living room. The day had begun.

When their needs were all met, and they were playing in their room, I washed my hair and rolled it up. Just as I secured the last roller, I heard voices in the front hall. When I opened the bathroom door, I saw Neal dart down the stairs, and Jack escort a young black woman up his attic steps. Stunned, I followed Neal, trying to blank my mind in preparation for an explanation.

In the kitchen Neal was busy lighting the stove under the teakettle and rattling cups. He didn't look up at me as I came down the stairs. I tried to keep my voice level.

'What's going on, Neal? Where have you been? I see you got Jack out – what was it?'

'Well, actually, you see – ah – you see Jack wasn't really in jail –' He laughed at this trivia and waved his spoon in the air. 'He was terribly drunk, and he thought – just as a joke, you know – it would be a way to get me to come out. He didn't mean anything by it, honey, honest.'

The sickening wave of familiar feelings welling up in me made me clamp my mouth shut and go sit down by the table. I was shaking and trying not to fly apart, but my dismay came through. I stood up and spat out in icy tones, 'You certainly don't think I'm going to put up with *that* sort of thing in my own *home*? With the children?' And I flung my head and rolled my eyes upwards like some biblical evangelist to indicate Jack and the girl. 'You just get yourself right up there and get – her – out – of – my – house – *right now*!'

In another second I would scream or break something, so I dashed for the stairs ahead of Neal and ran to hide in the bathroom. I'd forgotten how I looked. My face was there in the mirror with no makeup and the rollers, and what I saw was more like the violin teacher's face. I covered it with my hands. I could hear Neal knocking at the attic door and calling up to Jack, but I couldn't hear the words. I sat on the edge of the tub, trembling, and then I remembered the girls in their room beside the attic door. Grabbing a towel, I tried to wrap it around my head as I rushed out; I had to get to them first.

Too late. They were already standing wide-eyed in their doorway, and I got only as far as the foot of our bed when Jack and the woman jumped down from the steps and blocked my way. Neal was standing by the bureau between me and the hall, so I had to step back to let Jack and the woman pass. But the woman didn't pass. She lunged up to me flashing her black yes, narrowing them into slits or opening them wide with hate, the yellow eyeballs around the black centre like the eyes on toy animals. Slowly she uncoiled words around her tongue, and they slithered out between her teeth, smashing against my ears like a string of firecrackers gone wild. I didn't really hear what she was saying, I was so shocked. We all stood frozen like a stop-action film, while out of her poured snakes and toads of bitter words raining down around me. To stem the torrent, I tried weakly to insert that I had nothing against her personally, nor was it any concern of mine what Jack did, but this was my home, and I'd rather they went elsewhere. She didn't stop to listen, only mustered another barrage of adjectives, this time in a higher key. All the while the two men stood by dumbly, looking at the floor. I didn't feel at my best in my tattered robe, curlers and crooked face, but I sort of expected one of them to stop her and defend me a little. Neither moved a muscle until she ran down. She walked to the bureau haughtily and picked up our car keys, held them out to Neal, looked back over her shoulder for one last sneer at me and said, 'Take me home.' Neal obliged, took the keys and turned to the front door, Jack and the woman following behind.

Pain and self-pity got the best of me, and I couldn't stop the tears. I tried to hide them from the girls, but I had to go to them – do something. I swiped at my face and tried to blubber reassurances. What must they have thought? I hurried to get their lunch, restore normality and settle them down for naps, smiling at them, hoping they hadn't been somehow scarred.

I then went outside and sat on the back steps and looked at our little patch of green grass in the middle of the surrounding houses, and on up past the line of waving diapers to the square of blue sky above, hoping the sun would warm the cold ache in my middle. I just let my thoughts glide around without direction. I couldn't face the fact I'd have to go back and go over that awful last time, but what else was there to do? All there was to go on was the righteous indignation society demanded, and I was tired of that. What good had ever come of it? I could think of nothing to do, so I would do nothing, just see what happened next. This numbness was a kind of relief, and the Codeine helped sustain it.

Around five o'clock, when I heard them come in the front door, my heart contracted sharply; I hadn't expected them so soon – if at all. I didn't move, stayed where I was, and listened. In a few minutes all was quiet again. Curious, I went inside and up the stairs, leaving the girls at their play outside. Neal was asleep in bed, and Jack apparently in the attic, so I wasn't required to do anything for some time yet. I returned to the kitchen and began preparations for the children's dinners.

Neal was called to work, and when he was dressed, he came downstairs. I went on with the routine as though nothing were different, but he saw my familiar put-upon look and understood my silence all too well. He kindly enquired about my face, but I just shrugged. In the past something always told me that if I was cheerful or pretended nothing was wrong, he wouldn't realize how *important* the episode had been, and I shouldn't let him get away with it. But he was much better at pretending the sky hadn't fallen, and as he made remarks about the children I tried tentative answers, even ignoring the subject on my mind; I guess this time the horror was so stark to me, I figured even he wouldn't have to be told. Gradually, as I made his meal and watched him eat it, and nothing happened, I found I could converse a little, even with the sense of doom behind my voice. He must have been braced and bewildered, but he tried all the harder to be tender yet cautious, and at least he didn't try to make jokes. He left the house with the proper air of remorse.

That night the episode flitted back and forth in my mind among fragments of dreams, but I continued to push it away and refuse to deal with it. When Neal returned the next afternoon, I talked only about Jack and my concern that he had not stirred as far as I knew. Perhaps he had gone out while I was asleep, but Neal went up to see. I heard muffled voices, and Neal reappeared.

'Dumb guy; he's sulking, I suppose, but he says he's okay and not to worry; he's reading and writing.'

'But Neal, he hasn't eaten since yesterday, unless he has something stashed up there – and how does he go to the bathroom?'

Neal laughed, 'Out the window?'

'Neal, don't be ridiculous – not on the front porch.'

'Well, hell, I tried to talk him into coming down, but he just growled, so...' Neal shrugged and raised his hands in mock Yiddish gesture. 'I'll take something up after a while if he doesn't show – sort of casually. He'll get over it.'

Monday morning Neal stayed home, and I went to the hospital as early as possible. It seemed a month had passed since I'd called that doctor. The staff made me feel much better, and they promised me I wouldn't end up like the violin teacher. I began a series of treatments with heat, massage, exercises and electric needle muscle stimulation, which was no fun, but anything was worth it to know I'd be all right in six more months. They gave me a rubber band attached to a paper clip to wear over my ear and hook into my mouth, and an eye patch for my left eye, which wouldn't close, allowing things to fly into it. I felt about as unattractive as anyone could be, but I swallowed my vanity in favour of future healing.

When I got home, Neal and the children were outside. I took off my coat and turned back to the mirror to see if I looked any different. Then I noticed a book on the dressing table that had not been there when I left. I picked it up and saw it was my copy of *The Town and the City,* which Jack had inscribed to me when it was first published. I opened the cover, and beneath the inscription was a new note: 'With the deepest apologies I can offer for the fiasco, the foolish tragic Saturday of Neal's birthday – all because I got drunk – Please forgive me, Carolyn; it'll never happen again.'

So he had stayed upstairs, suffering with guilt and remorse as only he could. I was deeply touched, lifted up, so glad I had not behaved as before, and eager to show him all was forgiven. The thought flashed through my mind, 'unlike Neal?' Why could I look forward with pleasure to righting this situation but not if it had been Neal? Ah, well, Jack hadn't made any vows, nor was he responsible to me.

Still, I did blame Neal a good deal for the recent episode, and although it was now unlikely I would retaliate, this crime would join the ranks of all the others, ready to file in parade before him whenever I needed to remind him of obligations disregarded and my reasons for doubting his good intentions. My present state of suspended hostilities was not to be confused with 'forgiveness'.

After I'd re-read the message a few more times, I took the book downstairs to show Neal, who, after reading the note, bounded upstairs, and in wild jocularity released Jack from his prison with promises of total absolution from me. Together they came giggling down to the kitchen, Jack and I shyly smiling. Neal became master of ceremonies, opened the beer and some wine I had bought for his birthday when Jack was expected, and we gave up any thoughts of sorrow or condemnation in our efforts to restore a state of mutual comradeship.

After a glass or two, Jack bellowed, 'Hey! We gotta take pictures of us all! Come on outside; bring the camera!' I had only a Kodak box, but we used a whole roll of film (which has been a major part of my support ever since).

That evening after dinner there was no mention of their going out. They got high, laughed and talked into the tape recorder, and were eager to include me even more than I was inclined to be. For once, I wisely let the sleeping dog lie.

| TWENTY-EIGHT |

The old pattern thus broken, the climate of the household warmed. When Jack wasn't at work or busy writing, he'd now sit and talk to me, telling me of his childhood in Lowell, his mother's tenacity in working at the shoe factory, how he wished his writing would change that, and his regrets that his sister, Nin, disapproved of his writing aspirations and felt he should get a job and support their mother. Caroline ('Nin') was married, lived in North Carolina and had one son, Paul, Jr. Jack had a loyal affection for her, and he felt it was an odd coincidence our names were so similar.

Jack was still not satisfied with the ending of *On the Road*, and Allen tried to help. He wrote Jack his advice in a simple and straightforward way, listing a modus operandi in order to conciliate the publishers:

> Tell him in as few words as possible and in as least an alarming manner as possible that you have changed your plan or method of approach somewhat, but like what you have as a result...and say you are of course willing to make revisions as he suggests, compatible with your own ideas of integrity of structure...All I wonder is if you're trying to escape (as I always do) the sweat of patient integration and structure which you slaved over in T&C... Aside from that book sounds OK as is, if it is as you describe it.

His advice may have seemed simple to Allen, but it was maddening to Jack. Neal and I knew how sensible Allen's comments were and how much it could have relieved Jack's burden, but to him it was degrading. 'All this haggling!' he fumed. 'Bah! They can take it or leave it.'

I had only read random passages in the manuscript: I was too close to the pain of those events, and the more Neal chortled over it, the more fearful I became that I'd feel obligated to start something again. The only details I'd heard of their trips were those Helen had revealed, and I was blissful in my ignorance. Jack was still writing additional scenes, and he became excited with the possibilities offered by the tape recorder to capture spontaneous discussions or stories. I was beginning to think the '*Road*' might become an interminable highway. For each new addition, Jack found that with us he had an audience that believed he could do no wrong, and he was happy to share his daily efforts with me. He still carried the little notebooks in his shirt pocket wherever he went, and wrote impressions or new ideas, typing them up within a few days. One of these notebooks he later inscribed and gave to me.

The liquor store was around the corner on Hyde Street, and Jack sometimes bought 'poor-boys' (half a litre) of Tokay or Muscatel to sip late in the afternoon or after dinner, when he would share it with me – one glass apiece. Sometimes I'd go with him to the liquor store to buy these, and other times I'd go alone to buy beer for Neal. One time when I stopped for beer, the proprietor said, 'Your husband prefers sweet wine, doesn't he?' It wasn't until I was outside I realized he meant Jack, and I had to laugh. If only he knew – I had enough trouble hanging on to one husband, let alone two. I even mentioned this little drama to Neal and Jack at dinner, and we all had a good laugh.

One afternoon I was feeding John in his high chair when I heard the front door open and slam shut. Neal came clumping down the stairs dragging his jacket behind him. He threw it down hard on the couch and said, 'Shit!' He never swore in front of me, so I knew he was really angry.

'I've got to pack,' he said, 'I've drawn a two-week hold-down in San Luis.' He stood looking out the window, clenching his jaw.

This kind of assignment was the only kind he hated. On hold-downs he had to go to a neighbouring branch, and it meant staying in barren dorms, the 'crummy' (caboose) or a sleazy hotel. He had to work the same local freight early every morning for the two weeks, sometimes longer, as we'd learned to our sorrow in the past. Neal blew off some steam and then accepted his lot, reverting to his own cheerful self again. He hadn't much time. While he went upstairs to pack, I hurried with the dinner, and he called up to Jack to explain why it was to be early.

I was even more sorry than Neal at this unexpected development, and I suspected Jack would be too. When alone together, Jack and I had not found a firm footing in our relationship, and we needed Neal nearby as a buffer. Consequently, during this dinner we were both nervous, eyeing each other in a new and uncharted way.

Neal stood up from the table and planted his hands on either side of his chest in his Oliver Hardy stance, looking from Jack to me.

'Well, kiddies, I must be off. Just everyone pray I get back in fourteen days and no more.' He retrieved his jacket, kissed me and strode to the stairs. At the landing he turned back as though he'd forgotten something, but said with a grin, 'I don't know about leaving you two – you know what they say, "My best pal and my best gal…" ha ha – just don't do anything *I* wouldn't do, okay kids? Have a ball…' He bounded up the stairs laughing, knowing, as we did, what he was likely to do in a similar situation.

I wanted to crawl under the table and disappear, I was so embarrassed, and I couldn't look at Jack. Instead, I jumped up and began grabbing dishes off the table and putting them in the sink. Jack bolted for the attic.

To Jack marriage was a sacrament, even though he hadn't upheld all of that notion with his wives so far. I had no religious dogma to cling to; I just thought if a person accepted a set of rules and went so far as to make vows, they should keep to them as best they could, or shouldn't make them – nobody *has* to get married nowadays. Neal, on the other hand, was torn between his Catholic demands and his overpowering desires. He wanted to be the conventional husband, but he'd never known what that involved, as I had.

Jack's courtesy to me was because I was the wife of his best friend – or so we told ourselves, and, as he said in Denver, 'too bad, but that's how it is,' and we had accepted that condition without question.

The more I thought about Neal's remark, the angrier I got and the more it hurt. Well, maybe I was jumping to conclusions again – maybe he really did mean it only as a joke. It was no joke to me.

During the next few days Jack was gone most of the time and we rarely talked together. When he did agree to share a meal, however, it was so pleasant, we'd soon forget the circumstances while conversing, but the silences brought back our situation and our being alone together. And Neal's remark hung in the air around us.

When Neal returned, it was with great relief we welcomed him. He seemed a little reserved the first evening at dinner, and I wondered if he supposed we had behaved as he would have done. When Jack left us alone, I turned to Neal with my burning question: 'Neal, do you remember what you said when you left? How could you say a thing like that, unless you were joking? Were you? Don't you know how that hurt me? You made me feel I was no more important to you than – a towel or some object. Can you understand? Don't you know I'm proud to show you I deserve your trust, that I like chances to prove my loyalty to you? Tell me, did you sincerely feel we should have made love – Jack and I? Or were you just saying that to protect yourself in case we did?' I peered at him intensely, breathless for the answer.

He got up from the table, looking uncomfortable, and headed for the stairs. He paused and shrugged, 'A little of both, I suppose... yeah, actually... why not? I thought it would be kinda nice.' And up the stairs he went.

Damn the man! Well, I had asked for this second blow, but how could he be so unfeeling? I should know by now, I thought dejectedly. Hadn't he 'shared' LuAnne – even though after the annulment – and how many others? Again, I kept supposing I was different, meant more to him. Well, in my terms, the only ones I understood. To me this felt like a greater rejection than desertion.

Dolefully, I did the dishes, mulling it over, finding no solace. When Neal came down to tell me he and Jack were going out, I got a vision once more of the future as an incessant repetition of the past, and I knew I must do something to change that pattern. None of the old attempts had worked, so, defiantly, I said half-aloud, 'Okay, Neal dear, let's try it your way.' And the anger drained out of me. I felt another conviction torn away as though I'd shed another skin. Suddenly I felt exposed, but with that came a coolness and a spurt of excitement mingled with fear. Never had I known how to play female games of deliberately setting out to trap a man. At least in this case it shouldn't require much aggression on my part, just a few circumstances manipulated. After all, Jack knew better than I how Neal would react. It was worth a try; anything would be better than this.

| TWENTY-NINE |

An evening or two later I made a few plans – nothing elaborate or unusual, but admittedly I manipulated circumstances as best I could. I'd asked Neal about the train he was called for and its schedule. He'd be gone until the following afternoon.

When the children were settled for the night, I called up the attic stairs. 'Jack?'

He came to the top step, 'Yeah?' I tried to sound the way I always did when asking him to share a meal.

'I wondered if you'd like to join me for dinner tonight. I've made a sort of experimental pizza thing, and there's way too much. It won't keep too well, so, I thought maybe...'

'Yes, sure... uh... just give me a minute.'

'Oh, no hurry; it'll be another thirty minutes anyway, but there's some wine, if you'd like. Whenever you're ready.' I paused a second at my dressing table to check how I looked – mustn't be too obvious, although I was already feeling like a wanton woman and had butter-flies in my stomach. Too bad I could avoid his suspicions only by wearing my usual jeans and white shirt, but I had been more careful with my hair and makeup, and thought just a wee dab of cologne would be fair.

Downstairs I checked the munitions there: new candle in the bottle, table set as usual, radio set at KJAZ, the station we all preferred for its smooth jazz and ballads. The oven was ready, so I popped in the pizza dish. It was the first time I'd tried one with the thick crust à la Sicily. I had already made a Waldorf salad and some broccoli. I thought I'd better sample the wine to calm my nerves, and I fancied I appeared quite nonchalant when Jack descended from his attic to join me.

'Pour yourself a glass of wine; dinner will be ready in a jiffy. I'll have one, too.' I sat opposite him at the table, raised my glass to the success of my evil scheme and smiled at him. The wine helped put us both at ease and made us garrulous. Jack praised my cooking long and loud and plunged into stories, all self-consciousness out the window. For my part, I forgot my plot and was lost in genuine enjoyment. I loved listening to Jack, and I knew this pleased him. I had already learned he preferred talking about his life to asking questions about mine, and since I already knew all about that, I liked new stories in which he had been involved.

Tonight he regaled me with his knowledge and impressions of Bill Burroughs, his background, education, his brilliant mind and how they'd met in New York. Neither of us could guess why such a man had become so attracted to drugs and firearms. He told me about Edie, his own first wife, and the reasons that hadn't panned out.

He was looking forward eagerly to the coming summer when he would visit Bill, now in Mexico. He loved the Mexican laid-back lifestyle, the music, the availability of marijuana, the good cheap food. It represented an Utopian existence minus hassles – a timeless place. Both he and Neal favoured Spengler's word, *fellaheen,* to describe the culture, but since the term meant a people who weren't going anywhere but had already been and were resting before the next creative cycle began, it sounded to me like the impossible dream for these two men who loved dashing about looking for 'kicks'.

I knew I had to keep Jack downstairs until I'd finished what I had started; I'd never be able to repeat it. So when we'd finished eating I filled both glasses and walked to the couch which we kept opened out to double-bed size. As I sat down on its edge, I held out Jack's glass to him. He followed me, accepted the wine and lay back on the couch, balancing his glass on his chest. With his eyes closed, he hummed along with 'My Funny Valentine' wafting from the radio and tried out a lyric or two.

I said nothing until the silence became thick and warm, then asked him, 'Do you remember when we danced together in Denver?'

He turned towards me, opened his eyes and looked at me, tenderly. Then, smiling, he sat up and said softly, 'Yeah, I wanted to take you away from Neal,' and he kept looking into my eyes but had stopped smiling.

Barely audibly I asked, 'And do you remember the song we danced to?'

He leaned closer. '"Too Close For Comfort".' At that moment I knew plots and plans were foolish; my mind and will floated away, and just as in the movies, we both put down our glasses at the same time, not unlocking our eyes or looking at the desk beside me but making perfect contact. And so did we.

The first morning light awakened me, and for a second I didn't know where I was. Then it came back, and feeling Jack's body beside me, a wave of remorse passed through me. What have I done? I was married to Neal, and now I felt sorry for him, as well as afraid of what would happen next. The leather of the old couch was cold under me, and my muscles were cramped. As quickly and silently as I could, I slid out from under the blanket and ran upstairs to my own bed, hoping for an hour or two more of oblivion. It was no use. My mind kept frying the situation on all sides. I felt more shy of Jack than ever, and I didn't see how I could look him in the face – would he be sorry?

I heard him get up and come upstairs, so I pretended to be asleep. All at once I felt his lips on my forehead, lingering, and a flood of relief poured over me as he climbed his stairs. I now drifted into cosy sleep.

The relationship bloomed more rapidly than I had expected, but I was pleased my guilt was thus diminished somewhat. Jack was a tender and considerate lover, if rather inhibited, and sounded more sincere in his avowals of loving me than Neal. I suspected he wished I were more aggressive, but that I could never be. (Conditioned to think that sex was 'wrong', I had to be always 'taken' and thus innocent.)

Our temperaments and our guilty feelings made love-making infrequent, yet more passionate when it did occur. Although I could be romantically in love with Jack, my heart still ached for Neal alone to be enough. Also, my compassion for anyone in Neal's position made me feel more loving towards him, and I wavered in my resolve to teach him a lesson. I'd have sworn allegiance again in an instant, but I prodded my mind to remember his flippant words of indifference. I hoped sincerely that some lasting good would come from this, but for now there was nothing for me to do but relax and enjoy it.

Whenever Neal was home, Jack and I were extremely discreet, but there was no concealing the change in us. Neal couldn't help but notice, yet the only evidence we had that he cared showed in his increased attentiveness to me.

The hope that my gamble would change the pattern of our lives was well founded. Like night changing into day, everything was showered with new light. Butterflies bursting cocoons had nothing on me. Now I was a part of all they did; I felt like a sun in their solar system that all revolved around, and the variety was an extra added attraction; they were such different men, in spite of their closeness. Opposites that attract.

I tried to tune into the individual ways and preferences of whichever one was in residence. If they were both home at the same time during the day, Neal usually slept, and Jack wrote, or Jack would go out and leave the husband and wife alone. If Neal was at work, on occasion Jack and I made love in his attic if the children were asleep and I invited. He'd play host, sometimes with a poor-boy. I think of those times whenever I smell unfinished wood, and recall how the sun sometimes lay across us like a blanket, or, huddled under covers, we'd hear the soft patter of the rain close above our heads.

When both men became accustomed to the new arrangement, they dropped their defences and joined me downstairs in the kitchen. While I performed my chores, they'd read to each other excerpts from their writings-in-progress or bring out the Spengler, Dostoyevsky, Proust or Céline and read these writers aloud, interrupted by energetic discussions and analyses. Digressions were frequent in order to listen to and discuss a musician, riff or arrangement emanating from the radio. I was happy listening, butting in and filling their coffee cups. I never felt left out any more. They'd include me in their discussions, asking my views or getting me to moderate arguments, adding pats, smiles and gropes by Neal.

They still made forays together in search of tea or to buy necessities, but were never gone for hours and hours as before. If Neal was at home sleeping or writing, Jack and I took walks in the varied neighbourhoods nearby, such as Chinatown, where we marvelled at the weird food on display in the markets and the gorgeous embroidered clothing as well as the endless bric-a-brac on sale for tourists.

Spring was beginning to soften the air, but the wind from the sea could still be sharp. Jack found an old restaurant with a white tiled entry on a little street adjacent to St Francis Park. We'd buy steaming cartons of won ton soup for 35 cents, or fried rice for 25 cents. Often we warmed ourselves thus, and then sat close together on a bench in the park beneath the magnificent statue by Benny Bufano of Sun Yat Sen.

Other times we walked down the hill to Aquatic Park and drank Irish Coffee in the Buena Vista, or we walked down Union Street hill to Washington Square, taking French bread, cheese and wine purchased from the Buon Gusto market to nibble beneath the glittering gold spires of the cathedral. This reminded Jack of his childhood church in Lowell, St Louis en l'Isle, and his longing to see the original in Paris.

On bright days, too, we might hike the long way up Telegraph Hill to Coit Tower and gaze out over the bay, watching the ships from around the world and the little white dots of sailboats. I showed him the house in which I had once lived, and it was his cue to tell me of his seafaring adventures.

The times when Neal and I were alone were happier, too. We had the children's progress, illnesses and antics to discuss, as well as household economics and needs. I felt especially affectionate towards him now, and he accepted and returned these expressions in better grace. I wondered if it might be that he appreciated his women more when the relationship was threatened, or whether a rival made him seem less trapped, but at the moment I didn't care. Meals all together amused me, but also gratified my ego. Here the two men were like small boys, vying for the most attention, or the best story, and felt slighted if one held the floor too long. Jack was more sensitive, and since he loved Neal, and it was Neal's home, he sometimes felt offended, or he would sulk if Neal talked to me, excluding him as though he weren't there. Jack might stalk upstairs, and Neal would have to go after him and coax him back. Neal still had to prove he was the best man around. Taken by and large, my cup did runneth over.

| THIRTY |

Already, in the first couple of months since Jack's arrival, my self-esteem expanded when I found myself accepted as a desirable companion both mentally and physically. So I decided to go along with Jack's expectation that I would now join him, with or without Neal, on evenings out. At first I was apprehensive, conditioned by past experiences.

One evening Jack said he'd heard about a 'pay-the-rent' party, a frequent event artists or musicians put on for obvious reasons. This one was in a loft below the financial district. Musicians would be exempt from paying for admission if they would play instead.

'How much of a donation is expected toward their rent?' I asked. 'For three of us that might come to quite a sum…'

Neal interrupted with a laugh, 'My dear – have you forgotten? We have one of this country's best drummers right here visiting us from New York – and, of course, you can't forget how accomplished is your husband on the – let's see now – what'll it be? – I think – ah, yes, this is it.' Neal was sorting through the various native flutes and recorders and pounced on one. 'The recorder is my specialty tonight; this little number will do nicely.'

He made exaggerated motions in bringing it to his pursed lips, and tooted a few notes. I had never heard him play a recorder, but I wouldn't put anything past him, especially in these days of melody-less improvisations. The only drums in the house were tiny little bongos I'd given Jack as a joke.

'That's okay,' Jack brightened, 'I'll tell them I didn't bring my drums from New York, right? Maybe there'll be some there I can use to prove my claim.'

He was nothing if not confident on this score, and Neal said, 'Certainly, everybody has bongos – no self-respecting pad these days can afford to be without them.' And off we went.

This time, sitting between them in the front seat of the station-wagon was quite different from the first time. Now I was glad to try being invisible so I could listen to their party-mood nonsense, each trying to say something more preposterous, outrageous or mispro-nounced than the other, and both simmering in laughter which every now and then boiled over into chuckles.

Although street lights revealed the empty streets in this lower financial section, the alleys between were tunnels of dark, and into one of these we plunged in search of the vague address. Bright yellow squares of light revealed the building that had to be the one we sought. Neal parked in an empty lot, and we walked towards the wooden exterior rickety staircase, its stilts like toothpicks silhouetted by the light from the door above.

Now Jack and Neal talked seriously, intent on the story they would hand the hosts. We climbed the stairs and were met in the open doorway by a young slim girl in a long sack-like dress with a very determined look on her narrow face, her black eyebrows drawn together. We knew at once it was her responsibility to collect or show cause. Neal swung into action.

He strode past her with an even sterner look of authority to stand, hands on hips, inspecting the loft as though he intended buying it. The girl whipped around to catch him, yelling, 'Wait!' He turned to encompass her with his broadest smile and inviting eyes, saying sweetly, 'Why, of course, my dear – just checking – you see – I wonder if you might have a spare pair of bongos – or any type of professional drum, around here? Come –' and he took her elbow and guided her towards where Jack and I were standing by the door, her long black hair flipping from side to side as she looked at us and back to Neal, obviously dumbfounded and lost.

'Here – I want to introduce to you – this is – Jack Kerouac!' Neal pronounced the name slowly and softly in awed tones '...the great drummer who has just arrived from New York – and – this is my wife, Carolyn. Now – I'm sorry, I didn't get your name?'

She managed, 'Holly.'

'We-e-ll, Holly, we heard about your party, and we thought we'd show Jack some local colour. We trusted you might have some drums available he could play – oh, don't you worry – we won't charge you a penny! No, indeed – on account of your need for rent. We hope we can make that more probable, see?' He dazzled her again with his eyes and smile. 'I have my horn here – ah – ha ha, not my sax – it has a broken reed, but this will do, you'll see – wait till you hear it!' He beamed on her.

I was agog watching this performance. I had already experienced his expertise in conning, but this was a bit over the top. Still, I had to applaud. Holly opened her mouth to speak, but Neal was on a roll.

'So what do you think, Holly? Are there some spare bongos about?' He still held her arm and his smile.

By now the doorway and the stair landing were filling up. Holly was away from her post and totally flustered. She pointed to a couple of mattresses in the centre of the long wall of the room and fled to the door to stem the tide.

We walked into the enormous room – a loft over a warehouse. The roof was high, black night resting on the rectangles of glass set in the rippling tin between the steel beams. An attempt had been made to bring it down to earth by hanging bedspreads or burlap on wires over the sitting or sleeping areas. Most of the room was furnished with empty space, and most of that dimly lit by several candles on boxes that cast hovering ghostly shadows around the walls, the poor things seeming to hug their small circles of light around their glowing bodies to guard them against escaping into the great beyond.

The walls had been hung with huge abstract garish paintings, and the brilliant blobs of throw-rugs looked like spills or leaks around the three or four mattresses that served for couches and/or beds. In these areas the space was interrupted by burlap hung vertically on wires to differentiate kitchen, bath or living quarters. A cute little Franklin stove stood in the middle of the room bravely blinking and puffing, but failing to project its heat three feet beyond its belly, and I pulled my coat around me as I followed Jack.

Beside a mattress he'd found a beautiful sparkling new set of bongo drums, and was reverently turning them over in his hands. I sat down on the mattress opposite him. He looked up at me. 'They aren't tight – see? – the skins are loose as hell – look.'

'Oh dear – I guess we'd better ask Holly about it, hunh?' and Jack got up to find her.

Only a few other people had ventured or been allowed past the doorway as yet, so I wandered around looking at the paintings and tried to imagine what living here was like. Neal had vanished, and now I thought I should find him and settle the question of my own fee, so I walked over to the door as inconspicuously as I could and out onto the landing.

Beneath this platform was the sound of men's voices, and leaning over the rail I saw Neal, his urgent gestures telling me his mission: the everlasting search for tea. Not wanting to intrude, I returned to the interior, Holly making no move to stop me, having so many others to deal with.

I found Jack sitting with his back to me but looking over his shoulder frantically in my direction. The look of horror on his face made me quicken my pace. When I sat down beside him, he dropped his hands to the floor and his head to his knees and moaned. I put my hand on his head, thinking he was either sick or in pain.

'What is it Jack? What's wrong?' And then I saw the drums between his feet. A two-inch black-rimmed jagged hole disfigured the creamy skin of one of the drum heads. Very ugly it was.

Jack looked up at me and wailed, 'Jesus, what'll I *do?*' His blue eyes searched my face for a miracle.

I thought a moment, then said, 'All I can think of is to run. Come on, we can't possibly pay for those,' and I plucked at his jacket and made for the door, pasting on my party face as I darted and dodged through the little pack near the door, Jack right behind me. Holly was surrounded by a group of multicoloured hairy beings, and I guessed they were all musicians minus instruments like us. I mentally wished her luck with the rent as we clattered down the outside steps.

Neal was about to mount them, but when he saw our faces, he followed us running towards the car, threw open the door and had the engine started before Jack and I were safe inside. This once I was glad for all Neal's practice in driving first and asking questions afterwards. As soon as we were back into familiar byways, I quizzed Jack: 'How on earth did it happen, Jack? How could you have burned that hole in the drum head?' The next second we were bouncing off the dashboard and back to the seat as Neal hit the brakes.

'You did what?' He didn't yell; it was more like a hiss. Then he clamped his teeth, slammed the gears into first, his other hand dangling limply over the wheel, shaking his head. Neal regretted

Jack's frequent clumsiness, and I could hear him saying in his head, 'Leave it to Jack...'

Jack recounted mournfully what had happened, and knowing how Neal would regard it made him feel all the worse.

'Well, goddammit, it was that dumb broad's fault – she told me to do it. She said to hold the drum over the gas burner there, and I did – that's all I did, just as she said, but what she didn't say was there's a six-inch blue flame I couldn't see – what the hell, how should I know? Jesus, why didn't she tell me?' He was leaning forward waving his arm while he appealed to us as though we were Holly, and now he sank back and slouched down in the seat, leaning his head on his hand at the window. I know how very badly he felt – we all did. Instruments were precious, and the owner had probably sacrificed to get these. I tried to make sympathetic noises and weak excuses; Neal only shook his head and grunted. A silent gloom descended until we arrived back home.

Downstairs, after Neal had driven Mrs Davies home, we got out the wine and beer and let Jack go over it a few more times to wear it out, Neal now sympathetic and reassuring. The evening hadn't been a total loss, for Neal had scored a little tea, so he rolled a joint and talked about other crimes he'd known to make Jack get over it. In no time the scene in retrospect took on a comic aspect, and we ended up convulsed with laughter, Jack revitalized and his sin washed away.

Another night Jack asked me to accompany him to a party, this time with Neal's benediction, as he couldn't leave the telephone and was content to sleep until his call. The party was in a private apartment, and there were four or five other couples. The owner and hosts were Jordan Belson, a talented artist and filmmaker, and his wife Jane. The group had been invited especially to view a film Jordan had just completed. The living room was small but comfortable, and obviously decorated by an artist.

We were served wine and nibbles, and then the assembled company were seated in a wedge formation, Jack and I at the end point, he a little in front of me on my right. At the opposite open end of the wedge was a movie screen. I struck up a conversation with an art student on my left, and was intent on listening to her, not noticing that two joints of tea had been lit and were being passed down both sides of the formation – each joint ending with me before being passed back up the lines. So as not to seem prudish, I had been absentmindedly taking puffs on each joint as they were handed me, not realizing that instead of getting very little, as planned, I was getting twice as much as anyone else.

Soon the film was shown, and I was even less aware of my surroundings. This was the first film of its kind I'd ever seen, and I was totally fascinated by it. To the music of mambo, Jordan had animated line drawings and paint splotches to fit. It had everything: humour, pathos, despair, excitement, personalities, character types, yet all just single black lines – totally non-objective. I didn't want it to end.

When it did and the lights turned on again, I found myself unable to move a muscle; I was absolutely rigid. 'Stoned' came to mind – was this what it meant? But what was I to do? Rising panic made me icy cold as well. It seemed an eternity before Jack turned to me and said something requiring an answer, and his touch broke the spell. He turned away again, apparently not having noticed anything unusual about me. Could that be? I wanted to tell Jack, but now I was blocked again, couldn't think what to say, and the panic returned.

The party was breaking up. Jack and the others were moving about the room, collecting coats and making farewells. I sat like a rock. Someone was bound to notice, yet the nice student I'd conversed with accepted my smile as sufficient response to whatever she'd said to me. With an extreme effort I found I could lean forward slightly, but I didn't dare try to stand. Jack came towards me with my coat and held out his hand. When I saw I could reach for his, and with his touch I was able to stand, relief engulfed me. I was mobile; I was okay – not quite.

'Jordan asked if we can drive him over to Columbus Avenue, and I told him it's right on our way, okay?' I heard what Jack said, and it sounded simple, but *drive*? I hadn't thought of that, and Jack couldn't drive. But I must go on, and I said 'Of course' while climbing into my coat, my mind awhirl. Holding onto Jack's arm, I got to the door and down the stairway, the bright light on the stairwell illuminating brilliantly coloured paintings on the walls that made me feel I was floating in a surrealistic fantasy. Jack behaved as though I were perfectly normal. When we reached the car at last, I was about to give up and confess all to Jack and Jordan, when into my mind came Neal's original instructions at my initiation into tea: 'Remember, you can always do anything you have to do.' I grasped these straws, repeating the words again and again as I got in and started the car. I haven't a clue as to what the men were discussing, but, sure enough, I drove Jordan where he wished to go through the traffic, the busy streets and up the hill to home. I even parked with no greater difficulty than usual. I thanked God or whatever was responsible, but also I resolved that was my last tea party.

Neal was about to leave for work when we reached the house, so I said nothing of my experience to either of them then. Being close to Jack's warm reassuring presence was enough for now.

* * *

Work on the railroad was so slow now, Neal 'bumped' a newer man in order to hold down a steady job on a daily freight local, even though he'd make less money than he could on the extra board. My blossoming self-confidence developed into a daring hitherto unknown in my sheltered experience. To help with the finances, I decided to seek a night job. I wanted something fun and untaxing to the brain, a job I could quit without feeling guilty, and have a go at being a 'night person'. I knew I couldn't be a waitress; I'd nearly come unglued trying that at college.

After quite an education in the ways and means of night-time jobs, I finally had to settle for being a camera girl, even though the only income was from tips. The jobs I wanted, like cigarette girl or cloakroom attendant, required the girls to give all their tips to the management, humph.

The office was in the notorious 'International Settlement' in North Beach. This dazzling block of nightclubs and amusement stalls was neither a 'settlement' nor 'international', but everyone knew it was the last remnant in San Francisco of the Barbary Coast. It may have been shoddy, but by today's entertainment standards it was far from wicked. Now that the one secluded concentrated area has been torn down, the new lust factories have opened up on Broadway, once a nice street of restaurants and jazz nooks. Enrico's is the only survivor.

I went under the wrought-iron archway and found my boss, a big chubby man lounging in his desk chair chewing a toothpick. He gave me a quick resume of my duties and then yelled over his shoulder, 'Hey, Joe – here's a new one. Show her how to work the camera and give her one.'

I supposed it was that easy because there was no money involved. I soon learned what it took to earn any money in this profession, but for now I shouldered my camera and clicked my best high heels down to Sodom, or was it Gomorrah?

I was to cover three clubs: one was a small Mexican café which served excellent authentic food, had a good combo but very few patrons. The second was a block further along Broadway, an intimate, elegant club with a floorshow of female impersonators, the Beige Room, and no photos were allowed during the shows. The third club was in Chinatown, and a cab was necessary to reach it – on me. This one boasted 'exotic dancers', their word for strippers, but was frequented almost entirely by regular customers whom I was forcefully forbidden to approach. Later I learned these near-impossible assignments were given to all new girls to test their ingenuity.

I worked from six until two, and during this time Neal and Jack experimented with their 'voices' and the spoken word by enticing stories from each other into the Ekotape. I'd come home, kick off my wet shoes and head for the refrigerator, my appetite whetted from eight hours of tantalizing aromas of Mexican, Chinese and continental cuisines which I was forbidden to sample on the job. All the darkrooms were behind the kitchens; it would have been so easy to grab a morsel in one of them in passing, especially the Chinese, since all the food was laid out on big trays.

Jack and Neal would make me relate the continuing saga of night-life in the sinful city. At this time their own night-time ramblings had centred around the black neighbourhoods, and in years to come it amused me to think it was I who had first introduced them to North Beach.

For some reason, one night Jack was lying on the floor. I had a swift glass of wine and, holding my bowl of food, sat on top of him straddling his waist. It felt so good to be home, Neal only laughed. They were particularly curious about the Beige Room because, like me, they'd never been to such a club. I'd become friendly with the performers, and would listen to them size up each male patron on his arrival. 'Would he or wouldn't he?' and I wanted Neal and Jack to come down and be appraised, but they declined.

'Who are the customers?' they wanted to know.

'All kinds of people – even the Greyline Tours bring busloads of mid-western businessmen and their wives. It's always crowded, but when I go around between shows and ask to take their photos, they clutch each other and gasp "Not *here*!" even though I tell them I'll put it in a plain wrapper. I'm glad I can't work during the shows – they are great, not crude, and it is really amazing some of these men have very female features – waists, round hips, and one has a gorgeous alto voice.'

One night I had a public screaming match with the female boss, and I expected any minute I'd be fired – but I wasn't. I think she had accused me of taking a photo during a performance, which I hadn't.

Soon it was obvious I was putting in more nickels than I was getting out, so when a soldier gave me a $5 tip at the Chinese club, I decided to quit while I was ahead. I had 'done my thing' and found it boring, tiring and unrewarding, if temporarily educational.

| THIRTY-ONE |

Since Jack's arrival Allen had been writing more often. It was plain he envied his friends being together without him. He wrote long poems, reported the activities of everyone he knew, and repeated stories others told him. We enjoyed taking turns reading his letters aloud and discussing them at great length.

Jack was becoming more depressed by the hassle with Joan and her efforts to get him to send money he didn't have. He had given the $1000 advance for *The Town and the City* to his mother, and earned very little at the baggage room. Any mention of Joan made him angry, and he wanted to run. Allen offered sensible, fatherly advice:

> Carl Solomon upset you still starving, and that your mother keeps your money. Why don't you use it yourself? You are in a worse hole than your mother. I spoke to lawyer about wife and he said either change your address to keep safe or send her money (from another postal town) according to agreement. If want to stay in country safe and without anxiety, that's only way. You're letting yourself get too unnecessarily tangled up in sad fate. Let's figure a way to clean things up before it gets further, makes writing paranoid and life lousy... Am not being analytic-moral. None of us are fast and strong enough to battle society forever, really; it's too sad and gray. Just felt you

were feeling too crazy lately and am putting out friend-hand. Must not let situation drift to intolerability. We got too much else to do besides suffer. Burroughs has been writing. He is lonely. Write to him. Bill says 'Meanwhile, things seem kind of dreary around here, I want to get the case settled and clear out.' [A reference to the shooting of Burroughs's wife. His kids have been claimed by respective grandparents.]

Jack, please write New Directions a short note telling them how much you like Bill's book, recommending it for prose and archive value, and telling, as I did in 6-page letter, it's a great book. I have revised the version Bill sent up 2 weeks ago...smoother now, not so weird Reichian. If Laughlin no want, we'll peddle it to cheap paper covered 25c Gold Medal or Signet Books, like, *I, Mobster*.

Carl is serious about Neal's manuscript. Neal, get to it, honey lamb. He'll give you money, and you are a great man.

How I miss both of you and wish I were there with you so that we could share hearts again. I know I am hard to get along with and proud. I hope that you are not laughing at me when I am here away from your warmth. Write me. I think about you all the time, and have no one to talk to as only we can talk.

How or when will I ever hear your records? I sit here and my soul lacks you Neal and you Jack. I hope my ship goes your way to Frisco. I don't want ever to fade from your minds. Love, Allen.

His letter concluded with a poem.

Put a kiss and a tear
In a letter,
And I'll open it and cry
Over you.

Put a sperm and a wink
On the paper,
And I'll come when I read
I'm so blue.

Put a throb of your heart
In 'yours truly,'
With your names writ in blood
'Neal and Jack,'

And I'll open my palm
With my penknife,
And send you a bucket-
Full back.

    Done in 3 minutes
    A.G.

Jack's sights turned more and more longingly to the peace and simplicity of Mexico – and certainly a 'change of address', out of the reach of Joan's communications.

In the light of the past months of comparative compatibility and serenity with Neal, I felt our married life had achieved a more stable condition, and I let my thoughts return to plans for a family life based on the conventional patterns that had formed my own, still believing that's what Neal wanted too. Of course he did, and he didn't, but that I had yet to learn.

Now seemed a good time to solidify the tie with the grandparents, who had never seen the children but had shown a consistent interest in them. So we decided to go visit them in Tennessee, and give Neal a chance to see the farm as well. Neal, always ready to travel at the hint of an excuse, also thought it appropriate for me to accompany him on at least one 'road' trip. I had had no vacation of any kind for five years or more, and Neal thought this might also afford him a chance to contact his father.

There was now no doubt the trip was an absolute necessity, not merely a pleasure. I plunged into plans. We could survive if Neal took a month off from the railroad; we'd take with us all of the baby food and much of our own, takes spells driving, and keep the motels to a minimum. We'd drive Jack as far as Nogales and start him on his way to Mexico City.

Everything worked out beautifully. We took out the back seat of the 'woody' and covered the floor with a cot mattress behind the front seat, with John's small crib mattress across the back. This left plenty of room for the two little girls to stretch out between him and the front seat. Along the sides we lined up our bags and boxes of baby supplies and our food. There was a surprising amount of room.

Jack took a nostalgic farewell to his attic nook, leaving the bulk of his possessions in it, taking only his sea bag. He and I had no opportunity for a private talk, and we all bravely minimized the impending separation by making happy forecasts for reuniting in Mexico in the nebulous future. It was accepted by us all that we would share a home somewhere for at least part of each year.

Neal took the girls into the front seat and enhanced their excitement with a constant patter about every passing scene and his connections with it. Jack and I crawled into the back with John and sat crosswise facing each other. The space was somewhat cramped for two adults, but this made it possible for us to touch and look at each other, speaking with our eyes. We lapsed into silent reverie, aware how short the time left to us was growing. We could make no big overt moves towards each other without feeling sorry for Neal, so communication had to resort to longing looks and pressure on our adjoining thighs. The tension was nearly unbearable by the time we reached Santa Barbara four hours later, but it was a romantic agony willingly suffered.

We spent the first night with Neal's younger sister, Shirley, and her husband, and the second in Los Angeles, where Neal was able to locate two older half-sisters and brothers. We visited from house to house, and they were all very cordial, in spite of this sudden arrival of three adults and three children. I seemed the only one concerned about this breach of manners, and my objections were all silenced. I gave up and relaxed lying on the floor next to Jack in Bill's living room, where we watched the first TV I'd ever seen.

For all of the next day's drive I urged Jack to sit in front with Neal while the girls and I played games in the back. I had to smile as I listened to the men, thinking what a different road it was from the others they'd shared. It didn't sound as though the family presence was dampening their pleasure in the least; in fact, it seemed to add to it when they passed places remembered from previous trips. They would both talk at once to tell me embroidered stories.

When the children slept that night, we three adults sat in front and drove all night across the desert. It was a deep, clear night, and all of us were wistful, knowing it was our last night together. Jack could now put his arm around my shoulders and stroke my hair, and I could lean against him. We listened to the radio dramas, *First Nighter* and *The Whistler*, as we had done at home. During the latter, Neal became so emotionally involved, Jack and I had to laugh and repeatedly remind him it was only a play. He was probably putting us on, but his intense absorption made me uneasy.

Then when there was only music for background, we peered into the vast panorama of glittering stars all around us in the clear desert sky. Neal astounded both Jack and me with a detailed discourse on all the visible constellations and stars.

'Wherever did you learn all that?' we asked in unison. 'I didn't know you knew anything about astronomy!'

With a sigh Neal replied, 'I know everything about everything – how many times do I have to tell you?'

The stars dissolved into the pearl-grey dawn, and with it came a chill. The parting was near, and we grew silent. As if by accident I let my head drop onto Jack's shoulder, and he squeezed mine, his lips brushing my forehead – the best we could do by way of au revoir. Neal drove up to the wire fence on the Mexican border and parked alongside. I saw no guards or customs officials, only weeds, dirt and trash. Everything was grey and dreary, the weather, the edge of town and now our moods.

A few yards inside the gates was a white-walled café with chipping paint, and Jack said, 'Aw, come on; can't you have one last beer with me?' He stood forlornly beside the car, his sea bag over his shoulder.

'Sure, man.' Neal and I got out of the car. I checked to see the girls were still sleeping soundly, and that I could see the car from the café.

It was no warmer inside the one big bare room, and it smelled loudly of Lysol. A brown varnished bar lined one wall, and scattered in front of it were a few metal tables and chairs. Beer before breakfast was new to me, but this morning it was a good idea and helped calm me. Jack made a few stabs at cheery conversation, hopping from Mexico ahead to the adventures behind, but sensing only unrest on the part of Neal he fell silent too. I wondered if Neal's mood was less one of regret for Jack's departure than for not being in Jack's shoes. All he said was that in a few months we'd all be living there together.

Neal was eager to get going, and I wanted the separation over, so we said corny good byes and ran back to the car, turning to wave until we'd lost sight of the sagging figure by the border fence. Later Jack wrote us that we should have driven into the little town and surroundings, where there was a fiesta in the afternoon and all of it free. I was sorry we hadn't known; it would have been a far more fitting last time for us all to be together having fun and making another memory. For the girls, too.

After the melancholia of the morning, we set out on the rest of the journey confident our former problems were the errors of youth; we had learned our limitations and that freedom *from* gave us a new freedom *to*. Now I could concentrate all my attention on my own little family. We were together enjoying a shared experience; I didn't want to miss a minute of it.

Neal was all I could wish him to be. He drove slowly – almost too slowly I sometimes thought – but he explained he had some notion about a 'cruising speed' for the good of the car. Whatever the reason, I welcomed it as a deterrent to my bickering about his driving throughout the trip. My careful planning also appeared to have been good; the food was working out perfectly, and every few nights Neal and I could stop for a hot meal while the children slept. (We had a bottle warmer that worked for them.)

There was only one near-catastrophe on the way to Tennessee. At a drawbridge near New Orleans, Neal drove under the descending barrier, that then came down behind our car, not in front of it. I almost died of fright as I saw the concrete road rise up directly in front of the radiator. Hysterically, I began yelling at Neal, when a motorcycle cop came up beside us and did likewise. I switched from scolding Neal to defending him, and in my terror gave the full power of my indignation to the officer. Neal slid down in his seat between us, casting a helpless, henpecked look at the officer, who, also taken aback by my outburst, soon shot Neal a sympathetic look and rode off. My stability returned with the relief of not being arrested.

'Ha, see there?' I poked Neal. 'You have to admit there are times when having a shrew for a wife has its advantages. You do forgive me?'

| THIRTY-TWO |

The two weeks with the grandparents went smoothly. Neal excelled in good manners and thoughtfulness. He also impressed my parents by his affection for and patience with the children. He listened to my father's stories of the local folkways, the crops and animals with enthusiasm, and throughout our stay remained remarkably serene and agreeable. He showed an interest, along with the little girls, in the horses, cattle, pigs and lambs, and the sight of tobacco growing and hanging in the barn. A cowboy he wasn't, and I couldn't get him on a horse, much to my surprise. We took walks, played in the creek, taught him to churn butter, and toured the historic battlefields and ghost-infested mansions of the old South.

The girls ran all over the house yard excitedly. Cathy went out less often after the big gander lunged at her, squawking and flapping his wings. And Jami was like no other toddler I've ever run across. She preferred to wear only underpants, but she'd drop them any-where when they annoyed her, and we'd have to go hunting. She also would disappear, only to be found on her bed helping herself to a nap. Most children I'd known resisted naps.

Neal was once again my ideal companion. The only problem I had with him wasn't between us. He failed to get the proper slant on how whites had to treat blacks. He'd be naturally friendly and respect-ful to farm hand, coal man or drugstore curb-server, and they'd freeze in instant suspicion. To this they were not accustomed. I explained to him how I'd had to learn these techniques, although I hated them and the attitude of the southern whites – a major cause of my abandoning the south for good.

'Neal, darling, there is no use trying to reason with them; it isn't a matter of reason or intelligence. It's emotion ingrained from birth – just like some of your Catholic dogma. Both my parents and I have close friends who are wonderful people otherwise, but that is just one subject we have to avoid. It took me a long time to comprehend this.' But Neal couldn't, and I was glad of it.

Then one afternoon shortly before our departure, I caught Neal smoking tea in our upstairs bedroom. I panicked again, my confi-dence in him shaken. How could he risk even the remote possibility my folks would know, and after that I remained nervous and on edge until we were safely away.

The return trip continued as comfortably as had the incoming one for most of the time. In Kansas City he found his brother, Jimmy, against whom Neal surprisingly bore no grudge for his childhood atrocities. We had a friendly visit for an hour or two, but Jim had no place for us to spend the night, so we went to a drive-in movie and slept as long as we could before continuing across the endless plains.

Then disillusion struck again. Whether it was remembering his childhood miseries after seeing Jim again, or whether a reaction from his recent submission to conventional behaviour or simply his psychological imbalance I'll never know, but before we reached Denver Neal escaped from us twice for many hours or all night without any explanation. Back I went into the all-too-habitual reaction of righteous indignation and martyrdom, more bitterly this time because everything had looked so straightened out, so promising, and I thought I'd learned that lesson.

By the time we reached Denver, I was doing my best to collect the shattered pieces of our marriage again, and Neal behaved as though he wished to too. It was a bitter pill to have to acknowledge our differences had been overcome only through circumstances, not through inner change. With some reluctance, but trying not to show it, I agreed to take the children to see Neal's father. Not that I didn't want to meet him or have him see the children, but because he was living in a hotel in a neighbourhood that made me nervous, and I couldn't imagine what we could talk about. I knew I had to make the effort anyway; it meant so much to Neal.

As it happened, all worked out well. Neal decided at the last minute to stay in the car with the children, since they could hang out the car window in view of their grandfather's window and wave to him. I went into the hotel alone. It was just as well. The poor dear didn't really know who I was, but as long as I kept mentioning his son, he was happy. A wonderful floozy sort of a woman came in and out of the room full of cheer, clucking and fussing over Neal, Sr, and I was glad to be able to reassure Neal that his father was being very well looked after. Neal then went up to see his father while I stayed in the car. Neal's filial affection was appeased, and when his father died a few years later, Neal was able to return to Denver to arrange for his burial with a clear conscience.

We covered the rest of the way home more sombrely, and as fast as we could, resolving to return to Denver someday, see it properly and reminisce – he on his youth as I had done in Tennessee, as well as our own time there together. That seed-plan never bore fruit, much to my regret.

We were both considerably brought down by the setbacks, but when we reached home we agreed to continue to try. If only he could help me understand why he did these things; I wonder why he never tried. We promised each other we'd give analysis another chance. I also reached out for the hope that possibly a change of scene might make a difference. I really didn't know how to raise children in a city

– Neal had just seen the sort of natural environment I'd always been accustomed to, and although a city boy himself he concurred it might be better for us all to live in a more rural area. Cities were always available. It gave us something else to look forward to, more plans to consider, and as we settled into our own bed again, dim hope was recycled once more.

Two letters awaited us from Allen, one addressed to Jack as well. This was the first word we'd had from Allen for three months. He said he'd found a missing chapter of *On the Road* which he was forwarding to Jack, apparently unaware of our trip, saying, 'Jeepers, where is Jack?' The other letter, written later, said he'd just received a 'monumental letter from Jack in Mexico', and that we were to send back the 23 opening pages, while Jack was sending him the rest.

> Jack says you're mad at him or tired of him, Neal, is that true?…I'm afraid for him in Mexico, it is a kind of lostness…he's smoking with Mexicans in mudhuts… He says you are busy and obsessed with 'complete all-the-way-down-the-line materialistic money and stealing groceries anxieties.' etc., etc. also said he was happy there…are you in Frisco, even? What's going on around there, anyway?

Back in harness, Neal became depressed again. In those times I didn't understand his need for change and excitement, still judging others by myself, but he wrote Allen a nice note, saying, 'you're the same great wonderful guy and I'm more of a bum than ever…' and ending with, 'Why don't you come out here? Nice place if one likes it. Be brakie and make lots money. Or write in attic and make love to wife and me.'

Much to my surprise, Allen wrote a letter to me breaking the ice of five years:

> Dear Mrs. Cassady: How is you, after all…as I see things now I think maybe you been through the mill bad, always been sorry I contributed to the privation…Too bitter to forgive? Hope not. Take care of the children (that means Jack and Neal, too) as everybody will ultimately be saved, including you…I plan no imminent invasion of Frisco but would like to someday and hope I will be welcome to you and we can be friends. You always seem alright to me. Jack likes you but is afraid of you (you know?) I wonder how you feel about him, Yours, Allen the Stranger.

I answered him cordially, and he wrote Neal, 'Maybe a change of scene would be good. I may come out there yet.' He also replied to my letter and sealed our friendship.

> Much thanks for your letter. Didn't expect to be so well received either. So that dispenses that cloud. Was Jack's tip too; he not so dumb, with other people's female notions... Would be interested know your process of changes of love and thought. Don't realize too much of yr interior of last years except by conjecture. Thank you for child name. Never got the idea from W.C. Fields that you had anything to do with it, but now that you mention it does sound sort of inevitable that you might have had some hand in naming yr own children. Yipe! Consider my letters henceforth addressed to you, too. Would it be possible have my epistles (like St. Paul) read in state at dinner table in front of the children of the Church? Constantinople here needs me so can't get to Rome temporarily, am waiting for a Word. Understand your letter. Thanks. Shy. Allen

Immediately, I jumped at the offer to share my thoughts by pouring them out to him and requesting his comments and advice on my position with Neal and Jack. He further gratified me by setting down a thoughtful and thorough analysis of all our relationships.

> Jack's attitude:
> a) As I haven't got all his letters here, I'll send on an anthology of statements apropos his relations with Neal when I assemble them. What *I* think about it is, Jack loves Neal platonically (which I think is a pity, but maybe about sex I'm 'projecting' as the analysts say) and Neal loves Jack, too. The fact is that Jack is very inhibited, however. However, also, sex doesn't define the whole thing.
> b) Jack still loves Neal none the less than ever.
> c) Jack ran into a blank wall which everybody understands and respects in Neal, including Jack and Neal. It upset and dispirited Jack, made him feel lonely and rejected and like a little brother whose questions the older brother wouldn't answer.
> d) Jack loves Carolyn also, though obviously not with the same intensity as he loves Neal...considering their history together...Jack is full of Carolyn's praises and nominates her to replace Joan Burroughs as ideal Mother Image,

> Madwoman, chick and ignu. The last word means a special
> honorary type post-hip intellectual...Jack also says
> Carolyn beats Ellie [a girl in New York] for Mind.
> e) Jack said nothing about sleeping with you in his letters...

He gave a good deal more analyses of Neal, then,

> Mexico may be a good idea for all of us when become
> properly solidified...What we must make plans to do is
> all meet somewhere where it is practically possible for us
> to live, under our various pressures, when the practical
> time comes. Shall we not then keep it in mind to try to
> arrange for a total grand reunion somewhere for as long
> as it can last?...I am definitely interested in gong to bed
> with everybody and making love...P.S. Neal, write me a
> letter about sex. A.

Allen's attitude towards sex always managed to raise my Puritan
hackles, and I'm sure he knew it. It certainly pricked my romantic
bubbles, but in other respects his thoughts were reassuring, and I felt
accepted and safe, thinking that if we all lived together pressures
could be siphoned off in small spurts in a variety of ways. Deep in
my heart, however, I still yearned for a monogamous marriage with
Neal. If it weren't possible, perhaps this arrangement held possibilities hitherto unknown in conventional patterns.

After all, I had already learned some of those were nonsense. My
ability to analyze ended there.

We hadn't heard from Jack directly since we left him in Nogales,
and I wondered if he was feeling remorse, or if he was angry for some
reason. The first week of June, however, we received a long letter
denying all this. He said he'd read my letter to Allen, but also that he
had sent us two letters, one to Tennessee and one to San Francisco.
I couldn't believe we hadn't received them; I had to put the blame on
the Mexican postal service. He said he could never have enough of
the Cassadys, the children included. He also gave his thoughts on
our living together in Mexico – where he'd be sometimes at sea or
elsewhere, and Neal working in California part of the time.

He excused himself from analyzing matters of love, but he did
admit that often in the car he had wanted to hold my hand or kiss
me, but was afraid of Neal's jealousy as well as his own, so didn't do
what he felt like doing. He said he wondered how we both felt about

our three-way living, or I gather that was what he referred to. (He could beat about the bush so.) He said he was grateful to us for letting him share our life and was at our service. Of course, said he, nothing matters since all ends in death. But on his mind permanently now was eternity, and 'you are a part of it.'

He also said he'd written a third of *Dr Sax*, so he had another book almost ready for the publishers. He avowed his love for us both and hoped to see us soon off a ship bearing dry martinis and Shakespeare...and signed it 'Uncle Jack'.

He added a note to Neal, and tidied up any possible loose ends to the various relationships, reiterating their brotherhood, saying nothing had changed between them, their relationship always close and perfect.

One of his earlier letters finally caught up with us in which he wrote he had finished typing *On the Road*, and had made Allen his agent as advised by Bill Burroughs.

When Allen received the manuscript he wrote us: 'Jack's book arrived and it is a holy mess – it's great alright but he did everything he could to fuck it up with a lot of meaningless bullshit I think,' and he continued with a detailed analysis of everything he thought wrong with it:

> page after page of surrealist free-association that doesn't make sense to anybody...I don't think it can be published anywhere in its present state. I know this is an awful hangup for everyone concerned – he must be tired too – and that's how it stands I think. Your tape conversations were good reading, so I could hear what was happening out there – but he put it in entire and seemingly un-unified, so it just skips back and forth and touches on things momentarily and refers to events nowhere else in the book; and finally it appears to objective eye so diffuse and disorganized – which is, on purpose – that it just *don't make*. Jack knows that, too, I'll bet. Why is he tempting rejection and fate? Fucking spoiled child, like all of us, maybe, but goddam it, it ain't *right* to take on so paranoiac just to challenge and see how far you can go – when there's so much to say and live and do now, how hard it is, albeit. Jack is an ignu and I'll bow down to him, but he done fuck up his writing money-wise, and also writing-wise. He was not experimenting and exploring in new deep form, he was purposely just screwing around as

if anything he did no matter what he did was OK, no bones attached. Not purposely, I guess, just drug out and driven to it and in a hole. I don't know what he'll say when I say this to him – he comes back to NY this week or next I think – and how he'll make out with all this shit to shovel around, I dunno. I will try to help but I feel so evil when I not *agree* in blindness. Well shit on this, you get the point.

Before learning of Allen's judgement, Jack was feeling good. He wrote that he'd completed *Dr Sax* at Bill's. He was ready to leave Mexico and return to his mother, and thence to New York for a ship, ending with a sentimental paragraph about missing having wine and pizza with us (he called me 'fine, blonde kerouacass gal'), and hoping to land in San Francisco to see us soon. He couldn't know of Allen's reaction to his book yet, but his anger towards publishers was still fierce, and he told me that for me life with him would have been impossible, he was so unlucky. I couldn't remember any discussion he was referring to about our living together; all his idea.

The next word we got from Jack was two weeks later, a mysterious and enigmatic note. Had he heard Allen's critique? It sounded like a last farewell. He wrote that instead of returning to New York he was going off to a valley to live in a shack with Indians and a dog for he couldn't guess how long. He signed it with love and kisses but added a PS that he eventually wanted to go to Ecuador where fruit, flowers and wives grew wild, and no anger and hassles. He said to send any important messages to Allen, who would pass them on telepathically. Written along the side were kisses to me and the children, and an order to Neal to write his book and to love me sentimentally. Neal and I didn't know what to make of it.

'Oh, he'll come out of it,' Neal sighed, 'he's just paranoid again – misunderstood. Old Zagg will sit in his mud hut and have himself a regular orgy with Miss Green – the bastard; why doesn't he send me some? Awrg, fap.' He strode to the window and stood gazing out – not at our back yard, I could tell, but at a Mexican valley warmed by a lazy sun where there were no bills, no pressures, just mangoes and Miss Green.

| THIRTY-THREE |

In August of 1952 I wistfully bid good bye to the little house on Russian Hill where I had passed so many milestones and whose 'possibilities' had gone unfulfilled. Then I surveyed the new potential of the huge house we'd found for rent in San Jose, fifty miles to the south. We were still on the edge of a city – a city then aptly nick-named 'Nowheresville' – but the lovely valley surrounding it was too vast to explore from afar, so we'd settled on this lucky find until we could learn more about the area and Neal could see how the new location would affect his work.

The one-storey house was a 'hacienda' style, with white stucco walls and a red tiled roof. It had been part of an estate, then converted into a convalescent home. It had eight rooms of various sizes in a puzzling arrangement, high ceilings, but oddly enough no fireplace. It was surrounded with mature but neglected flowerbeds and set back far enough from the main thoroughfare, Santa Clara Street, to allow for a large front lawn dotted with fruit and almond trees. Behind the house was a paved courtyard that separated the big house from a newer smaller bungalow. Our decision to rent the big house was finalized when we met the young couple who lived in it: Dick and Marie Forest. They had a boy about Jami's age and a baby girl. Their eagerness to help us move and to adjust to a new town was a revival of neighbourliness in the old tradition.

The Forests had no notion of the kind of life their new neighbours had been living, but I confidently expected we would become as organ-ized, peaceful and conventional as they – except, perhaps, in one respect. Neal had talked away my fears and planted some marijuana seeds in the flower beds, tucked behind the large shrubs under the front porch and in the vacant lot next door, hoping to eliminate the constant search and high prices, but it would be a long time before the harvest. He was pleased the Forests were so 'square'; he figured they wouldn't know what the plants were.

Every room in the house had layers of old wallpaper, and I thought to get Neal to release some pent-up energy and steam by scraping it off the walls of our bedroom. It was a much bigger job than it looked, but he attacked it furiously, fighting every inch of the way, and once started there was no turning back; it had to be finished. When it finally was, he was proud of himself and the result, especially when I painted the walls a deep royal blue, the ceiling white, made white drapes out of old sheets with big horizontal tucks and put a white chenille bedspread on the box spring mattress against the wall. On the wood floor were yellow throw-rugs. Pillows lined up on the back of the bed were also yellow. I put a red bulb in the overhead light fixture, which turned the walls purple, the pillows and rugs orange, the ceiling, curtains and bedspread pink. 'Psyche-delic' we would have called it had the word been invented yet; instead we called it our 'passion pit', each of us projecting our own aspirations.

The change in location looked most promising for all of us. Neal seemed more settled and had more time at home to write. Besides the extra space, he enjoyed playing chess with Dick, a droll storyteller and a delight to the children, for whom he made toys as well.

The freight runs began and ended in San Jose, whereas formerly Neal often had to 'deadhead' from San Francisco; now he only went to the yard. He had taken great pains to teach me how to read a timetable when we first settled on Russell Street. I found that merely a means of distress when he didn't arrive at the times he should have, so now I gave that up. 'Whatcha don't know…' etc.

Now, again, Neal wanted to share this new house with Jack, plus which, of course, Neal was out of tea and had no connections here. We had heard no more from Jack during our move, assuming he'd gone off to his hut with the Indians and a dog. Nonetheless, Neal decided to write to him at Bill's address, fearing all along that Jack was angry with him for not being able to repay an old debt of $30. 'Damn you for being in Mexico without me. Why in hell not give up the Indians to come back and tell me about them and to still earn about 2000 bucks on RR before the year's out? You can easily live in our big 9 room house here in sunny San Jose and ride about in my new stationwagon.'

He then apologized at length for not having any money (new stationwagon to the contrary) saying, 'Sept. 26 this the first paycheck I'll have enough clear to even buy the 1 dozen light bulbs this house needs.' He understood that Jack was 'surely mad as hell at me. And rightly so, and I started letters and never sent them and I told Carolyn, who wants you back so desperately, to write you, and everything went to hell and I'm without even any help from Miss Green, and where the hell are you? I'll send you fare to get back here on, only hurry up or there won't be much Ring left…stay here until December then you'll have plenty to go east.'

Before mailing the letter we learned Jack was in North Carolina with his mother, and I added a note saying I hoped he wasn't mad at us and, 'Neal and I still not making it without you. He says to tell you he'll join you in December, and you'll both go booming on the Florida East Coast line. I shouldn't doubt it, and I'll be saying just what Cathy did the other night: "Daddy and Jack both went off and left me."'

Suddenly the SP came up with a new ruling that no new men would be hired who were over thirty. Jack had just turned thirty in March, so Neal rushed to write to him again and outlined in explicit detail not only how he could get around this ruling if he came immediately, but also how to travel on the trains at a minimum of expense – in such fine detail, in fact, that Jack would have had to carry the letter in his hand all the way to be able to follow the complicated directions.

Jack agreed to come, but he left North Carolina before Neal's instructions arrived. The next word we received was a card from Denver. Neal went into a fit of expletives, and dashed out to send Jack a telegram emphasizing the imminence of the hiring deadline.

My spirits soared, and my energy was electrified. Jack was coming back after only three months this time. Joyfully I hastened to make a room ready for him. We had brought the big plywood desktop with us, and it was reinstated in the bedroom next to ours. The girls' daybed was now his. Although the room was nearer the rest of the house than had been his attic, it had French doors into a sunroom which led to the hall and front door.

Across the hall from his room was the sitting room. Our San Francisco landlords had given us their awful couch, chair and carpet, but they were better than none. This room had a large open archway into what was probably another reception room, but which we made into a dining/family room with a big round oak table and a few chairs also from the landlords. This room had a very large bay window under which we put the historic couch. The kitchen was beyond it – rather spread out, with a pantry at the far side holding the sink, under a window overlooking the paved courtyard. The stove was on the opposite side of the big room. A back door at one end led to another screened-in porch for utilities, with steps to the ground below and the paved courtyard. No garage.

Oddly enough, a door opposite this door from the porch led to the only bathroom, and one from it into our bedroom. To the right there was a short hall from the kitchen past a huge walk-in closet to a large room surrounded by windows and a back door. We put twin cots for the girls in here and John's large crib in the closet, which had a window. This 'suite' had a door from the kitchen, so all kids could be shielded off from earshot at night. Under the kitchen window, onto the porch, we put our small table and four chairs for dining.

Saturday afternoon Jack telephoned from the City, and Neal told him to hop the 'Zipper', the train men's nickname for the Zypher, the fast freight train to Los Angeles that stopped at San Jose. He said he'd meet him at the yard office. Neal had been called to work a freight to Watsonville he could catch there. I realized Jack and I would be alone this first night, which for the rest of the afternoon caused a considerable lack of concentration on my household tasks, which now included preparations for him.

| THIRTY-FOUR |

I had to go along to the meet the Zypher since Jack didn't drive. The stationwagon wasn't running, but Neal had bought a Model-A Ford in the City for me. I enjoyed it, too, once I got used to driving it in traffic. It had presented something of a challenge on San Francisco's steep hills, however.

The night was inky black, and Neal parked near the far edge of the unpaved, weed-fringed lot next to the small wooden building that was the freight office. I stayed in the car while Neal went to check on his train, and the Zypher could be heard approaching. It then screamed to a stop, clanging its bell and snorting steam that billowed orange and yellow in the lights from the office windows.

Soon, silhouetted against the engine's powerful shaft of white light, I saw the two men coming towards the car, Neal's lantern making crazy zig-zags as he pounded Jack on the back and punched him, boisterous and exuberant. Jack tried to defend himself, chuckling and looking shyly at the ground then sideways at Neal. When he saw me in the car, he ran his fingers through his hair and shoved at his shirt-tail. I lit a cigarette to calm my nerves, trembling at the sight of the familiar hulk in the checkered shirt.

Jack climbed into the short back seat, dragging his seabag with him, and Neal got in the driver's side. I was glad Neal had to wait a while for his train and could talk to us a few minutes, putting us more at ease. He asked Jack for details of his trip, lamenting the lost directions. He went on to point out features of our new house, and its proximity to the playing field of a highschool directly behind the property, 'And all the pretty highschool girls and cheerleaderesses, and – oops, Ma, sorry.'

Jack giggled, I smiled, but we said nothing. Speech was even less possible when our eyes met, and by the time Neal bounded off to catch his train, the close air in the little car was fairly dripping with desire. The dark was warm and humid inside, and outside the fog wrapped a blanket around us.

'Let's don't go yet,' Jack said softly. 'Come back here with me.' As we embraced, all the memories welled up within me, resurrected by his sweet male smells, strengthened by his long journey. In my happiness I had to smile and broke away from his kisses, laughing.

'Honestly, Jack, I feel like a highschool girl myself – necking in the back seat of a car, yet.' Jack chuckled and groped for a poor-boy in his jacket pocket. After a few swallows apiece, he set the bottle on the shelf behind us and pulled me to him again. When he attempted to change our positions, his elbow struck the bottle, which flipped over to drench us both. The spell broken, we laughed and tried to brush off the wine, but soon his ardour returned undaunted. I was neither relaxed nor comfortable in these conditions, and when we were suddenly bathed in blinding light, we sprang apart, our breath suspended. 'Oh sorry, I was looking for...' came a voice from the fog, and the light faded away.

'Thank God that wasn't a cop,' Jack muttered. 'Probably a break-man with a lantern. Let's get out of here.' I agreed swiftly, knowing we reeked of alcohol.

As I swung the car around the back of the house, Dick was climbing his front steps, having just checked our children. I waved and called my thanks before leading Jack into the house. We had told the Forests of Jack's impending visit and that he was a published author. We had shown them *The Town and the City*, and they were impressed. Now, we told them, he was going to work on the railroad with Neal and continue writing. Nothing was said, of course, of our shared affection, and I hoped we could manage not to shock them inadvertently.

We made a brief tiptoe tour of the house, Jack pleased with its age and even its unique plan. He and I shared a mutual interest in houses – homes. He bathed while I made him food and poured wine. He ate with relish, and we lingered over our wine in the candlelight until our shyness was overcome, then floated to the magnet of his bed. His tenderness and appreciation made it almost impossible for me to leave him and return to my own bed, but that was my absolute rule, because often one of the girls would come to me in the night.

In the morning the girls were awake long before Jack, and could hardly keep still in their impatience to see him. Even so, they were both stricken with an attack of shyness when he did appear. After he'd greeted them with hugs and kisses and sat down to his breakfast and talked to them, they jostled each other to climb on his lap, which I had to discourage.

When he was finished, he asked them to show him around outside, and nothing could please them more. Off they went, a child hanging on each hand, both girls babbling at once. The first place Jack wanted to see was the highschool ballfield. They had to go through the Forests' yard, dodging the large cactus plants, and little Chris rushed out to join them. As I watched them out of the pantry window over the dishes, I mused on how cheerful Jack always was when with children. He relaxed into a naturalness that contrasted with his frequent discomfort with adults, male or female. With children he had nothing to prove, nothing to be more than just himself, still a child at heart.

When the little group came gaggling back into the house, the girls presented me with fistfuls of scraggly wild flowers Jack said they could pick, and took him into their big room. When they began dragging out every book and toy, I rescued him by giving them their lunch followed by naps.

Neal arrived in time for a celebration dinner of Jack's favourite 'pizza'. I had stocked up on some beer, so after a jolly dinner and the girls put to bed – Jack again reading their stories – we had the Forests over to meet Jack and asked the Hinkles to join us too. They had moved to San Jose before us and bought a house in a tract on the outskirts of town.

Everyone was compatible as if they'd all been old friends, Dick and Neal swapped Paul Bunyon yarns, the Hinkles were pleased to reunite with Jack, the bright energy was scintillating, and I felt happier than for a long time to see Neal happy and everyone – well – happy.

The next day the serious business of getting Jack hired on the railroad was undertaken. He was fearful and resistant, but Neal prodded, coached and reviewed the great benefits. In a day or so Jack was accepted, and began his two weeks of student trips. Every evening on his return home he had to be cheered and encouraged anew. The training over, Jack signed on the extra board, proud now to be a 'genu-wine' brakie and to sport the same paraphernalia as Neal: big freight lantern, retractable switch keys on a belt hook, iron-toed shoes, and the (gulp) obligatory pocket watch, which he had to purchase. Of course, the fat timetable and rule book as well. Another celebration was called for.

Jack soon found he much preferred stories about railroading to actual participation in it. His physique and kinetic responses were more suited to running on a football field than to the swift and agile instant moves necessary for 'freightcar switching. Here he couldn't let his mind drift into literary observations or notations; he must be totally concentrated on the conditions of the moment. His clumsiness was an agony to him, and although he loved the earthy railroad men as characters, his sensitivity and paranoia resented their practice of joking by identifying men by nicknames – his becoming 'Keroway', which degenerated into 'Carroway Seed'. He was sure they all scorned and laughed at him. Neal did his best to explain and encourage, but he too became more irritable, partly out of sympathy and partly because he wanted to be proud of his friend. Also, he was not pleased that Jack and I had more time alone together now.

At least a day would pass before Jack would be called for a job, and he asked me if the girls and I would go to San Francisco with him to visit our old haunts. The stationwagon was running again, and we all set off in high spirits on an Indian summer day, the air heavy with the nostalgia inherent in autumn aromas.

Our eager expectations were snuffed the minute we parked at Coit Tower. Cathy, trying to get out of the car, complained of extreme pain in her legs, so I took her to Mission emergency. She was diagnosed as having rheumatic fever, so I drove straight home. Our own new doctor disputed that, and said it was osteomyelitis, and treatment was begun.

In spite of lamenting our aborted romantic excursion into the past, Jack and I had lovely days at home, even more so when Neal was able to join us. We revived our pastimes from San Francisco – got out the Shakespeare, each taking several parts with changes of voices and many laughs, the men acting out parts with extravagant gestures. Out came the favourite writers, to be read aloud in turns and most of it recorded. Since we had so little cash and tapes were expensive, we used the same two or three over and over. (I'd rather not think of that loss.)

The large, bare dining room gave lots of space for the children to play nearby, while we three sat around the big table. Neal tried juggling the fruit from the centrepiece, sending the girls scurrying under the table to retrieve the ones he dropped. When the girls were not with us sometimes Jack read us passages from *Dr Sax* in a great booming voice, accented by W.C. Fields or Major Hoople imitations, while Neal, eyes sparkling above his grin, breathed 'Yeah! Yeah!' after nearly every sentence, and loudly whenever Jack made reference to sex, which would make Jack crack up in giggles. In turn Neal would read from Proust, making comments and ignoring Jack's attempts to correct his French pronunciation. (I still have a 10-minute recording of this – very precious it is, too.)

And there were lovely evenings when Jack and I were alone. We'd both put the children to bed; he'd read them stories using all his range of voices. Jami was still his special favourite, and she'd fling her arms around his neck and give him big kisses on the cheeks, dissolving him into self-conscious mirth. Jami was especially precious to me, too; she just about saved my sanity during the year of Neal's absence because she was so funny. Her hair was so long, I put it up in a rubber band on top of her head like an umbrella and her antics never failed to make me laugh. She was never any trouble, and was always agreeable and affectionate.

One night, when Jack and I had finished eating and I'd put the dishes in the sink, we sat dreamily sipping our wine in the flickering patterns of the candlelight, absorbing the music of blues and ballad, both of us silent and pensive. My mind was catching images drifting peacefully in the glowing atmosphere when Jack's voice broke the stillness like a great mellow gong, vibrating clear through me.

'GOD...I love you!' I looked at him to be sure I'd heard right and met his blue eyes, so intense and piercing I had to look down again, and I couldn't even smile, my breath caught somewhere, and all I could manage was a whisper I didn't think he heard.

'I can't believe it.'

Quick as a flash, but low and strong, he said, 'I could convince you.' (Now why were my wits so scattered I didn't take him up on that offer? Dammit.) I could tell his eyes hadn't wavered, but I could only look at my glass, then I closed my eyes. I slid my hand along the table to his and he grasped it. Then he said softly, 'Let's dance.'

He held me close, cheek-to-cheek, and for a while we swayed together warm and blending. But my joy was too strong, my heart beating so fast, I broke away, filled our glasses, and he loaded the phonograph with mambos. We danced and danced, grinning and abandoned, sparks flying when we touched. It wasn't long before a bed was required, and he expressed his love the more.

These golden weeks drift like clouds on a sunny day in and out of my mind and dreams in vivid little vignettes. If the baby cried and Jack's light was still on, I'd take John into his room and sit on the bed beside Jack. He'd pat John and talk tender baby-talk to him, then tell me about his mother, Memere, and how he'd like us to meet. He'd read me her letters, and I'd add notes to her on his. Then there were the long afternoons when he would sing into the recorder accompanying himself on kitchen pans, oatmeal cartons or the table's edge. The breeze through the open French doors to the side yard was fragrant with the smell of burning leaves, an aroma that never failed to transport me back to Michigan or Vermont and him to Lowell.

All this pleasure and my descriptions of it to Neal pleased him less and less. Jack was now more interested in Neal's family than in him, while lonely brooding on long runs stoked his jealousy and resentment. Where was his old partner in crime? Where his excuse and sidekick for his own private desires? Then the chill of impending winter arrived, and with it the colds in the noses. When jobs became scarce, the men were home together more often, and the feeling of confinement increased the restlessness and irritation of them both, waiting and waiting for the call that never came. There was nothing of interest in San Jose, and San Francisco was too far without a good excuse. It became evident that wanderlust was tugging at Neal again, and the Mexican sun at Jack, and in me the seed of dread began to sprout.

Neal found the necessary reasons to drive the new car (this time a grey Nash Rambler) to San Francisco more often after a while, but he still couldn't persuade Jack to go with him or cover up for him. For his part, Jack reverted to ranting and raving, growling and swearing at publishers, bitterly resenting his failure to be accepted and appreciated. He had only been writing in the mornings, mostly polishing *Dr Sax*, I gathered. Nor was Jack blind to the cause of Neal's growing irascibility and resistance to his attempts to continue their former intellectual games. All Neal would talk to him about was his responsibilities and the expenses of a family. Jack got the message.

He told me he thought maybe I should have one husband at a time, and insisted on moving to San Francisco and a skid-row hotel. Neal felt guilty but relieved, and drove Jack to the City. Yet after less than a month, he persuaded Jack to return, establishing a better balance in all our affairs.

| THIRTY-FIVE |

In December the railroad laid off the men with the least seniority, Jack among them. His paranoia ceased, and his mood brightened. He could turn his thoughts and plans again towards Mexico, and shared with me fondly remembered scenes. During one of these recitals he suddenly stopped and looked hard at me, a new thought springing to mind: 'Carolyn! Why don't you come with me? Come visit me in Mexico! Please do!' He hugged me, lifting me off the floor. 'You've never had a vacation from the kids – not since you married Neal, even. You really should, you know. You ought to get away from the children sometimes – it would do you both good. Just think of it!'

I did think of it, and at first the idea scared me. I was such a possessive mother and so opinionated about children, even though I knew the books said it was good for them to be without mother from time to time. But mine were so little. These thoughts spun in my head and then flipped over, and I played with the prospect of being in Mexico with Jack. For a moment the fear gave way to a tempting thrill of pleasure and suspense. Jack said he'd talk to Neal about it; we both knew neither of us would consider it without his approval.

Neal's response was not exactly enthusiastic. He said flatly, 'Great idea. Of course you should get away from the kids, Ma.' In a way I had hoped he might say no. Then after a few days of listening to Jack paint ever more enticing pictures of good times with me, Neal began acting strangely. He would put things down too hard, he said very little, even being short with the children, which he'd never been, and he was unusually distracted. When I'd ask what was troubling him, he'd look at me with that 'You know what you've done' look of accusation that I myself had perfected. If I got any answer at all it was sarcastic. Jack was faring no better – Neal wouldn't talk to him at all.

Jack and I conferred and decided to beard the lion. When we asked Neal if he'd changed his mind, if he really didn't want me to go – or what the matter *was*, he said, 'No, no, you must go, of course, I insist,' all the while looking the martyr. It took me some time to sort it out, because I never thought I'd see Neal being this jealous of me; it was quite different from his flash of possessiveness on account of Bud. It was an interesting phenomenon, and I watched him a day or two more until his behaviour verged on the farcical.

Jack could stand no more either. He said, 'Hey, Neal, forget it, man. It's okay.'

I said, 'I won't go, Neal; I never wanted to without your blessing. We won't mention it again.' We put on cheery faces and went back to normal. Then Neal became contrite; he was not as relieved by our surrender as we had expected. We were all playing pinochle one evening, and I could tell Neal wasn't with it; there was something on his mind. He got up to get a beer, then stood in the doorway and plunged:

'Tell you what, kiddies. I'll make you a deal.' He swooped into the chair beside me and took my hand, stroking it. 'You let me drive Jack to Mexico now – just so's I can get some tea, see? And when I get back *you* go – stay as long as you like, an' I'll carry on here – everything will be fine, long as I have Miss Green. You see, darling, that way poor Jack won't have to hop those awful freights and sleep out in the cold and catch who knows what, and he'll get there twice as fast and in one piece, and I'll come right back, I promise, so you can go even sooner, right? See? Isn't that the *perfect* solution? Whattya say?' He looked from me to Jack and back again.

I dodged the thought that I was being traded for marijuana and tried to be practical.

'Can we afford two trips that far?'

'Yes, certainly, my dear. It won't cost a thing – only the gas. I'll do nothing but drive down, pick up the stuff and drive straight back – less'n a week – nothing. The Grey Ghost is in great shape; she'll make it easy.' Inwardly I smiled. Practicality had nothing to do with it. Neal saw a chance to 'go' and was rarin'.

'Yeess –' I stalled. 'I'll think about it.'

Think about it, I knew, was all I'd ever do. Then I'd get angry with myself when I realized what a slave I was. 'Why not, you shnook? When are you ever going to get a chance to live like this? Other people do it all the time. What's to lose? You complain about being confined, and when you get a chance to break out, you won't take it?' It didn't work. I knew too well I could never leave the children and relax. Maybe if they'd been older. And I had lingering doubts about Neal's conduct. Oh why was I so afraid of life?

I said nothing of my doubts to either man. I would have hurt Jack to reject his offer, and I was intrigued with Neal as a martyr to me – wondering how serious this pose really was. Meanwhile, no use denying I felt good. I thoughtfully agreed to the bargain. Neal forgot his misery and returned to his customary cheer when anticipating another 'road' adventure.

The morning of their departure arrived. Jack had packed only his seabag again, leaving in a big trunk his manuscripts and books to be held until his return – inevitable, he always thought. Neal took very little – only the necessary razor, toothbrush, underwear, his change of socks twice a day and half a dozen handkerchiefs.

The early morning was cold and foggy, the children still asleep. The men stowed their gear in the car and returned singly to bid me good bye. Neal was first, and in top form. Had it been an audition for a silent movie, he'd have swept the field. He wrapped me in his arms and kissed me long and desperately, then slowly backed away holding my hand in both of his and scanning my face with a tragic, love-lorn look. Abruptly he turned, wheeled and strode across the back porch, pausing only once at the door to look back and give his standard exit line: 'I'll be right back, darling.'

I remained standing by the kitchen table, trying to keep the appropriate expression on my face; there was another round to go, and this was all so strange. Jack came to me shyly but lovingly, and I felt a wrench at his leaving me and all my wonderful times with him, knowing as he didn't that I would not be coming to Mexico.

He held me close many minutes before he slid his cheek down mine to kiss me slowly, sweetly, and then whispered in my ear, 'It'll only be a week or two at most. Please don't fail me, Carolyn, I'll fix a place for us, and Neal will hurry home, don't worry. It's just "au revoir" for now – I love you.' And with another brief tender kiss he too backed away, looking with eyes of love, and on the porch blew another kiss before heading down the outside steps.

I dropped into a chair, dazed. *Well*! Going back in my mind over the scene it struck me as funny, and I couldn't help laughing aloud, which was a release; I knew this was a level of flattery never to be again. You may be sure that farewell was branded on my brain and heart forever. I remained in a semi-dream state the rest of the day, going about my routines only half plugged in.

When I was able to think clearly again and reconsider the options, I knew for sure I'd never go to Mexico, never leave the children for weeks at a time. But I'd have to wait for Neal's return to find a way out, and not hurt Jack or lose the ground I'd gained. At least this trip of Neal's left me with no anxieties, no sense of loss, and warmed by the feeling of being so loved I was patient with the children, unhurried and serene. What a blessed change.

A day or two later I got an unusual letter from Neal – unusual in that it was so unnecessary in its reassurances, although this time these had more of a ring of truth:

> Dear, dear wife Carolyn, Dolly: Sitting in the gray ghost Nash in front of Bill Burroughs house in which Jack and he are sleeping. I write by light of Brakielanternfreightsize. My heart is bleeding for you.
>
> From S.J. to Bakersfield – *first* stop for gas – my thoughts of you filled my mind so that I knew I was composing great love letters. Naturally, I came by lovely things to say to you – mostly it came out – I love *you*.

He briefly catalogued the rest of the journey, putting in, 'I thought of you at every turn,' and ended with 'I have got to mail this now. Everything all O.K. Be home Sat. P.M. – leaving here Thurs. A.M. *This is truth*: I have not and *will not* touch any kind of any ole female – as I am with B.B. and Jack, talking only. Love, N.'

Saturday evening he spun into the courtyard right on schedule, but he walked into the house like a condemned man, grim and silent.

At first I was shocked and didn't understand. He was tired? He hadn't scored? The car was ruined? He spoke very little about the trip down, aside from a snide remark or two at Jack's expense and how he couldn't drive, 'couldn't even remember the clutch'. There was nothing he wished to relate about the trip back – 'just drove'. Then what was the matter with him?

We sat next to each other drinking coffee, when impulsively he leaned over and put his head in my lap, squeezing the hand that lay there. I stroked his hair and said, 'What is it, dear?' But instead of answering me, he got up and walked into our bedroom. I followed, and blinked at what I saw. There was Neal, standing in the corner, his forehead actually against the wall. (This man had obviously seen too many old movies.) Ah, ha! Now I got it – but I had to hurry out to stifle the impulse to laugh. So that was it: now that he'd had his part of the bargain, he was campaigning to get out of keeping the other half – my half!

Maybe this would be my out. I tried to play his game and pretend I didn't find anything unusual in his behaviour for a while; it was too fascinating to see what he'd do next.

A letter from Jack sent him into paroxysms of grief and tugged me in both directions. Jack told us he had rented two rooms on Bill's roof, had bought Mexican pottery to brighten it, and was buying delicacies and wine for impossibly low prices. He rhapsodized about the perfection of the location to write, as well as enjoy the vast sky, day or night. He looked forward to writing a great new novel there. He said he was all ready for my visit and was I coming? He sent love to the children one by one, and sent love and kisses to me. He then added a clincher to me, saying he had just received my letter.

He asked about Neal's return, and said how lonely he was and feared he'd never be satisfied. He said being with us he had regained his love of life and specifically of us – and then he begged me to come, since his new home was all ready, and again rhapsodized on what we'd do and eat. More kisses.

If I could only make this dream actually come true. If only it weren't so far away, and I could just *be* there, not have to traverse the miles between. But, ah, no, the idea of setting out alone on that journey was too much, and I couldn't watch Neal's apparent agony any more. Best to give up the game and get back to realistic living. So, I solemnly told Neal that of course I'd never leave him if he asked me not to. Nothing could make me happier than to see him smile, his brow unfurrow, the gloom dispelled.

'Now, how are we going to tell Jack without reactivating his paranoia?' I got out paper and pen to compose the 'Dear John' letter.

Neal snorted, '*Pah* – he'll get over it. Serves him right for stealing other men's wives.'

'You keep forgetting, Dear Heart, it was your idea in the first place.'

'How can you say an untrue thing like that? Not a bit of it. *Harrumph*.Why would I ever do such a stupid thing?' And he stalked around me waving his arms in mock seriousness.

'Well, there was LuAnne –'

'I never did. You're mistaken, my dear – besides, altogether different – I gotta run.' And he did, calling back, 'Tell the old boy to get his own girl.' I laughed and shook my head. What to do with these two? But it had been Jack once again who had furnished the cement to bind our little family closer together. I sat a long time musing and smiling and looking forward to the Christmas I could plan in this big old house.

The mail arrived before I'd thought of a thing to say to Jack, and with it came a note from him making it unnecessary. He begged my pardon for leaving Mexico to go back to his mother for Christmas. He said he hadn't done it on purpose, which I didn't quite understand. He said he loved me, and loved me for loving him, and what could we do. He said he'd write, and for me not to pass up my vacations. He signed it 'Awful Jack, fool', and asked about the children and me. Poor Jack. At first we thought it was just that he could not be alone for long. All had worked out for the best, and Memere would be happier too.

Neal showed his appreciation of my loyalty by giving us all a warm and bountiful Christmas, which we recorded, and his apparent contentment spread over all of us like a blanket. He was cut off the railroad on the first of the year, and was gone a lot seeking other interim employment, but he was home every evening for dinner.

I gave a good deal of thought to Jack's sudden change of heart, and after a letter from Allen I felt my diagnosis was correct. Allen said Jack and his mother had left Florida, she tired of the south and living in Caroline's family circle, and they had returned to Long Island.

Jack is back here. Have seen him not much, though. He's at his mother's house hiding out, comes in to see his friends seldom – never except thru my arranging – Came in in time for New Years, cried drunk & high in cab at dawn on way home. Couldn't tell why crying, except general recognition of the past and self back in N.Y. – older and (no?) wiser... and I feel there's some underlying battle somewhere lurking, tea, excitement organizing – have feeling he doesn't respect presence of individual he's with (me) and is creating artificial excitement. He solitary and excited overly – won't talk – though of course knows, sees what I am thinking, and says, 'I want to see you and talk to you 4 times a year... I think his writing, except for preoccupation with self as subject is advancing greatly. Maybe right preoccupation but wrong lament, lament, lament for him. I keep thinking he has no adult society & marriage world to write about and keeps repeating lament for Mother. New book about 17 year old Mary Carney love affair...

It seemed to corroborate what my analysis of Jack's sudden move had been. I figured Jack knew that if he spent weeks alone with me without Neal, he wouldn't want me to go back to Neal, but knew he had to let me. I felt he really did love me too much for his own good, but there was no way we could be together on a permanent basis (which I wouldn't want), so he was suffering from the loss. Years later when I saw him alone again, I asked him if I was wrong. He told me that was exactly how he'd felt, and his diving into his first love affair let him express the kind of emotions one feels so strongly for a first love and which he'd felt for me: a sort of purging.

We then got a letter from Jack himself, quite cheerful but also rather scatterbrained. He said he was burying himself in writing before he thought about railroad work, and his legs were bad. He then rhapsodized about winter weather in New York and long walks in the snow. He had no girls, no money. He just wrote and slept. He said the world ends with everyone alone, but that was how we started and it was good. He rambled on about nothing, how everything was in order, husbands lived with their wives, and said he still loved us.

Neal and I read and sighed. Dear Jack: one minute it's the balmy warm exotic nights of Mexico with the Indians, *fellaheen* or Faustian, that made life idyllic; the next minute it's snow and ice and winter storms. Before we could answer he wrote again to me. He asked why I hadn't written him, and was I mad at him for not trying to steal or take me away from Neal. He wanted to know how Jami was, and me. He said he was taking my advice and using tea for special occasions (in the previous letter he'd said every night). He hoped I was well, wanted a pizza, or the recipe, said otherwise to eat one for him, but write to him. All very urgent, with lots of exclamation points.

He then launched into rhapsodies describing John Clellan Holmes's new house in minute detail, He said, like him, I'd die seeing it. John was a close friend who'd just sold his book, *Go*, in which Jack, Neal and Allen were characters. Jack envied him on both counts. Neal and I agreed that if ever Jack was homesick, he was now – but for which and whose home?

He continued to write frequently. In early spring I got a long, rambling, tea-high letter he'd written at dawn, having been half awake all night thinking that maybe the railroad was beginning to pick up. He fantasized about bringing his mother to live in a trailer in a scruffy town at the bottom of the bay and working on the railroad. He interrupted his story by saying he would be my Valentine as I had asked him in a previous letter. After more fantasy he suddenly switched again and begged me to send him a birthday gift I'd offered – an ounce of tea.

He said if the railroad did call him he thought he would go, but he thought he should live alone in either a San Francisco skid-row place or one in San Jose. He would visit me, or perhaps only when Neal would bring him. If Neal didn't want to, then he had a right to be in California for his own reasons. He remembered being told that LuAnne's husband, Ray Murphy, was hunting Neal with murder in mind, so Jack said he wasn't a Ray Murphy and had reasons to defend his skull. He said he was all through with what he'd gone through with me, and no woman owned him, not even me, who should. He was starting on something new. He was longing to see his children again, and missed their walks. He wished his sweetheart (me) goodnight. He must get to work, and not goof off writing letters to other men's wives.

The next week brought another anxious plea. He hoped Neal had forgiven him, as he had done in October. He said if the SP didn't call him soon, he'd try Canadian railroads near his own people, but he would miss me and the kiddies.

To us it didn't sound as though Jack really knew *what* he wanted. In spite of his backward looks to our good times and his suffering for not having me, if he fantasized about me as a wife he wasn't thinking very realistically, at least at this time when he couldn't support a family yet. He had rejected his own daughter forcefully for the same reason; his freedom was essential to him if he were to continue writing his chosen way. He had such set views on how children should be raised (I often got suggestions), nothing less was possible for him.

As for me, he was far too moody, too touchy and too wrapped up in himself. This 'self' absorption might be what helped him to write so well. Locked up in the ivory tower of self he could observe and report all the details of life outside, but his efforts to join in and partake of what he saw were mostly disappointing; he felt threatened and thwarted.

Perhaps that was one of the fascinations Neal held for him. He envied Neal's ability to make life happen, to be a principal in the action, not a bystander. And when Jack made love, he had an air of apology, a victim of the 'whore/madonna' syndrome, I was sure. I felt he never gave of himself completely; I suspected he preferred the woman to manage the event, so he could play the innocent.

I felt the success of our relationship was due to my efforts to be alert to his moods and desires, not impose my own. I was allowed to share his observations, which I enjoyed, and he liked company – as long as it was sympathetic to him. I knew better than to express any criticism or suspicion of his inner motives – an area where he was seldom objective. Neal was such a perfect listener to my ideas, I didn't need Jack for that, but I'd never known a man with such a tender heart, nor one so vulnerable.

I wondered if he was ashamed to be gentle and compassionate. He sometimes put on a show of bravado and coarseness, which embarrassed me. The Sal in *On the Road* was rarely the man I knew; he seemed to be trying more to imitate Dean's behaviour or what he would like to be. In Denver he used to brag about getting into fist fights if some guy doubted his toughness. I supposed that came from having been conditioned, as I had, by a society that considered 'real men' were like that. Usually, he had to be drunk to behave so macho. In his last years, never without a bottle, he became worse, crude and disgustingly masochistic.

| THIRTY-SIX |

Neal failed to find a job right away, and by the third week of January '53 our finances were in a near desperate state again. Then he heard there was work on the Southern Division. A 'boomer', or freelance brakeman, could make up to $600 a month, really big money to us then. Neal burst in with the glad tidings, and prepared to leave the next morning, February 1. I accepted his decision sorrowfully, re-membering the summer of '48, but again the money was more important. We'd even miss his birthday on the eighth. The change in Neal since Jack left had made the past six weeks almost like a honey-moon, or the nearest we ever got to one. Now, when we were almost whole, another separation to endure. But sometimes a lurking thought told me our marriage would have been doomed without these 'spaces in our togetherness', had he chosen a different occupation.

We all had lingering farewells, and Neal telephoned me to say he had arrived safely in Indio, just like a regular husband. Daily we wrote passionate love letters, saying all the things we'd wanted to in the past when my disapproving attitude forbade them. He commented on my detailed descriptions of our domesticity and our struggles without him, recitals which soon took on my complaints and whining on how we'd been so happy together, how I hated being married and yet alone.

Again, he was to have been gone only two weeks, but when the second week ended, instead of Neal I got a dozen red roses and a Valentine card, on which was written, 'Double the days that 14 are, and that's the day that I'll be thar.' I was deeply touched by this unexpected sweetness, as I'd been with my wedding corsage, and had to brush away a sentimental tear.

In the midst of my self-pity came another long letter from Jack, shot through with wistful nostalgia, making a hard knot form in my throat as I read. Again he reviewed my possibly being mad at him for Mexico, and again he went into the living arrangements away from us were he called back to the railroad, and complaining about doing things Neal wanted because he always allowed himself to be led around and he'd trusted Neal, etc. etc. He said the publishers would publish his book if his name were Faulkner, and they said it would be at a loss, but they'd be interested in one that would make a profit. He said he had this great one about his first Proustian love story ready to go.

Then a detailed description of an old 1650 house near John Holmes's with 20 acres to farm and the original antiques to go with it. There was a sinking cemetery surrounded by trees blowing in the sea wind, only a mile away. Then he broke off and asked if I still wanted to go to Mexico, and he'd meet me next week when he was going for tea, then said no, next month, and that he was only smoking it in moderation. He felt he would just go to a dumpy grave and no one would care. But love was all that counted, and he would always love me the way we had loved. He asked if I wanted to get him to write to me instead of Neal, which was all he did now, but then laughed at the idea.

Neal was outshining himself in his daily letters too, telling me how lonely he was, with paragraphs of poetic compliments and longing: 'will you sing to me in our bedroom we depapered and painted? Love songs?'

Why couldn't I find the fulfilment of my own longings in one or the other of these men, both or neither? For here I still sat – alone. What good was it to be loved by two men if I couldn't be with either? Reading letters from the two of them, I pondered their differences again. Jack always seemed to be straining to subdue his real feelings, whereas Neal welcomed the opportunity to verbalize his love, even if he didn't feel any action was required to uphold his avowals. I supposed he wished he *could* believe in his words more. Jack had the feelings; Neal had the words, yet neither could bring the love directed at me into my experience, or join it with mine in any sustained constructive way. I hung on for another two weeks, at the end of which: 'Dear Baby: It's gone from bad to worse; hold onto yourself... THEY WON'T RELEASE ME! But they *must* before 13 March, cause that's when I have to be back on the Coast Division. So lookie here, it's really for the best...' And he desperately tried to convince me, outlining our need for the money, detailing his own loneliness, praising my help and planning all the household and garden tasks he was eager to engage in. 'I'm only sorry I'm not handy... and could make toys for the kids.' There followed three or four pages more of love.

But my house of fortitude was built on sand, and it tumbled down around me. I wrote more whingeing letters telling him the washing machine had broken, Johnny had a fever, and I should be celebrating the money he was making. I growled about having to play second fiddle to the damned railroad, but I sympathized with his trying to do his best with all the demands I made on him, and promised not to take out my frustrations on him any more. I told him Jack had written asking for a letter from him about the railroad and his fears of being disliked. 'B. Goodman playing "My Guy's Come Back"... thought I'd be singing that, too.' In spite of my efforts, my self-pity persisted:

> Sunday is too awful...our peaceful living room...all rearranged, is fine for funnies and the concert and the almond tree almost through blooming. I'm sick of telling you of things I enjoyed you are never here to share...I fear again you've found other interests and that's not so good an attitude.
>
> A big drunk just walked right in the front door. I'm still shaking. He said he wanted food. I gave him 50c cause I couldn't get him out. He grabbed Johnny and kissed him. Johnny screamed. The guy cried...(he has 3 of his own.) I called the landlord for a lock. Think of all the times, especially nite I go to the Forests for hours. Wish I had a husband at such times – damn the money...if it means this. I guess I'm incorrigibly selfish...I'll *try* not to be bitter again. Love, C.

Undaunted by my whining, Neal continued his cheer and encouragement. Although he gave me a factual account of his deadly hot days and cold lonely nights, he never complained. I told him it was part of my job to comfort him, but I guess the facts said it all. That spring I believed everything Neal wrote, since I knew people can and must change, and 'with love all things are possible.'

Now he was saying he can 'look at women without passion...I ain't spoke to anything resembling woman or female sorceresses.' I actually told him I would understand if he had a 'splurge' once in a while, and his response was he was 'horrified' by such a suggestion, and don't I do any such thing.

> I read Proust slowly and realize I really can write as he does. Of course he's better but I'm younger, and while less brilliant, still have a chance to learn how, with your help and patience. I'm terribly interested in life and wish you were here to share my musings and comments about living and dead things that pass so abstractly before me.
>
> When I get home we'll be in our rearranged bedroom and read to each other again all our love letters – all too

few they are, so we'll make up for it by telling each other,
mouth to ear, all the things we feel and all we want to say
and have wanted to say forever. Just remember this: I
have solved our sex problem. Don't forget to remind me
to tell you about it when I get home.

How eloquent he was; where did he find the energy? (I only learned
long after he'd died – thank Heaven – that he was as eloquent in
writing sex letters to Diana at the same time. He should have written
romance novels for bucks.)

Oh those glorious reunions – this one far and away the best yet –
and the harvest of the words we'd been sowing all these weeks. I
think Neal, too, thought a real change had occurred. Or so he made
me believe.

In any case three weeks were all we were allowed of this smug
complacency – and no sex solution – before we were presented with
another challenge.

| THIRTY-SEVEN |

Late in the night of April 10, 1953, the telephone's shrill scream
awakened me. The fear that overshadows all railroad wives was
actualized: Neal had been hurt. He had been taken by ambulance
from Millbrae to the SP Hospital in San Francisco. All I could learn
was that the accident involved a leg, but he was alive and would
recover. I was shivering in my thin pyjamas when I hung up the
phone. Wrapping my robe around me I walked through the moonlit
rooms, trying to subdue my quivering nerves and consider how this
would affect us all. I had little to go on, and had to wait until
morning for more information. Sleep was a bonus that night.

I left the children with Marie and drove the fifty miles to the
hospital. When I arrived, Neal was conscious but woozy. His story
lacked details. He could remember being on top of a boxcar that had
just been shunted into a siding. He was setting the brake when the
car hit the bumper and Neal flew off, landing on the toe of his iron-
toed boot, so the force of his fall tore the foot backwards, nearly
severing it completely. Most of the bones in his foot and ankle were
broken. The doctors had straightened it out and sewn it back together
the best they could for now. His leg hung in a huge cast and complex

traction apparatus, and the doctors said he'd stay like that for from four to six weeks. He would probably never walk on that foot again, they said.

Neal was too groggy to talk very long, just held my hand and tried to smile. Nevertheless, he told me he had been required to dictate and sign a description of the accident already.

On my drive home, I faced another long separation, building my life alone once more. This time I hung on to the fact that this summer he'd be home *all* the time if inactive.

In a day or two I began being bombarded by tales from other rail-road men of their accidents; how to file a claim, what to watch out for, how much money to expect from a damage settlement – no two stories alike, and the figures astronomical. It was all very bewildering, and nothing could be done just yet.

In another month the doctors completed all the operations possible for the time being, and Neal was strong enough to come home. He still had to stay prone most of the time; the cast was too heavy for him to use his crutches for more than a few minutes, but at least he could get to the bathroom and most meals. With great ceremony, the children and I settled him on the living-room couch, where he had an unobstructed view of most of the house as well as the front yard and the street beyond. I flooded him with books, magazines, news-papers and the radio, and he renewed his determination to work on his writing, so paper, pens and pencils were put at the ready.

First, however, he answered Jack, telling him to come out again and check with the crew-clerk. His attitude was cordial if not as demanding as on former occasions. He told Jack quite matter-of-factly that he was to stay with us. I did not add extra urging this time, not sure whether Jack's presence would help entertain Neal or widen the rift with jealousy.

In mid-May a welcome letter from Allen arrived, and I poured us each a cup of coffee and sat down to read it aloud. It was a long one, and we settled ourselves to relish it.

> Then Jack told me a few days ago about your accident. I groaned when I read. But aren't you fortunate having wife and children around to care for you in pain and distress? Oh, old father! What happened?
> (But not in T-hi incomprehensible detail) Are you getting compensation? Maybe you can read or improve your

knowledge with the leisure. I'll bet you sit around blasting and coughing all day. Someday we will yet be of all one family. Now I'm on a new kick 2 weeks old, a very beautiful kick, which I invite you to share.

Allen had discovered Chinese painting and hence oriental philosophy, and I suppose he thought he had a captive audience. 'China is a bleak great blank in our intimate knowledge...Much of the Buddhist writing you see is not interesting, vague, etc., because it has no context to us...' But through his study of the art and dynasties,

> you begin to see the vastitude and intelligence of the yellow man...I daily grow hunger on Orient...deeply impressed by a recording of Ghandi speaking...well, anyway, he mentions in his speech the great teachers: Buddha, Christ and (of all people – Zoroaster; who the hell that is I don't know...) Z in West is a vague magical name, somewhat of a seance joke.

I guessed Allen didn't know Ghandi was Hindu.

There was a knock at the back door. I handed the letter to Neal to read the long Chinese poem included, and went to see who it was.

'Jack! Why, how did you get here? Why didn't you call?' I didn't know whether to embrace him, but I put my hand on his arm. He looked at me shyly from under his brows, shuffling his feet.

'I jes' thought I'd surprise you – but I ain't gonna stay.'

Neal bellowed, 'Nonsense! Come in here and put your gear in your room.' Jack chuckled, and I took his hand, leading him in to Neal. Jack shook his head when he saw Neal's cast.

'There's the old crip – my God, man, that thing's bigger'n you are! What some guys won't do to get outa work, hey?'

I went for more coffee while they bantered, then Jack and I settled down near Neal. Neal showed Jack the letter from Allen and asked, 'What do you think of Allen's new oriental kick?'

'Oh, yeah – he's been filling my head full of it for weeks. Might be something in it – I dunno – I only read a little Buddhism, but I dig Gautama – don't know about the Zen stuff.'

'Hmm. Well, ha, we'll have to find some books, Ma, and brush up on our own vague rememberings; gotta keep up with ole Allen.'

Jack stayed for the weekend, but that was all. He and I had few minutes alone, whether by accident or design. At least I got the chance to ask him about my Mexico theory, which he validated, so we could now let it rest.

There was a heavy aura of sadness, and his presence was even more engulfing in its tenderness and warmth, perhaps because I knew it couldn't last. He had made up his mind. He walked with the girls and talked to Neal, and Neal listened more attentively, tuning his own awareness to Jack's and reaffirming their brotherhood. Both Neal and I were concerned about Jack's next move, but he said he'd go find Al Sublette, the mixed-race college student he had befriended on Russell Street. He had signed on the extra board, but he would stay in San Francisco. We could still visit each other. We all knew it was best, and it seemed we'd passed some sort of milestone, the kind that demands a sacrifice.

Jack's plan of settling in San Francisco was thwarted at first when he drew a two-week hold-down in San Luis, followed by a local freight run between San Francisco and San Jose. He always returned to the Cameo Hotel to sleep. This run meant rising very early each day, punctuality a must on the railroad, obviously.

A time or two he brought Al Sublette for a brief visit, avoiding any idea of we two being alone together. Although he tried to show enthusiasm for writing about his impressions of life around the Cameo, of digging the bars and music, everything had a hollow ring. It became obvious he was not happy, and was drinking more.

The strain and his lack of expertise, plus his antagonism towards the unempathetic conductor he was working under, finally got to him. As suddenly as he had arrived, he was gone. Al came for the weekend alone, and told us Jack felt the railroad was too slow or something, and he had gone home to New York and then shipped out.

'He didn't even call to say good bye,' I said sadly.

'Well,' Al explained, 'He was pretty drunk the night before he left; I guess he didn't know what to say. I'm sure he'll write.'

He did write, but didn't mail the letter for a week. For Jack, it was a singularly uninformative letter and brief. He was in a nostalgic mood. He was on a ship sailing in warm seas off the west coast of Mexico, looking at an isolated island with a beach, behind which were huge mountains. He thought it might be a Mexican penal colony. He described the colours in the sky and sea, the birds, shark fins. He said he had a new job as a waiter in the officer's saloon, and that they would be going south to Panama, then up between Yucatan and Cuba to 'dull, dumb Mobile', but he didn't know where after that. He wrote his lyrical, colourful prose describing the seas, the ship as if a sailing ship being directed by a shrouded sage in his imagination, and contrasting the southern seas with the cold northern ones. He begged us to write, and sent love and kisses. It was a relief to read the old Jack again.

Al Sublette was not in college this semester, but was to sail on a ship he was expecting, Jack having told him of the advantages of a seaman's life, especially financially. Al came often to visit and to keep up with Jack. He had never met Allen, but he'd heard so much about him he enjoyed reading his letters. One time Neal handed him the latest. After a minute or two, Al put the letter down, unfinished. He looked grim but said nothing. Neal and I looked at each other wondering. Neal picked up the letter and scanned it, stopping where he figured Al had. Allen had asked us about the 'unidentified darky'. Neal read it aloud. 'Ah, yes – now look here, Al,' and he explained Allen's nature and how he had no racial prejudices just poetic phrases, or something like that, but he had a warm heart and had suffered from prejudice himself.

This was one of Neal's traits of character I was proud of, even if he often made me cringe. He would bring any such misunderstanding out in the open to be aired and faced head-on, so it could be cleared up, overcome and not left to fester. On this occasion, Al did see the light, and from then on he felt comfortable discussing any racial situation he encountered, and was pleased to have someone with whom he could talk about it.

When Al got a ship on its way to Honolulu, he wrote us to say he had a job as a bellboy. 'Perhaps Neal would call this a "towel over the wrist" flunky job' (which was how Neal had described Jack's job as a waiter with misgivings as to his tenacity or success). 'But,' continued Al, 'when you conduct yourself right, you command respect.'

Jack was not as resigned to conducting *himself* properly in order to 'command respect'. He soon rebelled at his 'flunky' status, as Neal had predicted, and, with customary temper and paranoia, jumped ship in Panama and returned to Richmond Hill and Memere. Allen informed us of this and referred to Jack sadly as 'the thing from another world – of his own making, in which he'll allow only himself'.

In August I decided to write to Jack, concerned why he hadn't written to us. He answered at once, saying he had written a long letter a month previously and supposed we'd never received it, which was true. He speculated on how mail can get lost. Then he went on a paranoid trip, imagining that Neal wanted to remove the 'taint' of him and had probably destroyed my copy of *The Town and the City*, and had read and torn up the big 'gushletter' without telling me about it. He then suggested the FBI had taken it from our porch or it was in the dead-letter bin.

This was extremely frustrating, of course, but I knew Neal would never have done such a thing. I would certainly have liked to have read that letter, but I half suspected Jack had never sent it, afraid to reopen old dreams. I doubted letters got lost, especially with return addresses on them. All of Jack's letters were precious to us, not only for what he said but how he said it.

He sent another letter, somewhat watered down from that one, but still indicating his love was just as strong. He thought of me all the time and was haunted by our earlier days of love when he didn't hear of them, but when he did they gave him solace. He said his location was due to being restless and yearning to travel, not avoiding sweet eternity in San Jose.

Neal now turned his attention to pressuring Allen to come for a visit, an idea Allen had toyed with for the last six years. Neal used similar persuasions he'd used on Jack, and then 'Do your best in this, 'cause life so simple, good and easy here, that it's actually unreal seeming, like a joke or dream, no reason for worries, tho from old experience I try to, and all troubles of world are like mirage one reads about only to keep abreast and pass time.'

Allen replied that he came close to joining us after reading this letter, but he was still not ready. I was just as glad; we seemed to have reached another zenith of harmony, and I'd not had nearly enough.

| THIRTY-EIGHT |

No doubt a great deal of our peace was due to the fact that, as Neal had said, we had no financial hassles for once. The railroad had offered us $1800, a ridiculous sum according to the other conductors, so we decided to take their advice and hire the lawyer whose specialty was cases against the Southern Pacific Railroad.

Mr B. was a lively little Italian, brusque, outspoken (in loud tones) and confident. His crowning recommendation as far as Neal was concerned was that he had eight Cadillacs and allowed Neal to drive one to the San Francisco courthouse. We soon learned in what awe his name was held. He warned us the suit would take several months, but he would arrange for our support until the trial, the amount to be subtracted from the settlement. There was nothing for us to do but wait.

While home the first month Neal grew a goatee and shaved his head again. It made him look heavier, tougher, not as boyish and, as before, I felt I had a new man to get used to. He spent his days reading, either newspapers and magazines or Céline and Dostoevsky. He'd listen to every ballgame and guzzle coffee or beer, but when he was stronger he went outside with the children and watched them swing or play in the plastic pool. I marvelled at the endless patience he had with them; how I admired his reasonable approach and the calm, loving way he'd settle their disputes, with none of the anxiety that soured my supervision.

The biggest relief and pleasure was to be free of telephone minding. We could now go out to drive-in movies. We would collapse the back seat in the stationwagon so that Neal and his cast could stretch out, comfortably propped on pillows and covered with a light blanket. I was now the driver.

The first time we did this, however, I was mystified by the cashier's embarrassed double-take when I handed her the money. After parking I looked back at Neal and understood. He was lying on one side of the car, completely covered with the blanket so none of his cast showed – as though waiting for me to join him.

'Neal! You nut! That looks terrible – hunh – what a set-up. Everybody calls drive-ins "passion pits", but that looks a tad too obvious.' He only laughed, getting a kick out of the girl's shock, but he did uncover the cast while warbling, 'I'm in the nuuuude for luuve.'

One morning soon after Neal could hobble about some, the children came running into the house babbling all together in terror. I ran to the front window and saw fire engines everywhere. Two were parked in the empty lot next door, and a huge one was just swinging into our driveway. Marie came running from her house as fireman swarmed like flies over both our yards.

We all calmed down when one of them explained they had to burn the dry grass and weeds in the lot next to us, and asked if we would help. We agreed to hose our fence to stop the fire at our boundaries, and also to help them remove any articles that either wouldn't burn or we wished to save. I knew of one. Dick got out the hoses while Marie and I settled the children on their front porch, where they could watch out of the way, with strict orders to stay put.

I raced into the house to get Neal – not because we needed him, but because I knew he had planted marijuana in that lot.

I was wringing my hands. 'What'll we do? Will they recognize them? We'll deny any knowledge, right? Won't know what they're talking about, just like the Forests would do.' As I prattled I was trying to help him into his jeans. Rarely had I seen Neal so agitated.

'Great Caesar's ghost! We can't let them *burn* them! Come on, Ma, we gotta save the crops! Help me up.' This wasn't at all what I'd had in mind, but I knew it was useless to argue. For months he'd been proudly watching the plants grow, and they were nearly ready for harvest. We agreed that I would go over into the vacant lot, try to pull up the plants, and throw them over the fence to him. He would act as clean-up man for anything Marie and I tossed over. Naturally, we didn't tell the Forests about these 'weeds', and I must have put on my star performance acting innocent and busily occupied while I'd surreptitiously give a yank at the specified plants whenever I got the chance. They were firmly rooted in the dry ground, and it took me quite a while. Neal was positively apoplectic, and I nearly was. His sweat may have been cold, but I was closer to the fires, all sorts.

At last the largest plant let go. I dropped it quickly and reached for something else – a can, a piece of wood, a cigarette pack – sure someone was watching, guessing or recognizing the plant. One by one I uprooted them. Then the paranoid thought crossed my mind that maybe the whole purpose of this 'raid' was to find out who would try and save these plants. I knew dumb kids had planted tea in the park at the end of the street, and just that had happened. I quickly quelled my rising panic and concentrated on looking dumb.

When the firemen began rolling up their hoses and everyone's attention was directed elsewhere, I picked up the plants and flung them at Neal. With his 'pile of brush', he hastily hobbled around to the other side of the house and disappeared. The Forests departed to wash, I collected my children and was glad to go inside. Neal was making a great event out of the narrow escape – not ours, but the plants. He was overjoyed at our success, praised my heroism over

The author in 1946.

Schoolboy Neal, 1941. He played hookey the day it was announced that ties were to be worn for the school photograph.

below The two sides of Neal's first wife LuAnne, both photographs taken in 1946, the year of her high-school graduation.

In love. San Francisco, October 1947.

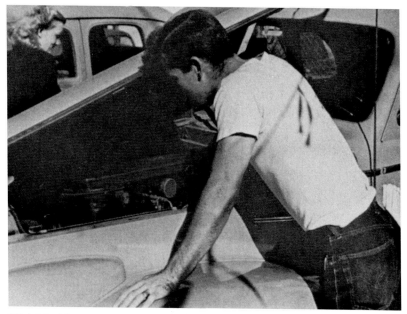

With Neal hunting a used car, San Francisco, 1948.

Neal with Southern Pacific colleagues, 1949.

Christmas 1949, with Helen and Al Hinkle, and Bill Tomson.

Neal with Diana Hansen and family, Tarrytown, NY, 1950.

With Jack, plus Cathy and, on Jack's knee, Jami, 1951.

Neal with John Allen and Jami, 1952.

Neal and Jack, 1952.

Neal, 1952.

Jack, 1952.

Neal, Jack and Cathy, 1952.

Jack, left, and Neal in San Jose, 1952.

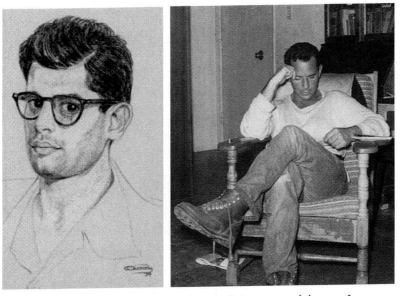

Portrait of Allen Ginsberg by the author, 1954.

Jack in the living room of the new Los Gatos home, 1955.

(left to right) Peter Orlovsky, Allen, Natalie Jackson, and Neal, San Francisco, 1956.

Neal, Los Gatos, 1960 – after a hard day at the tire recapping shop.

Neal as family man.

Taken to send to Neal in San Quentin in 1959. The sad expression was designed to make an impression on his jailers, though the emotion was real enough.

below Neal in heaven – a car and a girl, any time, any place (actually with Anne Murphy, 1960).

Gavin Arthur.

Neal 'hammer-
flipping' with the
Merry Pranksters'
bus, 1966.

Neal, near the end.

Destination 'Further.' The Merry Pranksters' bus on Ken Kesey's ranch in Oregon, July 1988.

and above, and gleefully showed me how he had hung the precious trophies upside down in the back of the coat closet behind the winter clothes. In spite of all our heroism, the crop was almost worthless. It seemed really unfair.

Not long after, the idyllic picture of our life Neal had painted for Allen began to pall for him. As the summer waned, so did Neal's satisfaction in idleness. He withdrew himself and his participation, smoked tea constantly and, as though mesmerized, lay for hours with eyes closed listening to music on the radio or the incessant ballgames. He moved his seat of operations to our bedroom, read less, slept more, increased the masturbation, and spoke hardly a word to anyone – except the children, with whom he could always put on a show of normality. I didn't think of it then, but later I wondered if the label manic-depressive, given by the psychologists, might fit him now, or was it the tea?

My own impatience and irritability grew from cleaning up the sheets of newspapers and magazines littering the bedroom every day and failing to rouse his interest in any subject, receiving only monosyllabic replies. Difficult for both of us was the continual postponement of the trial. I was eager to be able to plan the use of the money. Although Mr. B. had sued for $75,000, I knew we'd get only a part of that, but how much? When I'd try to pin him down to a realistic amount, he'd flare up at me, insisting we could get nothing less than the full amount. I still wouldn't believe it, and had to keep at bay tempting daydreams.

At the beginning of Neal's treatment, the SP doctors were confident he would never walk again. When the first cast came off and further repair was accomplished, they thought perhaps he could work limited service – passenger trains only. Neal decided otherwise. Full reinstatement was his only goal. Every day he worked on stretching and loosening the rebuilt tendons, exercising, soaking, massaging.

During the autumn, Allen and Jack also seemed to enter a gradual decline into the slough of despond. Although Allen's letters began with only his usual flux of restless frustrations, as winter approached his irritability and complaints increased.

> I was wrong not to have written since your last letter so long ago, so much more so since you invited me out – but the thing is, there is such a kind of confusion and hesitancy about life – moves in me that I kept putting

off...Jack here is worried you don't answer his letter, thinks you rejected him & wants word from you. If you talk to him straight whatever you think he will accept, so do...I am handling Jack's books – so far successfully & *On the Road* will be published except for whatever slips there are between cups and lips. Otherwise, except for the romance of cocktails with his publishers, my worklife as copyboy is grubby...you should maybe write a novel of such fatal dissatisfaction – your own (what is yours? any? or are you redeemed by your early settling down? What would you have wanted to do ideally?)

How I wished Neal would put some thought into and answer that one; how many times had I asked and would I ask the same question. Then Allen told us of a surprising action he'd taken: 'I telephoned Eisenhower last week (it cost me $2.00). "Rosenbergs are pathetic. Government will sordid. Execution obscene. America caught in cruxifixion machine only barbarians want them burned. I say stop it before we fill our souls with deathhouse horror." Didn't do no good.'

This marked the first time we heard of Allen *doing* anything outright about his political condemnations, and to us it was a drastic measure; we could not have imagined then what more it was to lead to.

| THIRTY-NINE |

As I've said, I'd had a fair dose of psychology in schools: psychoanalysis with Eric Fromm as well as clinical psychology in college, then abnormal and further clinical psychology as an occupational therapist. The psychologists seemed satisfied with testing and making pronouncements, but I never saw much effort going into helping afflicted people or their victims. There are hundreds of people with minor, borderline or serious cases moving about with us every day. Neal's diagnosis did nothing to change our ways of living. He accepted it as likely, and I tried to deny and soften. The psychiatrists made no suggestions or gave any advice as to how best to cope.

Jack had just discovered, courtesy of Bill Burroughs, Wilhelm Reich's book *Function of the Orgasm*. Needless to say, the emphasis on sex being necessary at all times appealed to Neal. As for me, Jack's suggestion gave me an idea.

I hunted up all my psychology books: Freud, James, Jung, Fromm and Horney, as well as textbooks. There had to be some answers to our repetitive problems, and I couldn't believe our failure to share a mutual obsession with sex was the only explanation. Up until now Neal had been the target under fire – could it be possible *I* might need some changing? Any alteration in my behaviour so far had been for self-preservation, not based on a change in theory. Well, I'd tried everything else I knew.

Gathering to my bosom a journal and pens, I settled down each day when the children napped. I reviewed Karen Horney's *Our Inner Conflicts,* and was able to identify everyone I knew, including myself, so I decided to give a concentrated effort with self-analysis. (Karen had been an associate of Fromm's, and he had highly recommended her.)

Daily I recorded faithfully my attitudes, anxieties, flare-ups, dreams etc. I thought I was pretty good at ruthlessly picking myself apart objectively. I probed and delved, and ended up months later with a notebook full of repetitious descriptions that thoroughly condemned me. The key to improvement lay in the requirement that one must have a 'serious incentive to change', and if one failed it was because one 'refused'. 'I can't' meant 'I won't'. I was positive I had that serious incentive, but beyond that what one actually *did* to change was vague and elusive.

Knowing was not enough for me, nor was the intense desire; neither of these wielded more power than the habitual reactions. A negative action thus amounted to a 'neurotic trend', and the more I called myself names, the more hopeless I felt.

During this time, adding grist to my mill and proving I'd accomplished nothing, Neal went to the City more often on some pretext or other. The family routine disintegrated; I never knew when he'd be home, meals went to waste, nights were spent in tossing and listening to every car, and if he did come home the relief was quickly dispelled by my need to freeze him out and fume in helpless sleepless despair while listening to his swaggering snores.

One afternoon, Al Sublette came to visit between ships, and I was glad to see a friend whom I knew to be sympathetic to me. Neal drove up soon after bringing his friends, the Fergusons, a couple I'd heard him mention. Although I had to scavenge an unexpected dinner for all, I felt encouraged by his wanting to share his friends with me and to show off his wife. How wrong could I be. Instead,

Neal openly seduced the wife in front of us all, and then took her out to our car. At least he didn't take her into our bedroom.

I turned to Al when we were alone and expressed my shock and dismay. Instead of consolation, he said impatiently, 'Look, Carolyn, you'd think you'd be *used* to it by now.' I'd have been no more stunned had he hit me. I fled to my room. '*Used* to it!' '*Used* to it!' I couldn't grasp it. Why wasn't I used to it? *Should* one get used to it? Then another cog went *click*. How could it be that here I was a blob of shaking jelly, every sense and sensibility outraged, yet no one else was the least bit ruffled? How could something so earth-shaking to me not matter a whit to anyone else? My psychology was no help here.

The next morning Neal had not returned from taking Al and the couple back to San Francisco, and I dragged through my routine with the children. Somehow, however, when Neal did return, I was able to modify my usual sanctimonious show of pain and mute silence.

I had been trying to interest Neal in my attempts at analysis, and hoped to encourage him to join me. Sometimes he had listened politely, sometimes been flip or indifferent. In the past an incident like this would be my cue to make him leave. This time I tried to get him to talk about it calmly, pointing out that something must be done. What did he think? Would he consider therapy again?

'Sure, baby,' his voice cold, his eyes hard. 'Here, take a drag off this and cheer up.' And he handed me a half joint, the tip brilliant with lipstick. My attempt at poise shattered like glass hit by a high note, and my defeat seemed complete. This was not like Neal at all; he usually showed some remorse, asked to be forgiven. After a few days of mutual silence, he must have felt confused and perhaps hopeless too, because he did go back to the clinic. Again, however, there were no results; we lived on day by day in a closed circle of habits.

Although Neal still couldn't stand with his heel flat on the ground, he could wear shoes comfortably enough to get around with nearly his customary speed. He found a job on a parking lot, much to our joy and relief, and all our spirits swung with another upward phase of our rollercoaster life. The family routine was re-established, his hours dependable. Once again he was his kind and considerate self, and he revived his correspondence with Jack and Allen, more eager than ever for them to visit.

Neal wrote explaining that when he was called back to the rail-road after the first of the year Jack could take over the parking lot until he too was called back, at which time Allen could take over. He had it worked out very neatly, and it appealed to Jack and Allen too.

After all these years, Allen suddenly decided the time had come to leave New York and start his pilgrimage West. For Allen, however, this journey had to be all-encompassing and significantly worthwhile. His excitement was contagious, and mirrored our own joy. Special delivery letters arrived every other day, the first before the parking lot plan reached him.

> I am leaving New York inside of a month...I will take my time getting there, as I plan a long *trip* across continent... Jack's novel rejected, I think for good...Bill's *sublime* work on South America will never see the light under the present structure of publishing in New York. I am sick of staying here and must leave...for every reason, especially that I want to go where it is sunny and the child I am can be happy. Carolyn: From the enclosed note you see what I want to do. I hope it will be welcome to you – I feel very well and full of vigor and have a whole load of projects both for living and writing – and depend very much in the immediate future on your welcome and Neal's...Jack (now in better mood) is casting around for plans and wants to know, 1) If he can work anywhere...2) Do you still love him?...I am excited and collecting maps. I will ship a trunk full of clothes and books ahead of me, and papers – you can open and read what you want. IS YOUR INVITATION STILL GOOD?

Then, being Allen, he explained every thought process and every step he'd take in disentangling himself from New York, and the financial picture before, during and after. He planned an extensive itinerary to Florida, Cuba, Yucatan and Mexico, stopping to look at ruins and archaeological digs, jungles, cities and then up the west coast to us.

Soon we heard from Jack himself. He liked the idea of the parking lot job, which surprised me, since he couldn't drive, but he wanted to be sure it was a genuine job and would be available when he arrived. He planned to leave December 26, arrive by the twenty-ninth so he could enjoy another new year's eve with us. He said Allen wouldn't be joining us until February or later. Allen had made the astonishing discovery that the New World had a Greece and Rome too, and you could get there by second-class bus. He looked forward to missing the eastern winter – and to seeing his Jami. Both Neal and I replied and approved his plan. Neal wrote,

> the parking lot is all ready for you to take over...when you feel good and ready to handle it, i.e. know all monthly parkers, how to set up lot each day, various ways of knocking down for at least lunch money – you keep job until spring rush, then give job to brother Ginsberg...Be careful, forget God (no such thing) forget being farmer (far too late or soon) say Hello to your mother for me, bring all your books, ideas of life and any amount of oolong tea you find to bolster stock at hand for New Year's eve party...

Allen sent us a final note at the time of his departure with explicit instructions on what to do with mail, packages, trunks etc. The day after Christmas, however, we received a letter from Jack who had learned he wouldn't get paid for his Christmas mail job until the first week in January, so he couldn't leave. He outlined every inch of travel – by way of Mexico for tea and counting on Neal sending him railroad passes from Nogales on.

Neal sighed, 'Well, here we go again. I can't get the jerk passes; he knows that. Lord knows when he'll get here now.'

We did know, at least, it wouldn't be for another three weeks at best, so we damped down our excitement. Now I was the one who was restless. I'd been deeply discouraged by having to abandon my hopes for psychology, though I continued to toy with the idea of returning to psychoanalysis myself. Each time I thought of it, the expense and time involved depressed me further, and I couldn't rouse the courage to act. Also, I felt vaguely this was not the missing piece to the puzzle. It looked to me that what Neal and I lacked most was a common belief in a set of absolute values. We couldn't agree on an authority we both respected. His study of philosophy, as well as his own life, had demolished his belief in the Church, and I had never had any – the Bible was a mystery to me, what little I knew of it. I felt paralyzed and resentful that everyone hadn't been handed a set of instructions. My parents thought they had supplied one, and Neal's church thought they'd shown him the way. Our experiences proved both of these maps unreliable. Ah, so, what to do? Neal listened to my woes and tried to cheer me up, but he couldn't help himself, let alone me.

PART TWO

| FORTY |

One evening soon after new year's, 1954, Neal came home earlier than usual and in a strange mood – looking as though some secret joy exhilarated him. He glowed with attentiveness to the children, and throughout dinner he kept smiling at me irrepressibly, less talkative than usual. I braced myself, afraid to ask the reason. He played with the children quietly while I washed the dishes, and when we had read to and put the children to bed, he ceremoniously sat me down and demanded my full attention. He then went into the bedroom and came back with a book, which he placed in my lap.

'Now, my dear, here's a book you have *got* to read before you do another thing. It is fan-tas-tic! I found it on one of the car seats, and I read the whole thing today. No, now, don't worry – the woman said I could borrow it to show you, and I'll take it back to her tomorrow. You'll never believe how amazing – not to mention the *timing* of finding it now. You may say it's coincidence, but you'll know better when you read...'

'What's it about?' I asked as I picked it up. The title was *Many Mansions*, and it was written by Gina Cerminara, a PhD in psychology, the jacket said.

'I couldn't possibly tell you – you'll see why. Now you just get reading and leave anything else to me.' He was grinning like the Cheshire Cat.

I was intrigued, and opened it at the first chapter, entitled 'The Magnificent Possibility'. All evening Neal was gentle, thoughtful, and every now and then he'd look to see how far I'd read. He continued to wear a slight smile, and his eyes were shining.

The content was chiefly a documentary of a man named Edgar Cayce (pronounced 'Casey', Neal informed me) who went to sleep and answered questions, at first about people's health problems, but later about anything. He was what they now called a 'channel' instead of a 'medium'. In due course the theory of reincarnation was put forward, and that these 'entities' who expressed themselves through Cayce were souls so far evolved that they didn't need to reincarnate on earth any more. They were on a higher plane, but contacted persons who were receptive in order to help them, and through them others, rather like the idea of Nirvana – once you've reached it, you go back and help others up the ladder of evolution. This theory gave a most satisfying purpose for our lives on earth.

Since the author was a psychologist, she was the perfect bridge from our studies to these new ideas. In time we left her far behind. But for now it was as though the door I had been pounding on and pushing against for so long suddenly swung open and let in a blast of light. On reading nearly every paragraph, I found myself saying, 'Why, yes, that makes sense.' Here at last was hope, real hope, altogether new hope. Here was a thrilling but logical explanation for all our troubles, and already I felt our conflicts were on the way to resolution.

The philosophy was all so positive; self-condemnation a primary sin, not a virtue. Yes, of course, I could see it all so clearly now. All that emphasis on the *wrong* I had been pursuing – to say nothing of Neal – going over and over the negative actions could only produce more of the same. I attracted it, asked for it by keeping it constantly in mind. A universal law: 'like begets like.' And the Cayce teachers declared, 'Mind is the builder.' 'A mind is as concrete as a post or a tree.' 'Thoughts are things.' I'd been brought up, as many of us are, to consider a positive attitude as unrealistic – we were kidding ourselves. 'Be prepared for the worst, and you won't be disappointed.'

Neal was overjoyed I was receptive to the ideas that came through Cayce. Oddly enough, both of us had easily accepted his clairvoyance, and at last we'd found a yardstick in common we could both accept. Far into the night we were of one mind, and shining our new light into all our dark corners. For the first time, too, we got a handle on religion, and all the overworked, hollow terms were filled with meaning.

Reincarnation as a means of evolution made perfect sense to us, and Neal's compassionate heart was pleased by the probability that handicapped people were not being unfairly punished but had created the condition themselves and were now strong enough to learn the lesson their affliction provided, as well as being an inspiration to others. What strength Helen Keller must have developed! It certainly made no sense for that to be her one and only lifetime. 'The stronger you get, the tougher the tests.'

Any sort of occult lore had been strictly off limits to us in the past, due to Neal's Catholic indoctrination and my scientific background. Now we were more influenced by what was logical, made sense and was practical. And any ideas we considered plausible were more so if we found the same ones in a variety of unrelated sources. We were also surprised to find the vast number of texts that had been available for decades and even centuries.

Neal quoted the Eastern saying, 'When the chela is ready, the guru appears' (when the student is ready, the teacher appears). So it would seem in our case. All other avenues had been dead ends. We never got over the fact that this new approach was embraced so completely by us both.

We looked up and studied as many uncorrupted scriptures as we could find, as well as spiritual leaders and teachers throughout the ages. We both left all new concepts 'out there' to be used or discarded by their application. Nothing was 'carved in stone' until we could prove a practical use or irrefutable connection in our lives today.

We'd often think in silence, then share a new insight. I asked Neal, 'Do you remember when Johnny was a baby and disappeared that two weeks? Do you suppose he was having second thoughts?' (The theory was that evolved souls choose the family in which they can best learn what they need to or with which they have had close connections in a previous life or lives.)

'Dunno – maybe. It was after that sickening and our only fight.' Here Neal reached over to hug me and peck kisses pleading forgiveness. 'But he must have known we didn't mean it, and he came back.'

'This many lives theory must explain why you and I got together at all; a more unsuited couple would be hard to find. That idea makes me feel better. But what must I have done to you to deserve this life? It must have been awful.'

'On the other hand, it could be that I did something awful to you, and you didn't forgive me then, so now I have to do more stuff so you'll learn to forgive me, hey? I can't make it up to you if you still hold a grudge.'

'Hmmm, yeah…I never looked at it that way. Karma is not just "an eye for an eye…"'

'No, no – that's the Old Testament, where some people's consciousness still is, to be sure; but the New Testament shows Jesus "fulfilled" the law through love, see? You don't have to pay for a mistake in kind if you can learn better otherwise, through your mind. That's Grace.'

'Well, it sure looks as though we can't get rid of each other until we do learn. I guess we chose to get it cleared up this time. You remember that every time I thought I could get free I'd either get pregnant, even if impossible, or the welfare would turn me down for no reason.'

'And remember how we wondered about you getting pregnant and not LuAnne? Yet she did as soon as she married another.'

Questions flooded in. I thought of another: 'Oh – and Cathy! What bliss to think there's some other reason for our hostility besides my failure as a mother to her. I wonder what it could be?'

We were now convinced we had found *the* road to salvation, and could hardly wait to enlighten our friends, and relieve them as well. Much to our surprise, neither the Forests nor the Hinkles seemed impressed. Dick made jokes about it, not from any disrespect to us, but just the idea. Both felt their own views suited them best, and of course they did. They were not ready for it as we were. Well, surely Jack and Allen would understand our views and embrace our exciting solution to the purpose of life. Jack, especially, who was so hung-up on death – 'We're just gonna die.'

January was almost gone, and still no Jack. We had assured Jami he'd be here for her birthday on the twenty-sixth, and she was disappointed. The next day we got his letter – from New York. He was having agonies of indecision, but finally made up his mind to come on the fifth on the Zipper. He said he'd learn the parking lot in a few hours.

Meanwhile, we received our first 'book' of a letter from Allen, written from Merida, where he had gone by plane from 'horrid Havana and more horrid Miami Beach'. His experiences were varied, and hardly the common tourist fare. A postcard from Jack in Mississippi assured us he was finally on the way, and on February 5 he arrived. At least he made it for Neal's birthday, his twenty-eighth.

To our sorrow, not only did Jack not grasp and support our Cayce revelations but he had simultaneously made a similar inspiring discovery that for him solved his problems with life: Buddhism. He too had hoped we would go along with him. Neal tried a compromise, telling Jack how the Hindu and Buddhist belief in reincarnation was reflected in the Judeo-Christian tradition, evidence of which had been deleted from the Bible at the 11th Ecumenical Council in Constantinople, but Jack interrupted him, saying 'I warn't no dawg.'

'No, man,' Neal hopped about the way he did when excited and wanted to make a point. 'That's not reincarnation – that's *trans-migration* – a dumb mix-up of perverted Hinduism. You've evolved past that if you're human now. You are a soul! Animals aren't souls – spirit, yes, the same that's in us; they're evolving, but they have group souls, see? That explains migration, for instance – but that's something else. What you don't understand is that man has evolved through *all* the kingdoms on this planet, from the mineral, vegetable, animal, each one nurturing the one above after absorbing the one below, so man is composed of them all. Eventually we have to evolve beyond our animal nature – as some already have, and Jesus did. But we have to evolve spiritually first – the physical evolution is the result. It is so beautifully simple, see?'

Jack didn't see it at all. He still thought in physical, here-and-now terms of animals being living sentient beings, and he forbade Neal to kill any more flies, now bellowing. Neal donned his most patient demeanour: 'Certainly they are, and the life force in them and us is the same...but I'm talkin' *soul* – you *are* a soul – just *occupying* a physical body. A soul is your unique individual self – the identity you've built from dozens, hundreds even – lives of experiences in this solar system – on different dimensions, even, making it or blowing it – "What you sow you reap." It's a Law, man. "God is not mocked."' And Neal stood with his forefinger raised gazing upwards.

Jack snorted and quoted Buddha that all life was suffering and pain, and the cause is *desire*. Jack emphasized the word sinisterly... and the way to salvation is the eightfold path. The world, said Buddha, is illusion, empty nothingness. And he sank back in his chair scowling. What a grim view of life, we thought. Why bother.

It would seem we had a schism. Each of us found it almost incomprehensible, and difficult to accept. Up to now we had all felt we were on the same wavelength, so to speak, as close as anyone could be. As the weeks went by we tried with extra concern to listen to the other's views, to understand and yet to sway each other too, to renew our harmony. Instead, in the end, we had sadly to concede that in the realm of theory we marched to different drums. This made it seem even more miraculous that Neal and I had agreed so readily in the first place, rather than Jack and Neal.

Neal and I had to learn to accept, however, that this new basis for agreement did not transform our lives overnight. The deep grooves worn by our habitual emotions and attitudes were not re-routed by intellectual enlightenment. The day-by-day frustrations continued. An entry in my journal a few days after Jack's arrival revealed:

> Jack here, and Neal and I edgy again. Neal is amorous but willing to disparage each of us in the other's eyes. I'm moody and resentful more. Got mad at Neal for lying about the Fergusons again, and because he put up the big nude poster in Jack's room, not thinking of the children first. I don't want Jack to hear us fight as of old, yet think it hard for him to watch us being loving. Neal has been better in some ways, though, and Jack is helping Neal to sidestep me again, probably to reinforce the shaky friendship. Maybe it's not good to have this three-way play against each other, because we want each other and each resents the third.

It was going to take a lot of work and much greater understanding for our new insights to become of practical use to us. At least, however, it was a beginning, and neither Neal nor I doubted the potential, nor could we choose but to go on with it.

Meanwhile, tensions grew with Jack. This time he was the one isolated from the magic circle. Also, he was not learning to handle the parking lot in the swift way demanded by Neal, and the railroad had not yet called him back. His reversion to helping Neal deceive me made me tearful and guarded. When Jack attempted to extend more warmth to me, Neal cooled. Jack couldn't play this role for long. Soon the private grumblings of the two men rumbled like inert volcanos that every now and then burst forth with little spurts of fire. Once more Neal vented his irritation in oblique cracks about Jack's presence as a freeloader in the family, again forgetting it was his own idea, while Jack's super-sensitivity and paranoia reacted instantly to an exaggerated degree. One night at dinner Neal referred to the pork chops *he* had provided, and Jack got up from the table vowing he would go out the very next day and buy himself a hotplate, put it in his room, buy his own food and eat alone henceforth.

I watched and listened in melancholy disbelief, as I'd done in October of '52, still no closer to ways or means to help. They too fought against the trend; one day sentimental brothers, the next snarling pups. The break finally came over a disagreement in the division of a batch of tea, and Jack decided to go home. We tried to persuade him to stay and wait for Allen, suggesting a fourth member might square the triangle, but he would not be deterred nor comforted. He left a week before my birthday near the end of April.

A few days later we got a note. He asked us to send on his mail. He had returned home hungry and angry, which he said helps you understand yourself. He went into a revised idea of 'emptiness', and hoped our karma would all come true, but he didn't believe in it. He wanted a means to be put to sleep, and wine and pork chops might be the way. Not only did he not begin with a salutation, he only signed it 'J'. Neal sighed and tossed it back to me after he'd read it.

'Well, I *personally* think the crux of brother Jack's trouble is that wish to just go to sleep...'

'To sleep, perchance to dream?' I added sadly.

| FORTY-ONE |

If Neal hadn't made a habit of reading every printed word in the newspapers, he would have missed the almost hidden advertisement for a series of lectures by Edgar Cayce's son, Hugh Lynn, to be held under the auspices of the recently formed organization to record and preserve the 'readings' Edgar gave. It was called the Association for Research and Enlightenment, or ARE.

After our discovery of *Many Mansions*, this was the second catalyst to the profound changes that were taking place in our lives. We embarked on our quest for knowledge and spiritual growth with this conference and our subsequent annual counselling with Hugh Lynn and his associate, Elsie Sechrist. We became members of the ARE, and were nourished monthly by the readings as they were transcribed, as well as other of their publications.

We also joined local study groups and worked hard to master the arts of meditation and positive prayer. We had learned a scientific controlled study had been done, which proved positive prayer really worked. For example, most religions use the Lord's Prayer as a plea – gimme gimme, whereas if you just add 'you' before each statement, it becomes positive: 'You give us this day our daily bread,' and so on. The Bible states God already knows what you need, and 'declare a thing, and it is done unto you.'

The new and complex worlds that now opened before us took a good deal of sorting and evaluating. Later on we learned the awesome power of our minds. Fortunately, Neal and I were of one mind about the multiplicity of information now flooding in upon us. Some of it we considered possible, some we rejected, and about some we were undecided. These categories were to shift and change throughout the rest of our lives.

For us, as I said, the object was always to find a concept that was of practical use in our daily existence – it was far too tempting to be swept into phantasmagorical realms that served no immediate or even long-term advancement. The first great joyous revelation had been that life – all life – is purposeful. This we embraced wholeheartedly; there are no accidents. One did have to keep asking, 'What is this knowledge *for*? What use will it be put to? The Cayce teachers said it isn't enough to be "good"; one had to be good *for* something.' Yes, of course.

Allen's trunks and books had arrived, and we stored them in the room Jack had vacated. In another long letter, he told us he had met a woman who had grown up in the Palenque area and owned a huge cocoa plantation where he was staying. He wasn't sure when he could leave. (Our world was taking on the bizarre on all sides.) This lady, Allen wrote, had been the first 'Jane' in the Tarzan movies, and he was immersed in the delights of the jungle and developing a new self-image, with a goatee and 'mustachio', long hair, heavy shoes – 'ride horses, go fishing at nite in streams with natives giggling with *focos* (flashlights) and long stick with prongs to catch great crawfishes size of lobsters.' He had discovered a set of drums, and 'play several hours daily, mostly very soft listening, and when a file of Indians ride in thru the trails from Aqua Azul Eden-like little town in hills an hour ride away I break out in African reverberations which can be heard for miles around.' He was known as 'Senor Jalisco'. I could easily imagine Allen's enthusiastic drumming from my memory of the metal tabletops in Denver.

In Allen's jungle paradise he had also been introduced to the possibilities inherent in meditation and the contemplative life. He ran across a book we had, *The Cloud of Unknowing*.

> Time spent here has been mainly contemplative of this
> fixed idea, and I had one day of excited agitation, thinking
> I should go be a monk, but no need to do that – can

develop anywhere and such agitations are passed. What hung me on *Cloud of Un.* was the lovely and obviously true idea that a contemplative doesn't have to do anything but what he feels like, sit and think or walk and think, don't worry about work, money life, no hangups, his job is to have no job but the unknown Abstraction and its sensations & his love of it.

'Ha, yeah,' Neal laughed, 'that sounds like every man's wish fulfilled.' Then Allen wrote, 'Forgive me for not answering your letter about spiritualism sooner.' We bristled. We had read about spiritualism, including Leadbeater's little book on the astral plane and its inhabitants, and though we accepted there are 'levels of consciousness', we couldn't accept communication with the dead via mediums or seances. If Allen meant 'spiritual', okay. We didn't think Edgar Cayce's clairvoyance was the same. But we knew we weren't schooled in spiritualism, so we withheld judgement. But Allen did say 'That Neal is religious is a great piece of news: I always wondered what he would be like with some overpowering Awful thought humbling his soul to saintliness.' Well, he had been Catholic.

A longer letter written the first week of April was the last we received for over a month. After a couple more weeks I wrote to Jack, thinking he might have heard something more; we were becoming uneasy about Allen. Jack answered at once, just telling us not to worry, and that Mexico wasn't dangerous. He then fantasized about thinking he saw him in New York. But he said it wouldn't surprise him if Allen had gone mad like his mother. Not a lot of help to us.

Jack was at his sister's home in North Carolina with Memere. He still sounded somewhat bitter and angry, even though he opened the letter with relief at hearing from me. He went on to say he understood all the mistakes we'd all made, but we three were all the same, and to fight was ridiculous. With his usual ambiguity, he declared he didn't think he would ever come back to California unless someone offered him a ride. He wrote further pages and pages extolling Buddhist doctrine and criticizing Cayce because of his misunderstanding and lack of definition of terms.

He had been collecting railroad unemployment, but now decided not to bother. No point in that, or even in life, because life wasn't worth living, yet you had to eat and be compassionate about loved ones. He took off again on Buddhist ideas, this time on people playing roles in life, such as he being Alyosha in *The Brothers Karamazov*, I Katarina Ivonovna. I didn't get any of that, but was flattered he thought of us that way. He then thought it so great that I'd told him something Karen Horney had said: 'You don't have to grasp or reject, just take what's given you.' This I didn't remember telling him.

He ended wanting to hear about the children, 'who know God is Pooh Bear', then blessed our house in Buddhist terms. He urged us to have a big back yard where he could live in a shack and grow vegetables, and signed it 'All my love, Jack'.

| FORTY-TWO |

Early in March of 1954 the trial date was finally decided. It was eleven months since Neal's accident, and it was then postponed for another week. The trial lasted for days, and when I was required to attend (with the children to add pathos to our plea) I was appalled at the performance my first time in court, yet everyone else accepted it as usual court behaviour.

It looked to me no more than a sparring match between the two sides, as the lawyers did their utmost to influence the jury by discrediting each other. At noon our lawyer took the entire jury to an elegant restaurant, charged to us. By the time the lawyers had quibbled, hashed and re-hashed the accident, no one had any idea what really had happened, and Neal was now so confused he contradicted his own original statement. No wonder, of course, considering he was half conscious the first time.

His recovery did seem miraculous, and the SP doctors, when describing the injury and Neal's recovery against all odds, turned out to be the best witnesses for our case. Neal, however, was so determined not to be handicapped he wouldn't even limp, and Mr B. said, 'Jesus Christ, Neal, that's the least you could do!' In the end we were awarded about one-third of the original estimate, and when the lawyer subtracted his fee and our expenses for a year, we ended up with $16,000 – not $75,000. I overheard him talking to his associate, and he sounded pleased, in spite of his word to me. But even that amount made us feel rich – and it was tax-free. The check did not arrive, however, for another two months. But it was all over at last, and Neal could return to work.

An annoying development was that the announcement in the press of our award sent hordes of barking hounds, each with the best idea of what we should do with the money. The phone never stopped ringing, as well as the doorbell. At last the check arrived, so that and the Cayce material kept Neal and me on an even keel, and for the moment the cracks in the mirror of the future were sealed.

We then got another adventure-packed chronicle from Allen. He said he was okay, had been at Xbalba, 'pronounced – dig – Chivalva', for a month, penniless, so couldn't get to town to send word. 'What unluck Jack is gone; I delayed too long, for one thing... but it will be sweet to see you at the end.'

Upon his arrival in San Jose I was extremely nervous in his presence, despite our warm correspondence. Seven years had elapsed since I'd seen him, and I still feared he didn't really like me. He looked much the same, more mature, perhaps, but he had shaved off his goatee, so he still had the same eager and youthful appearance. Very soon he put me completely at ease.

He arrived in the early afternoon, and hastily stowed his gear, eager to open his trunk and show us the goodies we'd waited for him to present. He had notebooks full of poetry and photographs of everyone in New York. While Neal was over these, Allen remembered he had brought me some masks and figurines carved from a soft white wood, and two colourful woven tote bags from Yucatan and Guatemala. There was so much he wanted to tell and talk about, he hardly knew where to begin, and we wanted to go over the books he'd brought back that described the ruins. We reminded ourselves there would be plenty of time ahead.

Meanwhile the family life must continue, so when the children joined us after their naps Allen turned his attention to them, to the house and grounds, and asked questions about Jack's stay and our affairs. I was getting ready to go to the market, but he jumped up and stopped me.

'No, wait – I'll show you I'm the world's perfect guest. Just you let me take care of all that. We'll have one of my culinary master-pieces,' and he asked Neal to lead him to the nearest food emporium – right across the street.

He was as good as his word, operating in the kitchen like a master chef, and produced a delicious meal. Afterwards, though he protested, I insisted he go talk to Neal, and leave the dishes to me. He hung about, helping to clear the table until I convinced him I really liked doing dishes: 'I like making order out of chaos, honest, Allen – although nobody believes me.'

When the children had been bathed, read to and tucked in, I joined the men in the living room. Neal and I insisted Allen tell us all about the plantation, the ruins and a mysterious mountain he had written about. 'Yeah, and what about that broad in the jungle, eh?' Neal's eyebrows did their Groucho Marx imitation, puffing his cigarette like a cigar. Allen grinned, then became serious and told his strange and exotic tales.

'And I took a lot of pictures; you'll have to tell me how to get them developed. I'll remember more when I get them back. Now then, tomorrow, if it's all right with you, I want to sort my manuscripts – you still have the tape recorder?' Neal nodded. 'Good. I'd like very much to do some recording – read my poems aloud, you know. I've never *heard* them – great kicks – poetry is supposed to be *spoken* or sung, you know.' He rubbed his hands together in anticipation, grinning, his black eyes alight.

Neal was busier on the railroad now, and Allen and I spent a lot of time together. Sometimes he wrote or recorded, and unless he asked me to listen, which he often did, I would leave him to it and keep the children from distracting him. Part of every day he spent with them and with me, and he was more considerate, aware, patient and kind than anyone I'd known other than Neal and Jack. He made each day a time filled with a variety of enthusiasms, always stimulating and amusing. Like me, he enjoyed sharing, and I was never bored or lonely. Once in a while we'd go to a movie in the evening – it was like having a 'date' again, and afterwards we'd sit at a café counter drinking milkshakes and bringing to bear our superior critical intellects on an analysis of every facet of the film.

He continued to do most of the cooking, and helped with the dishes. Although I had only a hazy idea of current real estate, I was hoping we could build our own home now, and I'd drawn detailed plans for it. I had studied architecture in college, so I knew how it was done, as far as spaces. Every now and then I'd get the urge to go look for a lot somewhere, and Allen would come along and tramp all over rough terrain and waving grasses, as intently involved as if it were his own dream.

When Neal was home, we'd bombard Allen with our new interest in metaphysics, and Allen listened respectfully. As with our other friends, he was not convinced it would solve all the world's problems, but he didn't bring us down. Like Jack, he didn't like the idea of coming back again and again.

'This life is enough – all I can stand, and anyway, I'd probably just sit around and do nothing if I thought it was a never-ending process. Why try?'

Neal explained at length the evolution of the soul through learning universal laws Jesus had taught and lived. Allen wasn't sold, and like Jack he couldn't separate the Christian metaphysics from theological dogma.

One evening Allen accompanied me to a lecture on hypnotism and trance. Neither of us was impressed, and the speaker made me uncomfortable. When we were outside again, I was approached by a man I knew to be interested in the Cayce readings. He was excited and wanted to talk to me alone. Allen began walking ahead of us.

'Listen.' His eyes were wide. 'That hypnotist could really help Neal. Let me make an appointment for him – the man's a Kahuna – you know, the ancient Hawaiian high priests – or he was in his last life.' He hardly paused for breath, but as he spoke the flesh was crawling up my back. I thanked him for the offer but said I'd have to talk it over with Neal.

Meanwhile, he invited Allen and me to the hypnotist's home in Sunnyvale. Allen was curious and agreed to go. Once there, we were no more enthusiastic. Everyone was more interested in occult phenomena, like pendulums and ouija boards, than in a philosophy to live by, which was my principal concern. We extricated ourselves as soon as possible, and discussed it all on the way home. We'd had something of a lark, but we felt those were muddy waters of which to be wary. When we related our adventure to Neal, he was glad to miss the 'cure'.

We often talked of Jack, and I had written him soon after Allen's arrival to let him know we were thinking of him and wishing he were with us. He answered me saying how much he welcomed my letter. He was sending Allen and Neal a big separate one, but this one was MINE. Apparently in theirs he talked about girls, and he told me not to get mad. He wanted to come back to California in September and give the railroad another try, this time for poetic reasons. He hoped Allen would still be with us, and if there was a possibility of Burroughs too he would definitely come. He visualized how wonderful it would be for us all to be together talking. Allen would have his index finger upheld, Neal with his tea, he and Bill with wine, me with wine and pizza. He also said Neal should take to the road again in his red and black boat (another new Rambler wagon), or what were they for? He said I should get a farmhouse in the valley. I had suggested I irritated him, and he said I never did, that I was a golden angel and he would always love me as he had, then asked everybody to write him and to say hello to Jami. He wanted news, too, of Al Sublette.

He didn't seem to resent not being with us, and said Buddha had convinced him that none of us were real, anyway, only 'ripples', as Einstein had proved 'mathematically'.

| FORTY-THREE |

Appreciating Allen's company as I did, and knowing his prime reason for being here was to see Neal, I did my best to make myself scarce whenever Neal was home and able to spend time with Allen. Although Neal liked to take Allen off to the City to show him his 'kicks', he also enjoyed reading Allen's poems and having intellectual discussions, as they had in the past.

Allen had hesitated to show me a notebook full of love poems to Neal, but I thought them beautiful, felt no threat whatsoever, trusting what he had written some years before about having overcome his sexual desire for Neal. I knew 'The Green Automobile' was a poem about their earlier love affair, and I knew how much it meant to Allen. When he could count on using the tape recorder undisturbed, he'd record himself reading it, and he must have done so a dozen times. (That should have given me a clue.) He and Neal got high occasionally and made recordings of Allen's new drumming techniques with Neal on the recorder, thereby catching up somewhat with the joys Jack had described of his stay with us in San Francisco.

As the perfect guest, Allen got along well with the Forests, and the Hinkles came over many times, when we would have wild funny card parties. Allen had come to dislike clothing, and although he was discreet when anyone was around, if he was sufficiently high and would embarrass no one, he'd doff the lot, usually after dark with the lights off.

One such hot night after I'd consumed quite a lot of wine, he persuaded me to join him. It was extremely difficult for me to shed my self-consciousness, and truthfully I am more at ease with some bodily wrapping, but I didn't like being a prude, either, so I gave in. We lay about a foot apart on the living-room rug like a couple of innocent children, enjoying the caress of the soft breeze that floated through the French doors open to the summer night, the moonlight laying cool white banners across us and the floor. Allen bellowed poem after poem to infinity, and I found myself relaxing and smiling in the security of being with a man intent only on his own body, not mine.

Allen must have been with us almost six weeks when one afternoon our idyllic life came to a shattering halt. Neal and he had been in his room for quite some time, and I heard no talking. I had a question to ask Neal, so I tapped on the door as a matter of courtesy and went in, but the question stuck in my throat from what I saw before me. The force of the shock nearly knocked my head off, or so it felt. I backed out and shut the door, my insides coiling and recoiling. In that brief instant the picture registered in toto. Allen lifted his head and turned to look at me, but I was gone – to sit, to tremble, pace, cry to heaven, wring my hands and fight down the revulsion threatening to make me sick.

By the time Neal had put on his jeans and came out, I was sitting on the edge of the couch, staring at the floor, wondering what to do next. I had known nothing of fellatio before, hence the added shock. Neal went past me into the bathroom, but Allen calmly sat down in the armchair opposite me. It was my move.

'Allen – I just don't know what to say – I'm so *sorry*! I don't really understand myself and my reaction. You know I have no prejudices, but – somehow – somehow – it's like having a *woman* guest in my home. Can you understand? I'd be pretty shook if I found her – well – I know you love Neal, but you wrote that you didn't desire him sexually any more – I trusted you – Oh, I don't know – I'm just afraid I couldn't handle it; I just want you to go.'

After a pause, Allen said, softly, 'That's okay; I understand.' He sighed but said no more. After all our lovely times together. I tried to look at it differently; even I knew I sounded like a bigoted bitch (a WASP I think they're called) – but that image. I simply couldn't help how I felt. If he stayed, I knew I'd be frightened, jealous, suspicious, not calmly overlooking however they behaved. I wanted to keep saying, 'I'm sorry, I'm sorry.'

'I'll pay your way anywhere you want to go, Allen, I'll help all I can. You know I champion homosexuals – what tremendous assets the great ones have given us through the ages, But then, of course, this isn't the same.'

When Neal did appear, and we were alone, I hit him with my standard line: 'How *could* you? Right here in our home?' It was a question never to receive an answer – the only possible one I wouldn't want to hear. Feeling stupid and miserable, with no help from Neal, I went on with my duties during the next day while Allen solemnly considered where to go, being gently compliant and sad. He had an uncle in Riverside, a city below Los Angeles, but that didn't make sense to any of us. I wasn't cheered by his final decision, which was San Francisco. He would now provide a haven for Neal when he wanted to get his kicks there. I could hardly object, nor make any more demands on Allen, and my heart sank prophetically.

I wanted to cry watching him pack his treasures, his books, notebooks and clothes. What a rotten state of affairs. The next week I drove Allen to the City, where he could visit old friends and make inquiries about Berkeley and the University of California across the bay. On the way, I apologized and begged his forgiveness in a dozen different ways. He was kind, said he understood, but I wondered what inner turmoils he was suffering – unless he was used to rejection and had been through the likes of this before. As he got out of the car he kissed me, told me not to worry and said he'd keep in touch. I drove home in a lonely blue funk, trying to forgive myself. If only they had been discreet; this time I'd have preferred to be deceived if our good times could have continued. Again – 'whatcha don't know don't hurtcha.'

I look back with even more regret, because now I would be able to deal with that situation for the good of us all. Then I was too conditioned and so utterly un-streetwise.

I didn't expect Neal to be mad at me, and he wasn't. Seeing me so distressed, he took my part, apologized, maligned himself and begged my forgiveness. Once more I turned to Jack, too, to find some comfort from the third member. I poured out the whole story, condemning myself and sure Jack would think me far too prudish. True to his good-hearted nature, he didn't let me down and answered at once.

He wrote he wanted to reassure me that he wasn't mad about my throwing Allen out and that it didn't surprise him. He reminded me I had thrown him out once too. He said Neal and Allen were close enough not to let this bother their long-time friendship, but I musn't be harsh with our Prophets. As for him, he said it wasn't his line. He continued a lengthy consolation far beyond my expectations, and wrote that Allen had not told him anything about it. He didn't think Allen's anger would be anything but standard criticism of American puritanical matriarchal repression and squareness, and he could hear him and Burroughs talking about it already. He said Bill prided himself on being disliked intensely by all his friends' women. He then asked me not to stay mad.

I didn't take much stock of these remarks at the time, but years later there was a biography of Bill Burroughs, and in it a vivid description of the scene in San Jose where Carolyn had thrown out Allen. It was completely distorted; there were quotes of all the awful things I'd said about Allen and homosexuals, etc. etc. Reading that, knowing only Allen could be the source, saddened me. No wonder Bill Burroughs would never give me the time of day. Of course I was never given a chance to defend myself – condemned without trial.

Jack's letter rambled on about the railroad, what he was writing – a science-fiction novel he expected to finish before new year's. He asked why he wrote like this, and said he thought he had heard me say to Neal, 'Write yourself to death,' and he felt paranoid that I didn't want Neal to follow his example to try to make good as a writer. He said he did feel he was writing himself to death. He concluded with his latest Buddhist visions, his ups and downs emotionally, but he kept coming back to my problem, then related Neal's mind to Buddhist concepts. As usual, I'd read the letter aloud to Neal.

Putting it down, I said, 'Well, at least it's good he's still excited about writing new works; surely he means a different *On the Road*? But I'll be damned if I can get a handle on what good it is to know there's a true unchangeable pure mind. We know that too, in other terminology, but what then? I still think metaphysics could help him more in his search for what to do.'

Neal sighed, 'Yeah, if he'd only listen. He'd understand if he wanted to and really thought about it. But alas, no; he's hung up on all those long names and sweet silence.'

Here, I thought, might be a clue to why Jack was so drawn to Buddhism and Neal to metaphysics. We felt the need of guidance in using our new knowledge in the here and now. Besides, neither of us could pronounce the names in Buddhism in order to become familiar with them and their meaning, as Jack and Allen could. Jack was enthralled by the colourful tapestry in the Sutras, and perhaps the remoteness took him out of this world as well. We couldn't see how it was helping him avoid pain and suffering or desire, although it probably added another dimension to his imagination. He was the dreamer, the be-er, the yin; Neal was the do-er, the yang; Neal and I had logical minds; Jack's more mystical. This could have had something to do with their attraction to each other. At any rate Jack's compassion always helped relieve my suffering, if only for a time.

| FORTY-FOUR |

In August of 1954 all anxieties were temporarily displaced by my finding a house near Los Gatos, a village at the foot of the coast range about ten miles south of San Jose and twenty miles from the ocean. The house was on a third of an acre on a short dead-end street in the middle of prune orchards, with only a few scattered neighbours and only a mile from the village. It had been built by an architect for his growing family, and had an unusual floorplan: the house was divided into adult and child sections. In front was the living room, with a big picture window from which – across a lawn, the street, a prune orchard and eucalyptus trees – one surveyed the rising mountains, covered in green and bronze ever-changing light. A small dining area next to it had French doors out to a brick patio, lawns and a flower garden with built-in barbecue and a swimming pool, eight feet by sixteen, and four feet deep at one end, three at the other. A fence surrounded this and shut it off from a field with a few prune trees, a fence surrounding the whole lot.

A hall led from the living room to a big family room divided from the kitchen to the right of the hall and the master suite to the left. Doors shut this section off. Next to the family room was a shower room and two bedrooms. The family room had a wall of glass separated by wooden shelves that overlooked the patio. I fell in love with it on sight, my only fear being its distance from the yard office and the depot, but Neal scoffed at such trivia and welcomed the challenge.

The first expenditure of the settlement money had gone for the 'black and red boat' – this car new and for cash. We had sent Diana $1000, and split the rest between investments and the down-payment on the house – $5000 each. We hadn't found the old farmhouse Jack had requested, to be sure, but, as usual, Jack's dreams were not compatible with Neal's job. Besides there weren't any in that area. I felt at home at last, and Neal had never had a home of his own. It couldn't help but inspire him to overcome his restlessness once he knew the joys of home ownership and the pleasure of maintaining a home that belonged to him. I was sure it would work wonders for my disposition as well.

As soon as I'd found the house, even before we could move in, I hurried to write to Jack. He answered that I must send him a complete description, and all the details of location and cost. He already knew of Los Gatos, because friends had lived there and he'd used it as a weekend retreat for the couple in *The Subterraneans*. He also wanted news of the kids.

Writing back, I was describing the property in the minute detail he wanted when it struck me like a thunderbolt that I had completely forgotten to consider a room for Jack. There was no guest room. I felt like a traitor, but Neal soothed me by suggesting we could find – or Jack could – an inexpensive house trailer to put in the back yard, which he'd like even better.

We now had our first television set, bringing more fun with Neal; he was interested in so many different things. He enjoyed my favourites, such as *Omnibus* and *Play of The Week*, British movies and documentaries, but enlarged my field with shows like Oral Roberts and others I'd never think to turn on. He didn't take Roberts's preaching too seriously, but he was fascinated by his style and the phenomenon of evangelists. Oral was much milder and had a broader insight than most, so he didn't make us wince. Just a lot of fun, and he didn't preach hell and damnation.

The children's viewing I strictly monitored. Sunday nights they could watch Disneyland, and the child in Neal rose to equal their excitement, and so enhance their enjoyment. It was the only time they were allowed to eat candy, so it became a time of indulging and a family ritual. During the week we all gathered for *Our Miss Brooks*, *Car 54*, *Ensign O'Toole*, *I Love Lucy*, *My Little Margie*, *Leave It To Beaver* and any suitable documentaries before their bedtime. Sports events I generally left to Neal. When he was alone he switched channels continually, taking in the full gamut of broadcasts all at once, a practice I found disconcerting but amusing. Late Sunday nights he loved to watch the girls' *Roller Derby*. At first I thought we'd have to move the set out of the bedroom, but after he'd persuaded me to watch some (like the midget auto races) I found it fascinating in its absurdity, and a treat to lie in bed with Neal and laugh at the shenanigans of our favourite girls. We still had our exciting discussions far into the night, now fired with new fuel by our expanded studies.

To decorate our living room wall I painted portraits of the kids, and over the fireplace went my great grandad, an excellent portrait in pastel, the history of which I had yet to learn. (At age nine I had begun formal traditional art classes, and sold my first portrait when I was 16.)

I entered both girls in the Los Gatos ballet school, where I paid for their tuition by designing the two annual productions and by taking class rolls. Neal took a keen interest in the productions, in which Jami always had a solo part, Cathy having given up after four years. Jami had an unusual talent. We made friends for life with the ballet master, although when Jami was a teenager I switched her to classes in San Jose with Dimitri Romanoff, the régisseur of the American Ballet Theater, in which he had been a premier danseur, and I had seen dance in New York in 1943. We learned to our sorrow that the first teacher had made her turn her feet out before she was 11 when the cartilage turns to bone, so a tendon grew around her knee cap not over it. Before she had a fall and this discovered, she was courted by every major ballet company when she took classes with them on their San Francisco tours. She spent two years in New York when she was 19, taking classes with Nureyev and Baryshnikov. Romanoff gave her a full scholarship, and wanted her in his company, but told her to join any other, any sort, so he could take her out as a soloist and avoid the years in the corps. She finally had to give it up because of her knees, and then she met Randy, and we've always been grateful she didn't lead that painful life. We had enjoyed the experiences – I had always wanted to be a ballerina, but that too was 'life upon the wicked stage', so I vicariously wallowed in Jami's classes and her success on stage as well as in the designing.

Neal showed her, or tried to, his skill in holding onto one foot and jumping over it with the other. It was always an hilarious performance, and I can't actually remember if he ever succeeded, but he never gave up trying.

Neal especially enjoyed the nice bathrooms, the first we'd had. Now Neal took a book or magazine into the tub and soaked for hours, turning on the hot tap with his toe when the water cooled. When he eventually emerged, he'd go into the other bathroom and take a shower to remove the soap.

This first year may have held some of Neal's happiest times, as it did mine too. He was proud of his home, and although not accustomed to care for one as had been the men in my family, he tried to help out to the best of his ability. He seemed to enjoy planting trees and shrubs, but when it came to carpentry repairs, he was hopeless, and his rage and self-condemnation were unmerciful if he bungled a job. For the life of the house there remained a fencepost bristling with a dozen nails when two or three would have sufficed. So I learned not to ask more than I thought he could handle, and I was a dab hand at carpentry myself.

Neal was popular with everyone in the ARE study groups, as he was with any level of social 'class;' he had schooled himself to fit in anywhere; no one would have guessed his past. I remember one party where we were invited by a friend of mine who had a large Catholic family, most of them either nuns or priests. Neal was the star of the show with them all (all the while making seductive passes on one of my friend's gorgeous aunts). I was so amused and awed by him.

We eagerly opened the monthly mailings and new readings. We adopted religious practices at home, long familiar but never understood, such as grace before meals and prayers at bedtime. John would be in bed, Neal sitting beside him, the girls on either side of him and me on the floor leaning against his knees, all of us touching. We'd say the new 'positive' Lord's Prayer and explain its relationship to the endocrine glands, the 'chakras'. Sometimes Neal would become inspired to give the children a lecture, so enthusiastic was he with the growing knowledge. After one of these, Johnny came out with thoughts on the same or even higher level, although he was only four or five. We were too awed to speak of that; something we couldn't explain at that time.

As I've said, we didn't join in experiments with occult phenomena and seemed able to spot charlatans quickly. We read about ectoplasm and all the varieties of other-dimensional or meditation results in order to learn, but we were still focused on logical, practical, demonstrable ways to grow. There certainly were 'higher' conscious states and hidden truths we accepted, but for us only as a means to our ends. For me, I could believe these actions and events did happen, but the idea of ever seeing or feeling any of these unearthly phenomena terrified me, and I prayed I'd never be confronted by any.

From a childhood experience of seeing a drunk race around our front yard in the moonlight I developed a terror of anyone not in control. During the war I visited many mental hospitals and from that came to some understanding of people in abnormal conditions, as well as from my own 'nervous breakdown'. Perhaps all this contributed to my abhorrence of mind-altering drugs. Why anyone would ask for that appalled me.

At least Neal didn't talk about ectoplasm, ghosts, amortizing or astral planes with the children, and when we retired to an adult evening our feelings towards each other and our problems had been uplifted as well. Even at times when we were at variance, we didn't allow our emotional stress to interfere with the bedtime ritual. A truce was demanded until we could be alone and the doors closed to the back of the house.

| FORTY-FIVE |

Neal's apparent contentment may have had another contributing source. With Allen in San Francisco, Neal had an anchor at that end of the line. Now he had enough seniority to hold down a regular daily passenger run. This meant taking a commute train from San Jose in the morning, then having a whole day in the City to do what he liked before bringing a train back in the evening. Perfect for him. He made new friends with poets, artists and wannabes. Our home was an oasis of strength and rest, and gave him the self-image of respectability he so desperately desired, but it made it so much easier for him to indulge in his ingrained proclivities all day in the City.

This comfortable and satisfying life made him begin to relax the boundaries, however, forgetting that my security lay in a conventional family life. Another weed growing in the garden of my delight was his increased use of tea when at home. I disliked the changes in his personality – he wasn't his 'real' self when high, and I became increasingly anxious the children would notice the difference, so I asked him to restrict its use to elsewhere. He did his best to comply, although he'd become so used to it it was difficult, and sometimes he'd become so irritable I'd be tempted to withdraw my objections.

Allen had found a new love, Peter Orlovsky, and Neal joined their circle of friends. It wasn't long before Neal would return to the City to play with them. He would describe the innocent but stimulating parties they had of intense intellectual discussions on art and poetry, while Neal propounded his Cayce obsession, earning him the nickname 'the Preacher'. All of which was easier to talk about than to act out.

He told me about an artist friend of the group, Bob LaVigne, who was painting a huge mural for a Foster's cafeteria. He used the locals as models, one of whom was a red-headed girl named Natalie Jackson, who was centred in one section, nude. What Neal didn't tell me was that he had met her and they had fallen deeply in love.

Judging only from what he told me, his pleasures sounded innocent enough, but his secrecy and evasion increased after he met Natalie, as well as his time spent away from home. Weekends became the only reliable time together, but as my suspicions increased these were less and less pleasant. It was no wonder he preferred the other end of the line. He still ardently shared our only points of closeness: the Cayce mailings and the children. We had abandoned the study groups. These few hours with him were as delightful as ever, which only underscored their rarity.

We never went to concerts or lectures any more; I'd not found babysitters yet, and Neal didn't seem interested in local events.

Alone I kept up my studies, and worked at learning meditation and positive thinking. Tiny revelations and successes began to occur, and although they sounded ridiculous in the telling they were magnificent to experience – little rays of the truth of the teachings, tangible evidence – and thus served to nourish my fragile faith and ensure my continued efforts.

Soon I began to dread Neal's comings and goings and the need I still felt to complain of his neglect. At that time I still believed there was a duty to married love, as well as believing one could expect as much love from the other as you were willing to give. I had to learn one can love only as much as one is able to. The Cayce teachers said the ideal attitude to everything and everybody was 'loving indifference'. I liked that better than Buddha's 'detachment', because love was there, and I understood it better than Krishnamurti's 'choiceless awareness', but I couldn't see how I'd ever achieve it.

Then one time I noticed that when Neal came in the door the children ran to him with open arms – happy just to see him. 'Be as a little child' came into my head. But I still didn't know how to function outside the mother–warden role I thought was my duty. Once Neal said, 'Why would I want to come home to that long face?' Neal never criticized or listened to gossip, so this was a one-off, and it shocked me into thinking, but alas not enough to change my attitude.

Often I'd gaze out at the patient, stately eucalyptus trees beneath the solid green mountain and think, 'I'll lift up mine eyes unto the hills from whence cometh my help,' knowing it symbolized the pineal or pituitary gland in my head, but the earthly counterpart was uplifting too. I wondered if Jack had read Buddha's advice to 'grow as a tree grows'. And the Cayce teachers had said the three dimensions on this planet were 'Time, Space and Patience'. Well, patience was a virtue I had a lot of opportunities to cultivate.

To make matters worse, Neal got a long letter from Jack – sent to the yard office! Neal saw nothing to hide, so he left it for me to read. I understood Jack's wish to get back to Neal from having been writing so long only to me, but still it made me feel even more abandoned.

Jack showed his paranoia, fearing Neal would think he was coming on all buddy, buddy (which was obvious) after seeming to be mad at Neal for some peeve. He described his activities that would appeal to Neal, and that he wished Neal were there to share. He said there was nothing to hide from me, but he wanted a more direct connection with Neal, himself, and no one else reading over his shoulder, even if it were Neal's sweet, protective Carolyn.

He had been thinking more about reincarnation, and said he approved of Cayce, really liked him, thought Neal might be his brother, Gerard, reborn, because he felt so brotherly towards Neal. He then went on about why he was so close to Neal's wife, because he really did love me and felt the kids were his. He insisted Neal was a great writer and must continue. He suggested Neal write him letters about sex and get them past me somehow, because I had all the wrong idea about writing about sex.

He declared he wouldn't talk of 'nuthin' means nuthin'' any more, and how sad that was. He'd rather be riding in the car with Neal to go get food and anticipating whatever Neal would say next. He would spend part of each year with his mother, part of it in Mexico, and part of it living with us. He painted more visions of renewed joy with Neal, remembering sentimental moments and begging Neal to forgive him for all he'd done wrong, ending with a blessing from Holy Angels.

His letter didn't exactly soothe my emotions, but along with feeling sympathy for Jack, I agreed with his belief in Neal, who was not writing at all any more, not even letters. We'd both lost him.

Apparently Neal didn't answer this letter either, thinking perhaps if he revealed secrets to Jack I'd hear of them. So Jack wrote one to me. He was afraid I'd stopped writing him because I was peeved at his suggesting Neal sneak letters to him about sex. He said everyone seemed to have changed; he frowned all the time and he had developed a very short fuse. He sighed and said we'd have so much to talk about. He wanted to come to San Francisco in the summer, stay with Allen and meet all the new friends after he'd spent a month in Mexico. He would naturally come to see me and the children. He was feeling quiet, lonely and profound on his way to the woods to write and meditate. He thought of me often, and hoped all was well.

It helped some to find he still loved me, but I knew there was no permanent relief from that direction, and I was far too eager to work things out with Neal. My reply must have conveyed some of those feelings unconsciously; his next letter was resigned and sad. He hadn't received the money he had expected for his trip to California, but allowed that the only good thing about it, anyway, would be to see me and the kids, and he was afraid they wouldn't remember him as before when they were younger. He was sentimental about our times with tapes, wine, kiddies, and when Neal respected him. Besides, he said, he'd only want to grab me, and he didn't think I'd like that any more, and even if I did it wouldn't be right – then there was Neal, so he'd better not make any moves. He thought I sounded more aloof in my letter. (How I wished he wasn't so paranoid!) As usual he urged me to admit my love for Neal (did I ever not?) and was more objective about our problems than I could be, all very kindly. He then painted visions of us talking all night with our wine, and declared we would when he had the money. I should be cool, blessed and relaxed like the roses he saw out his window in the rain. More Buddhist-inspired thoughts here and there, followed by a postscript of his daily routine in Rocky Mount, where Memere was living.

His lonesome thoughts only intensified my own. I missed him more than ever now – someone to talk to who was kind, yet I knew we had moved on, and nothing would ever be the same. In my misery and confusion I turned to Elsie Sechrist at the ARE and asked for advice. As always, I couldn't express the depth of my sorrow; I was afraid I'd sound too melodramatic, and my early training had taught me to make light of woes and not to express emotions.

Elsie answered immediately, thanking me for the confidence I'd shown in the Cayce work and her very small part in it. She and Hugh Lynn were planning a visit to San Jose, and she said she'd consult him. There would be plenty of time before then for her to pray about my situation. She had found help through aligning herself with her higher self through meditation. She said my efforts were in the right direction, and she looked forward to seeing me and Neal the following month.

The Cayce teachers had said no one meets a condition he hasn't the strength to overcome – if he will. This offered me some cheer, especially when I thought of all the people far worse off than I.

| FORTY-SIX |

That which I most feared came upon me ('What you fear comes upon you,' the readings said) in the form of two notes I found in the pocket of Neal's jeans I was about to wash. One was from him to Natalie and one a recent one from her to him. Trembling with cold shock, I read hers first:

> Dear N. 11:10PM – we're stimulated by pleasurable un-
> expected surprises, ie, I love you more now, but better.
> In the everyday. I haven't that yet or in another vein,
> 'the grass looks greener, etc.' I know your body – It's a
> mystery to me. I half forget about you then your body

surprises mine; another awareness of a solution to the non-existent a moment before mystery disclosing itself. I know every inch, mole, blemish, hair, scar, pore yet don't think of them really (except maybe a tenderness for a favorite or outstanding one) until I see them again – then the flash of memories, and how probably felt with my hands or touched and sensed and tasted all the feelings of your reactions to touch and the different tastes of the various parts of your body yet it excites me more than someone or something that is as yet unexplored to me. I love you. N. At 5AM this sounds like a label on a bottle of English lice killer for care and treatment of scabies. Is best over absinthe.

I needed nothing more graphic to define their relationship – and how could I compete with that? To leave no doubts whatsoever, the notes were wrapped around a bunch of snapshots of Neal, Natalie, Allen and Peter cavorting on a sunny street in the City, Neal and Natalie entwined or Neal joyously clutching her in a variety of sexual poses. His own half-finished note to her supplied the capstone to my grief.

How does one begin? Especially after so long our moment was too brief (as this train is too fast, the roadbed too rough, my penmanship too poor for good writing) yet my memory dwelling on those sweet brown eyes pouring out into me for that instant – a need matching my own intensity, a lack, simple and true of release of tension, resulting from our 'human condition.' I dreamt of you last night; rather, it was two dreams, one night, one morning. Among other things, including verification of validity of authentic vibration between us, as opposed to simple sex hunger, actually similar level of Mind – I met your San Jose girl friend in the train yard and suggested I take her to you just so I could see you again. Thinking back I find I've written almost no letters for maybe 5 years; a love letter for twice that; to begin again then – I believe it quite possible, but rare, to feel a perfect lover, one with whom you are one because each match, as radio stations attuned perhaps...

That was all there was, and it was more than enough for me. And how handy – this note must not have reached her – only me. No doubts assailed me then that this might be simply more of the similar rhetoric he'd written to me and countless others. I believed every searing word as genuine, as I always had his love letters to me.

Neal found me red-eyed from weeping, the incriminating evidence laid out on the dresser. I was too beaten to yell at him, but I asked him mournfully if he wanted a divorce, now that he'd found 'the perfect lover'. He said no, he didn't want a divorce, and I tried to understand. 'But, Neal, I just cannot take any more – *please*! You don't love me at all; what could be more obvious? Why on earth must we stay married? This is no marriage, etc., etc.' His answer was the usual sympathy and comfort, along with the intensity of his effort to explain Natalie away, insisting she was no threat to *our* relationship. 'What relationship?' I asked, and got only 'Now, darling…' This time his words fell on deaf ears; I'd heard them all before so often. I saw that I was going to have to make any decision alone – or almost.

Once again I poured it all out to Elsie Sechrist, sure that now she'd agree Neal and I should separate. I eagerly awaited her answer, feeling freedom was in sight. It was, in her view. She said she had given my letter much thought. She asked if she could forward it to Hugh Lynn, since he had dealt with problems such as Neal's, and that I should call our San Jose contact, Mrs Winter, to arrange a time for Neal and Hugh Lynn to get together. She also suggested she and I make an appointment to talk. Letters weren't sufficient; we could get more done by talking together. She said as long as there is any doubt at all about divorce or separation, the time is not yet. This karma seemed impossible to bear, but each soul is prepared to handle the load, because it is ready. She felt Neal probably suffered even more, for every soul desires to be good and do good, but some have strayed so far in the past they've developed grooves it is hard to get out of. A weak person in my place would have given up long since, but my inner voice and true love for Neal urged me to greater patience. 'No doubt there have been many times when you have cried out, "How long, Oh Lord, how long?"' On the other hand, she said, when a soul has done all it can, and its spiritual state is in danger, the Lord steps in and makes the separation.

She suggested Neal might be one of those souls with a high IQ and a superabundance of creative power who might have been a very advanced soul in the past when the power flowed freely towards good. If, when reborn, the power is still flowing but not directed, it can only return to one place: back to the gonads, and it then causes the person to run wild.

Well, this was certainly more to my liking than anything from the psychologists, and after reading it I felt torn and sorry for Neal.

> Above all, do not be untrue to yourself or your own principles!...the strong must uphold the law. Selfishness is the basic sin of all of us, therefore, 'Thy will' is of the utmost importance to direct the energy to the pituitary gland...Love overcomes all things, and love will also conquer the differences with you, girl.

She advised us to read Starr Daily's book *Release* for further help to us both. 'Pray together, the whole family – there's magic in that, too.'

I still felt caged, and I strained against the bars, but she made such good sense I trusted her judgement. Sadly, I handed the letter to Neal when next he was home, and he read it with intense concentration, eager to do his best to comply with her advice.

'Have you called Mrs Winter yet? Did you get the book? Maybe she has one she could loan us.' Well, if he was willing to seek further help, thereby acknowledging he knew he had a problem he wanted solved, I must encourage him. It brought a little hope, but my supply of hope was running low. Ah me. 'Keep on keeping on,' said the Cayce teachers.

Mrs Winter loaned us *Release*, as well as Starr Daily's other books, and she was right; they were very inspiring. We found it hard to believe anyone could actually have an experience like that accredited to St Paul's sudden conversion, but when Starr (not his real name) as a lifer in prison had the same sort while hanging by his thumbs, Neal desperately hoped he'd be next. He was particularly impressed, because in his youth Starr had been far more depraved, far more heartless and cruel than Neal ever could be. It was awesome, that when Starr had his vision, without anyone else knowing about it, the attitude of everyone in the prison changed too, and he was given a job in the infirmary and later released. As a felon, of course, he was a non-entity with no jobs open to him. Instead, he travelled the world visiting prisons and giving talks to inmates.

The now annual Cayce conference was on, and during these Neal and I were as one, and could view our situation more objectively and discuss it calmly. Both Hugh Lynn and Elsie were staying with Mrs

Winter in her large two-storey home in the centre of San Jose. On the day of our appointments we all had lunch together, and afterwards Elsie led me upstairs to a bedroom, where on separate beds we lay and meditated rather than having a discussion. I didn't feel I'd mastered this technique, so I didn't quite know what to expect. I did my best to quiet my mind and emotions, and after about an hour I felt a great wave of lightness and peace, but that was all. She rose smiling and assured me she now felt everything would work out in time.

We returned downstairs just as Neal and Hugh Lynn emerged from the study, Neal's eyes aglow. Hugh Lynn motioned to me to come back inside with him, and he shut the door behind us. We sat on either side of the fireplace, and he reviewed briefly what he had discussed with Neal, concluding that Neal must work very conscientiously at self-discipline with the help of daily meditation. He explained the difficult task Neal had chosen in this life, but he said he had the power to overcome, if he would. Suicide was not an option; Neal would never be allowed a solution that easy; he had come to face his past, and face it he must.

I had expected him to ask me my side of the story and give me sympathetic counsel. Not a bit of it; he was even slightly impatient at my attempts to tell him. I'd forgotten he had read my letter to Elsie already.

'Now, you.' He returned to his own train of thought sternly, 'There's only one thing you have to do, and that is to keep still.' Surprise and disappointment made my heart sink. Had Neal given him some wrong impression? Had he rationalized the whole mess? Keep still, indeed! Ha – keep still? – in the face of Neal's continual delinquency in our marriage – his constant infidelity? I tried not to show my depression, especially since Neal was so elated by his interview. Well, I still had Elsie.

All the way home, Neal held my hand and vowed he would succeed, repeating a dozen Cayce affirmations. When he asked me what Hugh Lynn had said to me, he agreed it was a curious bit of advice under the circumstances.

'I don't think he likes me at all,' I said sadly. 'And he is so fond of you.'

'Now, come on, darling. I'm sure that's not true. It's just, well, you know – the greater the sinner, the greater the challenge, that's all it is.' But I was not to be comforted on that score, and felt quite misunderstood. When I was so right, and Neal was so wrong, it didn't make any sense.

A few days later a lovely letter from Hugh Lynn cheered me considerably.

> You have been in my mind and heart ever since I left San José. Every morning at 6.00 I will spend a little time thinking and praying about you. This will help, but it will not take the place of your own work at both prayer and meditation. If you will begin now, both of you, to set aside periods for prayer you will find that there will be will-power enough to begin to apply the spiritual laws of discipline which you know are necessary. You, Carolyn, must do exactly what I suggested for you – pray and keep your mouth shut. You, Neal, have a job to do with yourself that will probably be one of the toughest you have ever tackled, but the goal of being able to serve others who really need help is well worth the price of discipline and self-sacrifice you must make. The only power that will be great enough to enable you to exercise choice at this level will come from within, when the divine in you touches the point where the universal divinity meets this inner self. Love to you both.

'How very nice of him!' I said when Neal folded the letter thoughtfully. 'Maybe he doesn't dislike me after all. If he can find time to be helpful, what's our excuse?'

'Yeah – he's a great guy.' We both fell silent, grateful for all the kindness and inspiration the week had brought.

Despite this, I was still not convinced Hugh Lynn's advice met my needs. It was strange how his words continued to pop into my mind whenever I was self-righteously reminding Neal of his accumulating crimes. They were irksome, like a pesky fly. I'd try, I'd bite my tongue, but I was never successful for more than ten minutes at a time.

| FORTY-SEVEN |

Neal was gone more and more, my life a lonely round of housework and the children, my sanity saved by their need of me and the lovely environment surrounding me. Doing dishes, from the kitchen window, I'd survey the hills rising above the village with their patterns of vineyards tended by the Jesuits from their white monastery, and higher up the firetrails scarring the serene bulk of the mountains. The pool, closer in view, was a godsend in summer as a childminder, and nearly every child in the neighbourhood learned to swim in it. It was a haven for me too. Just deep enough to submerge completely and long enough for three or four strong strokes. Then drying off beside it in the sun offered total relaxation. Its upkeep was a minimal expense.

Every other spare moment I'd search the readings for comfort and added stamina, trying to resign myself to Elsie's dictum that 'God would make the separation'.

In a way He did, although not in a way I'd have chosen. Neal announced he wanted to move to the City and live with Allen and Peter. The reason he gave was that the railroad was so busy it was easier for him, since he had to spend so much time there between trains. I wondered how long it had taken him to make up that one; one of his weaker attempts at lying. I knew, of course, it was Natalie with whom he would share a flat. On May 10 I woke alone; there was a note on the bedside table: 'Dear Ma: I hate myself, and you know it. But, I looked long and hard at my son last night, & I fully realize my responsibilities, plus, I am in full fear of my failings that once a man starts down he never comes back – never. N.'

A sudden chill made me shudder at his ominous tone. Did he mean to stop trying – to ignore all the advice we'd just received? One of his favourite and oft repeated Cayce dictums was 'You haven't failed yet.' Ah, the power of desire – both of theirs.

I dragged on, clutching at the edge of the plateau I'd reached. I leaned into 'long-suffering', not divorce. Neal came home every two weeks with his paycheck.

One aspect was that I knew so little about Natalie and the nature of my competition. The only clue came from the Hinkles, to whose home Neal had once taken Natalie. Helen said she was 'strange' and 'weird'.

'She just sat there; never said a word, just stared into space – catatonic, I'd say –' and Helen shuddered, making a face. Why, I wondered, would Neal be so enamoured of that? But then, most often he took up with women whom he felt he could help or heal. I suppose she could have been on drugs. Al said she was well-known around North Beach for certain oral sexual practices, and that made more sense, yet the notes testified to a much deeper bond.

One weekend Neal appeared with another man, stayed a few minutes and left alone. I assumed at once this was an effort to salve his conscience by submitting a substitute, although in his own mind I'm sure he thought he was also doing me a kindness.

Pat was a tall muscular Adonis, blond and bronzed and as unlike Neal or Jack as anyone could be in every way. I was not at all receptive to this development. I wanted to tell Neal to please let me choose my own friends and lovers, thank you. Still, I would have been delighted if I could fall in love with a man who could replace Neal in my heart, so I made no immediate objections. All in vain, of course.

Nevertheless, Pat came down from the City every Sunday, and although it was a change in my routine, he was little company. On first arriving he'd spend hours cleaning and polishing his Austin Healey. Then he'd take a portable radio and a beach towel out by the pool to lie in the sun and dip in the pool to cool off. Obviously the facilities were the chief attraction. He was good at playing with the children around the pool, and it made Sunday dinner more fun for them, but it made me sick when he'd make a big deal out of a slip one of them would make, calling him 'Daddy'.

In my efforts towards independence that summer, I forced myself to go alone to lectures and spiritually oriented events. I saw quite a lot of Mrs Winter, and one such opportunity presented itself in her discovery of a fascinating 'bishop'. He held services in a small auditorium in the 'Y'. He was a slight young man with fine black hair and a pale complexion. The hint of a French accent was credited to his being Swiss in origin.

He had been ordained in what was called the Liberal Catholic Church, which had no connection with the Roman, 'Catholic' here refering to its original meaning of 'universal'. Nonetheless, Bishop Romano dressed in the black habit and purple surplus of the Roman priests. There were very few of these churches in this country. Reincarnation was accepted but not stressed, the emphasis more on the universality of all religions in that the same basic principles underlay them all, the same one power behind them. Bishop Romano's favourite teacher was Sri Aurobindo, whom I learned to appreciate too.

The service consisted of a fairly long silent meditation at the start and one at the end, with the 'sermon' in between. When the Bishop spoke, his regular delicate features softened into a serene expression so as to look almost waxen and glowing, his dark eyes large and luminous. In his robes and with slim expressive hands he reminded me of Italian portraits of the early Renaissance. His voice was melodic, low and clear, and had a tone of authority.

After the service, as we filed out and paused to shake his hand, I could hardly believe my eyes; he presented an altogether different appearance. Now he looked fragile, his manner awkward and shy, lacking the elegant poise so striking when he'd spoken. His voice, too, was almost squeaky and weak, his face putty-like and contorted in a variety of expressions which flitted across it. Had I imagined what I'd seen before? Did they have some marvellous lighting system? I could hardly contain myself until I could get Mrs Winter alone.

She smiled knowingly, 'Yes, isn't it amazing? Well, you see, they say the reason is that when he's giving his sermon, he's well – being used as a channel by a higher mind – maybe even Sri Aurobindo? Anyway, he speaks from a semi-trance state.'

'You mean he's a medium?' I asked, appalled.

'Well, in a way, I suppose, but it could be his own higher self, you see. Anyway, nobody wants to be called a "medium" any more.' Like Cayce, I recalled. Now they were known as 'channels'.

I pondered this quite a bit, and discussed it with Neal on one of his visits. He was so curious he wanted to go with me the next time. We decided we were in no position to judge the man, and if his lectures were inspiring what did it matter? I wondered why we thought this different from Cayce, but somehow it seemed so.

When Neal heard the Bishop, he too was very impressed and noted the difference in the appearance when we left. Neal came to these meetings several more times, and somehow I managed to stay off the subject of Natalie and was able to 'keep still' – I liked pretending things were as they had been, and there was no point, anyway, Neal still insisting he was living with Allen and that she meant nothing. Besides, he was working hard on the railroad to support me and the children, right?

| FORTY-EIGHT |

It occurred to us that perhaps Sri Aurobindo, although Hindu, still might provide a bridge between us and Jack's Buddhism. We hadn't heard from Jack all summer, but just when I'd decided to write him about the Bishop, I received a note from him in Mexico.

More paranoia. He said he was going to go to Allen's cottage in Berkeley, which of course I knew nothing about. He would wait to hear from me whatever I chose to tell him, even by way of Neal. He said he often thought of me, but he had been purposely silent, not wanting to cause any pain to anyone. He felt awkward, but asked me always to tell him the truth and not pretend. He said he had no ego any more. He would come see me, the kids and the new house, but didn't want to surprise me.

Now what on earth had brought all that on? I had not written him, simply because I didn't want to mention Natalie, which I knew would pain him to hear and embarrass me to confess. Well, he'd be coming, so I would try to straighten him out. First, I'd send him a cordial invitation.

Neal met Jack in San Jose at the yard office and drove him home for dinner – our traditional one. On the way, I presumed Neal had brought Jack up to date on Natalie and his activities in the City. What with all the water under the bridge, or should I say women under Neal, we didn't exactly recapture the bright hopes bred of our former relationship, but if Jack and I were older and sadder, there was a mellowness from loneliness and endurance, perhaps even a deeper longing and warmer empathy we could now only express by tender looks, with which I hoped to dispel his doubts. I bloomed a bit with the three of us together again, and welcomed the crumbs of attention I had done without for so long.

When the children were finally in bed, and Jack duly impressed with our prayer ritual, we moved the television set into the living room. We hadn't shared TV before, and it would keep us away from personal pitfalls. Luckily, there was nothing in particular anyone wanted to concentrate upon, and none of us could stop talking for long, so Neal played his channel switching game with a running commentary, whether on commercials, situation comedies or musical variety shows, Jack adding his own highlights.

Jack had brought a large batch of tea from Mexico, and now produced it, Neal jumping up and down in anticipation and delight. Jack spread it out on a newspaper in his lap for the manicure, and Neal brought out the old Sir Walter Raleigh tobacco tin in which his always lived. Neal remained in action, hopping back and forth from the TV, and stopping to exclaim about the tight curly leaves of Jack's supply, urging him to hurry.

I went to sit on the couch across the room opposite the window. I saw a car turn into our driveway, supposing it was someone turning around. But no – it come on further and parked. Then I saw the flashing red lights.

'My God, Neal – it's the cops!' I ran to the window just as the Sheriff opened his car door. Terror shot us into action. I sprang to turn out the lamp, while Jack scooped the newspaper around the tea and stuffed it behind his back, turning his full attention to the TV. Neal sat in the chair I had vacated, also apparently engrossed in the TV. I answered the door, trembling from head to foot. The officer stepped into the dark entryway and asked for Neal Cassady. (There was no front hall, just a partition between the front door and the dining area, so the TV and living room were in full view.)

Neal jumped to his feet, all eagerness to please. 'Yes sir, I'm Neal Cassady. What can I do for you?' I knew I should turn on a light but, not sure how well Jack had concealed the tea, I didn't, and the officer turned on his flashlight and shone it around the room. I held my breath. Jack was still absorbed in the TV, having only looked up once at the cop and back again. I joined him, hoping the officer would not demand more light than the set emitted, and thinking I had a right to do as I pleased in my own home, rudeness included.

The officer was saying to Neal, 'I'm sorry to disturb you [what an understatement that was!] but when you came by the office this afternoon to pay the traffic fines, we made a mistake. Instead of two hundred dollars, it should have been two hundred and sixty – we need another sixty dollars.' You could almost touch the sighs of relief – so far! Poor Neal, he always somehow managed to get caught.

'Oh? Well, why of course,' Neal sprinted to our bedroom, calling back, 'Uh – dear – where is the cheque book?'

I hurried to follow him, saying, 'Never mind; I'll get it; it's in my purse.'

Neal returned to the living room and chatted casually with the officer, while I tried to keep my hand steady enough to write the check.

When that car finally backed out of the driveway and zoomed off into the night, we were all close to fainting. Not for long, of course. Neal and Jack were lightheaded and giddy at the narrow escape, retrieving the tea and carefully seeking out every fallen crumb while giggling and chortling at putting one over on the cop. I was considerably sobered; the episode had not only frightened me, but the revelation of the amount of money Neal had lost on citations unbeknown to me dampened my mood. Being poor at concealing my displeasure, I decided to retire, so at least the men could salvage the evening for their pleasure.

Neal slept with me, and Jack took the eight-foot couch in the living room. I allowed myself to cuddle Neal's body, so long deprived, but some time ago I had told him I no longer would tolerate sex with him. He had taken it in good grace, much to my surprise, both of us, however, aware he had many other outlets, hence my decision. Since his methods had always been painful it was a relief to me and no real loss to him. He had even told me he preferred masturbating, and thus not having to deal with a woman.

When he left for work the next morning, he said he'd try to get Allen to come back with him that evening to go with us to hear the Bishop. I was happy Jack elected to spend the day with me. The children, however, kept him so occupied by showing him all their new 'forts', climbing trees and any other treasures in the neighbourhood, we had little time to talk. In the afternoon he swam with them, frightening me but impressing them by doing jack-knife dives into four feet of water. Only when they napped could we touch – without sex, and I was able to reassure him I was not 'aloof', always told the truth, and had not changed nor ever would in my love for him. I was always grateful for chances to overcome his paranoia.

Neal arrived for dinner without Allen, because Peter and Pat wanted to come too, and they couldn't get here until seven. Although they'd miss the sermon, Neal urged them to come anyway. I wasn't in favour; it was hearing and seeing the Bishop in action I thought important. Neal had heard the Bishop sometimes went to people's homes after the meetings, so Neal asked him to come to ours that night. The Bishop accepted his invitation.

I was panicky, having to fend and prepare for so many guests suddenly, including the awesome personage of the Bishop. I supposed he liked tea – the liquid kind – and of that I had plenty. Jack had his wine and hoped the Bishop would join him. I was worried Jack had had too much already. This was not at all how I wanted him to be introduced to the Bishop.

Allen, Pat and Peter had already arrived when we returned home from the meeting, and I had barely time to put on the kettle and inspect the living room when the Bishop's car drove in. I felt anything but the competent hostess, lacking an upbringing to make me at ease with the clergy, and I was further unsettled when I opened the door to the Bishop and two middle-aged women as well. Struggling for poise, I didn't note their appearance in detail; my first impression was only that Dickens would have loved them. The Bishop introduced them as his mother and his aunt.

Our furniture was sparse, but we recruited some from the patio and sat the Bishop beside the unlit fireplace facing the room in a canvas 'campaign' chair, its high wing back creating a throne-like effect I felt suitable, if a trifle overwhelming for his slight frame. The two ladies sat together on the couch under the front window, now shuttered, and the rest of us brought in chairs from the dinette set – all except for Jack. He settled himself on the floor beside the Bishop, cuddling his bottle. At first he leaned back against the low bookcase, his eyes closed, and quoted a few passages from the *Diamond Sutra*, but little by little moved to lean against the Bishop's chair as he sipped from his bottle.

Bishop Romano took it from there, expanding, commenting and relating the content as though it was as familiar a topic as the weather. Jack then leaned against the Bishop's knee and sighed, 'I love you,' then sank back and took another swallow. The Bishop smiled; the rest of us pretended not to notice. This gesture happened frequently from then on.

As during the service, the Bishop's face was relaxed, his voice strong and resonant and his manner poised. I felt calmer, especially since everyone was giving him their full and respectful attention. Neal paced about at the opposite end of the room, searching his mind, I knew, for a relative example from Cayce, but still somewhat shy in the presence of a real 'preacher'. The two women gave me the strange feeling they had presented us with a magic doll, as in

Petroushka. They never took their eyes off the Bishop, and they never spoke.

I slipped out to prepare the tea, and then heard that Neal had found an opening to present *his* favourite sage. The Bishop was equally at home with this approach, and brought his comments in line accordingly, but he went on to explain that the harmony needed to develop the new age must come from an understanding of both Eastern and Western thought, and, like Sri Aurobindo and Parmahansa Yogananda, he stressed the compatibility of the Eastern teaching with those of Jesus on an evolving spiral of life experiences, the only difference being the terminology and images employed in expressing the same universal truths to different cultures in different times.

Allen had so far said nothing, and I had expected the closest rapport to come from him, he being considered the best informed among us on Eastern mysticism, although we learned later he wasn't at all. I wondered then if he felt some ego challenge from this ethereal young man. Whatever the case, he didn't introduce Sri Krishna; there was another topic on his mind. He helped me pass out the tea cups, and then marched over to the couch and squeezed himself between the two ladies.

'Now then,' he fairly yelled, 'what about sex?' I suppose I should have been grateful he didn't remove his clothes, but it had much the same effect. Even Neal fidgeted and looked at his feet. Jack giggled, 'Allen!' Pat's prominent jaw dropped, and Peter and I looked blank, as did the ladies.

Allen grinned, his black eyes peering at the Bishop, but the latter spoke calmly and seriously, never batting an eye.

'Yes, of course, sex is a vitally important aspect of the whole – the governing Life Force that must be understood for what it is and properly directed. The Adam-man uses this force, the Kundalini, to create new bodies for his own sensual pleasure, but when he rises to the Christ-man, he uses it to form creative ideas that materialize in benefits for mankind while evolving his own consciousness onwards beyond his animal nature. Our most powerful force, indeed. We are probably more familiar with it in its destructive power when it is misdirected in a negative sexual way.' I said a silent 'Amen', and remembered Hugh Lynn's admonition to Neal about misdirected power.

With this variety of nuts, and with Jack's intermittent 'I luuve you' to the Bishop, I was heartily glad when the ladies broke their silence decisively by indicating to their charge it was time to go. When the trio had departed, the serious tone swiftly changed to mirthful reflection, rebuilding the evening with hilarious might-have-beens, although I thought quite enough *had* been. Jack's chuckle grew into a hearty laugh with, 'God, Allen – you and your "now let's talk about sex!"' and he rolled over on the floor holding his stomach.

Allen shrugged and grinned, 'I was only trying to liven things up a bit. Those two gargoyles loved it; I nearly put a hand on each knee – they'd have loved that, too.' Neal chortled at the picture, but his reverence for the Bishop and subject matter kept him from taking that topic any further.

Neal had neatly arranged his own return to the City for the night, using Allen and Peter's need for transport as his excuse. Pat, he said, was going to visit friends further down the coast, so was no longer available. I wondered if Neal had thought of Jack and me and wanted to do us a favour. Jack and I had no idea we would have a night alone together; it was such an unexpected gift, and we looked at each other in awe as the others filed out. In bed we fairly smothered each other with our pent-up longing, our hopeless dreams and future fate. Somehow we knew it was a last time. We slept very little, not wanting to lose a minute of being together again. At dawn he gathered his sleeping bag to go outside, not to be found in my bed by the children.

| FORTY-NINE |

Next morning when I got up, Jack was basking in the sun on the patio, but came in when he heard me in the kitchen. The children had already left for school. He gave me a big hug and kiss.

'Here, have some orange juice; coffee'll be ready in a minute. Did you sleep at all?'

'Yeah, sure – that is, once I got settled. I started out here on the patio, but Cayce-dog kept licking my face, so I moved out beyond the fence to that lone prune tree. Beautiful unobstructed view of the stars and so quiet – you should sleep out there allatime – only – what's the smell?'

'Oh dear. We don't have sewers, I'm afraid. That's the septic tank. We're working on hooking up to Los Gatos sewers. But if you put your house-trailer back far enough...'

'That's what I'm gonna do soon as I sell a book.'

'Meanwhile, look at this while I do the breakfast dishes, okay?' I gave him a pamphlet by Sri Aurobindo. 'It's kind of an extension of the Bishop.'

He took it outside and read it carefully, making notes in the margins, and when I joined him he read me passages. His interest was gratifying; I'd missed Neal in that role for so long. I brought him a beer, since he complained of a hangover.

'The man's right, you know. Self-surrender is the key; you oughta surrender to Neal.'

'Whatever do you mean "surrender"? Just agree with anything he does or wants? Come come now, "This above all: to thine own self be true." Unless you mean surrender my personal ego, my attachment. I agree with that, all right, and I do try, but it's such a foreign concept from tradition.'

We continued a long, intense discussion in depth of our developing ideas. Jack didn't like logical analysis, preferring his ethereal mystical imagery and intuition, so whether we achieved more understanding on life's issues, I can't say. I tried to bring him back to practical applications: 'I guess all my fussing at Neal is really because I want him to be *mine* – want him to love me *more*. Oh dear.'

'Neal does love you.'

'Oh, I suppose so, in his way. As Starr Daily said, people love to the best of their ability at any given time, and that's all you can expect. So it's useless for me to demand Neal love me the way I love him; he's giving it his best shot for now. Dante said love is like a mirror; the more you give the more is reflected back. I admit I'm not putting out much love at present.' I thought about these sobering ideas then sing-songed, 'Cayce says if you want to be loved, be lovely.'

'You are, and I love you,' and he kissed me.

'Dear Jack. I do better loving *you* the right way. I think Neal and I must just have some karmic thing we have to work out. I know I could never possess you, so I don't demand more love from you – and you give me enough – and you and I haven't made great vows to each other, yet we both believe in marriage. How odd. You and I believe vows are to be kept; Neal that they are to be broken. Well, it's not quite that simple.'

'Neal gets mighty possessive when he thinks he might lose you.'

'Yeah, and all his other women, too, ha; you should know. Once his always his. I guess it all comes back to ego – self. Hard to get ourselves out of the way.'

'I just read that in the Aurobindo book – only he was talking about standing aside and watching your machinery work. That's also the basis of spontaneous prose and poetry; you don't say "*I*" do it; it's the gunas that work – aspects of God. That's why publishers have no right telling writers how or what to write.' We leaned close against each other, watching the clouds rearrange their shapes in the vivid blue above us, silent in thought.

'If only Neal could break the tea habit and replace it with meditation. We know there are no shortcuts. What a powerhouse he could be.'

'Yeah; I try to tell him, too, but he won't listen to me no more. Anyway, he's got to be active. You gotta go off by yourself alone. That's what I'm going to do – find a mountaintop and sit alone and meditate. But Neal, aw, that's the way he is, woman. Just do what he wants and know he's great.'

Jack turned on his side, his head propped on his hand, his eyes closed, scowling. A lock of hair fell in his face, and when I brushed it back the scowl cleared and he laughed softly. Then, jumping up, he reached for my hands and pulled me to my feet.

'Come on, let's get some wine.'

We got as far as the French doors to the house when we heard the front door slam, and Neal flashed past us into the bedroom, calling back, 'Come on, children, hurry up, we're going to the track. Can't miss the first race.' Jack burst into laughter now; this was the Neal he loved, and he went to the kitchen to get his wine, while I followed Neal into our bedroom, where he was changing his socks.

'The what? – did you say?'

'The track, baby, racetrack – Bay Meadows – you'll love it, c'mon.'

Jack came out of the kitchen and nodded to me, 'Ever seen a horse race?'

'Only in the movies. But how come, Neal? I didn't know you liked horseracing.'

'Never used to. But this is different.' He hitched his jeans, swiped at his hair, ricocheting from bathroom to me, 'I don't go to see the races, you understand – uh – ah – well, you see, I've learned of this marvellous secret system, yass, yass.' And he went into his W.C. Fields accent, grinning at Jack.

'Uh-uh, my dear; don't say a word; I know what you're thinking, but this one really works; I'll show you – prove it to you. Now leave a note for the kiddies and tell them where we're going. We'll be home for dinner. Hurry up now, or we'll miss the first race.' In the wake of Jack's advice, I let go and did what Neal asked.

On the way to Bay Meadows, Neal briefly explained his 'system'. You simply bet the last minute on the third-choice horse. The theory was that the first and second choices are often over-rated, but the third choice was likely to be just as good sometimes, and by the law of averages it had been proven to be so; it won frequently and consistently, and the odds were better. The trick, of course, was to bet each time enough money to cover any previous losses. Neal began with $2, and it usually hit before he lost very much, thereby getting it all back plus the winnings. He had been doing this a month or so (I groaned) and had begun to keep detailed records by checking the daily race results in the paper. So far, the longest period of loss was eleven consecutive races. Well, no, he hadn't had the capital to cover that – 'But think! If I *had*! Honestly, darling – think of it. Now, in time, I'll have other guys covering all the tracks in the country – every race! But, you see, it must be done scientifically, no getting interested in the horses, no listening to tips from touts – it's hard work, not fun.'

'Well, I guess I've heard everything now. I'd never have believed you'd become a gambler.'

'No, no! Of course I'm *not*! This isn't gambling; I just told you – it's scientific. Just a job. You have to keep your ears shut and just watch the tote board until the very last instant, run for the window and bet the third choice. Then wait for the next race, and so on. That's why nobody does it, dig? It's really tough.'

Not to bring him down any further with my doubts, I rode the rest of the way in silence, while Neal rattled away to Jack the latest statistics. I could tell Jack wasn't altogether convinced, either, and Neal was putting even more conviction into selling him – his brother.

At the track, after Jack had shown me the paddocks, the tote board and the betting windows, I stayed in my seat while they ran back and forth. I found the people fascinating, as always, but the races quite different from those seen in movies. In those the suspense was built by dragging out each race to what seemed at least fifteen or more minutes, but watching them live the race was over in a flash, and the time between races interminable.

Neal didn't win that afternoon, and he was thoughtful and quiet on the drive home. Directly after dinner he left again for the City, this time taking Jack with him.

* * *

One morning a few weeks after our day at the races, I received a telephone call from the banker who had set up our investment funds. We had felt unusually lucky, since our initial investment of $5000 had doubled in value in just one year, so I greeted the gentleman warmly.

'Mrs Cassady? I'm sorry to bother you again, but when you and your husband were in the office yesterday to cash in your investments, I forgot one paper for you to sign.' My mind went blank.

'What do you mean? You what? Oh, you must have the wrong Cassady,' I laughed. 'I haven't been in your bank since we came to invest originally. My mother is fine – well, obviously, this is a big mistake.'

I expected Neal home that night. In my condition I felt it was safer to leave him a note, not start talking. I thought of Hugh Lynn's 'keep still', knew the written word was just as wrong, but I considered it a tiny bit of progress. I wrote it out several times, and when I was satisfied it was as unemotional as I could manage, I left it by the bed:

> Dear Neal, In case I'm too sleepy to keep you awake tonight, I'll talk at you by this less painful method. What did we say about getting greater tests as we grow stronger? It sure happens fast. The good Lord decided I should know about your deal in Cupertino, too. I keep wondering why, but am going on the assumption it's to give me an 'opportunity' to overcome rather than one to get even. Poor guy, when he called I said, no, we hadn't gone East nor had my mother died. I really thought he had the wrong Cassady. Anyway, when he persisted, I had to admit ignorance of the deal (clever boy, why must you make things so complicated?) He wanted to sell the stock immediately and swear out a warrant for Natalie's arrest. I hastened to collect the children from their schools and dashed over there to countersign the whole thing and told him to hold it. He assured me he'd be standing by if I ever wanted to bring the guilty party to justice. I tried to

explain that you thrive on punishment, so nothing to do but try something different, and hope the horses come in. No wonder your parties are so renowned, wow! By the way, is the identification card of mine she used something I'd miss? She did very well, I must say, but could use a bit more practice on the C's.

Like you say: I ain't dead yet.

Guess I've said all I can keep from. Wake me if I won today. C.

It took every once of grit I had not to let fly all the vindictiveness I felt. I'd never have believed he'd go so far. Not being able to sleep, I spent the night working on myself, repeating every affirmation and Christian principle I could remember, even when I heard him come in, read the note and slide into bed to sleep. Still I hung on, keeping the mouth shut but filling my head in constant rote: 'Bless those who despitefully use you' etc.

At last I could accept it in a kind of fatalistic light. After all, I told myself, it was really *his* money to begin with. We were no worse off than if he'd never had the accident – better; we still had the house.

Next morning Neal was overcome with contrition and remorse, both for getting caught and for the act itself. My note (and my closed mouth) seemed to have helped that much anyway. He, too, was amazed at his action in retrospect, but he'd been so sure he'd win it back in no time, replace the money, and no one would be the wiser, only richer. He planned to show me proudly that the system worked, and we'd be set for life. Instead, he had not been able to follow his own advice; he had listened to touts and tips, missed races, and lost nearly all of the $10,000 in close to a month.

'Neal, what dumbfounds me – aside from the idea you can get something for nothing – is you always manage to get caught. You'll slip up on some little thing every time. Do you suppose subconsciously you demand to be punished? You're always dropping clues about for me to find, like Natalie's notes. I don't even have to be a nosy wife.'

He pondered. 'It sure looks that way.'

'Well, *I* don't want to punish you. Get somebody else to be your warden or mother – go to confession. It's a role I detest, though I've played it to the hilt, I admit.'

Nor did I give up the role overnight, but just to be able to see some improvement in my behaviour was a blessed relief. I still lost patience with both Neal and the children, and we often skirted the crater of despair, but with our growing knowledge of life's principles and purpose, there was something to turn to, a direction to follow, and we'd already learned that when we managed to act on the theory, in never failed to work. So, as Winston Churchill said, 'To survive is to have the chance to begin again.'

| FIFTY |

On December 1, I sent the children off to school and sat down with a cup of coffee and the morning paper. On page 2 was the headline 'Woman fights off rescue, leaps 3 stories to death.' I don't usually take any notice of that sort of news, but this had one of those compelling photographs of a building with a dotted line superimposed from roof to the sidewalk below. As my eye followed the arrow, it ended at a car – just like Neal's. The familiar sickening wave of fear made my hand tremble so I could hardly read the article.

> An unidentified woman about 35 years old slashed her throat on a rooftop at 1041 Franklin Street yesterday, then kicked free from the grip of a husky policeman and jumped to her death from a third-story fire escape.
>
> Wearing only a bathrobe and T-shirt, she stood poised outside the railing of the narrow fire escape walkway as Officer O'Rourke lunged through a window to grab her. 'All I could do was dive through and grab,' he said. 'I got a grip on one arm and her robe just as she tried to kick loose. But I couldn't hold her. All at once I was just holding the robe, and she had fallen.' His partner said she might have slashed herself with fragments from a broken skylight.

'Unidentified'. Could it be Natalie? Why would I think that? It could be anyone's Packard, and I thought Neal had said Natalie was 24. I must be imagining – dramatizing. But the apprehension lingered. In another hour Neal telephoned.

'Carolyn – Natalie – Natalie is dead.'

'I saw the paper, Neal. I'm so sorry. Would you like to come home for a while?' He didn't hesitate.

'Oh, could I?'

'Of course, Neal; this is still your home, like it or not. I know you loved her; it must be awful for you.'

Later that day he dragged into the house looking grey and gaunt. I'd never seen him so unhinged and defenceless. I poured him a cup of coffee, and he slumped into a chair. I got the feeling he wanted to talk, but it was hard for him to discuss her with me after denying her for so long. Maybe if I sounded matter-of-fact he could too.

'I saw your car in the photograph. Where were you?'

'I was asleep, see? She got up and went out. I'd no idea, but when I heard the sirens, I thought of you and the kids getting involved and just grabbed my stuff and ran out the back way.'

'I am truly grateful for that! What made her do it? Was it suicide?' I hated to suggest it, but that might explain some of his misery. He'd become convinced by the Cayce readings that suicide was the worst crime against yourself. It would mean a severe karmic lesson in learning to appreciate the gift of life. Neal groaned.

'I don't know – partially – no, I don't want to believe that. She had become completely paranoid the last couple of weeks, and she already had an obsession about cops. Part of it was the guilt she felt for forging your signature; she's been agonizing ever since – and she did that for me. I kept telling her it was all right, you weren't mad, but it didn't help. She got so bad she talked of nothing but sin and guilt and how we were going to be arrested for our sins. Last week she tried to cut her wrists, but the knife was dull, and I told her all about suicide and never to think of it again. I thought she was better – and she was her old self last night when we'd talked a long time. I'll never know if she really cut her throat on purpose; one paper said she fell on the skylight and could have done it that way. And she didn't actually *jump*; she was afraid of the cop, so when he grabbed for her she must have backed up and off...' He stared blankly into space.

'Well, maybe – look at it this way: perhaps it was an out for her – a chance for her to change course, to start over. She seemed to have boxed herself in. It could be a merciful release, couldn't it?' Neal brightened a trifle.

'Yeah, maybe; I suppose it really is better for her. She was insane – I couldn't help her.' I persuaded him to take a hot bath and rest.

Next day Neal moved his things back home. He was considerably sobered by grief and guilt. He had loved her very much, and now she had become something of a martyr in his eyes, on the verge of being a saint (I feared). The papers were still saying she had not been identified, and we thought it safe enough for Neal to do it and get the poor girl settled. That grim task set him back some more, and he called LuAnne, who met him at the depot. She told me he held on to her hands and talked it all out again. 'He sounded as though it had impressed upon him his downward path to destruction.'

I told her about the note he had left with me when he moved in with Natalie. Violence and death he had succeeded in avoiding until now. He felt the incident represented a powerful warning or punishment. I resolved to work even harder to make him happy now that this obstacle had been removed.

During this time Jack had been visiting in San Francisco and Berkeley, meeting Allen's friends, including Gary Snyder, with whom he'd spent a couple of months climbing mountains in the Sierras and enjoying Gary's Zen practices. A book resulted, called *The Dharma Bums*.

Jack had known Natalie slightly, but was frightened by her insanity. On his way back to North Carolina for Christmas he stopped to see us for a few more days. Now that it was cold and wet we made fires all afternoon and evening – another new experience to share, and we often sat on the floor drinking wine and talking.

On evenings when Neal was home we'd bring in the TV. It was cosy and genial, but I was aware that Jack persisted in feeling in this house he was an outsider. He had to sleep on the couch, and the house was all too open; no private room where he could shut the door to nap or write, and now he couldn't escape by staying outside. I know he didn't intend to, but with his habitual paranoia, he gave out the impression we'd done it on purpose, and he spoke more often of his homelessness.

Neal's obsession with the races continued to grow. He insisted now he was obligated to continue the system in order to atone for his guilt of having lost our savings and for Natalie's death. He turned a deaf ear to reason. Every evening he spent an hour with the newspaper race results, calculating every race, keeping exact scores with hyroglyphics in the margins.

Then, folding the sheet meticulously with the chart uppermost, he'd place it carefully in order in a beer carton and return it to the closet shelf. I'd watch the cartons accumulate and sigh, wishing all that mental genius and concentration were being directed towards a more constructive goal. Jack agreed, but said nothing to Neal.

The week before Christmas, Jack left to hitchhike home, and he looked forlorn and lonely starting off in the cold, grey fog. I received a welcome postcard when he reached North Carolina to let me know he'd arrived home safely, and telling of hopping freights and communing with truck drivers at night. He wanted to know how Neal had made out at the races on a Monday and the next day, when Jack was supposed to have played for him – just so he could figure what karma might have befallen him. He wished me a happy new year with kisses.

On Christmas Day, Allen, Peter and one of Peter's brothers, Lafcadio, came to share our feast. They were the most gratifying of guests to cook for; I watched a twenty-pound turkey melt away as though by time-lapse photography. I wondered how frequently they ate. We had a jolly time, Allen always so helpful and considerate, and Peter too. We all liked Peter. He had craggy features, his eyes were warm, his manner gentle and quiet yet alert and intelligent. He spoke only when he had something to say. I couldn't imagine him being as boisterous as I knew Allen to be at times – even on the night of the Bishop's visit, he'd been so quiet I'd hardly known he was there. Maybe he was Allen's straightman then, but not, I learned, in years to come.

I wrote to Jack about it, and he was horrified at the men attempting to clean out our food stores. And, sadly, his mother was called away to a funeral, so he spent Christmas alone. He regretted not staying with us, especially since he learned Malcolm Cowley had come to California with his manuscript of *On the Road*, ready to put on the final touches, only to find Jack wasn't there. He reminisced about fires, wine, playing catch and relaxing with Cayce readings, now all having to wait for later – ever 'later'.

| FIFTY-ONE |

In January 1956 an event took place that surprised and delighted us: a book was published entitled *The Search for Bridey Murphy*, and it caused a furor. It supported the evidence for reincarnation, but to us it was perplexing that this book should receive so much attention, rather than a book like *Many Mansions*, written by a modern scientist. And so many others before. Neal jumped for joy.

'See? See? Cayce was right! He said that between 1958 and 1998 there would be a renewed wave of interest in spiritual matters throughout the world!' And so it would seem. Everyone in all walks of life was suddenly talking about *Bridey Murphy*. We were intrigued and amused to watch a debate on television by a panel of psychiatrists, unanimously debunking the whole preposterous idea. Why then, we wondered, didn't they ask themselves why they got so emotional about it? They were positively apoplectic. If it were such obvious nonsense, why bother? Why not indifference?

Two months later an article appeared in *True* magazine by Morey Bernstein, the author of the book, and here he stated that he had originally been fascinated by the work of Edgar Cayce, but he knew no one would listen if he wrote about him, so he decided to do some experimenting on his own. Now he could acknowledge the debt to Cayce. Apparently Bernstein had pushed the right button at the right time, for from then on, we witnessed an astonishing rapid increase in interest and investigation in the spiritual and the occult, and in the next decade we were to accept as commonplace events that would have been considered miracles or trash in our youth.

Then, a few years later, Arthur J. Lerner made a wonderful starstudded movie from his fascination with the Edgar Cayce readings. It is called *On a Clear Day You Can See Forever*. Designed by Cecil Beaton, Barbra Streisand has never looked so beautiful. And Lerner did it exactly right – the best way to sell an idea – with humour and great songs, so the idea was inoffensive to everyone.

Jack had heard the news of *Bridey Murphy*, too, and wrote at once. He gave a detailed account of all the previous lives he thought he remembered while meditating under his back yard tree, as Buddha had done under the bo tree. Shakespeare and Balzac were prominent memories, he declared. He asked for the address of the ARE, because his sister was so interested and wanted literature. She had begun the study of astrology too. Neal and I were excited by this, hoping Jack might come around. Alas, no, he still preferred Buddhism, which provided him with an instant remedy for any painful situation that challenged him. And now that he was drinking more, the more he repeated Buddhist phrases, allowing no communication on a human level.

Jack had also been investigating Oral Roberts, and asked if we knew he was a Cherokee Indian. He said he didn't disbelieve him and his compassionate heart. He told how he, Jack, had healed a cough his mother had by hypnotizing himself to find out what was wrong, and had had a vision. He planned to ease his way into this method of healing as a channel of God. He didn't seem to note the similarity to Cayce. Sickness, he believed, was an opportunity for punishing one's self (forever guilt), and his phlebitis resulted from his cruelties in football. My own suspicion was that these Catholic-reared boys could not abolish 'punishment' – actually an Old Testament doctrine.

He then wrote that he'd written a new novel in 16 days, about his brother, Gerard. He felt it was his best yet, and so powerful it should make Shakespeare 'raise an eyebrow'.

Another letter soon followed with good news. He'd be able to meet with Cowley at Stanford University to begin the process of getting *On the Road* printed and published – as the first 'rock 'n' roll' book. Then he said he was homeless. Nin's husband was becoming irritated by his presence, and Memere had finally decided to accompany Jack to California.

Another letter came with even better news: he had been offered a job fire-watching in the Northwest Cascade mountains. He had even asked the ranger to take him back every year for the rest of his life. He rabbited on about having a hut there, an apartment in Mexico City, and twice a year coming to us, with fires and television – then asked me to let him take me and the kids to the Sierras, where he knew just the right trails and lakes.

I looked up at Neal. 'Do you think he'll really like being alone on that mountaintop?'

'Hell no, he'll hate it. That guy's lonesome in a crowd. He doesn't like his own company that much. Imagine him completely alone; he needs people; he'll go mad from boredom. Pah.'

Almost as proof of how much Jack needed someone to talk to, I got another letter within the week, a long rambling one full of possible incarnations and Buddhist prayers. He said what a joyous moment this was in his life, and how he felt great happiness in store. He said Memere was going to write me to ask Mrs Winter if she knew of any shoe factory in the area. We seriously doubted that, but he said everything was going to be just fine, the way he wanted it. He would see his 'sweet friend' soon.

Neal and I were both relieved and happy for his joy, and we both would have welcomed him and his mother settling in a cottage nearby, but some doubts did assail us. I had been thinking, and I tested these thoughts out on Neal. 'You know, Neal, what I think is that Jack's going on about how he wants to be alone because he is so moved by sensory pleasures – of all sorts, right? I can't think of anyone who can describe so sensually every kind of life in its many manifestations so intensely and lovingly, can you? Well, to the Catholics, sensory pleasure in any form is a sin. I think deep down what he wants is a way to avoid temptation in his enjoyment of sensory pleasures. There are none when he's alone. Whattya think?'

Neal nodded. 'Yeah – you may have something there.'

| FIFTY-TWO |

When Jack did come to California, I saw him seldom. He was busy with Cowley and catching up with Allen, who had improved his lot and his art and had been travelling through the Northwest reading poetry and lecturing at colleges. Jack renewed his Berkeley friendships and tried to show Neal some interest by going to the races with him and grumbling about the system. Then he said good bye to everyone and the world and went off to his mountaintop – rather prophetically named Desolation Peak.

The solitude affected him just as we had predicted. Although there were moments he cherished, he nearly did go mad with loneliness and boredom. He let loose in San Francisco on his return, wallowing in drink and 'sensory' pleasures. And he knew he would never go back. He was further disillusioned to have to face this truth about himself.

When he came to see us, Neal wasn't home. Worn out from partying in the City and depressed from his revelation, he asked me to drive him through the redwood forests in the Santa Cruz mountains between our home and the coast, hoping to find a secluded spot to set up camp and try again, not so far from friends. It was a grey damp day, but I packed a lunch and we stopped for wine in Saratoga, the little village on our way, then headed up the winding road beyond the town.

Jack had started out already gloomy and resentful, but when I told him – and I had to repeat it several times – that it was unlawful to light fires in these mountains except in designated areas, his disillusion was complete. On and on he ranted at so-called 'progress', 'civilization' and the interference of bureaucracies in private lives. It was useless to argue with him, so after a stab or two at more cheerful conversation, such as pointing out the beauty of the scenes surrounding us, I gave up and retreated to noises of agreement.

Then he growled, 'Well, if that's it – hell; there's no use going any farther. Drive up that dirt road and we'll eat our lunch.'

The sun had begun to peep through the fog and filter golden shafts between the trees to steam the ground. I loved the variety of smells of these wooded hills, and tried to get Jack to accept the conditions, forget his woes and join me in a jolly picnic. In the middle of a redwood grove we found a tiny clearing, the ground covered with soft brown and auburn leaves now warmed by the sun. He tried to be more cheerful, then fell to reminiscing about us and became glum again.

After we'd eaten, he stretched out on the ground while I removed the picnic debris and folded the cloth on which I'd laid it. He reached for my arm and pulled me down beside him. I sensed he wanted me to make love to him, but in spite of the romantic setting, the picnic, the new sun, the wine, his having sung the blues all morning and dwelled on his rootlessness, I'd formed a lump in my throat and couldn't relax enough to feel at all sexy. He was too shy to make the first move, as was I, so I pretended I hadn't read his signals and just lay close to him, my head on his shoulder. We sipped more wine, stared at the treetop leaves glittering in the sun and dozed a little, he clutching my arm over his chest.

When we got home he built his fire in the fireplace, and I poured him more wine, so by the time Neal came home for dinner, Jack was happy once more and ready to indulge in an evening of Neal's brand of television. Again he slept outside, lugging his great pack that so intrigued the children, and in the morning he accompanied Neal on his train back to San Francisco.

* * *

Gregory Corso was in the City. He, Jack and Neal went to the races together and joined other friends in parties, but Jack was unhappy that Neal and Gregory didn't get along as well as he had hoped, so Jack asked if he might bring Gregory to our house for the weekend.

Saturday afternoon the three went to the track, but Gregory wouldn't follow Neal's instructions on how to bet, which didn't help bring them any closer. As it happened, Gregory would have won, but since he broke even he remained neutral, Neal disgruntled. Neal won, so at least he was in good enough spirits to be patient with Gregory. They rode to San Jose on Neal's train, and he drove them home in time for dinner.

Gregory made me nervous. He had a perpetual offputting scowl, and he didn't talk sense. Actually, he didn't talk – he'd just suddenly blurt out or shout some sentence I couldn't connect with anything. So I tried to shrink into the background for fear I'd antagonize him further. After dinner, with everyone somewhat ill at ease, we watched Neal and television, all sitting on our low bed in the dark bedroom with Neal perched on the edge ready to pilot the machine from channel to channel.

Gregory didn't understand this game and bellowed, 'How can I see the show?' Neal explained you always know what's going to happen next, so this way you could watch all the shows, and Jack added, 'It's all one show.'

Gregory paced between the bedroom, the hall and other rooms, grumbling, every now and then looking in through the bedroom door to see what was on the set at the time.

Next day no further rapport was forthcoming between Neal and Gregory. I saw that Neal couldn't talk to him any better than I could; we didn't know how to penetrate Gregory's brooding facade. Both Neal and I were withdrawn in the face of disapproval and discontent, and Gregory seemed disgusted with everything and everybody. So Neal went on doing what he did normally: lying on the bed reading newspapers and magazines, watching television and answering my queries, or those of the children and Jack. He was capable of taking in all stimuli at once, sorting them, and answering accordingly, still aware of the TV and his reading.

Today he was watching a sports event, so he didn't change channels. Meanwhile, Gregory wandered around aimlessly. He didn't even seem to want the big breakfast of bacon and eggs I prepared for him. He picked at it and pushed it around, still scowling. Jack took the children on their usual walk, and shortly after lunch Neal herded us all into the bedroom to watch Oral Roberts, one of Neal's regular rituals. Gregory was more disgusted than ever.

'You don't *believe* all that crap, man?'

Neal replied, 'Just watch; he's great!' and leaned forward avidly, taking in every word, muttering 'Yeah, yeah' every few seconds and bowing his head when they prayed. Although the Baptist terminology didn't mean much to me, I liked Roberts's sincerity and joy, which was unusual in the orthodox sects, whose hymns, even, were mournful, not joyous. Jesus came to bring joy, we believed. I knew Neal liked these same sincere dramatics, and we'd heard Roberts had opened a university and achieved some really good things. He did nothing to change our basic metaphysical beliefs, just added more colour to them, and was fun.

Jack and I obliged Neal for a while, then retired to the living room, leaving Gregory to growl at him. I was glad to get a chance to talk to Jack.

'Dear Jack – after five long years, *On the Road* is finally going to be published. When will the finished product actually be in the shops?'

'Yep – they said May or June, but now I suppose in the fall. Maybe then I'll at least have enough money to bring Ma out here. We'll find some place near enough so we can all see each other often, visit back and forth, hey? We'll have big Sunday feeds – chats across the fence? A real home at last. Course I'll still travel and go to Mexico now and then, but to have a place to come *back* to – and you being near, I'll feel better knowing you're looking after her.'

Although I said how much I'd like that and how much happier we'd all be – and really meant it – I never counted on his prophecies any more. He'd made so many hundreds of plans that had never materialized. I was tired of all the disappointments, and I hadn't forgotten all our grand expectations through the years of sharing a big old house together somewhere. I'd thought that was really going to happen. Why couldn't these men ever stick to anything? They still dreamt of the same eventual ends, but they couldn't persevere or give up a small new idea for a bigger dream, just scattered their energies fruitlessly. Jack and I couldn't discuss religion any more either. We'd each found our path, and he was no longer seeking – felt no need, as I did, to keep testing my tender, green beliefs. He knew all the answers he cared to.

That evening I fed the children first and put them to bed, then served the rest of us buffet-style in the living room by the fire with wine and candles, hoping to mellow Gregory a bit. Neal tried to please him too, by challenging him to a game of chess while Jack helped me with the dishes. Then, since Neal and Gregory couldn't converse, it was back to the TV. This time Neal let us stay with a movie, one of our favourite activities in the past.

About half way through it, Jack heard a noise in the front of the house and went to see. He let out a shriek when he opened the front door to Allen, Peter and a girl who had come to collect Gregory. They looked in the bedroom at us to say hello, then Jack took them out to the patio, whereupon Peter instantly shed his clothes and dived into the icy pool. When he'd dried, they left, taking Gregory with them.

In the morning there was only time for a brief kiss good bye before Neal took Jack to the yard office to begin another trek to Mexico.

Later that summer, when Gregory was in Amsterdam, he wrote to Neal apologizing for his actions that weekend.

> You, my friend, did offer me a fortune by placing my bets on your choice – I did not follow you – I was an ass – but reason I did not…was because I felt that you inspired in me a shot at what number illumined before me. The number lost. I lost. I will never forget the loss. Not that I lost 30 dollars, but that I lost your power that you so kindly bestowed upon me. I now ask you to forgive me and give me another chance. I am expecting 20,000 francs and will take it to the races and bet anyway you say until you tell me to stop. I'll tell everyone else to do so as well. You will be a millionaire in no time because you deserve to be – what I learn from Jack & Allen and my short life with you is that you are a wonderful human being – As I write this letter I am happy to remember that you were kind to me and liked me – the mad no brakes car ride – the track – your home and television – your suddenly transformed actions when you were in your RR garb – your love of women – your sad face – our great conversation in McCorkles shack when I first realized your mind – I love you – Gregory.

Like most of us, I thought, Gregory had hidden good resources, and I regretted my condemnation of his manners.

| FIFTY-THREE |

That spring we attended the ARE lectures as usual, and had our private counselling with Elsie Sechrist and Hugh Lynn. In the summer we went to a conference where the featured speaker was Starr Daily, whose books had so inspired us.

Starr was dynamic – a no-bullshit ex-con with blazing blue eyes in a tanned rugged face beneath a shock of grey hair. He was of medium height but sturdily built, with an air of authority and determination. Neal had high hopes that this perfect father-figure who knew about prisons would give him the magic he needed to mend his ways. He felt Starr had been 'sent' to him.

But when Neal did get to speak to Starr, he, like Hugh Lynn, could only tell Neal to use his own inner faculties to pull *himself* together. This meant a dedicated effort to reach these qualities through meditation and positive prayer. Poor Neal, there was no magic spell – just DIY, do it yourself.

Starr told him, 'You have just as much of the Spirit of God within you as did Jesus – that's what He came to demonstrate. "Ye are Gods," He said. "Anything I can do, so can you." Now get with it, boy – pray like the very devil and discipline yourself on a daily basis. Keep that light glowing. It will take time. You didn't get those lousy habits in a day, and you won't get rid of 'em in a hurry, either, but don't fight yourself – *revere* the life that's in you, for that life is God and rebellion is irreverence. Start with that. Keep that thought. You take the first step and God will rush in to help. You must choose.'

Alas, Neal's heavy indoctrination into Catholic dogma – just the opposite of this truth – made him unable to surrender his belief in his unworthiness and guilt. His prayers were apologies and supplications, not from a God-filled vessel affirming his divinity but of a miserable worm – a guilty sinner. We had Starr sign his book *You Can*, and I hoped Neal could.

Then he began consistently losing at the track, which deepened his feeling of failure and desperation. In my efforts to change the pattern of his thinking I found myself virtually insisting we didn't need any money – a strange declaration considering we were scrounging to live from hand to mouth. It was such a bizarre fixation for Neal to have, too; he'd never been acquisitive, and everyone knew he either gave money away or spent it on a good cause, yet here he was obsessed with the need to make a fortune. All to expiate his guilt. He even confessed he'd considered faking another accident, which of course horrified me, and I begged him to banish such a plan.

'You know you can't get good from evil causes!'

He smiled at my outburst. 'I know,' he said sadly. 'Don't worry, baby; I know the karma I'd be asking for.'

Imagine my reaction, then, when only a few weeks later I got the dreaded phone call for the second time. Neal had had an accident, had injured a foot and was back in the SP hospital. I'd learn no more until morning. Now I feared for his sanity.

Next morning I was torn between rushing to find out more and fearing to see him, but when I hesitatingly approached his hospital bed, Neal was smiling knowingly and nearly fell out of bed in his eagerness to grab me.

'Wait now – I know what you're thinking –' He silenced my forming question. 'No, darling, I did *not* do it on purpose. But isn't it fantastic? I had had that *thought*, right? Wow – talk about instant karma! Wait till you hear how it happened – you'll never believe! Sit down now and listen.' He was chortling with delight and awe at what he saw as a perfect 'demonstration'.

'I was facing the car, see, hanging onto the handhold by the passenger car steps, you know – ready to drop off when we'd slowed enough, and like a dummy I let my foot hang off the step. I'd forgotten about the metal mile-posts beside the track. Now, can you imagine my doing such a thing? Don't I know every little thing about getting off a train? Haven't I done it so much it's second nature? Now, honestly, darling, do I ever make that kind of mistake? *But I did*! – and my foot hit that thin metal marker. It sliced it neatly – right through my shoe – we musta been going about thirty miles an hour.' I winced and looked over at the enormous white cradle holding his right leg from the knee to the toes. Seeing my look, he said, 'No – now get *this*, baby, – not one bone was hit – not one – just flesh. Now is that possible? *And* it's the *other* foot! I'd be a gonner for sure if it had been the same one as before, right? But wait –' His grin broadened. He was relishing his tale and my absorption in it. 'On top of all that, I can't collect one red cent! We had just *barely* passed the yard limits, and I was *off duty*. How about that?' he asked in a hushed voice. 'Isn't that the most fantastically, perfectly clear and precise demonstration lesson? *"God is not mocked*!"'

Wheweeeew.' He sank back on the pillows, his eyes looking upwards in wonder.

I almost collapsed with relief. Not only had he committed no crime, he wasn't insane either. Best yet, he'd seen proof that a power beyond his conscious will could affect his life. Even if he wasn't sure God loved him, he marvelled at His shrewdness and appreciated His mercy. (It didn't seem to me a good time to try to point out that the power he had just witnessed came from nowhere other than himself; instead of lifting him up to view his own Spirit, it would have diminished his respect for God – since he couldn't yet see they were one and the same.)

*　　*　　*

During this time Allen was preparing to move on. He'd been in the bay area nearly three years, and could now justify his existence as a 'poet without a job'. He'd even made some money. So at last Allen was not the 'sick blank' he had once declared. He planned to return East and then reach out still further by invading Europe. (I tried to comfort myself by thinking perhaps my sending him away to Berkeley had produced these good results.)

Jack was in Mexico, and Allen, Peter and Gregory made a detour to visit him there. But Gregory was again soon grumbling; he disliked the shabby living arrangements, and insisted on moving into a posh hotel. In the end he gave up altogether and took a plane out, while the other three found a share-the-ride deal and drove across the wintry USA. Once in New York, Jack and Allen wrote a letter together in a light mood. Allen began it.

> Here's Allen and Jack writing you a letter on a nice type-writer in a big yellow airy apartment on 15th street and 6th avenue with a Hi-Fi set, Chinese matting, Picasso... big cats... Jack has a pretty girl who clings to him constantly so he has taken refuge in R's apartment to type novels for which there is a constant demand from thousands of pub-lishers clamoring over the telephone for our stories and poems... Please send immediately one huge metaphysical manuscript to circulate among the fairy editors of Manhattan. How is your foot?... How is sweet Carolyn? God has forgiven her (tell her) so how can I not?... Please tell her to forgive me for that night in her house. The

money you owe me, since you are sick you can have it for
keeps...but in half a year when we are starving to death
in Europe...I will write you big demanding desperate
letters, please do not let us starve to death, please, otherwise the money is yours...

Jack added a paragraph of his own to tell us he was going to
Europe with Allen to see Burroughs in Tangiers, to write in Spain
and spend April in Paris. He planned to read Joyce in the Trinity
Library in Dublin. He had somehow found Céline's address and
hoped to visit him. He also planned to make a lot of money, buy a
Mercedes and give it to Neal. He said Allen loved Neal, always
would, and so would he. Allen would marry Neal in Heaven and
would court him again on his return. Jack didn't know what to say
to Neal.

In February of 1957 Jack left to go directly to Tangiers and await
Allen and Peter at Bill's. In spite of his promise to write, we got only
postcards. Neal and I did so hope he might be inspired to write a
book less preoccupied with himself, but from what we read and
learned after his trip he had taken himself along, and home was
where his heart remained.

Not long before this trip, Allen had read a poem called *Howl* in
San Francisco at the Six Gallery and whipped the audience into a
frenzy. In that audience was Lawrence Ferlinghetti, owner of the fairly
new City Lights bookshop, and who published paperbacks of poets.
He arranged with Allen and others to publish *Howl* with some other
poems in a limited edition. This edition soon sold out, although it
received little attention from anyone not already familiar with these
poets. When a new edition was printed in England and shipped to
the bookshop, U.S. Customs seized the book as obscene literature.
Both Ferlinghetti and his clerk, Shig, were arrested in May.

The 'Beat Generation' was launched. The hearing opened in August,
and the furor kept the papers selling until October 3, when a decision
was reached in favour of Ferlinghetti. Neal got to look in on the
proceedings frequently between trains. In his passenger uniform,
doubtless no one in the crowded courtroom of North Beach bohemians
suspected he was the 'N.C. secret hero of these poems', part of
Allen's dedication.

I had to follow along with the daily press. Besides a front-page
article, every columnist had a comment or a point of view, either on

the issue of censorship by Customs, freedom of speech or poetry. Most fun were the pages of letters to the editors day after day – people even arguing heatedly with other letter-writers.

As an example of how unknown either the poetry or the poets were before the trial, one columnist casually made a note of the seizure of the book, spelled Allen's name wrong, and called the book *How*, 'A sort of do-it-yourself thing,' he guessed. It wasn't long before the national magazines picked it up, and the success of *Howl* was assured.

Since Allen was in Europe and missing the circus, I carefully clipped every word I could find so he could reconstruct his rocket-trip to fame. By the time I saw him again, it was ancient history and he was far beyond the launching pad. I hadn't considered the fact he must have a clipping service.

Before the arrests we had received a letter from him with his prophesied plea for money. Here was poor Allen scrounging for sustenance, when already the spinning wheel of fate had picked up his thread and was rapidly converting it into gold.

| FIFTY-FOUR |

Just before Jack left Tangiers for Paris he finally wrote us a long letter, first about the Arab tea smokers all over and the veiled women – although cheap, he couldn't afford them. He apologized to me for mentioning them.

He then went into a long dissertation about moving his mother to California, repeating most of what we'd already discussed, but saying his mother would like Neal to come help them move, for which Jack would pay him. He complained that Neal never wrote him any more. He worried about Neal being recognized too much in *On the Road*, which would be out in the fall. He said maybe it would be a best-seller and we'd all get rich on third choice. He sent his love to me and the kids. He wrote postscripts on all the flaps of the fold-up airmail envelope, one to me praying he could finally get to his true home, and signed with kisses.

Of course, as usual, this road trip was never made. Neal had now been promoted to conductor, and between runs was always at the track, playing his role at home, and involved with more women in the City. I also wondered if this proposed trip didn't appeal to him as had former ones because it was all planned out – no suspense or conflict.

Jack returned to Florida, where Memere was living in Orlando soon after the trial in San Francisco. He swooped her up, shipped their furniture, took her on a long bus ride via Mexico, and thence to Berkeley. I never knew anything about it until we got a postcard from Berkeley saying he was now at home with his mother for good. He couldn't find Neal nor any news of him. He said to send word or stop by, and had we received his telegram from New York? He wrote he hoped soon to see me.

Neal and I looked at each other, puzzled. No telegram. Jack said he understood – what? Paranoia sprouting again? But why? So Neal hunted him up, taking LuAnne, Al Hinkle and the Fergusons to Berkeley. I knew nothing about this, either, until Neal brought home an advance copy of *On the Road*, only telling me Jack had been opening the box of them and tossed one to Neal. In those days we knew nothing of first-edition signed books, so Neal tore off the dust jacket and didn't ask Jack to sign it.

I had been frantically busy designing costumes for 200 little girls plus the several soloists for the Christmas *Nutcracker* production, and I assumed when that was over some arrangements would be made for us all to get together, and I could at last meet Memere, a long-awaited pleasure.

The next bit of news was that Jack had left Berkeley and taken Memere back east because she was unhappy in California. I was stunned. 'But Neal – he never brought her here – she might have liked this area better. Why didn't he?' Neal couldn't explain it either. I was very hurt; it was an episode Jack never explained to me, and years later I was more dismayed to read in one of his books that I'd been mad at him and 'refused to see his mother'.

On the Road was in the bookstores in September, and about a month after Jack left we received a frenzied letter to Neal, begging him to write him. He told us of his trip back to Florida for four days and nights, how they now had a $45 pad. He had gone to New York and the publishing parties a week later, his agent had turned down $110,000 offered by Warner Brothers for a film in which he would play himself and Neal could play Dean if he wanted to. His current girl, Joyce, had told him not to wish a movie-star's fate on Neal.

Then he described a play he had written act by act, spawned from his experiences in Los Gatos, part of which became the amateur film *Pull My Daisy*, vaguely related to the evening the Bishop came to tea. Jack was also being besieged by magazines for stories, and had sold three so far. He had appeared on a TV show, and Broadway producers brought beautiful models who sat on Joyce's bed, and how he yearned to have sex with so many of them. He then said he wondered what all this was doing to Neal, and was he being stalked.

He described wild parties, and was always drunk, but had switched from wine to whiskey. He then launched into dreams of the future, when he'd stay with us and flood us with purchases with all his money. He blamed a lack of funds on his reason for not seeing much of Neal when last in Berkeley. He was now eager to renew his close friendship with Neal, money being no object.

Such fruits of fame were shortlived. Although the first review in the *New York Times* was highly complimentary, it was the only one. None of us had anticipated the incredibly hostile and bitter attacks from others – all over the country. Being so sensitive, paranoid Jack took every word personally and was cut to the quick. He was cast into a hell he could never have imagined, so sure of his worth as a writer. He sought oblivion all the more in Mexico, Buddha and whiskey, the last two at cross-purposes.

Neal and I were shocked, as well, at the ferocity and cruelty of the remarks. These journalists were like snarling dogs threatened by a wolf. We commiserated with Jack ourselves, feeling so close to him, and all so soon after the rejoicing. One journalist called it a 'barbaric yawp of a book'. But perhaps the ultimate in violent and negative reactions to the activities and feelings of Jack and his followers was most typically articulated by Art Cohn in the *San Francisco Chronicle*, although he was by no means alone in his denunciation. His title was 'Sick Little Bums.'

> In a nation that lives by labels and slogans it was inevitable that someone would hang a tag on the new batch. THE BEAT GENERATION is catching on and, with sufficient repetition, will become part of the language like the Gay Nineties, the Jazz Age, and the Lost Generation.
>
> It figures. It is as meaningless as they are.
>
> What is the Beat Generation? Even, or especially, its high priests are beat for a definition.

The 35-year-old prophet of the sect, Jack Kerouac, says...'we're in the vanguard of a new religion. I want God to show me his face.'

'The truest lingo of narcotics,' claims Herbert Gold, one of its historians, 'because this more than anything gives Little Boy Beat what he wants – release from imagination and the body – a timeless browsing in eternity. In other words, a cool simulation of death.'

'The cats play everything cool,' Sam Boal, another biographer, reports. 'The girls half denude themselves and are indifferent to their nakedness. The men must be similarly aloof, cool. Remember, these cats are beat. They've had it. Nothing matters. Why bother, man? Who needs anything, cat?'

Time out to open a window.

Kerouac...prattles: 'Spengler prophesied that in the late moments of Western Civilization there would be a great revival of religious mysticism. It's happening.'

This, then is the new religion, the Jehova of the Beaten handed down from his Mount: Thou shalt kill for the sake of killing. Thou shalt defile all flesh, including your own. Thou shalt deny thy birthright and resign from the human race. Thou shalt contribute nothing to the world except scorn. Thou shalt destroy the innocent. Thou shalt make a mockery of morality, justice, law, common fairness and, most of all, love. Thou shalt dishonor thy father and mother and curse them for giving thee birth. Amen, you pathetic, self-pitying, degenerate bums, amen!

There were many many more along the same lines, and we grieved for Jack. I tried to figure out why these men were so violently hostile. One writer friend said he knew of no other author who had been so viciously attacked. I wondered if maybe these men were frightened by exposure. That is, many of them were probably as guilty of such thoughts in secret while pretending to be upright citizens and snowy white. We'd never know.

When Neal had brought home the advance copy I was now far enough removed from the events to be able to read it through, and I was as curious as everyone else how Neal felt about it. He said he enjoyed Jack's descriptions of what they'd done together, and got a kick out of reminiscing by reading it, but the glorification of his antics in print also made him sad. He wasn't proud of this side of his nature; he was trying so very hard to overcome all that, and the review in *Time* magazine hit too close to home:

> In contemporary terms, Moriarty seems close to a prison psychosis that is a variety of the Ganser Syndrome. Its symptoms, as described by one psychiatrist, sound like a playback from Kerouac's novel: 'The patient exaggerates his mood and his feelings; he "lets himself go" and gets himself into highly emotional states. He is uncooperative, refuses to answer questions or obey orders…At other times he will thrash about wildly. His talk may be disjointed and difficult to follow. The significant thing about sufferers from the Ganser Syndrome is that they are not really mad, they only seem to be.

It hurt Neal deeply to find himself exposed as that kind of nut. 'And why don't they ever look at my work record? Uncooperative? Not answer questions? Not obey orders? Hunh.' I wanted to fly to the defence of both men, but there was no way, and besides, here was another test of 'Bless those who despitefully use you', and the lesson Neal had taught me that no one can hurt you if you don't let them tell you how to think or feel. It is your response that hurts you; you have a choice; you don't have to take on their problem.

| FIFTY-FIVE |

The process of growth is almost imperceptible at times. Three years elapsed before I was able to score a solid win by applying Hugh Lynn's curt and decisive command to 'keep still'. My efforts before had been consciously willed, and perhaps had failed because I was trying to 'fight one force with another'. A no-no. This time there was no conscious plan on my part, more a weary rebellion against the conditioned response I'd always made.

The day in question remains in my memory as the most vivid demonstration – aside from Neal's accident – of the veracity of the laws we'd read and heard again and again.

The winter was one of the wettest we'd had in years, and freight work was almost at a standstill, so more often the men with more seniority were able to 'bump' Neal from his regular passenger run if they were qualified. One morning after the children had gone, he came home to announce – or try to announce, after he'd beaten about the bush a good deal – that he wanted to – um – go to – uh – Mexico, 'just for a short trip, understand – I'll be right back.' My adrenaline surged through its well-worn channels, but all of a sudden the thought or feeling came to me that I was so *tired* of feeling like this over and over again. It was a strange sensation, rather like skydiving, I imagine, floating in emptiness with no bearings, or like suddenly stepping off a cliff.

I did not reply, just continued making the bed. Neal, taken aback at my unusual silence, may have thought I didn't hear him, because he continued speaking in his own defence, just as if I'd responded with the familiar barrage of objections. In a moment I began to feel the change in me from the relief of not behaving as I usually did. I was in control; I could tell I now had the advantage, and I kept on keeping still, but I also had to keep busy, emotions warring within me. I walked past him into the bathroom and brushed my hair. Neal followed.

'So? How about it?' The mystery made him nervous and irritable.

I sighed wearily, 'Neal, you know as well as I what the situation is here. I don't have to tell you about our finances; what is there for me to say?' Was I really saying this so calmly? I spoke without emotion or bitterness. He couldn't figure me out. After nearly ten years of a constant pattern? And neither of us knew the rules to this new game.

He then stamped around the house, slammed the refrigerator door, and worked himself into a fury, while I held my breath. He came back to me. 'Damn it, Carolyn, why not? I'll only be gone a few days; it won't cost that much. I've been working solid all year – I gave up going to get Jack – a man deserves a vacation, doesn't he? What the hell!'

This was my cue to say, 'What about me? Don't I ever get a vacation?' But now I had no desire to say it, and I continued to straighten the house, somewhat anxiously, not knowing what was supposed to happen next. Neal noisily poured himself a cup of coffee, but again turned to me in his frustration. For the very first time ever he actually made critical remarks about me, but they were aimed at how I used to act, not at my present stance.

It was all I could do not to lash back in defence, but I didn't look at him, and hastily loaded the washing machine, hanging on for dear life. Then I caught on to what he was trying to do, even if unconsciously. 'That won't work, Neal.' I was still calm! 'You're just trying to make me mad so I'll throw you out again. If I tell you to get out as before, then you can skip off with a clear conscience, right? And then return humbly and beg my forgiveness. Forget it. I won't make your decision for you this time; it's entirely up to you.'

With every statement my insides seemed to expand and become lighter; knots untied in slow motion and strings wafted away. With it was an unfamiliar sense of power. Or something – I don't know; it was all so new. I wanted to share it with Neal, but the game wasn't over yet. Part of me still felt the defeat and sorrow of his desire to go, but the stronger sensation was one of resignation with a trace of triumph. Neal could see what I said made sense, and dropped his defences, but now he was at a loss as to how to proceed.

He sulked to his closet and began banging hangers and shoes around. I assumed he was packing; I'd never doubted his decision would be to go. When he came back out, however, he had changed into his old work clothes. And just as though there'd been no discussion whatever, he pleasantly inquired,

'Did you say once you wanted that stump removed from the front yard?'

'Why, yes, I did, several times, dear.' What now?

'Better give it a go, then, I guess.' Gruffly he marched out the front door. When I looked out the front window, there he was with a spade and pick-axe digging away with a vengeance in the cold fog, his frustration flung at the wet ground through his flying pick. I gazed in wonder and admiration, smiling all over. It was then it dawned on me I had done no more than follow Hugh Lynn's wise advice – and it worked! He had understood all along.

The next time I looked out, Neal had completed a deep trench around the stump, backed the big old Packard within a few feet of it and was trying to attach a chain to both – a chain that looked suspiciously like the dog's leash. Could it possibly be strong enough? Misgivings rose, but I brushed them aside. 'He'll find out; don't interfere.'

Soon I heard the motor of the car racing and grinding. I went to the window again to watch the extraction. Oh no – dear Lord! The Packard was spraying grass and mud high into the air as it easily ground itself into the lawn, half way up to the hubcaps. The chain had snapped long since. As I saw Neal jump from the car, I hastily retreated. I didn't doubt he could solve getting the car out with boards or something, but I knew the setback would anger him.

In another minute or two I checked his progress. I could hardly believe my eyes. Anger had obviously distorted his reason, for there he was, backing the Rambler stationwagon into position on the lawn to tow the Packard! Could he not see the futility of that? I couldn't watch. I went as far away as possible, back in Johnny's room, and became very busy, bracing myself for the inevitable explosion. I could hear the second car churning, then silence.

To my surprise, Neal came in the house slowly, quietly, not slamming the door, and walked back to where I was. He dropped onto the bed, defeated but humble.

'What is it, honey?' As if I didn't know.

'Well, it just shows you. I should have gone. I just blew everything, that's all – everything.'

'Oh? How's that?' I went into the living room to look. Sure enough, there were both cars deeply embedded in the green turf, the stump secure. It was all I could do not to laugh; Mack Sennett would have loved it. But at that moment I didn't think Neal would find it amusing. So I hung on and rallied round.

'Now Neal, what's done is done. No good lamenting. Tell you what, maybe the triple-A could get them out with their tow truck. Shall I call them?' Neal opened up like a sunflower. He could never get accustomed to these services I wouldn't be without.

In a matter of minutes, the tow truck not only dislodged both cars but the stump as well. The day was won. Happily, Neal filled in the hole and the ruts with dirt. I reassured him the grass would repair itself, and by the time the children came home from school, he was glowing and serene, proud of his contribution to his home, and I heaped on the gratitude.

For the rest of the afternoon Neal sat on the couch in the family room, the children clustered around him, and right before my sceptical eyes he created intricate toys out of toothpicks and string. He was patient, skillful, emanating warmth and his special sparkling humour. Here was the man I'd married – the same man who'd spent another afternoon stringing tiny glass beads on silver wire to make a spider's web.

He continued to give of his best throughout dinner and the bedtime rituals. When the children were tucked in, we returned to our room, and I thanked him for giving us all such a lovely day.

'You know what I think, Neal? That saying – or the law that says the greater the negative impulse overcome the greater positive energy released in a constructive way, like a kick from a gun, remember? Maybe because you overcame your desire to go to Mexico you set that law in motion. You were certainly a blessing to us – don't you feel good too?'

'Yeah – sure. You're right, of course.' He didn't take up the discussion eagerly as was his custom, and I wondered why. He went into the bathroom for quite a long time, and my uneasiness returned. When he came out he opened his closet and stared into it. I sensed his restlessness, but pretended to study the *TV Guide*.

'Anything in particular you'd like to watch tonight?'

'Well – actually, sweetheart –' He sat down close to me on the bed. 'You know there's a Cayce lecture in town tonight, and I thought I'd go hear it – uh – would you like to go, too?' From his manner I knew my answer had to be no. My high spirits took a nose-dive.

'No, it's a bit late to get a babysitter, thanks anyway.' I couldn't look at him.

'Well, then – I really do think I should run down to Mexico – you see, I'm out of tea, and I promised Doug –' I needed to hear no more and dashed for the bathroom, shutting the door with one hand and my mouth with the other. So it had all been for nothing! No, not all, I couldn't believe 'nothing', but didn't the cure last? It wasn't until years later I learned that once you think you've got it the tests begin.

When I'd composed myself and revived the show of resignation, I returned to the *TV Guide*. He meanwhile was throwing socks and shorts into his suitcase. He closed it and came over to hug me – back to the original script.

'Now, darling, don't you fret. If I go, I'll be home no later than a week. First, I'll go to the lecture, and maybe afterward I won't want to go. I'll take these clothes just in case – no sense 'doubling back', eh? Heh, heh.'

He winked and grinned, wobbling his eyebrows. I was not amused, and had reverted to stony silence.

When the front door closed behind him I let loose the tears. I knew, even if he pretended he didn't, what his decision would be.

What was the use of anything – even learning to 'keep still'. What difference did it make?

I was just dropping off to sleep at last when I was frightened wide awake by thinking I'd heard a door softly open and shut. I froze in terror. But who should softly tip-toe into the room but Neal. The miracle really was complete, regardless of my lack of faith. We couldn't let go into sleep just yet, so cuddled together; Neal told me about the lecture – which he really had attended. 'Actually, you see, darling, today we both did what the lecture was all about: crucifixion. By "crucifying" our selfish desires, we were lifted up – "resurrected", see? Into heaven, hunh, baby?'

| FIFTY-SIX |

One evening in early February, after the children were in bed and I had taken some mending into our bedroom, Neal came in and sat beside me, fidgeting. Ever since he'd come home from work he'd been behaving as he did when something was on his mind he was debating whether or not to tell me, and I was braced.

He took a deep breath. 'Carolyn, there's something I think I should tell you.' He had been much more open and communicative since Natalie's death and our 24-hour 'heaven', but that was about the only notable change in him. This was a serious matter by his tone. 'You see, I was at a sort of party this afternoon at the Fergusons' pad in North Beach. When I left to get my train, a couple of guests said they'd drive me to the depot. When we got there, I offered them a couple of joints in return. I got three out of my locker and handed these to them. Then on my way home it hit me; something told me they were narcs. I'm positive now they were.'

I didn't know what to say; I'd no idea what it meant.

'Do you mean you think they'll do something to you? What?'

'That's just it. I think it was a trap. You see, a couple of months ago some other guys asked me to buy them some tea. They gave me $40, and I said I'd try. I was sure they were narcs, so I took the money to the track – which, of course, let them know *I* knew who they were. Now, somehow, I think it's all connected. Damn.'

To that point my experience with law enforcement agents had been limited to a parking ticket or two, and I still considered them public servants. My ignorance left me unable to offer solace or suggestions to Neal. I wasn't as affected as him simply because I didn't know the consequences, whereas he did. As the weeks went by and nothing happened, Neal relaxed, and I forgot about it.

Gradually, a bizarre change began taking place in Neal, behaviour altogether new to him and me. He became hard, cocky, swaggering, sharp and cynical. He'd answer my questions or comments with a smart retort or callous remark, obviously not 'with' me. I couldn't figure him out, and my apprehension grew. I talked to Al and Helen about it. They admitted they had noticed it, too, and were also concerned. They'd never heard him be boastful about risks before, nor smart-alecky.

Helen felt somehow he was afraid of something – something physical.

'It's almost as though he's afraid for his *life*!' she said, puzzled. Al looked serious and shook his head sadly,

'He's really asking for it this time,' was all he'd say, but I suspected he knew more. All I could do was grit my teeth and get through the encounters with Neal's boorishness the best I could.

On a chill foggy morning the first in April, after watching the children walk to the school bus, I was clearing the breakfast table when the doorbell rang. At this hour? Probably some neighbour child or a mother. I opened the door to face two men dressed in hats and topcoats – one, of course, a pale belted trenchcoat. As they asked politely for Neal Cassady, they snapped open and shut what I presumed were their IDs. I didn't see anything specific, but I'd seen enough movies to know what the gesture meant.

I turned away to go call Neal, my heart pounding with dread, but they followed right behind me into the bedroom, where Neal was starting to dress.

'You're Neal Cassady? We have a warrant for your arrest; you'll have to come with us.' These hackneyed words are familiar to all from theatrics, but their impact is utterly different in reality.

At first I didn't remember Neal's story of the previous February. I knew he was on a three-year probation since a 60-day sentence for traffic violations had been suspended, so my first thought hooked onto that. But when I heard 'San Francisco', I knew it was more serious. My naivety blossomed forth in full flower as the shock and disbelief brought out a storm of stupidity. Seeing those two stony monsters standing at the open bathroom door while Neal shaved, I hurled words at their backs. 'How is it possible you people can walk in unannounced and snatch a man away from his home, his family, his job – just like this? How can you support your own families by destroying another's? How can you sleep nights?' Oh, I was a tiger, and a pitiful one. Suddenly I was afraid I'd go too far, and they'd take me too – why not? They didn't care.

Neal didn't say a word, but I was sure his mind was racing. He was not allowed to close the door, the men hovering, watching his every move. Each time I'd understand what was in their minds, the horrible purpose of their manoeuvres stung me anew. And I also saw they were actually afraid of him! How could I have seen this acted out on the screen and not realized the baseness of it?

I could stand no more, the tears welled over. I ran to the living room to wring my hands and choke back the tears of rage. When the men came out I flung myself on Neal for one electric kiss, no words possible.

Through the window I saw them walk to the waiting police car, and the final hideous sight was branded on my mind forever; the man I loved, the father of my children, a man I knew to be gentle and kind, shackled in steel chains being hauled off by other men as though he were a dangerous beast.

'He's a *man*,' I wanted to scream, 'a son of God, whether you *like* him or not!' He looked so forlorn, humble and defenceless. Oh Neal, Neal – no one could be so evil as to deserve such humiliation. I sobbed and moaned, but this was only the beginning. How blind I had been to all this.

I fell back on affirmations again, but now they weren't enough; my faith was too green. So what to do? I wandered around, shifting between pity for Neal, for myself and the kids, and rage at the law. I sat and stared, wandered through the house some more, sat and cried. When I had reached dead-ends in every line of speculation and my emotions were numb, I did what I always did at times of crisis: I drove over to Helen's.

By the time the children came home, I had reached an appearance of stability. Not having the faintest idea of how best to tell them about their father, I said nothing. Each time I looked at them and thought I should, I felt it would be the equivalent of telling them there was a live, fire-breathing dragon in the closet and expect them to believe it. In my efforts at normality I almost convinced myself it was all a bad dream – only to awaken when I'd bid the children goodnight, the painful scene having left its aura with Neal's clothes still lying around in the bedroom.

In the morning Helen telephoned as soon as the children were gone. The *San Jose Mercury News* had a short article on the second page, which she read to me. Boy, that reporter had been busy working on his 'story', and no doubt on a promotion as well. He wrote that he had talked to the SF police, SP officials, to some of Neal's fellow trainmen and the DA. Since no one knew any real facts of the case, his colourful report was sheer guesswork, all wrong and made as sensational as possible, with no concern for truth. He said Neal was part of a gang of smugglers who brought marijuana on the SP trains from Mexico. None of those people he talked to had told him Neal's trains didn't go as far as Los Angeles, let alone Mexico.

When I'd hung up, I was startled by the doorbell. On the stoop stood a short, dark-haired man. He spoke quickly, 'I'm Sam Hanson from the *Los Gatos Times Observer*. I wondered if I might ask you a few questions? I...'

I cut him off fiercely: 'No, I'm sorry – you'll have to find some other way to sell your papers besides my personal tragedy.' The false words of the San Jose paper were still ringing in my ears, and I vented my fury on this representative of the press, but he hurried on before I could shut the door.

'That's just it, Mrs Cassady, we saw the item in the *Mercury*, and we have to print something. I thought it might help if we got the true story and were able to present it in some other way.' I stared at him, mortified, and meekly invited him in. He stayed and listened for at least an hour, while I – still a jumble of nerves and confusion – tried to reconstruct some sense of our life that would mean something to other people. I don't know what all I told him – too much I feared, after he had gone; or was it too little? For hours I remembered things I was sure I hadn't explained properly.

That evening I hung around the front of the house to be sure I got the paper before one of the children did. When I opened it, I got a surprise. The whole bottom half of the front page and two columns on the second were devoted to our plight. This little local paper rarely even mentioned such events in the lives of subscribers, and there had been a few.

I learned that Sam Hanson had recently left the *Mercury* because he disagreed with their policies, and turned to writing special interest columns for our village paper, but this was nearly four times the space usually allotted him. It was certainly a difficult subject, especially since 'dope' in any context was the most heinous of human degradations in the eyes of the general public. And such a serious crime was unknown in this upper-middle-class community. I was amazed at Sam's and the newspaper's courage.

In the article, Sam did his best to play down the drug angle, stating truthfully that the story in the *Mercury* was untrue, and as yet nothing was certain. He emphasized Neal's ten years of steady service with the railroad and my community volunteer activities, such as Brownie Scout leader, collecting for various charities, working to access sewers, the four years of designing for the ballet school, and my portraits. These activities had brought me into close contact with a large number of residents of both Los Gatos and Saratoga, and now I didn't know whether to be glad or sorry for that. The last sentence in the article read 'Let's show Mrs Cassady she lives in a community that can and will help.'

Later that evening Helen came over to read the article and comfort me. She suddenly got the idea we should search the house for tea, in case the authorities might beat us to it. Such an idea would never have occurred to me. But Helen was right. In one of Neal's shoes, we found an envelope containing five rolled joints. Helen made a fire at once and threw them in it. To my astonishment, I found I was feeling like a traitor to Neal, knowing so well how hard the stash had been to come by and how much it meant to him. I felt as Neal would have, watching those five sticks glow red. I almost cried out to save them, but stopped short, appalled at myself, considering the price I was paying for the brothers of those babies. Helen prodded them with the poker and swore, 'Look at those damn things – they refuse to burn! Standing straight up there defiantly – like five fingers, Jesus!'

I still couldn't bring myself to tell the children. What do you tell children aged nine, eight and six? I didn't know, but I knew the next day I'd have to think of something; everyone would have read the article, and I didn't want them to hear it first from some other child on the bus. But at breakfast I failed again. I decided to drive them to school and pray. If I told them before school, they'd be no good at their lessons, and I didn't want them to stay home mourning.

When I picked them up in the afternoon, Cathy came out to the car, tears streaming down her face. Oh Lord; it's too late! She climbed into the back seat, and I turned around, holding out my hand.

'Cathy dear – I'm so sorry – tell me...'

'Nothing, Mom. I think I've caught cold. My eyes and nose began running last period.' Relief flooded in, but the scare was enough to ignite my resolve. So after dinner while they were still at the table, I told them as off-handedly as possible that their father had been arrested and would be gone for a while.

'What for?' they chorused.

'We're not sure yet – oh, don't worry – he hasn't hurt anyone or stolen anything; you all know he couldn't do anything like that. It is just something to do with cigarettes – a kind that aren't considered legal at this time.' When my voice broke, Jami started to cry, and Cathy and Johnny stared bewildered into space. What were they thinking? All I could say was, 'Everything will be all right; you mustn't think about it. We'll get it sorted out, you'll see. I only hope you don't have a hard time at school. If you do – anything at all – please let me know and call me at any time.' I took up our usual routine, and talked cheerfully of other things.

Then the second phase of the miracle hit. After I left them at school the next day, I was to learn that Sam Hanson had succeeded beyond belief. The rest of the week during school hours I was kept at a constant trot between the telephone and the front door. Old friends, casual acquaintances, total strangers, teachers from school and Sunday school, past and present, friends of friends, brakemen and conductors – hordes poured in and out of the house, while others called on the phone to wish us well and provide help of every kind. Cards and notes arrived in batches, each containing money and blessings – even one with $2 from the local 'hermit' whom I'd never even seen.

Some of the visitors arrived in startling combinations, such as the rough trainmen with their earthy language, who told shady stories in the presence of neighbourhood mothers or Christian Science practitioners and teachers. My minimal poise was keenly stretched. All levels of society seemed destined to meet in my living room, harmonized by the mutual magnanimity of their purpose. As I recounted later to Neal, they all appeared really hungry to give, as though starved for any opportunity before.

They were often entertaining as well. Many had one or more skeletons in their closets, and evidently welcomed the opportunity to let them out for air in order to commiserate with me. I just hoped in future they wouldn't hold these confessions against me.

Along with good wishes and encouragement came not only cash but food – and more food, so much in fact I had to hurry and stash it out of sight in the garage before each new arrival, lest they think their gift superfluous or unappreciated. Near the end of the first day, when a friend reported the spectacle to her husband, his response was, 'Groceries, fine, but what she really needs right now is a bottle,' and he dispatched one forthwith.

I had postponed telling the children about this mountain of food too, so as not to alarm them, even though I regretted not being able to share the experience.

There was a third aspect of this miracle. I had continued driving them to school the following week, and remained braced for a call from one of them. None came. When I asked them if any child had been curious or cruel, they all affirmed the contrary. Mystified, I asked my next-door neighbour what she thought about that.

'Well, I don't know about anyone else,' she replied, 'but we burned our papers the minute we read them, and our children know nothing about it.' Could everyone in both villages have done that? I felt mighty humbled that the population had all had the same thought that night. Never were any of the children accosted at school, then or later when Neal was gone.

| FIFTY-SEVEN |

Al Hinkle drove me to see Neal in the San Francisco city jail, where he was being held pending indictment by the grand jury. How could I have lived so long, I wondered, without any knowledge that such places existed? Details didn't register, so shocking was the total picture to my stunned senses; I do remember an impression of looking up above me at hard, cold bars from floor to ceiling in tiers like cages of grey steel, behind which shadowy figures paced or cowered or slumped – all dark, all sound loud, echoing and reverberating hollowly. The officers were brusque, rude and tense. The sombre atmosphere was oppressive, heavy-laden with bristling hostility.

They had Neal's name spelled wrong, and for some reason that made me furious. His true identity was obviously of no importance; he was just a disagreeable object they were put upon to deal with.

I waited for hours, but at last I was able to see Neal. Visitors and prisoners were herded onto opposite sides of a long counter above which were panels of glass and steel mesh, about two feet wide, where we stood elbow-to-elbow with fellow visitors and tried to establish some kind of personal communication through a speaker system, everyone wailing and trying to out-shout the others. Neal looked cheerful, and his talking eyes were at their best.

'Don't you worry, baby – Carolyn – hear me? Everything is cool. Terrible place, I know, but God is with me. I'm way above it all, believe me; I feel great, not antagonistic. I'll tell you all about it later, just don't fret, Mommie, promise?' I started to cry, but got control. He gave me the name of the Public Defender assigned to him, a Mr Nicco, and told me where to find him. 'Don't hire a lawyer; this guy is terrific – all I'll need.'

A week later Helen went with me to see Mr Nicco. My hopes rose at once when we met him. He was sharp, dynamic and under-standing. He felt sure Neal's chances were good, and asked about our situation at home. Much encouraged, Helen and I walked to the stairs that led down to the street. We heard footsteps clattering down the flight above us and, pausing to look up, I reached for the handrail, close to a good old-fashioned swoon. It was Neal! He was bounding down the steps two at a time, a big grin on his face. He caught up with us, put his arms about us both and pulled us down to the hall.

'Neal, wait – wait – what are you doing out?'

'Ha, *ha* – I'm freeee! The grand jury couldn't find enough evidence; they just laughed at the charges. I *told* you, didn't I? Huh? Ha ha – where's the car? Come on – *let's go home!*' What a rollicking ride that was. We stopped at the depot for Neal to sign on the extra board and sailed gleefully home, the world alive and spinning once more. On the way, we took Helen home to tell Al all about it. When the children came home and found him there, they fell all over him, and we all pampered him the rest of the day and evening. Our bedtime prayers that night were highly charged, and filled with thanksgiving. Daddy was not a criminal; he was a good man.

Afterwards he and I lay close together on the bed and talked. He was awestruck by my story of Sam Hanson and the community response.

'But – uh – now that I'm back – what will we do with it all? We can't give it back, can we? They'd feel cheated; they gave it just for the sake of giving – hmmm.'

'Oh dear, I hadn't thought about that. Darn – what should we do? Well let's think about that tomorrow – now I have to tell you how proud and delighted I am about your attitude! You see, of course, how powerful it is – it's true! It's how you *respond* to a situation that determines its effect on you, right? Oh gosh – we've had another beautiful demonstration of the laws – bless you – you taught me that, and look how it works! You knew!'

'You're right on, love, but listen, that's not all. Wait till I tell you. Why, do you know I did the most amazing thing? You saw those cells? God, are they awful? The toilet is right out in the middle of it, you know – no seat on it, of course…'

I interrupted with 'Why is that, pray tell?'

'Why, my dear – terrible weapon! I suppose they figure you could tear it off and bash someone's head in – God, who knows how they think? Anyway, I was in a cell with three – yeah, three – other guys. One was a heroin addict on withdrawal and sick as hell – but the other two started fighting – I mean with fists! One was a huge spade, the other a Mexican, and believe it or not – before I even thought, I jumped up and stepped right in between them and they backed off! Gad, when I sat down I nearly passed out. Only then did I think what I'd just risked – they could have killed me on the spot. But it was an instant reaction instigated by my peaceful state of mind, dig? Beautiful…' And we mused on this further wonder in silence.

'But why did they arrest you, if there's so little evidence?'

'Oh yeah – well, I found out. Two detectives, see, kept bugging me. They wanted me to tell them everybody I knew who smoked marijuana and where they got it. Sure. Guess they'd seen me enough and thought I knew most. I wouldn't tell them anything. They took me into a private room and got madder and madder. "Cooperation", baby, that's the key word around there. "If you'd just *cooperate* Mr Cassady…" They hit you in the stomach so it doesn't show…'

'Oh NO, Neal, no-*no-no-no*!!' I wailed and put my hand over his mouth. He kissed and held it.

'Yeah, hunh, well, when they wasted their week, they were really p.o.'d and said, "We'll see you in San Quentin, Cassady, if it's the last thing we do." Ha, the bastards! Yes, sir, my dear, that was a terrific warning and example to me. I know now. I'm free of that crap forever, hear me?' He grabbed my shoulders and shook me, his teeth clenched in determination.

'Oh yes – I do I do hear you! Hallelujah!'

But Anslinger's boys on the narcotic squad were not so easily diverted from their vow. The following morning the doorbell summoned me to the door once again, to be faced by a second pair of trenchcoat vultures. My night of renewal gave me confidence.

'You're mistaken,' I smiled, 'he was released for lack of evidence.'

'Sorry, Ma'am, we have a new warrant. He'll have to come with us.' This time I simply sat down in complete bewilderment, letting the principals repeat the second performance without me. Only this time Neal was furious. He didn't accompany them humbly as before, but strode on ahead of them, his head high, muttering curses under his breath. A new wave of foreboding swept over me. Now what? I called Helen, but now we had no basis for speculation.

One thing was sure: I could not tell the children again. It had been so perfect to have him back, the dark cloud dispelled, their father innocent. So, trusting the good people around us, I told them he had been called for a hold-down north of San Francisco and would not be home for a long time, but he'd write, as he always did. I didn't make this sound too definite, because I still hoped he'd be released as before. I tried to be vague enough so as not to propagate a big lie for them to discover later. They accepted my explanation. This was one time I was grateful for the erratic schedules of the railroad.

My faith in the community was justified, and unbelievable as it seems, the children knew nothing of his incarceration until they were teenagers.

Next day I hurried to the City to learn the reason for his recall. The filthy jail was the same, but Neal was not. He was seething in defiant anger, practically twitching all over at the effort to control his fury and his language. Futile were my attempts to remind him of the lesson he'd learned about attitude, from which he'd benefited before. He was deaf to my pleas.

All he had found out at present was that the two detectives had demanded a special session of the grand jury at midnight the night before. They had trumped up 'new' evidence and witnesses. He'd find out more and write to me.

When I returned home I immediately sat down to write to him, praying to find a way to reverse his attitude. I stuffed in as many Cayce quotations as possible. Two agonizing days later I received his reply:

> Henceforth, restrict your letters to two pages, one side only. I've read all of *Science and Health* with Key to the Scriptures by Eddy. She has something, not enuf in toto, tho. Reread all New Testament, refreshing as usual. Am now finishing all the Bible, without pronouncing the names, of course. Have attended all available church services: confession, mass, Protestant and 1 Negro fundamentalist. Say numerous rosaries daily and have memorized 7 gifts of Holy Ghosts, 12 fruits of same, prayers for Dead, sick, unity, confidence, adoration, love, life, Angelus, various litanies, various arts, 10 Commandments, 11 mysteries, etc. – so well up in Spirit, highest *ever*; only Grace beats Karma etc. However, ahem, uh & gulp: *please save* form charts, most important. Mostly disturbed about John. Pray constantly. Even believe can now father him correctly and girls, too. Bless them…

In other words, he was telling me I needn't shovel Cayce quotes at him; he could handle it himself, but I wasn't so sure. It looked to me that he was just frantically filling his mind with as much rote and words as possible so as to prevent his anger from surfacing. He wasn't giving it much thought, really; his attitude hadn't changed, and that was the key. His paramount use of energy was being spent in finding a way to outwit the detectives.

He was able to read the transcript of the grand jury session, and was confident he had the upper hand. He learned all of it had stemmed from the two agents who'd given him the $40, which we had suspected. But they had neither the drug nor a receipt. His bail was set at $12,000. He intended going to court to try to get it lowered. The DA had made 'wild' claims which clearly showed the DA had 'facts' (his exact words) taken from some newspaper source – these being word-for-word from the *Mercury News*. 'All this is to show the judge I am dangerous outside.'

I marvelled at the amount of bail, as did Helen when I called her. This sounded far more serious than the comparative triviality of the 'crime.'

'Neal says it's to "keep him off the streets".' Helen asked Al to explain further.

'Yeah, that's it, see? Now Neal knows their identity as narcotic agents, he can "blow their cover" – tell his friends, and they'd lose their jobs.'

'Humph,' chimed in Helen, 'tough titty; what about *Neal's* job? And his family – Jesus! He wants you to put up the house as a property bond. Will you?'

'Gosh, Helen, I don't know what to do. How can I do that? It's all I've got, and now no income; I can't even hire a lawyer. It cost us $7000 for the SP trial – where would I get that kind of money? And I just can't risk losing the house, can I? If I could only trust Neal's word. But you remember how oddly he was behaving before all this? Once free, can you imagine he would surrender willingly and not split across the border? I would.'

'Frankly, no. That would be hard to believe, and he has vowed so often he'll never be put in jail again. I don't know, gal; I'm glad I'm not in your shoes.'

So I sweated and strained. One thing I didn't know was that the Fergusons had also been arrested. He had been begging me to put up the bail so he could have a jury trial – alone, not with them. I didn't understand this. I also didn't know until too late that for the emergency meeting of the grand jury or after, the whole cast had been changed to men loyal to the DA. Even Mr Nicco was gone without my knowledge, he whom I had expected to iron it all out. Of course, I was still ignorant of how our system of 'justice' actually worked, not at all what we had been taught at home and in school.

Al investigated the attitude of the SP towards Neal, to learn they wanted no part of him ever again. They said they didn't care if the newspaper story was true or not; just because the SP had been in the press was enough. We wondered if they were in some way 'getting even' for his suit against them earlier. They had a lot of felons on their payrole. Neal used to bring some home. One guy kept checking out all the doorknobs in the San Jose house, so I asked Neal what for.

'Oh, he's an ex-second-storey man – burglar, y'know. Just seeing if everything's okay with the locks.'

So with no possibility of future income from that source, with debts already past due, with no income at all in sight, I couldn't bring myself to risk my only asset – the house. I wrote to Mr Nicco, and he did answer. He told me he was no longer Neal's defender, but in his opinion Neal should be free in about three weeks. Ah, the answer to my prayers. I thought.

When I told Neal that I didn't dare risk losing the house, he wouldn't believe it. At first he just kept repeating his request for me to act, mildly ridiculing my objections. When he saw I was in earnest, he became frantic and angry; his only means of persuasion lay in writing. He had been transferred to the county facility at San Bruno, and told me not to visit, the only day being Saturday, when the children would not be in school.

I flinched at his letters, but I read them avidly, hoping he could find a reasonable out for me. But his final desperate attempts to convince me only made matters worse:

> Carolyn, I'll never forgive you. How can you be so blithely demented? *What* are you afraid of and where is the risk? *Calm* yourself *face* it simply: I show for court and house is *safe*, period. Do you *really* fear I'll run away? No? Then what's wrong?…I assure you all problems will be quite solved during my bail-procured freedom by a method necessarily unrevealed, as it involves the *big* money. If you hesitate because the P.D. said 'only three more weeks,' I *know* he is incorrect by *months*;…Remember, *now* is your *only* hope to avert the deep sorrow you'll forever have in knowing it was you *alone* who prevented $100.000 & that by your *absurd* fear that I'd run off with our precious house!…But aside from this *concrete* 100 thousand is the *fact* I can successfully handle this case only if I get out *now*. Please 'know' that McNamara is *not* Nicco & Superior Court is also something else, so believe me, without *instant* bail, I'm Quentin bound.
>
> The one silver lining, when *that* happens, is that the state will grant you an uncontested divorce for only 1 dollar…

He then wrote that if I wouldn't put up the house I should call LuAnne, Al's uncle or anyone who would, after which he chattily veered off to describe the books he'd been reading as though nothing else were on his mind. But the final paragraph vented his spleen once more:

hence, o distaff nemesis, just because I'm screaming for immediate release to make us rich, keep my job & clear our name, please don't presume to 'know' that I'm not progressing...Could you show it cost anything to get me out, I might listen (tho I won't with $100,000 & 100 days of freedom at stake) but since you can't justify your treason, I therefore 'know' you're completely NUTS... Good bye. N.

Every word stung me to tears, but now I feared for his sanity. Could he seriously believe I'd think he could suddenly raise such a sum – legally – if he had not done so long ago? A much smaller sum might have caused me to hesitate – had he lost all reason? I debated with myself over and over, and I didn't altogether agree with those who kept saying, 'He should have thought of that before breaking the law,' or 'If you can't do the time, don't do the crime.' I could never willingly contribute to penning up anyone in such inhumane conditions, but with three little children dependent upon me, I could hardly risk what little security they had. As it was, my naivety caused me to assume a debt of guilt I am still paying for.

No further word came from Neal. I understood his rejection, but if he were as innocent as he said, I counted on the trial to prove it. I waited for a call from Mr McNamara, who would want to talk to me, and I scarcely left the house; any day he could call, and I waited for him or Neal to tell me the trial date.

| FIFTY-EIGHT |

The next communication I received from Neal was a full month later – the trial was over. The wounds of his rejection and my own self-doubts were reopened, and streamed afresh when I realized he hadn't wanted me to be there, salted now by his own bitter acceptance of his fate, from which I had refused to save him:

Dear Wife: Your husband, tho still imperfectly contrite does freely forgive you for his now being a felon whose recent conviction by jury could so easily have been averted by bail and a separate trial...I realize your sin of omission hardly balances mine of commission, yet rest assured that in the ensuing years we'll both still suffer

proportionate Karma...again, too, you may be paradox-
ically consoled that through your refusal, I'll hand back
most of those 10 bad years you've endured, since on *first*
conviction, the law prescribes 5 to life on each of my 2
counts...understand that this sentence is quite mandatory
for those who go to jury (during the whole 2-day trial, only
15 minutes of which concerned me)...my bum P.D. proved
himself an ace D.A. collaborator by entirely ignoring points
in my defense throughout & in summation didn't even ask
for acquittal, tho there is NO PROOF, only a marijuana
exhaling agent's word, so probation is quite out of the
question...

He held out one frail hope: I was to write to the judge pleading on
his behalf and get anyone else I could find to do so too.

Enclose good snapshot of kids (Cayce dog?) & plead a
minimum sentence...I repeat, for all else has failed now,
your letter is my one last chance to escape the pen and
subsequent parole for the rest of my ruined life...get these
mailed immediately as I get sentenced next week...Flatly
unpersuasive...so seemingly bitter and beyond hope...as
this final letter is...there is yet a further glimmer of unlikely
insight for it to report; I *desperately* need to see you. *Not*
to berate, belittle or bewail, but to speak...about our
future. This Saturday, then – my last here – let kiddies play
in park across from building while you go in...as soon as
possible after 1PM. Thanks...'Beat' is even in Catholic
pamphlets now; poor Sublette, I pray every hour now,
have for weeks; it's wonderful. If it wasn't for kids, would
enjoy prison, just what I need. Don't miss sex, driving or
freedom, but must confess still hunger terribly for candy
bars and cigarettes. *Please* forgive my last two brutal letters;
they were obviously meant to snap you out of your folly
in time, but they failed, alas, just as your attempt to awaken
me before it was too late. See you Sat. Be strong, patient,
peaceful. I love *you*. Neal

Given this new hope, I shot into instant action. I wrote the judge
two single-spaced pages of the best arguments I could muster, without
any bitterness. I didn't want him to think we believed in getting
away with anything, I just asked for a realistic choice of correction
that would benefit him and society the most. Five years in prison could

only produce one hardened criminal and three possibly delinquent children – not to mention a whole family for the state to support unnecessarily. It wasn't as though he were dangerous. I wanted to mention the fact we were wise to the real motive for his arrest, but decided to curb any criticism. Also, I still trusted lawyers and courts.

In mentioning Al Sublette, Neal was referring to another tragedy that had splashed across the newspapers just before the trial. Al had been living with a girl for over a year when he decided to break off with her. 'We're dying together,' he'd told me. He had taken an apartment on the other side of town from hers. One night late she tried to go to him, but in the alley beside Al's apartment she was raped and murdered by a black seaman. The seaman was now in jail with Neal, and told him he had not known he had killed her. According to him, when Al refused to open his door to her, she enticed the passing seaman and led him to the alley. There she disrobed, folding her clothes carefully over the wire fence (as they were found by the police) and offered him her bottle of whiskey. She was partially crippled, an alcoholic and a wreck of a woman – why Al had left her – but the seaman didn't know her condition that night. He said he had only clutched her throat to curb her irrational screaming. It probably took very little to extinguish her dim light. He thought she had just passed out. How they found him I don't know.

Al became involved in the mess, not only emotionally, since he blamed himself for her death, but publicly, the whole sensational scandal annihilating his upward striving and turning him, too, into a hopeless alcoholic. I wrote Jack the sad news.

On the day Neal was to be sentenced, Helen and I hurried to the Superior Court, and in the hallway outside I found McNamara bearing down upon us.

'Oh, Mrs Cassady, I'm so glad to see you. I'd like to ask you a few questions.'

I cut him off sharply, 'Don't you think it's a trifle late? Why haven't you contacted me before?' I gave him a scathing glance.

'Well, you see – since we haven't actually any proof of your husband's guilt – let me see –' and he began shuffling nervously through papers.

'Then what is he doing here?' I retorted, and was so angry and close to tears, I turned on my heel, and Helen and I bolted for the courtroom, where I supposed I'd see our revered democratic justice system in action.

After the judge was duly honoured and seated, about a dozen men were herded in, shackled in pairs by their wrists, looking like a scene from *Les Misérables*. Neal's partner was none other than the seaman, the horrible murderer of Al Sublette's girl, but he looked more like a weak, terrified black rabbit. His sentence was postponed, and even though we were sure he hadn't a chance, we were grateful not to have to hear of his fate. The man sentenced just before Neal had been apprehended with a car full of marijuana and had received money from from an agent for its sale. He was treated with respect bordering on the friendly. Later we learned he had 'cooperated', and implicated several other people. He was sentenced to one count of five years to life.

The proceedings were carried out quite casually, with a taint of boredom, not the awesome solemnity portrayed on the screen. The judge spoke softly; it was difficult to hear him, but he seemed serious and concerned enough, so my hopes rose. I wondered if he'd ever received my letter.

Neal was called up, and I leaned forward. Neal stood straight, his manner respectful, answering calmly when spoken to. The judge read off the data concluded at the trial, but most of it too fast and low to hear well, but we did hear one incredible statement. Neal had denied ever having smoked marijuana, and now when the judge asked him again, Neal denied it again. Helen and I looked at each other in dismay. What could he be thinking? For what reason? (And why did I never ask him later why he had said this?)

The judge said, 'In that case, I must assume you were a dealer.' MacNamara lunged from his sideline in a vain attempt to interrupt, pulling on the judge's gown and insisting, 'But, your honour, there is no proof!'

The judge ignored him and began addressing Neal again, his voice rising, his colour mounting until he was practically screaming insults at Neal about his 'double life', despicable character and lack of 'cooperation' with the law. Aha. That was the bit that really irked the judge. I knew he had been trained to believe a good citizen should report infractions by his neighbour, but we knew that Jesus, quoting Divine law, said, 'What is that to you? Follow me.'

There stood Neal, his head bowed, poised, cool and respectful, and there screeched this man who believed himself worthy to judge his fellow man, absolutely hysterical with vindictive rage. MacNamara went up to the judge and pawed his gown, shouting now, 'But, your honour, we haven't any *proof*!' several times, trying to get the judge's attention.

When the latter ceased ranting, he heard McNamara, stopped to look at him briefly, then turned back to Neal with 'Yes – well – *I don't care*! I am sorry for his wife and children, but I don't like his *attitude*!' And with no hesitation he sentenced Neal to two counts of five years to life in a penitentiary, both sentences to run concurrently – this double the sentence for the recently dispatched cooperative proven dealer.

Neal sat down quietly to be reshackled. I came unhinged and had to clutch my bench with all my strength to keep from racing down the aisle to tell that judge what I thought of him and his unbiased administration of 'justice'. The more fool I. Instead, I ran outside to tremble against the stair rail until Helen joined me.

'Jesus, what a farce,' she said, and put her arm around my shoulder. MacNamara came bustling over to us, but I didn't dare speak to him, and only glared. He stammered and mumbled something about making a motion for a new trial, but I knew he was only trying to save face, so we walked away from him, and I called back, '*DO* that!' but without any hope he would. It was obvious the two agents had triumphed; they could ply their trade with no further fear of Neal's exposing them. It was all like something out of *Alice in Wonderland*.

Now disillusioned with the wonderful American system of justice, Neal looked even more the martyr to me. He had shown an integrity and dignity far beyond the honourable men, and wouldn't dream of implicating others even to save his own skin.

Ironically, Neal began serving his sentence on Independence Day, 1958. As naive as ever, I assumed sentences are what they say, so I believed he'd be gone at least five years. I learned sentences mean nothing. 'Five' years means two, 'life' means seven years with innumerable variations. The whole process is an intricate game; one should study the rules and get a score card before participating. I became more and more disgusted with the good old U.S. of A. More was yet in store.

Before investigating how a prisoner's family was supposed to survive, I wrote to Jack and Allen, and they answered with sympathy, distress, questions, suggestions and encouragement. As a bonus I received an unexpected note from Gregory Corso. He explained first his behaviour while visiting us that weekend, saying his attitude towards breakfast had been due to a bad dream about eggs, then ended with:

> This is hard to say, yet I feel I have the earthly journey that is miles and miles of vision and sorrow and awakening to say: Neal's walk in life has always been pyloned by roses, and if a great old sick rose blocks his walk, he'd certainly not sidestep. That's what is so true and lovely in the man. When you see him please tell him for me that I well know that all things render themselves; I never knew this before, because when I used to come upon that obstructive rose I'd not sidestep, yet would I continue on, venture on, but stand there and complain; well, I learned enough this last year in Europe to dispense with the complaints; how absurd I realized to complain that which is life. I hope this makes sense. I want it to, because I am very unhappy about what has happened to Neal. I'm almost apt to say 'Poor God' and not 'Poor Neal.' My love…

My only other consolation lay in the fact that Neal's letters were so full of religious fervour, even if only as a muzzle. Possibly this could be an enforced monastic interlude that could help him, which he insisted was the case.

First he was sent to a medical facility at Vacaville, where prisoners underwent psychological studies, supposedly to discover the best method for their correction. A good idea, but as far as we ever learned this remained in the realm of theory, but Vacaville was a more humane institution than most, and he stayed there in comparable decency for several months.

Over a week passed before I heard from him. Then on July 22 an explanation arrived for the delay.

> Unbelievable as it may seem, I've written you half a doz. letters since being here. Oh, I know you've received only one (the second I wrote; first was rejected for writing above lines) besides this, the sixth so here's the abridged story of my 3rd, 4th and 5th ones: Wed last, after devouring your 6-page beauty, proving more than mere karma spouse devotion, began preparing what I considered an equally uplifting missive manifesting mutual matehood. By writing

every spare moment that day & the next, I managed to
get it mailed Thur. night, but because trying to cover
everything at once, I had conserved space by crowding
lines on back of unruled page (just as I had on the letter you
received.) It was rejected. Expecting to be 'pampered,'
like a fool, I proposed to sgt in charge that it be allowed
to pass, 'just this once,' and, of course, I'd not write tiny
again. After consulting with Capt. the hour I cooled my
soon-to-be subversive heels in the horseshoe pit, he
recalled to tell me the letter seemed full of 'double-talk,'
secret answers to your secret questions, and thus couldn't
be sent; so ended letter 3. All day Friday, with natural
resentment tempered only by what I thought was the
humor of it all, I composed an awkward biting satire on
'double-talk' and tried mailing this farce to you. But no
go. Instead my supposed wit proved a bad mistake of
judgement when Sat. AM I was called in and chewed on
for openly insulting the Capt. So, this letter, the 4th and
funniest I thought, was the most sternly rejected, as well
as being quite probably put in my central file to show I
disrespect authority. Anyway, Sat. nite I mailed another,
the 5th attempt to get thru a 'message to Garcia;' this new
one was a most sorry affair, reflecting much of my deep
disgust over the whole sad hassle in which I'd stupidly
involved myself, so despairingly blah was it that, altho
already 5 days late in answering you, I quickly regretted
having written at all, but, hurray, my prayers working via
a bum memory, it was returned this morning for forgetting to put my number, etc. on the flap of the envelope.
Well, now that I've wasted nearly a page by explaining
somewhat my delay in writing – tho have been scribbling
so furiously all week I've writer's cramp – I'll begin anew
this long retarded reply to your #1.

I put the letter down here and tried to figure out why – if, they'd
refused all the others – why did this recap get through? I could find
no answer, but at least the Gilbert and Sullivan score brought both
Neal and me some laughter. He went on to say I was not to try any
more ways of releasing him or getting a new trial. He said he wouldn't
even know how much time he'd have to serve for another 18 months,
when he'd go before a three-man board to have it set. I studied
all he wrote again and again, but, like Alice, all I could think was

'curiouser and curiouser'. It doesn't please me now to have learned too late that had I known how then, I could have hired a lawyer who would have had Neal out in 60 days for only a misdemeanour.

He went on to say he had been seriously composing prayers of his own, and was memorizing the names of all the popes to help

> hasten my growth as well as all mankind. To better emu-late these leaders, I am memorizing their names & add a new one each day to the prayer, i.e., today's Pope – the 21st in order (I began July 1st) is St. Cornelius, who reigned from 251–263. Next week will get back to your wonderful first letter, the first paragraph of which is all I've managed to answer so far. I love you, sweet strong Goldilocks. N

This wasn't at all what I had thought would be the best use of his monastic life. These 'leaders' he wanted to 'emulate' had nothing in common with their 'Lord', Jesus, and slaughtered everyone who tried to live according to the teachings of Jesus. And what had those 'leaders' done for him except burden him for life with unworthiness and guilt. Ah well, I was grateful for his explanation of some of the rules of the prison game, which, even if still a mystery, at least meant he wouldn't be away five whole years.

Neal was consistent in writing each week when he could, often practising word games and imitations of Proust's non-stop sentences. When I mentioned his religious ardour, he saw beneath my casual comments an anxiety that he might be overdoing it somewhat, and in his usual way brought it right to the surface for discussion.

> One last bit on the religion 'kick' (& indeed it is this, whether in or out, it's really the only 'kick' left, true?) I read that a Postulant in Cistercian monastery spends 90 days at least as such; this corresponds to my 3 months in SF jail; 2 years as novice, equalling my term inside pen, 3 years under 'simple vows,' my period of outside parole. So just as they take 5 years in all before finally accepted, I'll be completely discharged & accepted back into society only after a similar passage of time. Interesting, what?
> By the by, *On the Road* is in library here, and Doug Ferguson bewails it's always checked out, so he still hasn't read it, as I wish no one would, frankly…

In most of Neal's letters when describing his conditions he managed to maintain an objective, sarcastic or satirical tone with one eye on the censors. My penance demanded I visit him, always a torment for me whether or not Neal was hostile, which he often was, and I'd drive home in tears. Nothing could be more depressing than the prisons themselves. Vacaville wasn't as bad as San Quentin proved to be, and provided a gentler introduction. The grounds were not as formidable, the building less of a fortress. Still, the two-way mirror on the wall and the order to 'keep your hands on the table' (which I continually forgot and got scolded) were humiliating. The 'don't touch' policy was the cruellest of all. The only possible benefit I could conceive from these encounters might have occurred if you could just hug each other and sop up by osmosis what we both really needed. Ah yes, punishment.

Vacaville wasn't deliberately degrading to the inmates; there were psychological games to play as well as a more balanced life physically. Soon after he was settled in he wrote,

> I look out cell window and watch trains meeting and passing a half mile away, and within a few 100 yards there daily comes creeping a local frt. over Sacramento Northern Branch line; ho hum, let 'em work – I'm on vacation. Took gym test today, ran 250 yards back & forth in 53 seconds, chin-ups 37 – all in the 'very good' category, Took 900-question quiz on attitude and comprehension; then spelling, I.Q., mechanical apt. Scholastic, math, vocab., voc. skills, etc. Now all tests over & am in 2-week doz.-person 'Group Behavior Adjustment' class. Our ball team (tell Johnny I'm a Giant, too, just like on his cap) won 2 of last 3 & now in second place in league. Each Sat. go to confession to receive on Sun. the Holy Eucharist from fine German priest here. Gained 10lbs! Feeling increasingly purged of old desires, especially of flesh.

He had volunteered to participate in a psychological study called 'IT', 'Intensive Treatment'. (We laughed at the ironic coincidence in view of the descriptions of Neal's searching to find 'It' in life.) In spite of the accusations that Vacaville was a 'country club', I did so wish he could stay there. The confinement and regulations would have been punishment enough, but the more humane conditions could strengthen his character, his self-respect and dilute the bitterness.

He said he hoped to be sent to Soledad, where 'the kissing facilities are better', but I suspected that idea was because it was beyond the visiting range. As in the armed services, I suppose, the place you request or that seems reasonable is the only one you may be sure you won't get, and so he was sent to San Quentin, and I received a poignant account of the transfer:

> Dearest Dear Carolyn, Wonder Wife: Even as they were striking my leg irons, that had, along with two side armed officers, locked door, barred windows & snow-white pajamas worn – minus the half-expected bright red and yellow bullseye on back – most adequately subdued any wild urge to disembark during the short bus ride from Vacaville, I began experiencing generation of a not inconsiderable self-pity, soon to become, while procedure progressed, almost overpowering by virtue of those repeated shocks every new dismal view bordering sheer disbelief administered in separate but accumulative blows to my oh-so-sorry-for-myself sharpened conception as, now buffeted from both within and without into a bewildering numbness, I at last encountered, when first stumbling across the 'Big Yard' – as the 'cons' call it – in that characteristic state it seems to engender, a paradoxical one of haze-like concentration, the main source of what gloomy emanations my all-too-sympathetic mood had rendered it recipient; that physical wall each convict's despair-ridden tension made to exist inside the, high and wide though they be, far weaker stone walls of this infamous old – 1859 is chiselled atop the facade of one still-used building – prison, at which, accompanying 23 more, I finally arrived last week...

(I saw he could still enjoy creating Proustian sentences.) In the bunk above him was a 'thug who'd escaped 8 times'. The next day the newscast revealed the death of the Pope, which ignited a painful realization of how self-centred, he said, he'd been in regard to me, and to end the day with a final 'depressing and shared sadness' of the demise of the Milwaukee Braves in the World Series. Above all, however, he experienced the 'balancing factor of compassion...truly, I've never seen nor is there elsewhere in this noble country concentrated...such an assorted assemblage of absolutely pitiful misfits as are the 5,042 felons – latest count, which KROW announced on the 6PM news as largest since 1942.'

San Quentin, whether viewed from the inside or out leaves no doubt as to its purpose. It's an ugly eruption on a jut of land beside the bay, a rare barren blemish in the otherwise lush landscape. In what seems a desperate attempt at camouflage to deceive the visitor, exquisite rose bushes closely line the concrete walk from the gatehouse to the small entrance – turned sideways as though hiding in shame. Wooden steps lead to the door, and inside are more steps to a small, dingy waiting room containing too few old, hacked benches as rigid as pews, hard, cold and crowded with the pitiful collection of family and friends; old and young mothers, girlfriends, brothers, babies and every age of child and a smattering of old fathers.

Next to the steps is a low counter where, if the officer happens to be there, you give the name and number of the inmate you wish to see. After checking a file, the officer hands you a 'chit.' You then wait, wait and wait some more. I spent as long as three hours expecting 'Cassady' to bark from the loudspeaker. I tried to time my visits so that Neal could get out of work, not a meal, but sometimes he explained they 'forgot' to tell him I was there. First, inmates had to go to their cells to wash and change clothes.

When the welcome name is called, you go up four to five more steps through the formidable steel door attended by an armed guard who takes your chit and allows you to sit at one of the tables in the huge echoing room. The windows are high and heavily barred, the several burly guards bristling with armaments stand about the cracked ancient wall. Another thick steel door opens to a window-less passageway that curves down to some lower depth from which the inmates emerge.

One day when I was trying to talk to Neal, an unusual blaring alert suddenly set all the guards to nervous activity, their hands hovering near their pistols, their eyes filled with fear. My heart jumped at this display, and turned to Neal for an explanation. He looked back over his shoulder just as up the ramp of the passageway came a small, frail black man, huge armed guards at his sides. As he drew nearer, the guards in our room leaped to slam the two steel doors with reverberating clangs.

'Probably a death-row inmate come to see his lawyer,' Neal guessed. 'There's a private room just outside there.' Neal was used to all this; I was not.

'What a fantastic performance! That defenceless little man half the size of those big bruisers – not to mention the guns. What did they suppose he could possibly do to *them*? You'd think he was a wild boar! They're afraid of him!'

'Yeah, well, they like being dramatic, you know how it is.' I was learning how it was, and I'd wonder all the way home each time *why* it was.

Neal wrote touching letters to the children on their birthdays, Christmas and Easter. He'd tell them the history of Mother Goose rhymes and the origin of words, like 'sincere'. He'd correct the grammar in their letters to him, and tell them some of the things he did at their ages, etc. Most ironic to me were the lectures on behaviour, emphasizing 'obedience' and 'truth', and when John reached seven, 'the age of reason', Neal outlined for him the difference between 'right' and 'wrong'. I sighed and thought of the Cayce proclamation that 'knowledge not used is sin'. When I received letters from him to them, I cut off the top two inches with his number and the famous name of his residence. On the back of this strip would be a note for me.

Instead of learning a useful trade, Neal was put to work sweeping the floor of the textile mill,

> which reminds me how I've been using prayer lately, how this very ex-beatster beats a beat bastille: Rule: blank mind/desire proportunately to each bodily nullification. Example: Hearing. To overcome eardrum-bursting racket made by the cotton textile mill's 4 million dollars worth of 1745 RPM, 68x72' hi-speed looms, whose constantly collecting flug is my weary job to sweep all day from beside and beneath, I, thus, noisily assured safeguard from eavesdropping, deadening surfaced thought to equate the deafness, incessantly shout into that accompanying roar every prayer known, & since saying them hurriedly, it takes just one hour to complete their entirety, each minute after the first 60, finds me repeating the very one I said on that very moment last hour. Don't demur, it at least eliminates clockwatching.

Then on our first anniversary apart, he tried to convey to me the conditions under which he existed in his four-and-a-half by seven-and-a-half by nine-and-a-half feet cell:

> to get some better idea of what lying so encaged is like you might put the car mattress in the bathtub, thereby making it softer & if not as long, at least much cleaner than is my bug-ridden bunk; bring your 200lb friend, Edna, or the more negative aggressive Babs, then lock the door & after dragging 11 rowdy kids into our bedroom to parallel the 1,000 noisy ones housed in this particular cell block (of course you must remove the toilet seat, towel racks, cabinets – anything other than a small mirror & 4½ shelf) remaining almost motionless so as not to inadvertently irritate armed robber, Edna, ponder past mistakes, present agonies & future defeats in the light of whatever insights your thus disturbed condition allows.
>
> April 2 got heartrending Easter card from John and Jami...Tell John how pleased I was he got right number of humps (his drawing of a sand container) on top of the engine. Don't tell Jami how tragically ironic I found it that she...spelled 'Hey, hey' as 'Hay, hay' to innocently twist deeper in firmer fix the sharp memory knife cutting my remorse anew by her unwittingly giving such appropriate name to the vile weed used in that selfish habit of vice putting me here...

We learned with great disappointment and wonder that Hugh Lynn was not allowed to correspond with Neal, nor could he send pamphlets from the ARE; the best we could do was for me to pass his messages on. Only after Neal's release did I learn he was allowed communication solely with women.

Does that make sense? More 'punishment'?

In spite of Neal's generally loving letters, his resentment against me for not having furnished his bail lay like a coiled serpent in his heart, and every so often he was unable to prevent its striking out. As time passed, I grew to sense its constant presence, and although I desperately wished to believe his rebirth, I dared not rely on it completely, his hate affected me so strongly.

The first indication of the continued vitality came as a sudden blow in a note to me on top of one of the children's letters exactly one year from his sentencing. It was at the time when we were getting people to put in a good word for him to the Adult Authority prior to their setting his time: 'now's the time, probably too late already, in fact, of course all this means as little or less than did my bail so maybe better forget such help, like the folly of entering the State's employ at this crucial time, and just go ahead and spend a buck to do that which I advised a year ago...' (get a divorce).

The 'State's employ' referred to an attempt by the welfare department to force me to become a social worker.

The next letter bore a humble apology and a long dirge as to how much my love for him had dwindled as evidenced by the few letters I'd written and fewer visits, immediately justifying my actions by taking the blame himself for not having written and for asking me not to visit. Then more depressing words of his being a felon who would damage the children, an ex-con the parole officer could send back at any time, my woes being married to one, etc. I wondered how much real satisfaction was afforded him by tormenting me – love and hate so entwined; pushing me away, hauling me back. I'd have done anything he asked now, visited as often as he wished, even though the few times I did were traumatic. The sight of me roused the serpent, his forked tongue lashing out. As usual, Neal was fully aware of his actions, and, as usual, felt apologies would change their effect. After the last one, he described our visit being so unproductive from his 'stiff-necked adolescent gawk', so he concentrated on analysing 'WHY WHY?' Then followed a long review of everything I'd ever done as a homemaker and mother, besides 'countless other tasks above and beyond', all listed and counted. There was no lack of humour as well as drama in this tale, and when I thought he had finished, he wrote, 'I will at last get down to the business at hand; an analysis of resentment with examples of how I've taken it out on you, titled WHAT IS RESENTMENT?, subtitled, "I'm not angry, but just look what you've done to me!"'

And so he did, filling a page now with every critical insight about himself. I hoped it was purging for him, but doubted it, even though I appreciated the effort. I wasn't sure exactly what that exercise was for, except to try to make me think he was no longer resentful. I knew he was and would be. I had done a truly unforgivable thing. I could understand that.

| FIFTY-NINE |

On the home front during this time, confusion vied with bewilderment. Cayce said, 'Why worry when you can pray,' but I had not yet learned the difference between a positive declaration of what was wanted and concentrated worry, so worry I did.

I found it very strange that one bureau of a social system could remove the supporting member of a family and give no thought to the innocent dependants thus deprived. Instead, it was totally up to me to find means of survival. Through friends in the know I was directed to the Welfare Department. I hadn't thought of them, because of my experiences previously with this august body. But there was no other choice.

Their programme provided 'emergency rations' while considering your case. These took two months to arrive, and were pitifully inadequate for a family of four, but my stocked garage kept us alive. After another two months my application was refused. I felt that since my situation was within a specified temporary time limit I was justified in turning to the government that had created my need. I, myself, had been a contributor to the programme for years through my taxes, and had thought it a wise proviso for persons in exactly my dilemma. Again, such simple logic eluded the agency.

After another two months of 'string pulling' by influential friends, I was finally awarded Aid to Needy Children, otherwise known as ANC. The parent was not included. The monthly sum for us was $184.50. The house payment alone came to $105, so we'd have $74.50 for utilities, food, gas etc. To compensate somewhat we were issued surplus food. This consisted of butter, cheese, dry milk and occasional seasonal vegetables. There was always a lot of corn meal, and although I never mastered the art of making tortillas, I could do corn bread and corn meal mush. We ate a lot of corn meal. And making milk from powder was soon an automatic chore.

Some months later, this policy was discontinued, due, they said, to a lack of interest. It didn't occur to them that the distribution point was ten to fifteen miles from most of the needy, few if any having cars, and public transport non-existent. I had been collecting as many as I could while the policy was in effect.

During the six months before receiving anything, I was kept busy worrying about the debts we'd been caught owing. Aside from the house and utility regulars, there were a few scattered charges for children's clothes and instalments on appliances – all within the budget of Neal's earnings. I wrote or called everyone, and performed the disagreeable duty of explaining my lack of funds, while assuring them they would all be paid if they could be patient. A few wrote off the debts, like children's clothing.

To compound this problem, I discovered via missed payments that Neal had acquired three loans unknown to me, totalling close to $800 in all. One company agreed to wait; one wrote it off, but one said 'Tough', and sent the Sheriff to collect my car. That cost $10 to take it to their garage and $5 per *day* thereafter. I couldn't figure how I could earn the money to pay them without a car. No one cared.

Except one: Jami's ballet master's father had formerly owned a loan company, and was now in insurance or something, but all these people knew him. He paid off Neal's loans, chastised the lenders for making them, collected my car, and gave me an interest-free loan to be paid whenever I could. Many of the townspeople also ordered portraits, so I avoided foreclosure, and the hours spent painting revived my spirits.

My first welfare check in September (I'd had no income since March) looked enormous, but the $74.50 didn't go very far. Along with it I got another social worker, who was to review the whole thing and re-evaluate my needs. He was an ex-Baptist minister, and I looked forward to stimulating discussions on religion. Well, no. After his initial appraisal, he reported I had a car and a swimming pool, resented my surplus butter, and I lost both him and the aid.

Why, I know not, they informed Neal that his family was no longer receiving aid. 'Your name will now be removed from the restricted commissary list by the Finance Officer,' and he went off at a tangent, condemning all the agencies, but most of all himself, and wallowed in remorse and guilt. I couldn't help a slight suspicion that most of this Dickensian letter was aimed at the prison officials. He said there was nothing he could do, because he was entering the hospital himself, but did not say why. He ended with 'Cathy Crosby to star in *Beat Generation* by MGM. Imagine a "Beat" Crosby, revolting what?'

I was allowed to visit Neal in the infirmary, where we were left alone and relished a good long hug, but I came home in tears again, this time for him. His operation was for haemorrhoids, and because he carried a card stamped 'DU', not for Denver University, he told me, but for 'Drug User', he was denied anaesthetics. This senseless sadism and his stoic acceptance drew tears of rage at our helplessness.

At home I returned to the battle with the welfare to reinstate the aid. This time they dispatched their head man to deal with me. He had a reputation to uphold, and boasted he had been 99 percent successful in getting lone mothers to go to work, and I became his target for today. His first suggestion was for me to hire a babysitter whom I would have to pay the exact same amount I was earning, which, of course, made no sense. He then proposed I divorce Neal, because 'divorced women have a better chance in the marketplace'. I assumed he meant with men. I refused that option too. Then he said I should become a social worker, since I had a college degree. I tried not to, but did pass the test. When I then faced the grim examining board, one asked me if my experience as a recipient for aid myself would have any bearing on my attitude towards the job. My answer was swift: 'You bet it would!' My name was put on the bottom of the list, never to rise again, and he finally threw in his towel and my aid was reinstated.

Another blow awaited, however: from the incessant misunderstandings of the rules, I had not realized that any money I earned could not be used to clear my debts or fund my living expenses but was subtracted from their allowance. I had dutifully and honestly reported my portrait earnings (long since spent), and the bitter truth was made known to me when my December check totalled $13.

Now what to do about Christmas? I had downplayed all of this, of course, to the children, but how to tell them Christmas wouldn't happen this year? My anxiety was misplaced. Instead, I had more difficulty explaining the ever-mounting flood of gifts from strangers – some expensive items like watches, and most with sad tags like 'Boy – aged 7' etc., which had to be yanked off. My concern, too, was how we could ever live up again to this Christmas in future! We were on the 'needy' list of every organization, and were evidently the current bandwagon.

Two incidents showed the paradox of human nature: one was the good intentions of a men's club in Saratoga. The children had been chosen to be 'honoured' at a club luncheon, and we assumed they'd won some kind of drawing. I found it humiliating to learn they were 'special' only because they were unfortunate, and I had a hard time giving the children a reasonable explanation of my refusal without revealing Neal's whereabouts.

The other was from a women's club which chose us as their target for a huge Christmas dinner. I begged them to give their generosity to a friend's family who had been 'needy' for 25 years and had never received such a gift. Her response was, 'How do we know they are worthy?'

| SIXTY |

In between such hassles, and over and above the necessary house, child and school activities, I became involved in theatre design projects besides the ballet school. In the fall my friend Margaret, a speech therapist and acting teacher, put together a unique and exciting summer theatre group, and she asked me to design the costumes and makeup. She was an authority on the western theatre of pioneer days, such as were performed in mining towns by travelling players.

She had recently met a couple who had been performers in Wild West shows, and after they retired they built a model Old West town and museum. It was about ten miles south of Los Gatos, surrounded by a high stockade. It provided the perfect setting for Margaret's project, and I was eager to join the 'Wagon Stagers'.

The 'stage' was a flat-bed wagon, flanked on either side by covered wagons – 'calistogas' – which served as dressing rooms. The audience was seated on benches under the stars, and nearby was a campfire over which hung a huge pot of coffee sending an authentic aroma through the summer air. By stagecoach the can-can dancers arrived in the nick of time, squealing and hooting at the whistles of the 'ranch hands' standing around.

At intermission a startlingly real gun-fight broke out, the shot victim falling off the saloon roof to be carted off to Boot Hill.

For me the long drive and these lively evenings in the country were a soothing balm, so long had I been immersed in our depressing life at home. The children often came with me. They loved the whole scene, the museum, the horses, and sometimes they were included in the 'Oleo' sketches that followed each play performance. Cast parties, either at a nearby roadhouse or Margaret's home, took me further away from my stifling conditions.

And, well, another attraction and distraction had evolved. When I had first gone to rehearsals at Margaret's, I had put my hair in a bun and was resigned to middle age. I was now 35, pushing 40, I felt, so I was on the shelf.

Much to my astonishment, two young men in the cast began making intense passes at me. I saw them as practically teenagers, even though they were only five years younger. I really had a difficult time adjusting to this, I have to admit, although it was wonderful suddenly to feel so young and desirable again.

When our first successful summer season was over in the fall of 1959, Margaret found me another job, this time with the drama club at the University of Santa Clara, where she taught and acted. It was a Jesuit all-male university, and I was hired to costume their quarterly plays and make up the principal actors. (I had stopped declaring my home-made income to the Welfare people.) Here I also enjoyed the intellectual stimulation of the discussions we had on philosophy, religion and the arts. Most of the boys I dealt with were in their last year, and well schooled in logic. They didn't scoff at my weird ideas from metaphysics and psychic phenomena, but were amused by them – so opposed to their accustomed Catholic dogma.

Other than Margaret, who was considerably older and not platinum blonde, I was the only woman they encountered while at school. There were periodic dances with a nearby girls' convent-school, but that didn't offer them much release. They treated me like a queen, and not a queen mother either. Testosterone at its height, a couple of these lads fell passionately in love with me in time, which was flattering, but they really did seem too young at 18 and 19, so I had to repel their advances, fun though those were.

I learned the best cure for hiccups one night after one of the year-end banquets. These were held in Capitola, a small coastal town in a wonderful restaurant sunk below a cliff next to a river – you reached it by cablecar. Once, when being driven back to Los Gatos, the young man next to me in the crowded back seat kissed me non-stop for the entire 22 miles, and my hiccups disappeared.

Thinking of the future with Neal, I wrote that I hoped he would like my new friends. I had stressed the Jesuit connection, and he approved this climate for my work, but he answered bluntly in the negative, not, he insisted, because they were chiefly male, but 'Don't you think if I wanted more friends, I could make them from among the 5,000-odd miserable wretches in here? I've seen enough people to last a lifetime and can't seem to work up any desire to renew old friendships, so certainly don't want to form additional ones.'

His response was at such cross-purposes to my intent, I suspected he was resenting my freedom in spite of my efforts to the contrary. He was more at ease with my reports on activities with the children, their problems at school and mine with sadistic PE teachers and daffy counsellors as well as Jami's triumphs in ballet. She had already exhibited an exceptional talent, and he wrote her his approval as in his Easter letter to her: 'even though you can't be the Easter Bunny, I'm happy to hear you are to be the White Rabbit in "Alice". You know I'll expect you to give the role your very best, don't you?'

Jami hated the role for some reason I never understood. At dress rehearsal a mother noticed she was limping, so I got her off the stage and had her take off her white tights. The bottom of one foot was raw and oozing, like a blister from which the skin had rubbed off, the foot of the tights red with blood. I took her home, soaked it in Epsom salts and told her to lie down and keep it raised. I was harassed with mothers coming for their children's costumes, and couldn't think what to do. She had no understudy. After I'd told one of the mothers what I'd tried to do, it suddenly struck me that she was a Christian Scientist practitioner. I apologized, but she asked if she could talk to Jami. 'Be my guest.' She stood in the doorway and simply told Jami she was afraid of the part, but she must believe she would be fine and do a good job – something like that only more. She just told her to wrap the foot, keep it up, and forget it.

I guess Jami took that in through her pores, because the next morning her foot was perfectly normal, not a mark on it. Once before she had totally 'turned off' extreme flu symptoms in the presence of the doctor, so afraid was she of shots. Back home she began the dripping and coughing as before.

When I reported these 'supernatural' events excitedly to Neal, again he didn't respond as I anticipated, and I got the impression he didn't believe me. I had so wished he could have been present, because I felt a real demonstration would have strengthened his faith, as it had mine. Still, he must have done more thinking along those lines

on his own, for a confession of renewed self-appraisal came in a
letter soon after:

> I've found that all my metaphysical reading and thinking
> cannot create that understanding so desperately sought in
> order to *believe*! Rather it is vice-versa: I must believe to
> achieve understanding...but when faith fails and virtue
> vanishes, what then? Patience, I guess, for, small as it is,
> that's all I've got left...

He went into a vicious condemnation of society and its attitude
towards alcohol and drugs:

> as stated in a recent Chronicle poll that they would rather
> hand out the death penalty for selling dope, including my
> nemesis, marijuana, to minors than they would for sexually
> molesting same, so just as I condemn the chronic or
> otherwise marijuana user, so too do I condemn a society
> that has so rejected reason as to prefer seeing their
> children raped before allowed to smoke Mari. Altho last
> paragraph reveals resentment still to be overcome, am
> sure can do it in next half-thousand days with His help
> and yours...

I was not so sure. I could tell the last sentence was there for the
censors, but his bitterness was clearly still a very active force, and I
knew I headed the list of the guilty. I, on the other hand, had one
more gripe against the Church who had so branded him with guilt
that he could never feel he had a spark of divinity in him. No mark
of Cain, dammit.

As the variety in my life increased on the one hand, on the other
I felt guiltier about Neal and his miserable condition. Through it all
I wished more fervently than ever that our pleasures could be shared.
Yet, a new realization began creeping into my weary bones: for the
first time in ten years I knew where Neal was and what he was
doing; I wasn't constantly on the defensive, continually fearful and
braced for the next unexpected jolt or suffering over the last one. I
cannot deny this was an indescribable relief. A blessed reprieve, I
assumed, because I had come very close to the end of my tether
when 'God made the separation'.

| SIXTY-ONE |

As Allen and Jack had requested, I wrote to them occasionally to keep them posted on Neal, and this spring I also inquired about the typewriter Jack had promised to buy long ago with his new wealth. I received a long and amusing letter from Peter and Allen in New York, Peter full of sympathy for our plight and Allen revealing new plans. He was coming to read at the University of California in Berkeley and at the San Francisco Poetry Center, and hoped to find a way to help Neal:

> don't know if I'm considered officially a Nice Person out there or Juvenile Delinquent but with Professorial address it ought to be OK. See if you can get Neal to fill out forms for me to visit... and write if possible. Reporter from NY Post doing sympathetic 12-part literary story on 'Beat Writing' been interviewing me... and going out to Calif this week to see Snyder, Ferlinghetti, poets... will probably look you up... I assume anyway he's sympathetic within the limitations of journalism. See him if you wish or not. He might eventually, if his story is sincere enough, be able to help – he sees Neal as sort of a martyr, given bad deal by Wicked Opinion and Law. Reporter's name is Al Aronowitz... finishing new book of poems, main long poem about my mother 50 pages long & higher and wilder than howl...

A few weeks later I heard from Jack, the first letter in a long time: he wailed about the awful, cruel prison authorities, how he couldn't correspond with Neal, nor could Allen. He asked if he could mention it in his column for the *Escapade* magazine, or maybe not mention Neal. He told me to tell him how much money I needed to buy Neal a typewriter, which he would do to make up for all the pork chop dinners and pizzas he'd had in our 'dear sweet kiddie kitchen'. He was afraid we'd think his book contributed to Neal's arrest, and if all the fans knew where 'Dean' was they'd be deluging SQ with letters. Then he declared his book was a paean to Neal, and hoped I agreed.

He expressed his wish to see me when next he came to California with our pizza and wine, but said I would find him jaded. He said he could now see too much attention is worse than none, except for the money. He mourned the fact that the critics and press had built him up to the point where his relatives in Lowell said he had disgraced their name. Again he was dreaming of a solitary cabin in California, so he wouldn't be seeing me much. Ah yes, the same old dream, poor Jack never got the message. Still, he said, he thought of me the same as ever. He had paid his income tax and ended with $30 in the bank, so he wasn't as rich as portrayed, but he had enough for the typewriter. He prophesied Neal and I would be blissful in our later lives, 'so don't despair...' He didn't qualify as a prophet, for sure.

When Allen came to San Francisco, he took care of the typewriter himself, and then came to see me over the weekend. He had finished *Kaddish*, the long poem about his mother, and read it aloud to me. I was very moved, far more than by *Howl*, convinced it was a likely masterpiece.

One day, too, I went to the City to see him, and to discuss what action, if any, we might initiate to hasten Neal's release. We had lunch at Moore's, a posh cafeteria, so I could see the murals by Benny Bufano, the creator of the sculpture of Sun Yat Sen that Jack and I had so admired.

Allen offended the other 'square' diners with his torn T-shirt and loud complaints. He repeated this behaviour later when we went to the *San Francisco Chronicle* office. I asked him how he expected people to be persuaded to his way of thinking if he offended them, rather than extending his avowed attitude of 'kindness to all'. He seemed to think me quaint, and I doubted he understood my suggestions that he set a good example or my views on non-resistance – like Ghandi.

Then I received three postcards from Jack on consecutive days. The first one told of sending Allen a check for the typewriter, and had some notion Neal could get out early. The second one asked if I wanted his new book of poems, then criticized all who were taking away his money and the USA, and the third one just said he loved me.

After Allen had left the area, Al Aronowitz, the journalist Allen had foretold from the *New York Post*, came to interview the members of the 'Beat' movement here on the coast. He went to San Quentin, and was allowed to tape a conversation with Neal, as well as take photos. Neal's reaction was not favourable: 'Had a 3-hour interview with Pagan Reporter, no rapport. Every time I began to go into the spiritual reality, he forced return to physical one, ugh, when will they leave us alone?'

A few days later, Aronowitz called to ask if he could talk to me, and I agreed. Maybe I could get in some licks where Neal had failed. Al was a stocky brunette about our age. I soon saw what Neal meant when I, too, tried to explain some of our beliefs and how we'd changed. He didn't seem to comprehend a word of it, so completely fixed was his mind on the physical-social level. I felt as though I were speaking in tongues. He did try, I suppose, but apparently had no point of reference. I could remember being in that same place once myself. Consequently, we talked in circles and I wondered if anything had been accomplished. He was personable and pleasant enough if I stayed in his groove.

A day or two later he called me again, and asked if I'd go with him to Big Sur to try to find Henry Miller. Miller had written some sympathetic comments on Jack's work, so Al thought him related enough to include in his story. I could hardly refuse, and the day was sunny. I always enjoyed the ride through the redwood forests, the rolling truck farms around Watsonville and the rugged cliffs of the coast. Our conversation eased without the intrusion of the tape recorder, and it was fun to talk to someone from New York again. Al had all that big city's tensions I'd forgotten people lived with; life was mostly a laborious and depressing rat-race, but he'd written some fascinating articles, one recent series on Zsa Zsa Gabor, and would soon be doing one on Frank Sinatra. I was envious.

We drove for several miles before finding Miller's property, which was reached by a winding dirt road straight up. When we reached the open space below which was his house, we parked the car and walked up stepping stones to the top of a small hill, below which lay the picturesque Spanish-style adobe house and tiled patio. To the left of it was a long shed-like building. We were met on the patio by a tall pretty young girl with shoulder-length black hair, but I had difficulty keeping my eyes from wandering to her lower half. Beneath a loose, low-cut blouse she wore nothing but snug light blue ballet tights. With these I was very familiar, but never without trunks or a leotard on top. She might as well have been in her underpants. With her was a taller young man, swarthy and handsome, almost too pretty – like a mannequin.

The girl (whom I assumed to be the latest Mrs Miller) told us Henry was busy writing in the adjacent building, and not to be disturbed, 'but he should be out soon; you may wait in the house if you wish.' We walked into the huge living room, the floor terracotta tile like the patio, and sat in rattan chairs placed together beside a small table and exotic plant. The room was dark and cool. The other two sat across the room near the fireplace, and were intent on their own conversation, ignoring us. I had the feeling they had remained in the room with us to be sure we didn't swipe the silver.

At least an hour passed, and Al and I were about to abandon our quest when the girl said it was nearly time for Mr Miller to join us. We returned to the patio to watch for him, admiring the painted plaques and other artifacts decorating a wall which, Mrs Miller informed us, had been done by the children.

Like a burst of sunlight, Henry Miller suddenly opened the door of his writing shed and bounded towards us down the steps to the patio. Al informed him quickly of his mission, and more quickly Henry said, 'No,' he was sorry, but he couldn't give us an interview because this was the time he played ping-pong with his children, which he considered a sacred obligation. We saw no children nor ping-pong table, but no way could we object.

Most courteously, however, he walked with us to the road, where our car was parked. He was only mildly interested – more amused, really, by Jack's spontaneous prose style, saying, 'That sort of thing works only in relationship to the mind behind it; if the mind is of genius, good; if not – trash.' But he then reviewed the history of literature in relation to spontaneity from the Greeks onwards. How we wished the tape recorder had been running.

I was particularly gratified by this brilliance, since I'd never been able to get past page one of anything he'd written, most of which sounded pretty 'spontaneous' to me. This charming, cultured, genial gentleman didn't fit my preconceived image of him at all, and I was pleased to find it so.

When Al's series was completed he sent me tear sheets, and I thought them remarkably well written, with a sincere effort to understand these men who lived lives so different from his own. Even if he missed the essence of our spiritual search, he did a good job in repeating some of what we'd said. The chief drawback was the sensational nature of the *New York Post*.

When Jack read it he had a mixed reaction. He thought it was scary, but also that it might do good. He liked best Neal talking of the pineal gland and its function, and the references to Cayce and Aurobindo.

| SIXTY-TWO |

When Neal's time was officially set, and we knew he'd be released in June of 1960 – if not a couple of months earlier, he hoped – I began searching for a job he could do – a prerequisite for parole. We had expected he'd learn a trade during the two years, and he had been taking as many offered courses as he could.

He had begun with psychology, but switched when music was offered. When he had learned to read it and was about to be issued an instrument, 'the order initially instigated last year finally came through... Yes, music school and cotton plug are now forever in my prison past, for from here on out (it's a three-year course at minimum) I shall be learning the printing trade.'

Were they this disorganized on purpose, or just stupid? A whole year wasted in manual labour, and now when he might get something to use outside, he gets shifted so often he can never learn enough of any one of them to provide an occupation. Maybe just a game of punishment for them.

I had already asked everyone I knew for ideas or open jobs. Well, of course, very few if any were open to him, since he was a felon and unbondable. Can you believe all this from possessing illegal marijuana? I remembered Starr Daily's telling us of expecting your 'debt to society' to ever be paid; the 'punishment' never ends. He said he had tried conscientiously to obtain employment by honest means, only to be rejected time and time again, whereupon he just bought another gun.

Although no marketable skill was involved, Neal's favourite course in prison was 'Comparative Religion and Philosophy', taught by Gavin Arthur. This man became a bright star in our lives from that time on. Neal loved him dearly, but wrote to me satirically:

> Last Saturday 'Uncle Gavin' Arthur, grandson of our 21st
> President, who, Republican though he was, could hardly
> have been more conservative than is Gavin underneath all⁻

his Occult Astrology, failed to show (again for the third time in six weeks) to teach our class…about three dozen regularly in attendance, on account of a death in his group at Global House, which he bought by selling newspapers on Market Street for ten years; so again it was my pleasurable duty to instruct the boys in Caycehood – a task they always urge upon me whenever our respected and illustrious Leader, who knows literally everyone important in the Metaphysical and other fields (his talks range from taking Yoga enemas with the great Gurjieff to making horoscopes for Mrs Winter's old crony, Dr Blanche Baker, and Lottie von Stral, whom he now suspects is losing her psychic power because of using it exclusively to get money to keep her husband, the Baron, who's dying of cancer, alive despite his oft-repeated desire to go.) Our Leader either oversleeps or runs out of gas, as he did on two previous times…

Neal had not heard Gavin's story of their initial meeting, which Gavin told me when he paid me a visit to collect data for our horoscopes. In the course of the conversation Gavin gave me his impressions of Neal, and recalled how he had first heard of him.

'I had read *On the Road*, of course, and I was driving Gary Snyder down to visit the Onslow-Fords near Carmel. Gordon Onslow-Ford is an English painter who paints far-out things and wrote a book about "instant" painting. He and his wife, Jacqueline, admired Gary Snyder's poetry, and were going to give him a letter of introduction to a Japanese sculptor in Japan. So I said, "Gary, I know you're the hero of *Dharma Bums*, but do you happen to know the hero of *On the Road*?" And Gary said, "Oh yes indeed, I do; he's one of my best friends," and then he grinned and slapped me on the knee, saying, "And you are going to meet him at ten o'clock tomorrow morning."

'Well, I was flabbergasted! How could he know such a thing as that? With a sly grin, Gary said, "Didn't you tell me you are opening a class in Comparative Religion at ten o'clock tomorrow morning at San Quentin?" and I said, "Yes, but what has that got to do with it?" So then Gary told me that Neal was in "Q" for exchanging a joint for a ride, and "he'll be the first one to sign up for your class – you'll see!"

'"Well," I said, "will I recognize him? I've never even seen a picture of him," and Gary said, "Oh, you'll know him all right, don't worry about that." He was sort of chortling, you know, pleased with himself. So I went to class the next day and looked up at the sea of faces – there are about sixty cons who take my class – and there was one face that was really *shining*!

'There was something about Neal when he wasn't taking dope that was absolutely angelic. I could easily recognize him out of all those sixty faces. And, sure enough, when the talk was over, he shouldered his way down, you know, with that impetuosity of his, and he said, "Mr Arthur, you read my name as Neal Cassady, but you might know me better as Dean Moriarty." "Oh yes," I said, "your friend Gary Snyder told me you'd be the first to sign up for this class." "I was, *I was*!" He was so enthusiastic, like a jack-in-the-box – so delighted Gary would know that. Really, his enthusiasm was just – just breathtaking. I loved him the *moment* I saw him.

'Then from time to time I would bring guest speakers to the class. One day I invited Varda.'

Yanko Varda was a prominent artist who lived on an 'ark' in the Sausalito Bay. I later went to parties there with Gavin. He was a Greek by nationality, and Gavin had him speak on the Greek Orthodox religion. After the class, Varda turned to Gavin: 'I suppose you know you have a saint in your class? He has a halo around him.' Varda believed in auras, and according to Gavin painted halos around his subjects as did his genitors. Neal had been the 'saint' he espied.

'After that,' continued Gavin, 'Onslow-Ford came one time, too. He's a great friend of Braque and Picasso and so on, and he, too, was very much impressed with Neal's shining.

'But the visitor that topped them all was Allen Ginsberg. One day Neal said to me, "Allen's in town. Do bring him to the class. You really should have him." And I said, "Do you think for one minute the authorities would allow the author of *Howl* to come to San Quentin as a speaker? You're *mad*!"

"No," said Neal, "I doubt if they've ever heard of him, and if you can get the Chaplains to okay it, I'm sure you can do it." I doubted it, but I did broach the subject at lunch the next day. The Catholic Chaplain never came, but the Jewish and the two Protestant Chaplains comprised a quorum, and they said they'd love to meet Ginsberg, and would see what they could do.

'Well, in a few days they called me to say the pass was going to be all right. So I called the place where Allen was staying, but they said he was visiting Margaret Mead's husband for the day, so I left word for Allen to call me the minute he got in no matter the time. He took me at my word and called – it must have been nearly three in the morning – and I told him Neal wanted him to speak to my class, and that I felt it would be very appropriate, because it was Mother's Day, and I understood he had just written a poem about his mother. Allen said, "Oh, I'd love to do that, and it would give me a chance to talk to Neal without all those bars." And so it was arranged.

'I picked up Allen on the morning of the class, and being very sleepy I didn't notice he was wearing jeans. You know, of course, no free man is allowed into the prison in jeans, that being what the cons wear. We got to the west gate where I go in, not being a tourist, and the guard said, "I'm sorry, Mr Arthur, but we cannot allow your guest to come in wearing those blue jeans."

"Oh dear," I said, "It's all scheduled, and well – call Chaplain Eshelman and ask if he could lend us a pair of trousers and bring them to the gate, would you please?" He did so, but the Chaplain is much taller than Allen, so Allen had to roll up the pant legs three times.

'When we were walking through the "Garden Beautiful" on the way to my class, I overheard one of the gardener cons say to another, "Who do you suppose Mr Arthur is going to bring as his guest next time? Last week it was a Yogi in orange robes, and this week it's Charlie Chaplin himself."

'So Allen stood before them, and to my amazement, all three Chaplains were sitting together in a row to hear him. I felt so downed – they wouldn't do that for *me* – but Allen got up and stared at those sixty cons, including Neal, through those thick spectacles that make him look like a black goldfish looking out of a goldfish bowl, and he did what is ab-so-*lute*-ly *de rigeur* – impossible to do if you are a free man – he used the most frightful four-letter words in describing his recent accomplishments with the navy – and well, I just wanted to *die* – literally; I wanted the ground to open up and swallow me, because I thought – I *knew* certainly – that Allen and I were going to be sequestered in San Quentin for years and years and years.'

I was confused: 'What do you mean, "accomplishments with the Navy"? The Merchant Marine?'

'No, no, my dear – *sailors* – you know – *sexual* exploits! But then – I suddenly saw that all sixty cons were cheering. You couldn't hear yourself *think* – and I finally dared to look up, and there were all three Chaplains on their feet cheering and stamping – well! I knew then everything would be all right.'

'Were there guards in the classroom?'

'Yes, certainly. That's just it – amazing!' Gavin shook his head, chuckling to himself.

After that episode, Neal wrote to Jack, through me, urging him to come speak to the class, too.

> Dear Bro. Jackson…On the night of the 20th, Herr Beat Brendan Behan Balzac better not guzzle too much wine, because the next 9AM you'll be following the lead of G. Snyder and A. Ginsberg – ask him about that scene – by addressing our class…tho the room, indeed the entire building, would be overpacked to fire hazard proportion if I dared let out that YOU were coming, why, they'd stampede, honestly. I'm sick of overhearing your nigh-notorious name being always mispronounced in 'Big Yard' conversations EVERY day…

Personally, I couldn't imagine Jack standing before such a class – he was too shy, far too self-conscious, far too 'sinful' for that, and he couldn't drink beforehand. I somehow knew he never would. And he would be crucified with damning reportage if he didn't. Judgements minus understanding.

Jack had come to California at the end of November – or so I heard via the grapevine, because he didn't call me. Also a *Life* magazine had a story on the 'Beats,' and in it a squib about Neal being in prison. My family read that magazine from cover to cover, and I was worried they'd learn of Neal's internment. I had not told them; that was way too much to expect them to accept. I wrote Neal of my anxiety, and also asked news of Jack:

> no, I didn't see Jack; yes, I did see the *Life* – rushed to me the AM it arrived by the local Herb Caen of our newspaper, who, for the upcoming 'Bastille-by-the-Bay' column wanted permission to do a vignette on the exiled 'Prime Minister' of the 'Beatnuts,' etc. bah, bum bunk like the rest of it all, pure puke. Sorry about your folks and the possibility of their hearing via Luce's lousy rag…

The following week he passed on information he'd received in a letter from Jack via Gavin. 'Uncle is bringing the famed Alan Watts over next Saturday to make up for the defection of Kerouac, who, as he said in a long letter…met Uncle and was set to come here until 3 parties the night before caused the drunkenness I predicted in the postcard to him…'

Jack had given plenty of excuses, which I had predicted, but he also said his condition shamed him into not seeing me from countless parties at famous addresses. He wrote that it was strange how good writers have always been drawn to each other, but in the past no big deal was made of what kind of stimulants they used. Coleridge became an opium addict among other things. Jack enjoyed his trip back to Memere, this time indulging in motels and good food every day, so different from previous trips.

I agreed with Neal it was a terrible shame, and likely to get worse. Already had, for Gavin told me Jack had been called on stage at the San Francisco Film Festival where the film *Pull My Daisy* was being shown. He was so drunk he fell down twice. Gavin had tried to set up his appearance at his class for the next day, but Jack was too overhung. My heart ached for him; such a beautiful person bringing all that disgust upon himself.

| SIXTY-THREE |

As I contemplated Neal's release I was less and less inclined to return to the life of deception, suspicion and loneliness I'd known with him, to which now was added the real fear of his resentment of me and the bitterness he felt towards the law. I was becoming more and more afraid of him.

One day the Hinkles called, and proposed a bold plan. They wanted to go abroad, and suggested I join them. They had saved some money, and thought I might have enough equity in the house to enable us to work out a feasible financial arrangement with their help. It was a wild idea, but the more I thought about it the more appealing it became.

We agreed it would be more beneficial if we didn't 'tour' right away, but instead picked a country to settle in and took side trips when finances permitted. We chose Scotland, a country with traditions dear to us all, and we figured it would be less expensive, the schools were said to be the best, and we wouldn't have language problems. We did overlook our antipathy to constant cold and damp, even though I'd missed seasons and snow in California. The whole scheme was really in the land of dreams, but it did serve as hope for me during the last year of Neal's confinement. We studied maps, saturated ourselves with history and travel articles, and taught our children the currency. We wrote to schools and generally researched as thoroughly as possible. I had Scottish ancestors – Sir Walter Scott a great uncle. I loved the pipes and the kilts and everything that went with all that, the romantic I had always been and would remain.

When we'd worked out the essential details, I set upon the task of justifying this move to Neal without revealing my fear of his future behaviour. I suggested he could use the time of his parole to find himself and to test his conviction that a family life was really how he wanted to live his life – which had previously aroused some doubts. If our experiment was rewarding, he could join us when his parole was up, and start a new life with us himself. If not, we would return, everyone more confident of his true desires.

My first attempt to sell Neal on the idea in late July 1959 did not bring the response I had hoped for, but the one I dreaded. His letter was resentful and filled with self-pity. Again he asked me not to visit or write, and ended with

> that peace that even a prisoner needs – and which can't be gained from even the most reassuring letters, as yours have always intended to be, for which I thank you again as I close suggestions that 4 years (until parole is up am stuck in S.C. County you know) of you taking the Hi road & me the Low – to Scotland – will never get us together – unless Life – does begin at 40, ha, bah, Good Luck, from your lousy husband, Neal.

I answered by reaffirming my greatest desire, which had never changed and was for him to be my only husband and all the rest of it, and his next two letters were apologetic and positive. He asked me to visit him so he could express his devotion, what I'd learned about a job and my exact plans, what was the latest with the 'kiddies' etc. Although I wished desperately to believe in his 'devotion', my resolve often wavered, and now I had older children to consider, and I didn't feel confident in my ability to handle my own tensions as well as theirs – or his. I even wrote to Hugh Lynn for advice.

He answered as expected, that Neal had to decide how to live his life, if he wanted a family etc. But he also said, 'It is important that you be firm about any decisions which are to be made. Part of the difficulty has been your willingness in many directions giving way to him and constantly retreating when he failed to live up to his part of the bargain.'

Well, that was true enough. So it was, again, strictly up to me. And I couldn't make the visit Neal requested; the car broke down, and Neal's response tipped the scales in the direction of my going away: 'rather than being sorry, I was quite relieved you couldn't make it up here Friday, pimples on the probuscus pushing pride until preventing any desire to be seen; so I'm glad the car isn't fixed, that visits have pretty well vanished like hope itself.'

He gave me a long sarcastic tirade because the promised photos of the kids had not arrived either. In a postscript he asked what I'd do with the dog. 'I'm sure it's too risky for him to go, because if he ever fell overboard, he'd not be bailed out either.'

The Christmas season depressed him even more, understandably, capped by my letter written on the twenty-first that didn't reach him until the thirtieth, for which he blamed me. We kept up this gut-rending correspondence, he sometimes hateful, sometimes loving, but always with avowals just to work himself to death on release and eventually become a hermit if I didn't come back. He urged me to find a Scottish mate if I liked. My emotions rose and fell as I read every innuendo in his changing moods, his restraint, his sorrow, and I could easily sense what he was holding back – and that was what I feared. If only I could believe he was true to his affirmations. What could I do? Where turn? At that time I felt I could only run. Past efforts to be of help to him had always failed, leaving me holding the empty bag.

He had told me on occasion that parole dates were advanced a few months if there was sufficient reason, so I sat down to plead my case in a letter to the board. I told them of my pre-arranged plans to leave the country on July 1, and since his date for release was June 1, it would give us very little time together. This time was important, I wrote, because I was undecided whether or not he was psychologically fit to take over family responsibilities again, and I referred to their own and other tests that had indicated he was pre-psychotic already.

> No one knows what degree of stress would turn the tide and cause this affliction to develop into violence and/or psychosis...I am vitally concerned with observing his behavior under as little strain as possible to help me judge if the family can remain united without danger to the children and if his prognosis appears good...

I therefore pleaded for a few more months, which couldn't possibly affect his 'punishment'.

Al Hinkle had been trying throughout the year to soften the attitude of the SP superintendent without success. Retribution for Neal's 'crime' did seem unnecessarily severe and counter-productive, and I knew Neal's bitterness rose in direct proportion, fanning out to include the world and life in general.

Easter of 1960 came and went, and we had no 'new beginnings'. My appeal was turned down. When I received a notification of parole requirements, however, my plans for Scotland were brought to a sudden halt. One of the prerequisites for release, besides a job, was that he must have a home to come back to. Otherwise he would not be released until such conditions proved adequate. Well, there it was; we would stay home.

Somehow in my heart I'd always known I'd never go, even though I already had the steamship tickets. I sent them back for a refund, and called Helen with the news. She and Al decided to go anyway, but they would tour, not settle down. I wondered how I'd get along without them.

Neal was resigned to the change, and to lessen the disappointment for the children he suggested we take a shorter trip to visit my family at their summer cottage in Michigan on Glen Lake, where a reunion was planned in July. If we agreed, Neal would then have some free time to re-evaluate his life on his own.

His initial reaction to the news of my remaining home had not met with the enthusiasm I'd expected, and I asked if he had been disappointed too. 'No, I'm NOT disappointed – on the contrary, my heart sings to know – YOU'RE NOT LEAVING!! Hip, hip, hooray!!' But he added, 'Besides, my tensions always spoil my intentions even here, so who knows to what depths my dreadful desires might plunge if I were free of you and the children for a year or more?' Now what did he mean by that switch? I didn't dare think about it.

From now on our letters were full of only one plan: what to do on his release. His spirits had risen, and stayed fairly consistent once the actual date was in view.

> Here is the way things shape up now…giving a tentative schedule for your approval: arriving between 9:30 and 10 on the morning of my exit, you drive me to see Mr. McKinnon in the SP building on Market St.; after my appeal – it should be some time before we know if it succeeded…we drive home in time for me to take Johnny to the Cub meeting…fix Cathy's scientific models and help Jami with her homework. Early the next morning (like the fade-out of a Hollywood movie, I skip describing *that* night, leaving it to your and the censor's imagination, ahem take a bus to S.J. and report to parole agent, after which…look for a job, unless you've already found me one, of course…[I had found one tire company in San Jose that agreed to risk hiring a felon.]…we'll save money, sell house and go to Europe in summer of 1963 when my parole has expired and more important, when kids are old enuf to appreciate it & without their psyches getting all fouled up in the process, right?
>
> I CAN stand the costume mess and am terribly interested in them. THANKING GOD you're not going…

Heartily I approved of every word – if only I could believe it would happen as he said. Now I wished he could go with us to Michigan, but when I inquired about it, I learned he would have to have written permission from every state we passed through. Naturally, there wasn't time for such nonsense. As it happened, I was to learn this was a very good requirement.

Neal's mood sky-rocketed as the time drew near. And I put forth my best efforts to calm my fears and earn his forgiveness. Wisely, he asked,

> Just what the heck am I to tell the kids when they ask where I've been for 787 days and nights? Try and remember exactly what lies you've told them, so I can make up some to match (sickening, what?)…Just felt a BIG surge of love for you, realizing afresh how gamely

you've struggled thru all these years without money or help not to mention affection, understanding or concern; all the things you crave, which your EX-dope *will* DELIVER till his time for the grave – only, as Cayce said was best, it's to be cremation, *promise?*…Put buttermilk and sour cream on dinner menu…and more later, all can think of now is what I don't want (beans, etc.); let's buy matching rings BEFORE you go East, OK?

Strange, I thought, Neal should mention death just when we had something pleasant to think about and communicate – then more tragedy struck. This time it was the dog, Cayce. He received an injury to his spine and had to be put to sleep. I hated to have to tell Neal, especially right now. He was always so sentimental about our animals, and many's the time I'd been jealous of the affection he lavished on them but not on me. He had written of the dog so often, and was so looking forward to seeing him. His reply to my report made us all break down once more as he described again all I had told him about Cayce's last hours.

When I had learned the date of Neal's release I wrote briefly to Jack, and he answered. He said he hadn't written because Aronowitz thought I was leaving Neal. For some reason known only to him he thought I would want no more to do with him either. He didn't like to think of us being apart without having our intimate discussions, which even Corso couldn't interrupt. Of course, he meant himself, since Gregory never found us thus engaged. He thought we'd laugh at his descriptions in *Desolation Angels* of the races, the Bishop etc. He wished us well together in the future. He complained of many ailments now: he'd hurt his elbow in a drunken fight, his phlebitis was bothering him, and he had neuritis in his hands. I suspected that was arthritis. He also complained about journalists hounding him, for he believed anything he said would be all twisted in the papers. He welcomed getting a letter from 'my darling blonde aristocratic Carolyn', and visualized us all together again with a fire, wine, television and laughter. I was to show his letter to Neal, and tell him he loved him. Then he told us in the Italian *Life* magazine, *Successo*, they had printed a photo of Neal with the caption 'El Santo'. The letter was so like a summation, I hoped it wasn't an ending.

| SIXTY-FOUR |

The day finally arrived: June 3, 1960, exactly one month less than two years from the time Neal began his sentence, not counting the two additional months he'd already served. The 'times and half times' were over.

The highway was crowded with holiday traffic, and as I drove onto the dusty narrow road to the prison for the last time, my dress was sticking to my back from the heat of the plastic car seats as well as from my nerves. I had only just pulled into a parking space when I looked towards the gatehouse and saw Neal striding briskly towards me and freedom. His expression already told me that having been released from an undeserved hell, the joy was eclipsed by the resentment. Otherwise, his appearance was much the same in his prison-issued clothes. (I had asked him if I was to bring anything for him to wear, and he'd answered, 'Do you think they send us out naked?')

He jumped into the car, and would only indulge in a brief passing kiss before urging me to get away as fast as possible. I'd expected we'd jabber like jaybirds, but very little conversation passed between us on the drive back to San Francisco. I had so rarely been in the driver's seat, my nervousness increased. My mind was spinning, as I presumed was his.

I actually found a parking place close to the jewelry shop where we were to get our new rings as he had requested. First, however, he told me he had a message to deliver to an inmate's mother, so he'd better get that over with first. He was gone nearly an hour, and I wouldn't let myself speculate until many years later, when I could face the fact he had undoubtedly gone to one of his female correspondents to get what he'd missed most.

We then went into the shop that sold the original and artistic jewelry by Peter Macchierini. There we chose matching gold rings, sculpted in uneven fluid circlets, his thicker than mine. We put them on each other's fingers, but not at all as I had rehearsed the scene; we were too self-conscious in front of the proprietor to do more than squeeze hands and smile at each other. (Neal never removed that ring as far as I know, even when working with dirty heavy tyres, and two of my children were married with them.)

Neal told me Gavin insisted we come to Global House for lunch, and I was delighted, not only for this manner of celebration, but to help normalize our emotions through a third party. Neal's mood lightened with something like happiness as he took my hand and bounded up the broad stairs to the porch. A young student admitted us to a sunny white-wainscoted, plant-filled conservatory where a table was set for three. Gavin joined us, and after a warm welcome to Neal as well as me we were served a delicious lunch of seafood salad and wine, waited upon by the young men who lived in Global House and studied astrology with Gavin.

At the time of our first meeting Gavin was 59 years old, but the longer I knew him the longer these years seemed to stretch to accommodate the vast number of experiences he'd had and the persons he'd known. He'd fought in the Irish Rebellion with a price on his head, and the Spanish Civil War. Names of the famous and infamous peppered every conversation, yet his 'name-dropping' was legitimate; he felt no insecure need to impress, and each personage was regarded with equal respect, except of course real villains against human rights. No field, no social class and no section of the globe was excluded. Consequently his company was not only entertaining but inspiring, his zest for life contagious. Later I taped incredible stories I regret I can't include here.

Gavin had lost his father's millions from his mother's divorce, his own second wife, worldwide adventures and poor investments. Never did he give the impression of being 'poor' in any sense of the word. His bearing was always that of the elegant, cultured gentleman. He was tall and graceful, fine-boned and slender, his features of classic proportions, barring a rather short nose. His skin was smooth and transparent and wrinkle-free. Fine brown hair was turning grey when we met, and during the 12 years of our ensuing friendship he groomed it in the current style – long, short, bearded or shaven. Gradually, too, his mode of dress changed from immaculately tailored shirts and slacks to the colourful garb of oncoming generations. His dark brown eyes twinkled in good humour and kindness, flashing sparks only if someone was rude or ill-mannered in his home; his remarkable tolerance ended there.

Gavin's lodgings were always on the verge of condemnation and destruction by the City, and he would be forced to seek another – in an equally doomed building. Moving was an Herculean feat. 'How I wish I were a Shiva instead of a Vishnu,' he'd wail at moving time. His students and friends helped out by decorating the decrepit structures wherever possible with imaginative paintings, astrological schematics, pictures cut from magazines, mind-boggling to survey, especially as the ceilings were high and the rooms large so there was an awful lot of wall space. Among all this were photos of famous people in present and previous times. The cut-out pictures covered every imaginable subject, earthy, celestial, sacred or profane.

One corner of a smaller room was orderly and consistent: the 'presidents' corner'. Here were signed photographs of all the presidents since his grandfathers' day, some of their wives, some of foreign dignitaries or monarchs, and personal souvenirs, such as his grandfather's cigar clipper and his father's branding iron from his Texas ranch. Flanking the photographs were eighty looseleaf notebooks containing their letters. Other orange-crate bookcases around the rooms contained Gavin's extensive library, and some were filled with the 6000 horoscopes he'd done to date, all filed in colourful notebooks identified by every known alphabet in the world.

After lunch Neal and I wandered hand-in-hand throughout these rooms, now and then asking Gavin to explain a photograph, but the stories were so incongruous, I cannot repeat them.

Gavin came to appreciate me, or so he said, because I stuck with Neal and thought first of keeping the family together in spite of Neal's infidelity and errant ways. This was important to him personally because of unhappy childhood memories of when his mother divorced his father for the same reasons. He had broken his mother's favourite record three times, a love song that proclaimed 'the heart of my loved one is small, very very small; it has room in it only for me.' Gavin knew, even as a child, that no heart can be so small as to have room for only one other person. Little did he know how long it would be before I came to learn and accept that truth.

The first week or so of Neal's return was all joy and gladness; the ice had melted. We clung together often as we became re-acquainted. He began work in the San Jose Tire Shop, drawing the night shift as the newest employee, which he declared he preferred. We all appreciated having him around during the day between naps, and he'd get up for breakfast to see more of the children. An almost equal joy for me was to kiss the welfare people good bye!

Strange how an absence can make you forget the personal habits and mannerisms of someone you've lived with for so long. For two years I hadn't had to pick up endless match books with covers torn off, a habit Neal acquired early on to keep his women from knowing where he'd been or whose telephone number was written thereon. Back, too, was the litter of magazine and newspapers beside the bed (some underwear ads he used for masturbation), the ritual of his feet that required an ever-ready supply of clean socks along with abundant handkerchiefs for his problem nose. I'd forgotten his passion for pinching blackheads – he giggling, me protesting – and the long hours in the bath. Some of these amused me, some I thought might have been abandoned.

The one idiosyncrasy I always welcomed was his appreciation of food. Our garbage disposal was back. Neal cleaned up all odds and ends of leftovers as though they were special treats, and dove into every meal as if it were a banquet.

It didn't matter to him that his job was rough and dirty; he still had to be the best worker, and he still paid careful attention to grooming, patting and fussing with his hair, warning me not to muss it when we kissed good bye. It was his hands that took the worst beating, and I regretted seeing them become thick and calloused with ground-in grease and rubber. I tried to get him to leave his wedding ring at home, but he wouldn't.

By the second or third week it was as though he'd never been away. He was making special efforts to be considerate and affection- ate, and live up to his extravagant prison-letter vows, succeeding enough to allay my fears. The new schedule of regular hours posed a challenge he declared he welcomed. Since he was not allowed to leave the county, and the racetracks were all elsewhere, he was obliged to follow his system only on paper. He insisted he wanted nothing to do with his former acquaintances (the law forbade it as well) and, in spite of his written denial, he was gracious to my new friends, and with some developed lasting relationships. With these friends looking after Neal, my mind was more at ease when the children and I took off for Michigan.

| SIXTY-FIVE |

My sister Margaret met us at the Traverse City airport alone. During the twenty-mile drive to the lake, I asked her the burning question: 'Did the folks see that *Life* magazine about Neal being in prison?'

'Oh, my yes, indeed they did.'

'Then why didn't they say anything? That came out last November, but their weekly letters never mentioned it.'

'You know them; it's not a subject they're likely to discuss. Just like when I eloped with Carmy, remember? Or your early pregnancy.'

When we arrived at the cottage neither my parents nor my eldest brother Joe and his wife showed any difference in attitude towards me or the children. I was encouraged, but the next morning when I found my mother alone on the beach I told her how sorry I was to have been the cause of another added burden of sorrow. I asked her if there were any details she would care to have explained, either about Neal's arrest or our management without him. Her face was grim, her hands trembling as she snapped, 'Is it true?'

'Well, yes, but...'

'That's all I want to know!' and she hurried away to her own cottage next door. I had, of course, so hoped I could tell her how good everyone had been to us, how unjustified Neal's punishment – but there was nothing to do but pretend it never happened. My parents never knew or would believe there was any sort of corruption in the institutions of the USA. My father had told me banks never made mistakes, for instance. I had to learn for myself.

Only one other time near the end of our three-week stay did I make a last effort to reach her. We were sitting in the car, and again she was furious, shaking all over, and fumed, 'It would have been far better if he had hit every one of those children in the head!' She meant, of course, 'death before dishonour'. I had no conception that this mother of mine, who had shown some compassion now and then when I was disciplined by my father, could possibly believe so strictly this old Victorian principle. Dumbfounded and very saddened, I gave up my appeal. She was even less streetwise than I.

In spite of this blot on the escutcheon, they were all nice to us and we had a good time. I was pleased to be able to share my most precious childhood memories with my children, even though the area had changed so much I would never want to return.

We had ridden a variety of airplanes on the incoming trip. We had a return ticket on United Airlines to San Francisco. The plane stopped in Denver, and there I was told that's as far as it went. I'll spare you the amazing convolutions I had to go through to find a way back to San Francisco. We ended up trading the remaining air fare for a couple of roomettes on the wonderful Vista Dome train – like my family relationships, soon to be extinct. It was a fabulous ride. That extraordinary scenery down the gorge, our cute little rooms. Adventures – such as an announcement that the train was going to be washed, so no one should cross the open areas between cars. Cathy, John and I were in the dome, and we knew the sound system was off in the room where Jami was, so she wouldn't know that. We fretted, but she didn't get wet. Then, in the dining car, I mistook a pitcher of cream for one of syrup, and liberally poured cream on my pancakes. We had a waiter who always catered to us, and he did well to cover up my embarrassment. There was a mother who tried to con Cathy into babysitting her child, which Cathy didn't want to do, so every time we passed this lady's room, we all crawled by it. Thank God we were never discovered in these strange postures, but we did have an hilarious trip, far better than a flight.

Neal was as welcoming as expected, the house was in order, and I had no reason to suspect he had been engaged in anything but his work and the housekeeping. Other activities would be revealed later, but for now all was serene and I was at peace.

| SIXTY-SIX |

Near the summer's end we heard that Jack had returned to San Francisco, but I rarely wondered any more if we'd even see him. Neal showed no particular interest, either, as far as I could tell, and since he was restricted to our county it only made him grim to remember past binges that had led to his present state. Part of Neal's feelings about Jack was the sorrow of seeing him get more into alcohol. Neal had already gone through that trauma with his father, and knew the inevitable conclusion.

So I was very surprised one Friday evening to hear a loud scuffling and banging on the patio door. Before I could reach it, Jack staggered in drunk and bellowing, surrounded by three motley men. I greeted him warmly, of course, and put my hands on his shoulders, intending to hug him. He shoved me away, and I backed up, mortified, thinking my behaviour must look odd to the assembled strangers.

These were sorted out as Lew Welch, a poet originally from Reno but more recently from Reed College in Oregon, Paul Smith, a friend of Lew's also from Reno who played guitar, bass fiddle and sang, and a roustabout who had come to the City in advance of the Barnum & Bailey circus, by whom he was employed. I never learned where Jack found him, why he was with them, and I never learned his name. Eventually, I learned the visit was a spur-of-the-moment whim of Jack's to see Neal and to introduce him to Lew, as usual wanting to share people he liked with 'brother' Neal.

Jack had been staying alone in Lawrence Ferlinghetti's cabin near Big Sur, and Lew had driven the others down to fetch Jack back to the City. I told them Neal would be working until 2.00 a.m., but I would telephone him. Neal couldn't talk long, with all types of tyres to time in their cooking processes, so he suggested they come to the shop and talk, or watch him work after the boss left around midnight. Meanwhile I asked if they were hungry.

The children had eaten early with their father, and were now asleep. After taking a consensus of opinion, and Jack had patted his pocket, embarrassing us further by loudly complaining to me that people were only interested in him for his traveller's cheques, he nevertheless insisted on buying a dinner 'to go' they could bring back to the house.

There were few such places in Los Gatos, but I called a nearby Italian restaurant that had been established for a long time and had a reputation for excellent food. They agreed to prepare a specialty to take out. The men were gone so long I feared the worst, and I was nearly right. When they did return, Lew, Jack and Paul tried to tell me about the chaos they'd created at the restaurant, but were laughing so hard I'm not sure I know yet what really happened. The restaurant was as 'square' as is possible, and the clientele quite elegantly so.

In walks this startling group: Jack in his lumberjack shirt, sagging rumpled jeans and hiking boots, his hair wild and falling in his partially closed eyes. He was obviously drunk and disorderly. Then there was Lew with thick short red hair, also unruly, wide bright blue eyes; slight of frame but wiry, and although clean enough, dressed in well-worn jeans, tennis shoes and a casual knit shirt. Paul Smith was the personification of a Roman athlete, and even though his appearance was the opposite of Jack's he was nonetheless equally out of place. His golden hair was full and wavy, blending into a short gold beard. His eyes looked gold as well, almost yellow. His muscular chest and arms were hairless and tanned a deeper gold than his hair. He wore no shirt or shoes, the only visible garment a pair of tan chinos, the composite image that of a single tone, almost too youthful, healthy and gleaming to be real. The fourth member, the roustabout, was shorter than the others, thickly set and wore a tight red and white striped T-shirt taut against bulging muscles. He had short black curls over his forehead which reminded me of our white-faced cattle at home.

Afterwards I thought they should have told the management they were actors from some local play, rather than wasting so much time and energy in an attempt to downplay their appearance and to impress the staff with Jack's fame in order to promote the reliability of his cheque. Understandably, no one had ever heard of him, and seriously doubted their story. At this particular time in our lives, our own name was also useless as a character reference. But traveller's cheques are less risky, and I suspect the tide turned in favour of speed in order to remove them from the dining room, where Jack was earnestly engaged in an attempt to seduce a waitress.

While they were gone I built a fire and set out silverware, plates and glasses for wine. The food turned out to be a superb veal scallopini. The three principals made a game of honouring me as the sole woman among such attentive and attractive males. Lew Welch was a great delight with intelligent, erudite patter, often the essence of satire. I was impressed by his sharp insights, quick wit and poetic imagery, even if the occasional earthy expression was added for spice – or to shock me. Jack tried to keep up with him, but he was too drunk to express more than unintelligible roars or grumbles. The roustabout never spoke, not even to answer my query if he wanted coffee. I passed him some anyway, and he drank it without a word. Paul said little either – just sat smiling at me or hovering, his eyes waxing and waning, now shining gold, now shaded bronze. I found him a trifle worrying – that magnetism rearing its head again.

When we noticed it was nearly one o'clock, they all scrambled into Lew's Jeep 'Willie' and rattled away to find Neal. I could imagine that scene well enough. I'd seen the tyre shop, a pre-fabricated aluminum structure all open to the street in the middle of San Jose's industrial quarter, with a radio blaring country and western music over the din of the re-capping machinery and Neal blaming and slamming the huge truck tyres from the piles to the floor, looking like a creature from the deep in his goggles, grime and sweating bare chest.

While the men were gone I did the dishes, straightened the living room and dug out blankets and pillows until I heard the roar of the two cars spinning into the drive. Lew was an acclaimed driver, like Neal, so no doubt some competition had taken place on the way home.

Neal was exhausted, the others overstimulated with alcohol, tea and each other, so bed was all anyone wanted now. Neal went to shower, and I allotted spaces. Jack insisted on the back yard again, Lew would sleep in Willie, so Paul took the couch. I indicated to the roustabout he was welcome to the daybed in the family room.

Lew said, 'Good night, Mommy,' and kissed me as he went out the door. Jack giggled and did likewise, so I took it up, playing the mother coyly, and kissed Paul on the forehead as I 'tucked him in'. I went back to the family room so as not to have anyone feel left out, but the silent one was still sitting in the dark in a chair by the table. I leaned over hastily to plant the peck when his great arms shot out and like a vice encircled me, indicating better than words he wanted no cute games, he was all business. Rigidly, I disengaged myself and tried to laugh. He let go, silent and stern as ever, and I fled to climb in beside Neal, grateful for his presence.

Next morning everyone slept late, and Jack came inside as I was making coffee. Now that he was sober, he was pathetically happy to see me, gave me a big hug and kiss, and I was relieved he seemed to have forgotten our initial encounter. He asked me to come out to the patio where we could talk alone. Once more we sat on the grass in the sun, as we had so often in the past. He was overflowing with clinging nostalgia, as though he knew somehow we would never get back to the simple pleasures and sweet dreams we'd anticipated ten years before. No longer did he make staunch vows to stop drinking; he knew he was being slowly pulled down into the quagmire, and his will was too weak to resist. His tormented eyes foretold the future, his face like a character from Poe.

The usual admonitions blinked on and off in my mind, but I knew now it was too late, the shame and isolation he felt deep within too powerful to uproot with overworked answers.

'Ah – why do we settle for pleasure when we could have bliss – and we've known what that is,' Jack groaned a Dantesque wail. 'I know, I know. What'll I do? We all take the path of least resistance.'

'My unbelief is a belief to be transcended.' I quoted aloud.

'Yeah, well, I know now my Buddhism doesn't help – and why Buddha forbade alcohol – but I'm just too weak. Thinking of those critics and the rubbish I've gone through with publishers starts filling my mind, and I reach for the bottle...'

'But these past three weeks you've been at Big Sur. Didn't that help at all? Although I know you don't like being alone.'

'Naw, you know how it is. It was okay at first, then I got bored. Why is that? Why can't I be content?'

Lew came bounding out the door doing some hilarious charade concerning 'Aunt Harriet', his equivalent to Mrs Grundy, and the scene exploded into slapstick shenanigans between the two of them until my stomach ached from laughing. The roustabout had to get back to sign in with the circus, and Lew wanted to see his girl, so they were eager to return to the City. First, however, Jack needed more wine, so I rode between them in the Willie to show them to the nearest liquor store. All the way to and from they kept up a fast and witty dialogue, replaying a mythical baseball game that did nothing to ease my stomach pain. Returning home they collected Paul and the Quiet Man and said good bye to Neal, who was still in bed.

The following Friday night, when Neal came home from work, I got up to get him something to eat. He told me he had been laid off. The boss had financial difficulties, and had to let some men go. He said he hated to lose Neal, but since he was the last man hired, he had to be the first to go.

Now what? The house payment was due. Over my reservations, Neal thought it was all right to ask Jack for a loan, and the next morning he telephoned him. Jack welcomed the chance, or so he said, having so often written of supporting us all, and said he'd get Lew to drive him down with the money.

This time two Jeeps appeared in the driveway. Lew and Paul were in one Willie, and Lawrence Ferlinghetti drove Jack, Philip Whalen and Victor Wong in his. Victor was the artist son of a prominent Chinatown family, and delighted me with multicoloured pen drawings as I sat beside him on the floor. I liked Phil Whalen very much, too, although I was unfamiliar with his poetry, and he certainly didn't look like the current poets. A professor, maybe, being rather stocky, tweedy and pipe-smoking. He struck me as an extremely kind and gentle person, quiet yet openly friendly and definitely not 'beat'. His presence was reassuring, as was Ferlinghetti's, whom I'd already met and liked.

Since Neal had no work to go to, and since they were all on their way to the cabin in Big Sur, they mock-pleaded with 'Ma' to let Neal go off with with the boys for the weekend. This time I was glad for Neal to have a respite, a time to 'dig' nature, and in good company. I forgot, as did he, about the ban on his leaving the county. He was overjoyed, and gushed promises to hunt for work 'first thing on Monday'.

Before setting out, however, they invited the whole family to share a pizza dinner, and we all piled into the Jeeps. Our large group took over most of the pizzeria, but luckily there were few other diners. There was one huge room with long tables, and we filled one in the centre of the room.

The acoustics in the vast high room amplified the noise, so what with Lew, Jack and Neal we were a conspicuous lot. This time I was proud to be a part of their party. We consumed platters of pizza and tankards of beer, no one in any particular hurry. The children loved the clowning, and once home we wished Neal a happy weekend then took off ourselves for 'Old Town' and the Wagon Stagers.

Sunday evening Jack and Paul stayed on at the cabin while Lew drove Neal home and Lawrence drove Phil and Victor back to the City. Lew stayed a few hours with us to rest midway in his journey. No longer was he the comedian, and I supposed he, like many gifted 'clowns', had a serious side as sombre as his wit was sparkling. Neal turned on the television to await the news, and Lew stretched out on the low bed with me at the foot. No sooner were we settled than Neal said he was out of cigarettes and asked Lew if he could 'make a run' in Willie – another thing he shouldn't do with no driver's licence. While he was away Lew quoted some of his poems to me, which I was surprised and glad to like. He was so open and unself-conscious too.

I have been haunted ever since by the disappearance not long after of this unique and gifted man.

| SIXTY-SEVEN |

On Monday morning Neal went to the Los Gatos Tire Company on the recommendation of a friend, and those wonderful men agreed to hire him, even though they weren't especially short-handed. Well, what a relief. He was close to home, his hours a regular day shift, and we could live a more normal life (in my terms) again. As usual, at work Neal astounded everyone with his speed and efficiency. Employers, employees, customers – and even the cop on the beat – watched him in unabashed awe. But when he came home so physically exhausted, I feared he was using this labour to work out much of his bitterness as well as in a penitent flagellation of himself. How I wished he could find an occupation which would employ his remarkable mind. A writer would have been ideal, had that ambition not been eclipsed by 'kicks'. All I could do was to keep his home life as peaceful as possible; I could do nothing to vanquish his boredom with that. He did appreciate his home, and although he liked mountains better than water, and never swam, some evenings after his long bath he'd take a beer and float around in the pool in one of the huge inner tubes he'd brought home from the shop.

Our Rambler wagon was finally in bad enough shape for Neal to admit it was useless. We hated to let it go; it had served us long and well – and it was paid for. But now that Neal had a driver's licence again, he was eager to use it, and the first chance we got after his return to work we hunted another car. To our joy we found a Jeep, just like Willie, only maroon instead of blue, and we got an exceptional deal with our trade-in.

To check it out we decided that on Friday after work we'd all go to Big Sur to show it off and surprise Jack. I made a picnic supper for us to eat on the way, and the children and I sat on a mattress in the back which was low enough so I couldn't see the cliff-hanging roads of Big Sur. Neal's driving scared me enough on flat roads.

When we turned off the highway onto the dirt trail that led down to the cabin, I looked out once and only once. The road was chipped out of the hillside at a downward slant; one lane and no guard rails. Neal yelled back to me, not looking at the road,

'Sure hope we don't meet a loggin' rig, Ma, 'cause I'd have to back up all the way to the highway to let him pass.'

'No, Neal, don't!'

On flat ground at last, Neal parked beside a barbed-wire fence with an iron gate. He explained we'd have to walk to the cabin to get the key to the gate, but it wasn't far. The sun was hot on the sandy trail that led through a pasture, where munched a lone donkey, named, we learned, 'Alf'. We soon saw the cabin nestled in the pines by a rushing mountain stream that seemed in a great hurry to reach the ocean. Over rocks it splashed noisily close by the cabin porch, and then slithered off like a green and black snake through the trees. Neal lustily knocked on the cabin door, but before there was a response he flung it open. I could see nothing but darkness and the dim flicker of a fire. A second later we heard a great roar from Jack, and he bounded towards us, laughing.

'My God! It's a band of *angels* – with St Michael at the head!' He couldn't get over our unexpected appearance. He had been sitting in the dark room, and the sudden burst of sunlight on all the blond heads shining kept him exclaiming for many minutes, and referring to the scene ever after.

Inside the cabin was one large room. In the centre against the back wall on a platform of bricks a fireplace had been built out of oil drums on their sides, with the front cut out. A flu had been welded to the top side, and continued through the roof. The smell of the wooden cabin and the burning pine logs perfumed the warm atmosphere. The only windows were large ones with shutters on the front, shaded by the porch.

'Yessir, Ferlinghetti built this in *four days*, Carolyn,' said Jack when he noticed me taking it all in. 'Imagine that – four days! There's no bathroom, however; we all use the beautiful outhouse out in back, and Neal and I have taken care to put a can of water and some soap out there, so you needn't worry about that. We'll teach these heathen yet about proper bathroom hygiene – like us Frenchies have always known forever, right?' This feature of the accommodations so intrigued the children they had to run right out and investigate their first ever privy.

Against the wall on one side of the room were two folding cots, and on the other side was a small table and four chairs. Paul Smith had stood up from the hearth and now greeted us, quietly smiling, his eyes still melting. At the table sat a pretty dark-haired girl in tight jeans holding a small child, and beside her sat a slim young man with black curls framing a handsome face. We were introduced to Mike McClure and his wife Joanna.

Mike had been discussing a poem with Jack, and Neal was now asked to read it for his comments. Both Jack and Neal expressed extravagant approval, and then handed it to me. The title was the first jolt: 'Fuck Ode' – and about half way down the page embarrassment and revulsion made me barely scan the remainder of this long 'poem'. I hoped no one was watching my face, but the others were busy talking about the gate key, and thankfully no one was interested in my opinion. I looked sideways at the lovely delicate girl and her cherubic child, and wondered how she felt to have her husband describe in such relentless and gross detail sexual acts between them that to me would be considered too personal and private – as well as holy.

Neal and Jack took the children to get the car, the McClures went to the beach where we would join them later, and Paul poured me a cup of coffee. I was somewhat uncomfortable to be alone with Paul, who emanated that well-known energy of physical attraction. He was such a pleasure to look at, I would have liked to paint him – his every movement was harmonious and graceful. He was such a perfect 'specimen' it was all I could do not to touch him, as one would a piece of sculpture. I knew that would be like putting a match to tinder; together we created that aura of magnetism that made conversation halting.

So it was a relief to hear the rattle and bang of the Jeep when Neal backed it close to the stream and the porch. He and Jack stomped up the steps, and it was evident even before I saw his bloodshot eyes Neal had indulged in his favourite smoke. The children ran in with them, and all eagerly told me of petting Alf. Now they were itching to go to the beach.

'All right, children, come along.' Neal took control. 'Come on, we have to go by the stream here…' and the little group clustered around him as they started down the path. Jack grabbed my hand and pulled me to the door, quite purposely away from Paul.

'Come on, Ma, I'll show you my meditation cove.' Paul smiled and ran ahead to catch up with Neal and the children. Jack and I ambled slowly beside the stream. He told me incidents and observations from his previous stay, and I was sopping up the smells and sights of the sun-dappled woods and water. The stream opened out and spread itself over a clean, narrow sandy beach in a broad secluded cove far below overhanging rocks and cliffs. Neal, the children and the McClures were already enjoying the beach.

High overhead was the thin ribbon of a silver bridge that made me shudder – with good reason, it would seem, when Neal pointed out the remains of a car lying upside down beneath it, rusted and mute on the nearby rocks. Neal joined Mike seated on a rock in the shade of the cliff, while Joanna and the child dug in the sand at their feet. Paul took the children to explore caves further up the beach, then helped them build dams in the stream and find pieces of driftwood to sail down the strong channels.

Jack led me around a jut of rock in the other direction. We sat on his 'meditation rock' near the warm sand in a snug little cove while the reddening sun slid into the water and stained it, the surf a brilliant pink.

Leaning against him, his arm around me, I asked, 'Did you do any writing while you were here?'

'Only some poetry. I wrote a great poem to the sea – Cherson! Cherson! Shoo – shaw – shirsh – Go on, die salt light, you billion-yeared rock-knocker…like that, see?' He hugged me and whispered in my ear, 'St Carolyn – by the Sea.' I drew away and smiled up at him, a bit baffled. He just kissed me again. 'But I haven't been able to write much else since all this awful attention – everybody at me.'

'Do you still carry those little notebooks everywhere? I cherish the one you signed to me.'

'Naw – I forget. But hey, let me tell you a funny thing that happened. When Neal and I went to the hot springs up there with a bunch of poets – you know, that weird far out psychological healing centre. Esalon? Something like that. He and I were the only guys who wouldn't take off our shorts! I thought at the time, ha, the big Road heroes, and they're the only modest ones in the bunch!' We both laughed at that incredible picture.

He looked at me suddenly, pulled me to him and kissed me in a desperate sort of way. Then we lay back and in silence watched the sky cool and the stars pop out one by one. I became too chilled to sit longer, and the tide was creeping in, so we searched our way back to the cabin, clinging to each other over the rough ground and sudden springs in the darkening woods.

The hot coffee by the fire was welcome. I sat down in a low-slung canvas chair beside the fireplace, Jack in a chair opposite. The children found some cards and sat at the table to play, Neal lay down on one of the cots. Mike and Joanna announced they were going back to the beach, and would sleep there. Paul folded himself cross-legged on the floor beside me, leaning back against my chair.

He began to sing softly. He had a low mellow voice and a technique much like Mel Torme's. Absentmindedly my hand strolled through his hair from time to time, as one would acknowledge a pet. Everything seemed so cosy and relaxed. Then little by little Jack began to fidget, change his position, and now and then spit out a remark I would either ignore or try to answer without noticing his tone. I couldn't figure out what was eating him until he got up and fiercely threw a log on the fire, sending sparks flying, then burst out with, 'My God, Paul, haven't you got any consideration for Neal, man? How can you be so unfeeling?' and he smashed another piece of wood against the first. Paul stopped singing abruptly. I should have been more aware of Jack's view of what I thought an innocent act on my part – it just didn't occur to me because Paul was so young. I tried not to laugh.

'Neal?' I said quietly. 'If you look closely, Jack, you'll see he is so concerned he's fast asleep – honestly, honey, what's the problem?' Jack just growled and stamped over to the kitchen area to look for wine. There was none. He hesitated, stomped about a bit more, then went over to wake Neal.

'Hey, Neal – Neal? Come on, man, drive me into town for some wine, okay?' He was gruff and obviously angry. Neal stirred and sat up, good-natured as always.

I spoke up: 'You men said you wanted to build a big bonfire on the beach, remember?'

Jack replied, 'Yeah, well – you and Paul do that while we're gone, and we'll join you when we get back. Come on, Neal.'

'Right,' said Neal, calling to the children to come along for the ride if they liked, and everyone scrambled to the Jeep and rumbled away. Paul and I put on sweaters, collected matches and paper, and walked with flashlights back to the beach. The waves were now lapping and shushing among the rocks and smoothing the sand in glassy reflections of the moonlight. I'd rarely seen a night on the ocean without fog, but tonight the stars hung over us so glittering and close it looked almost artificial, like a ballroom dome. We stood close together for warmth for a minute while absorbing this wonder, but when Paul's hands began the restless seeking, I hastened to our stated purpose – the fire. It kept him busy until it was lighted and roaring. We looked about for the McClures, but they were nowhere in view. Paul couldn't resist grabbing me, and I allowed a lovely smooching session for a minute, but disengaged myself with difficulty when it became too hot. We then sat back to back, hugging our knees, while he sang until there was only a bed of coals left of the fire.

Neal and Jack never appeared. My anxieties surfaced again, so we hurried to bury the fire and trudge back to the cabin through the now cold woods. The Jeep was parked beside the porch, and inside it I could see the children snug and asleep. Jack was a lump in his sleeping bag on the porch, and inside the cabin Neal was asleep on a cot. I was relieved, but also disgusted they had left me to be alone with Paul, much as I had enjoyed that. Paul got his sleeping bag, and on his way out to the porch kissed me goodnight, in spite of my effort at half-hearted resistance. I climbed in with Neal, narrow though the cot was, but the smoky aroma in the stuffy warm room soon put me to sleep.

| SIXTY-EIGHT |

Next morning Jack and Neal were grouchy and furtive, and I was annoyed. When Paul left the cabin I asked Jack, 'Why didn't you come back to the beach? Here we had that big fire going, as ordered, and all for nothing.' My tone was petulant, but his was harsh and accusing.

'Neal thought you and Paul wanted to be alone.'

'Oh, *Neal* did! That's just dandy. He might consult me once in a while instead of pushing me off on any male who happens to look interested. Why doesn't he *protect* me from wolves, not *encourage* them?' I wanted Jack to know my protest included him, too, but my outburst served only to brighten his mood, although he was still suspicious.

When Paul came back, Jack stopped him on the porch and I hurried to make breakfast for the children. In a few minutes Jack came in all smiles again; Paul had banished his fears, but his doubting me didn't improve my disposition. As for Neal, he didn't care enough even to ask; he just assumed what he wished – another act of 'sharing'

I supposed, which now looked to me more like cowardice, or worse, indifference.

The McClures returned for a late breakfast, after which Joanna and I cleaned up the dishes and the cabin, and we all climbed into our respective Jeeps. I had to be back for the Wagon Stagers performance, and the McClures were headed for San Francisco.

I was excited at the prospect of sharing my enthusiasm for the Wagon Stagers and Old Town with Jack. He had been interested in my theatrical activities in Denver, and I knew he'd enjoy the stockade and museum too. Neal had already accompanied me several times, and had applauded with genuine approval and apparently real enjoyment, so I expected him to sell Jack on the scene as well. It was too late, the timing all wrong; Jack had had a jug of wine and was well on the way to his now daily intoxicated condition. When on the ride we found we were ravenous and early, we stopped at a roadside café near our destination, and I hoped Jack would sober up. Instead, he refused to eat. In Paul's presence, Neal maintained his aloofness towards me, and had left Paul and me to linger over our coffee when a siren wailed and a fire engine screamed into the parking lot. The children came running to me out of breath to report that our Jeep was on fire. We all ran outside, and I felt panicky – we could hardly afford to lose our new car, and certainly not before the show, which, of course, must go on.

Fortunately, the fire was out by the time we reached the car. It had been mostly smoke, caused by a smouldering cigarette in the mattress. Jack had been sitting on the tail gate with his jug, so the finger of suspicion pointed at him, but no one voiced the accusation; we were so relieved it was no worse. The mattress was now thoroughly soaked, the smell awful, so we were glad we hadn't far to go.

By the time we arrived at Old Town, Jack had reached the stage of singing with half-closed eyes, so all I could hope for from him was that he'd be subdued. Neal parked the car by the back gate of the stockade while I went to obtain passes for them. I found Frank, the owner, erecting scenery, and Jack was standing in the centre barking some story at him in an exaggerated western twang. I cringed and made signs of chagrin to Frank behind Jack's back, and ran to get Neal. He and the children collected Jack to take him on a tour of the town. I ducked into the men's dressing room, now quite late for work.

The actors were all good friends, and kidded me about 'famous' Jack's behaviour as I applied their makeup and beards. I knew they sympathized with me, but were also disappointed not to get to talk to the great writer, which now appeared quite unlikely. As each one finished dressing, he'd go out and report back to me what the great man was up to now. In a way, I was glad I couldn't see for myself. The children had taken him to the saloon, and on seeing the piano Jack had pounced on it and started banging out great dissonant chords while bellowing tuneless western songs, his behaviour still smacking largely of mockery.

The audience was beginning to straggle in, and Frank came to ask Jack not to play the piano and disturb the other saloon guests. Jack became defensive and defiant, and yelled back about his rights as a customer in his most obnoxious way. Frank had something of a temper, it now rose, and he ordered Jack off the premises.

Neal had taken advantage of my having to work to go back to the car and smoke more tea, and now Jack strode angrily out to join him, growling and swearing. When one of the actors reported this to me, I ran to the back gate and around to the Jeep, sick with disappointment, chagrin and fury. 'Is it that I demand so damn much of you guys that just *one* time in all these years you couldn't manage to do me the courtesy to even *pretend* to be interested in something I care about? And which I thought of as a treat for you? Oh no, everybody's supposed to fall all over *you* two – just give give give to you – while *you* – oh to hell with it.'

I had to stop to stem the tears, and Neal did look sheepish but said, 'Uh – maybe you could get a ride home with someone? Don't you think I'd better take old Jack away – so we won't bother you or embarrass you further, my dear?' The last bit allowed sarcasm and ridicule to enter his tone, and I was hurt and disgusted. I slammed the car door and ran back through the gate. I glanced back to see the tyres spin in the dirt, and the Jeep swept out of the driveway with a cloud of dust peeling behind it. So now they'd managed to have their time alone together.

'Huh,' I said aloud, 'you deserve each other. Good riddance.'

There was no problem finding a ride home, and I now appreciated Paul and his warmth all the more. On the drive he told me how much he'd enjoyed the evening, and that it had struck him as a sort of celebration – for the next day was his birthday.

'Your birthday? Why, Paul, why didn't you tell me sooner? How old will you be?' I had expected him to say twenty-five or six.

'Seventeen,' he said shyly. Seventeen! I was stunned.

Neal did not return with the car, so Paul was stranded at our house the next day. Without the excitement and now the future to think of, the rose colour began to fade from his glasses. I could see it, even if he couldn't yet. I'd been here before, and had known it was inevitable. He became embarrassed for having made sexual advances to an older woman.

To ease his growing restlessness, and keep us seriously occupied, I offered to paint an oil portrait of him for his birthday, and that evening friends of his came to take us out to dinner. In the morning Neal had still not returned, so Paul set out to hitchhike down the coast. The next I heard of him was a letter from Gavin some months later, when he was visiting a commune near Santa Barbara:

> had a wonderful Xmas lunch at my nephew's mother and a fine bearded friend of yours was there among the 20 – Paul Smith and his red-headed chick. We talked much of you and Neal and came to complete agreement. *You* are the saint. But Neal, in spite of the fact he has never realized that it is inevitable that one horse or car can run faster than another, he remains one of the great human beings that we have ever known – a kind of wunderkind, as the Germans put it. If we didn't love him so much we wouldn't worry so about the seeming inevitability of his going back to the Big House.
>
> I was driven to a wonderful jazz combo at Paul Smith's last night and we have promised to go to a Subud combo evening with them on Wednesday. Wish you both were going to be with us.

When Neal returned he blamed his long absence on Jack, of course, and told me that that night he'd taken Jack to see a girl named Jackie – one of Neal's former lovers. Neal was telling me about it to prove to me he was through with her. How reassuring, but I knew it meant nothing. I foresaw, as well, that his restriction to our county was at an end, and my peace of mind with it.

The following Friday evening Jack and Lew appeared again at the door, this time accompanied by Lew's girl, Lenore Kandell. Her appearance was striking. She was much larger-boned than Lew, quite

Latin looking, and 'fertility goddess' registered in my mind. Jack had been drinking, but was still coherent. Conversation centred on their plans for the coming week, again at Big Sur, and I wondered why the threesome. As with errant schoolboys, the truth leaked out that Jackie and her child were outside in the car. I was horrified.

'Now really, Jack, how could you leave her out there in the freezing cold? What's the matter with you? Bring her in at once!'

'Uh – are you sure it's all right?' Jack actually looked fearful.

'Of *course* it's all right! What can you be thinking?'

'Uh-oh –' Lew sing-songed. 'Bring in the saucer of cream!' I was dumbfounded.

'You guys! Are you nuts? Or do you watch too many soap operas? You "innovators" – new age prophets – rebels from conventions. Ha – do you really think Jackie and I are going to tear each other's hair out?'

Jack had now gone out and sheepishly returned with Jackie. I asked her to sit down, inquired about her child, who was asleep in the car, and we had an ordinary short give-and-take about children and motherhood. Jack was sitting opposite me on the couch under the window, and began sending me unmistakable soulful looks and suggestive remarks, which irritated me even more. I did my best to ignore him and my inward sobs of regret, and keep my attention on this pitiful mother-in-the-middle, Jackie.

Neal started in on his jealousy routine I'd first seen in my Denver hotel room and many times since. Pacing, glaring at Jackie, growling, breathing hard, humphing, this time for her benefit, not mine, although Jack thought Neal was mad at him. It was all so insane.

Lew became bored and eager to be on their way. At the door Jack said to me, 'Now Neal's mad at me because of Jackie; I can tell – but it was *his* idea!'

'No, no, Jack – it isn't you he's mad at – oh never mind; run along.'

The whole episode was so depressing and silly. At least I didn't need to condemn Neal; Jackie was punishing him this time, and he'd asked for it again. Little did I know this was the last time I would ever see Jack in person.

Many months later he sent a letter, the first of many more throughout the remaining years of his life. In all he expressed his constant longing to return. In this one he said he was writing to me not because he had just dreamt of me 'and *quel* dream' but because he wanted to explain why he hadn't in so long. He had written from Mexico suggesting he come to see me, but never sent it, figuring he'd just get involved with San Francisco friends instead of me. It turned out for the best, however, because during the weeks at home he had finished writing *Big Sur*, in which he recounted that summer. He said it was an answer to my last letter, and went into a nostalgic review of our time together then. It is the only book in which he tells of our affair and my having two husbands at the same time. Well, it was now the Sixties, no need to protect anyone's virtue. Before then it wasn't done to write about having an affair with your best friend's wife.

Now he was afraid he'd be condemned for writing about us all as we were, and explained how he always tried to clean up anything by changing names, times and places. And in the case of this book about him and me – a 'gentle karma that hasn't even started'. He said he was so ashamed for bringing Jackie to my home that he'd never returned to get the shirt of his I'd mended. (Whatever happened to that shirt?) Anyway, he begged me to write him as of old, and signed off, only to begin again, saying 'I ain't finished yet.' He recapped more of the events of that July, his being thrown out of Old Town, reminiscences about me, the children and our home, and how there was always the undercurrent of the muted romance between us. He hoped I wasn't mad at him, but he was worried Jackie might be. He said right out that she bored him, whereas I never did, and on and on, thinking of repeating our times around the fire talking while Neal played self-chess.

He wrote several more letters about working on this book; it evidently excited him a good deal, and when I finally read it, such a tragic story of his decline, I thought it a turning point in his writing. He seemed far more honest and objective about himself in describing his true emotions. In many of his books I cringed when he'd be bombastic or play to the audience – much of it not the way he was in person.

PART THREE

| SIXTY-NINE |

Neal's resolve to stay home and avoid people was shortlived. After the episodes of Old Town and Jackie I had to face the fact he was reverting to the old habits. Only to be expected, really, and probably with more gusto. Occasionally his resentment towards me flared, revealing its enduring presence, and I sometimes wished we had gone to Scotland.

The first infraction was 'only to the track' on Saturday afternoons, but this time away soon extended into Saturday nights, and gradually more nights were added.

Sometimes we went together to John Gourley's, one of the friends I'd made in Neal's absence. John was an engineer, poet, musician, actor, disc jockey – well, a man of many talents, and often the children or Johnny came with us to play in John's gym or with his elaborate racing-car set. He and Neal were so compatible, the friendship grew until Neal was using this 'acceptable' friendship as a springboard for clandestine affairs of many kinds. Neal could meet girls, write others letters, have a cover for runs to the City, a car to borrow and a source of acquiring and smoking tea – now being called 'pot'.

I accompanied Neal less and less, and the last time we went to John's together I happened to be reading a *Holiday* magazine in which was an interview with Neal. In it he declared Natalie had been 'his only true love'. I had not known of this interview, and reading it in a national magazine somehow stabbed me with intense pain. Later I could see why he would have said that, but at that particular time I couldn't. Later, too, I would have argued that LuAnne was his greatest love, but I guess each woman had her special trait, so a bit of each would have made up his 'true love' – if any. But under these circumstances it revealed the old burning jealousy had only been sleeping, not banished. Another test flunked.

And I had thought I'd been making progress, slowly but steadily. Neal had been changing too; he'd grown calmer, less defensive, more open with me, even telling me his feelings and fears. This article seemed to prove my failure in achieving 'loving indifference', but also to verify an about-face of my own. Formerly I had insisted 'truth' gave one a choice; now I firmly adopted 'whatcha don't know don't hurtcha'.

It dawned on me that I had been concentrating on his vices, and I felt ashamed to have cast aside all the unusual virtues that had made me love him in the first place, and which were still there. I needn't continually tell him what he was doing wrong; everyone knows that about himself. This exercise allowed me to love him even more, but in quite a different way. In exchange for this improved 'detachment' or 'indifference', I traded in the dream I'd fought so hard to hold on to, the reason I believed for my living. Neal would never be the husband and father I'd counted on. He was being true to himself. He was Neal being Neal, which he had every right to be. And I still had a choice.

I'll never forget the moment this revelation came, even though I tried to dodge it, so long had it been my central core. I knew well the pain of trying to hang on to a lost cause, and I musn't forfeit the peace of mind I'd now attained. At first it was an isolated and lonely peace. A bridge had fallen between me and Neal, and I looked at him now from the opposite bank of the gulf between us. Was this 'loving indifference'?

For the next two years I fluctuated, sometimes managing positive reactions, sometime falling back, ego-wounded and resentful, even though I was better at concealing my feelings. Our home life was peaceful, but there wasn't a great deal of it, and I didn't know how much this was related to Neal's bitterness against me or merely a continuation of his former need to spread himself thinly. He wanted and appreciated a home and family, but he wanted everything else as well – his cake and to eat it too. And he never took me out; now we never went anywhere together, to a show or concert.

As he became more entangled, I became less so. My theatrical activities still kept me busy designing, sewing, attending performances for makeup, but some were diminishing. Now that the ballet academy had added the annual *Nutcracker* to its regular spring production, once the first production was finished, only a few new costumes for the soloists were required each year, and now I costumed only one or two plays for the university. The Wagon Stagers had succumbed to the inevitable 'democracy' in the company, with disagreements, factions and failure. Other groups started rival companies, less authentic, more corny and hyped.

I had a brief season as artistic director of a new San Jose Opera Company, for which I designed *Die Fledermaus* and four Puccini operas, only one of which, *Madame Butterfly*, was ever produced before they went bankrupt, I escaping just in the nick of time. By 1960 and Neal's freedom, I made costumes only for individual performers, and gave up my classes in makeup. I still painted a portrait or two now and then.

During the first two years of Neal's three-year parole, the Santa Clara students still came to the house for parties, and some were often there when Neal would come home in the wee hours. He would cheerfully join the group sitting on the floor around the candlelit sandstone coffee table in front of the fire. Through this I felt less the abandoned wife, and the young men welcomed him, knowing a little of his reputation although few, if any, had read Kerouac. How charming he could be. I'd watch him as he entered the discussions of philosophy or the latest bands etc., listening and nodding with earnestness, not asserting himself in an overbearing way, yet keeping up his end brilliantly to everyone's enjoyment. At such times the sharp pang of my lost dream would thicken my throat with remorse for what might have been.

One such night, the boys had all begun to filter out of the house to go back to the campus, when my niece, Judy, who was staying with us at the time, drove in, bringing with her Hoyt Axton. She had attended his performance in San Francisco, and rather offhandedly invited him home. Much to her surprise, he accepted. Naturally, everyone filed right back into the house, and the remainder of the night and well into the morning was a new delight. Neal played the gracious host, and Hoyt was completely at ease, insisting on playing his guitar and singing between conversations, food and wine. As the sun rose and the students left, he and Neal had discussions of a different sort, or so I gathered when I overheard Hoyt say to Neal, 'Well, I'm an ass man, myself.'

| SEVENTY |

Neal's pay was far below his railroad earnings even without his gambling losses, and our debts continued to rise, periodic refinancing of the house or a loan now and then saving our skins from time to time. Most of this I arranged, as usual, since Neal wasn't familiar with all these legal matters. I decided I'd better go back to work at a regular boring job. In this way I thought perhaps I could gradually lose my dependence on Neal financially, as I was doing emotionally. I brought in little income, but it helped. I began on the switchboard of a local newspaper, a skill I'd learned at college and with the Army. I liked that job, but I was soon drafted into display advertising, which I didn't like. Now my only goal was to wait out the children's growth and keep a roof over their heads.

The location of that roof continued to sustain my spirit and my sanity, and not a day went by I wasn't grateful for it. It was worth even Neal's bad behaviour and resentment, for I never really believed I would have gained him in exchange for bail. Sometimes as I looked out at the ever-changing colours of the hills beyond the orchards, our youthful expectations of life and the plans we'd all made would parade through my mind, and I'd trace the fates of the major protagonists. Was there any hope for Jack or Neal?

Allen, on the other hand, was going his own way, and well. At least he was happy doing what he liked. We heard from him seldom, but when we did we knew we were still in his thoughts as he was in ours. At the end of 1960 we had received a wildly scrawled letter from New York:

> Merry Xmas... Forgive my silence. I will write you. Peter and I were at Harvard last week eating synthetic mushrooms... very high. *The Revolution Has Begun...* Stop giving your authority to Christ & the Void & the Imagination... *You Are It*, now, the *God*... I will have babies... all's well... we're starting a plot to get everyone in power in America high – Hurrah! – I flipped my lid last week at Harvard & rushed out stark naked to telephone Jack and wake him up – he's always wanting to die – I stopped vomiting up the Universe last week. My book *Kadish* (all Death Death Death) (hymns) done and will be out in a few months. How are you? and Caroline & the

Babies? I love you in Life's sweet July. What kind of money work you doing? Why don't you write again to communicate the holy news to the world... you are *needed* – stop hiding your light in a bushel. I'll sit down & write you a long gossipy letter soon as I can... Always, always, always.

He and Peter took off again for Europe soon after, and we only got postcards until they got to India, when Allen wrote,

When'd I last write? I forgot... Met some weird saints on streets, but no guru. We (Peter here too) know a lot of people, poets, businessmen; go around on streets in indian clothes & I got long black hair down to shoulders & a beard & Peter long blond hair, we sure look looney. But everybody here also looks looney so we pass unnoticed more than if we were in slacks & U.S. hair...

One of the few close ties Neal and I had left was to read Jack and Allen's letters together, and it was one reason I welcomed them more than ever, yet they were arriving far less often now. Of course, the main reason was that Neal never answered them. Jack wrote only two or three times a year, and occasionally we'd get two in a row that began how he was now writing letters without remembering, and he'd repeat the news he'd sent in the last one. He was still seeking a home, always planning to come see us, and steadily lamenting and drinking his life away. Once in a while he'd try to reach Neal directly again, but without much hope. He'd tell Neal he needn't answer; it was just that he felt like talking to him. He thought we should know that Joan had married an Arab and had twins, but left him. She was suing Jack for child support and giving damning and untrue interviews to the newspapers. He said he wanted to know more about Cayce, but I suspect that was just his way of trying to make Neal write to him. Didn't work. Neal was disgusted, and said how Jack never listened anyway.

For a long time we got no such chatty letters, only notes he'd add to a few fan letters he'd received for 'Dean'. He said to tell me to write him if Neal couldn't. Sometimes the fans would ferret out Neal's address for themselves; but they made Neal flinch with guilt, and he didn't answer them. Once, however, a letter came from a student in an American school in Germany. I nagged Neal to answer it, partially hoping thereby he'd get interested in using his mind again and in writing. (I was unaware how heavily taxed these faculties already were with his love letters.) He obliged me this time, and wrote a nice answer. Then instead of hearing again from the boy, Neal got a letter from the boy's female teacher. A circuitous route, but his magnetism got through.

Few and far between though Jack's letters now were, when I'd feel lonely and wanted someone to talk to who knew Neal, I'd write to him, and this would keep me together and keeping on. He had written he was going to Europe, then wrote he hadn't and he'd tell me all about it in front of the fireplace. Once I wrote in October and received the answer the following January. The next summer I poured out my woes again, and he responded in October, he too pouring out his woes, in regard to being insulted by critics, and feeling like not publishing anything more – that is, after *Visions of Gerard* and *Desolation Angels*, which he'd already written. He advised me to support Neal's absorption in anything on TV, because he was studying the culture. Jack said he did that too, and all of it important. Also newspapers. He said Neal should never leave us, because he could have his freedom just the way things were. Which, of course, Neal was already doing. Jack told me to ask Neal for a romantic weekend in the City at a Chinese restaurant and a show – so like Jack but not Neal, I had to laugh.

Long since I'd lost track of how often Jack had moved with his mother back and forth from New York to Florida. I thought they'd just gone to Florida when he wrote to say he couldn't stand the subdivision there, and had bought a 'modern ranchito'-type house in Northport. I was puzzled, since he was always complaining he hadn't the money to pay Joan, but he kept buying big houses. He wrote that he felt *Big Sur* was just lightweight, but now he planned to write the 'horrible tragedy' *Vanity of Dulouz*, which would be much better. 'Come May, I come see you – (TRULY, just wait and see).' Wait I did; see I did not.

| SEVENTY-ONE |

Early in the fall of 1962 a Cayce conference was to be held at Asilomar, a conference facility in our favourite vacation spot of Pacific Grove. Neal encouraged me to take the children for the weekend. I had a few qualms, but in the end decided to give him a break, and he insisted he could handle things at home. We rented our usual cabin in the pine woods close to the conference grounds and the beach. Each morning I walked to Asilomar to attend Elsie Sechrist's class on meditation, and the children swam in the motel's pool, beachcombed, climbed the dunes or read.

Late Sunday afternoon we drove home, sunburned, sandy, refreshed and relaxed in body and spirit. Then WHAM! We entered the house to a macabre version of Goldilocks and the three bears: the living room gave no particular clues, but my bedroom, John's room, the patio and family room displayed a series of sickening jolts. My bed was stripped, the blankets in a heap on the floor. I found the missing sheets stuffed hastily into the washing machine and splotched with blood. John Gourley had given Neal the prized racing-car set, once the star attraction in his home, and Neal had presented it to Johnny with loving glee. It was an extravagant toy, and occupied almost all of the free floor space in Johnny's room. Or did. Of course, Johnny cherished it both for itself and as a gift from Neal. Now Johnny stood in his doorway, struck dumb. A mini tornado must have whirled through that room. The bed was a mess, his books and papers scattered all over, and the racetrack a twisted tangle of metal. Some cars were found around the room, around the house and in the bottom of the pool.

The patio was in a similar condition. In addition to the cars, the pool contained sticks, stones, tools, dishes and silverware. It was obvious an unsupervised child had had a lot of time on his hands. Only then did I remember when a man at the tyre shop had confused me with another woman and inquired about my three-year-old son. This woman and her son must have been Neal's weekend guests.

My supposed progress in 'loving indifference' vanished in a flash of shock and fury. All the worst of the old emotions flooded over me, plus some new ones I didn't know existed. When Neal's devilry hit at the children, my maternal instincts blotted out all else. What thoughts were in Johnny's eleven-year-old mind, I never knew. Naturally, I said as little as possible to the children about the cause of this mayhem, but I could not conceal altogether my displeasure and pain, which I'm sure they understood and shared.

That night, when they were all asleep and the house in order again, I sat in the living room in the dark and looked out on the lush moon-washed lawn and the shadowy stately eucalyptus swaying in the distance below the towering hill. 'All answers come from within.' I tried to match the peaceful scene by silencing my crowding thoughts and raging emotions and grief, but it was no use. Self-pity was as strong as ever. I felt utterly ineffectual in my own life and in those of the two men I cared for the most. A total loss.

The next day I wrote a long agonized letter to Elsie, but it was never mailed. I knew already what her answer would be: 'God will make the separation,' and I could no longer accept that. Even if I were wrong, I just didn't want to take any more.

Another nagging worry had assailed me since Neal's return from prison. These older children were living under a double standard. On the one hand was Neal's complete lack of any discipline, and on the other my strict rules. I had a sneaking suspicion we each needed aspects of the other's ways, but I was too insecure to try loosening my habits, gleaned from my own childhood, even if I was not altogether convinced they were best. I didn't even know how to begin.

When Neal dared come home after the grisly weekend, I made little effort to conceal my disgust. No emotional tirades; it was too late to hope for hope, too late for strategy. Even he didn't go into his usual song and dance to explain it all away. Grimly I told him it was now time for a divorce. In the year and a half since his return from prison I had several times mentioned the disparity between his theories while there and his subsequent practice, as well as my growing desire to set him free from the drudgery of supporting a family if that wasn't what he wanted in life. He had steadfastly refused to discuss it.

I didn't like the idea of divorce in any sense. I didn't think marriage vows were very realistic, but since I was convinced Neal was and would be the only great love of my life, I hadn't minded making those vows. And vows they were to me. Now, however, since Neal and I did not share one life, none of that signified. I didn't speculate as to whether I might meet another man to replace him – none could, although an agreeable companion…

Here is one of those times in a long life you look back and say 'if only…' I thought my decision to divorce Neal was based on motives entirely for his good and my peace. Seeing him beat himself to a pulp every day at work tore my heart. But it was only decades later I was to realize how wrong I had been – at least in his case.

I've had to look back so often to describe these men to others, new insights have occurred to me. Looking at Neal's life, I suddenly recognized the thread that he clung to and tried to strengthen was – to become respectable. I saw that from his earliest childhood he had dedicated himself to improving his mind and his acquaintances. He had read and studied avidly; he met Allen and Jack, and here were men who could teach him a 'respectable' career – writer! He had the brains; he had read a lot – why not? And when I came along – well, there was the woman who could partner him in a 'respectable' union.

Neal poured all his energy and ingenuity into securing them and me, and succeeded beyond his original hopes. I gave him a respectable home in a respectable neighbourhood, and even learned enough about economics to handle things like taxes and insurance.

With all these aims accomplished, the regular work on the railroad became another source of pride for him, knowing he was the best at it and the most reliable, and it was a respectable job guaranteed for life. I suspect all of these achievements diluted his ambition to become a respectable writer – so much hard work and solitary confinement. He found he had not only achieved his social ambitions as a respectable homeowner and family head, he had also found this arrangement supported even more freedom for his other interests. There is no freedom without fences, and here Neal had them both. Until he lost the balance.

The two pillars of his support were the railroad job and his family. His imprisonment cost him his job and removed that pillar, and when I divorced him he lost the other means of support. In five years he was dead.

At the time I thought I would be doing him a big favour. He would no longer have to burn that energy in a nowhere tyre job to support a family he didn't want to live with. He could go where he liked, do what he liked and be unburdened by responsibility. In other words, in my ignorance I removed the fences. But it took a lot of persuading to get him to agree to the divorce. This time I had new ammunition.

One of my advertising accounts with the newspaper was the owner of a local music store. I had met Bernard (let's call him) before, when I knew him as the father of one of the ballet girls, when he had still been married – he was now divorced. He was twelve years older than I, but witty, good company, played drums and sang in a local nightclub band, and was financially secure. He could hardly have been more opposite to Neal and the boring, straight/square life he lived looked to me at that stage like sheer paradise. He was president of a local men's club, and I could wear a cowboy hat to the BBQs – yeah!

To augment his wooing, Bernie had arranged for Johnny to have piano lessons, and 'loaned' us a piano from the shop. He knew I was unhappy with Neal, and when he began to pressure me to marry him I wondered if he were God's agent heaven-sent to 'make the separation'. Reluctantly, at last Neal agreed sadly to the divorce, only, he said, because he felt Bernie could do more for the children than he could. We made the decision a year before his parole was up, but I told him I'd wait for that freedom first.

I wrote to Jack, suddenly realizing it would probably be the end of his friendship as well. It did give me pause. I was the one breaking up the old gang, as it were, but on the other hand I had little hope for Jack either, and was determined to put the past behind me and begin anew. Jack answered sadly, thinking it was all a question of money. How strange; we'd never ever discussed money, but I guess he was nearly constantly involved with it himself. He said he wasn't much of a counsellor, since he wasn't sure he could manage his own affairs for the next day or two. He said he'd retired from New York scenes, but was a happy writer and would answer my every letter. He offered me advice on raising the children, and all around the margins added notes to Neal about how positive he was the system wouldn't work, and to please give it up. At least he hadn't abandoned me altogether.

Four days before the expiration of Neal's parole, I went to court. This time it was all very simple and smooth, the lawyer carried the ball, and good old Helen once again agreed to be my witness. Now we had a year to wait before I could marry Bernie. Neal behaved as though I'd been to the dentist, and made no other plans, at least none he confided to me.

I called the children together to try to explain what it meant, and I felt a worse traitor than ever. I did not believe in single-parent families. One after another my ideals fell, like so many tenpins. They sounded understanding as far as I could tell, none of us knowing what changes were or were not in store, and many of their friends had divorced parents. I didn't urge Neal to pack up and depart, not wanting to rock the boat too suddenly, even though it was hard for me to look at him without remembering that weekend. Now I'd done what is expected of wronged wives – retaliated with divorce. Me and my advanced philosophy. Humph. And I later wished I hadn't done it.

Since I had always disliked sex with him, I had stopped that many months before. I was surprised he took my ultimatum so calmly, understanding my motive only as his having so many other outlets for that; I never was able to discuss his technique. Another 'if only…'

When Neal's parole was over in the summer of 1963, not surprisingly he expressed his freedom by blasting off on a cross-country trip. This time he took friends unknown to me, and gladly so, judging by Jack's description of them in a letter soon after their visit to him. He had wished Neal had come alone and stayed indefinitely in his mother's house. But the rude friends disgusted him. One helped himself to anything in the ice box, another put his feet up on the kitchen table and threw bread around. This didn't sound like something Neal would have sanctioned either, but I suppose they were all high. 'But Neal alone with me for five minutes was as sweet and gentle, polite and intelligent and interesting as ever he was…' He said he himself was older and bored. He wished me luck with my new marriage, which he now understood better, seeing how Neal kept taking chances. But he said, believe it or not, he still thought about Neal and me daily, from habit and from unchanged affection for me, but not for the hangers-on. He wrote he hadn't had a drink since Neal left.

| SEVENTY-TWO |

Neal's interest in the ARE and other metaphysical studies continued, and he did discuss these ideas with me still. Bernie wasn't 'with' any of it, as I'd expected him not to be, so I was always grateful when I could talk with Neal.

The previous year, during the time I was convincing myself to divorce Neal, and after an errand in San Jose, I stopped by Mrs Winter's. On this visit she was all excited to tell me about a woman who had recently been in town, a Dr Neva Dell Hunter, who had a PhD in Psychology but had become a 'channel' for a 'teacher on the seventh plane'. He called himself Dr Ralph Gordon, the name he would use in his next incarnation on earth.

Mrs Winter had always staunchly believed no one could ever match Cayce, but after much critical consideration she agreed to have a past-life reading from Dr Gordon. This consisted of a review of past lives that related to the present one. Everyone had many more, but not all were related to the present one at this time, so naturally they would mean little to know of now.

Mrs Winter was very impressed, although she still wasn't sure if Dr Gordon had as wide a contact with the Akashic records (records etched on the ethers of every thought, word and deed of each person throughout his or her existence) as did Cayce's many teachers. Still, the range was far wider than most 'mediums' who were used by a 'guide' – a disincarnate entity whose knowledge could be limited, so she felt those she'd heard and her own might be quite accurate.

Mrs Winter asked us if we would like to hear her reading to get an idea of how Dr Gordon operated. We were eager to do so, and arranged an evening to listen to her taped recording, and in the ensuing weeks we heard several others. The readings lasted ninety minutes, the longest a channel could relinquish her own consciousness without harm to her, said Dr Gordon.

Many lives were given in amazing detail, often with even more on daily life in past centuries than had some of the Cayce readings. We were so impressed, we had to get readings of our own. Neva Dell would be returning each spring, and we could make a request. Dr Gordon had to vet applicants in advance, since some would not be 'ready' to hear or to benefit from this knowledge.

When Neva Dell did return, Mrs Winter held a small reception for her to introduce her and the applicants for this session. She was a plump blonde, unaffected, warm, poised, humorous and glowing; we loved her at once. She told us the strange story of how she had become a channel, and told us Dr Gordon had an assignment to establish men's 'light teams' throughout the States. To pay her expenses, he gave these readings for $25 each.

At that time the readings were divided into types. The first ones were of lives concerning your physical and emotional karma; a second reading could be requested for a year later, which would give lives related to your spiritual development and your gifts. Neal had his 'physical/emotional' reading first. He came home afterwards red-eyed and sombre. He insisted I listen to his tape at once, even though it was eleven o'clock. We settled on the bed and started the reel. Neal lay with his eyes closed, and soon his face was glistening with tears. For ninety minutes I sat transfixed, often moved to tears myself. At the end of the recital of about six or seven lives, Dr Gordon asked Neal if he had any questions, and I heard Neal's voice on the tape sobbing so he could hardly answer, 'I think you've covered everything.'

These lives were so awesome, we were both silent for a while after. Dr Gordon had said many requests from people with lives as tragic as these he would have to turn down, but he felt Neal was advanced enough to take it, and could benefit from knowing about them. Well now, did we believe these stories were true? Throughout these readings, I felt a kinship with those men – I felt I had known each of them a little through Neal, but I didn't dwell on this.

We had never accepted as absolute any psychic information, as I've tried to emphasize. We did believe 'all things are possible'. We did not believe it was necessary for anyone to believe in reincarnation to live this life properly; it is, after all, simply a formula or means of soul evolution, not an end in itself. The same principles apply to this life – only there is no death of the soul after. This theory was a joyous one for me, and erased so many regrets. I resented having only one chance at a wedding (me thinking one was all that was real), my only chance at children and a home – and think of those who could have none, or far worse circumstances, etc. My chances had been a mockery of my expectations. Nor would I have put up with many of the subsequent disappointments had I not accepted the maxim that everything happens for a reason and lessons must be learned. Neal was totally convinced these lives were true; he had been touched so deeply by them. I can only encapsulate them here, but they were long and detailed.

In the first life, Neal was a Bedouin. A rival tribe killed his mother, and to avenge her he managed (after a lot of events) to pass himself off as a prince of that very tribe. The strongest attributes were deception and a desire for revenge; I could relate to his expertise in deception, but not to a fixation on revenge. Perhaps he'd overcome that meanwhile. Here he learned from experience there is no 'death'. After more adventures he was unmasked, and his own son stabbed him in the back. The tribe left him in the street where he fell, and every passer-by hurled hatred and curses on him, of which he remained conscious, even if 'dead'. That life contributed to his restlessness and fearlessness, as well as a deep sense of guilt. (Guess I can't blame the Catholics altogether.)

In the second life he was a general in the army of Nebuchadnezzar. He raped an enemy Hebrew woman, was caught by her officer husband and publicly castrated, then discharged in disgrace. He never returned to his own family, but watched his children grow from afar (as in this life, and then, as now, they didn't know of his crimes). In defiance, Neal became the vice king of Babylon and amassed a fortune by exploiting every human weakness. He owned brothels and gambling dens, dealt in magic and drugs, led a band of cut-throat robbers and fenced the loot himself. He backed all the most brutal blood sports. Again, 'to get even' was his driving ambition, as well as to prove he could excel and be successful as a man even without his 'manhood'. Dr Gordon said in his present life Neal didn't seem much concerned with competing with other men, only himself, and his women can testify where getting even was concerned ('I hate women; they're my weakness'). We thought the impact of the castration might be a contributor to his excessive sexual needs now.

The third life was in China. He was the sickly son of a rice grower who suffered from arthritis. Neal was subject to nose bleeds (his 'problem' nose now?), and found relief with the wild poppy. He tried to persuade his father to take it to relieve his pain, but the father refused. As Neal's opium addiction increased, he deteriorated both mentally and physically. He killed his brother and ploughed him under a furrow in the rice paddy, then told everyone the boy had run away. He then became haunted by dreams and hallucinations of his brother rising from the ground.

As his mind grew weaker, he turned himself into a fakir, and amazed the townspeople by throwing himself on a bed of spikes, glorying in the pain for penance and pleasure. He was afraid of water, but one day when he went to a pond to apply the mud to sores (syphilis?) he let go and allowed himself to drown. In his present life he shied away from water and didn't swim. Dr Gordon said he was still subject to the chemical imbalance he acquired then.

If anyone knew or encountered Jesus in a past life, that life was always given, because that experience could be a source of spiritual growth and inspiration ever after. Neal had been raised in an Essene community. As a boy he was often disobedient, and roamed outside the walls of the commune. One day he came upon a group who had been listening to Jesus speak. Jesus was an Essene, and recognized Neal's Essene garb; he knew his stepmother well. Neal was desperate to hear the 'Raboni' speak, and Jesus told him to come to the hills that evening, where He would be speaking again.

That evening Neal ran to find the meeting place, but when passing a jewelry shop he saw a big red ruby sparkling in a display and promptly stole it as an offering to Jesus, then, as now, feeling unworthy in himself. The shopkeeper pursued him and struck him on the head with a sharp stone from his sling-shot. Neal fell unconscious, but so many stones were red from his blood, the shopkeeper failed to find the ruby. When Neal came to, he crawled up the hill, stumbled through the crowd, and fell dead at the feet of Jesus, the ruby rolling from his hand. Jesus was saddened by this, and after the lecture he carried Neal and the ruby to the shopkeeper, returning the ruby and showing the man the sacrifice Neal had made to hear Jesus speak. Dr Gordon told this story in such a soft and reverent tone, it was moving and sad, and both Neal and I were crying. Dr Gordon said this life showed a soul seeking approval, and since Neal had received a personal blessing from Jesus, this power would release him, if not in this lifetime, then in another.

Both Neal and I had found a new view of Jesus from our studies than the conventional Catholic one. I had formed no fixed opinion of Him, but of course Neal had the dogmatic view, which he had never liked, and was so very happy to have found a way to really appreciate Him now. So this reading meant much more to him than it would have before.

Neal went into the bathroom to blow his nose, then came back to lie beside me again, whispering in my ear:

'I'm sorry for this next one – forgive?'

In or around 600 AD Neal lived in the Pyrenees. I was his wife and Cathy his daughter, then as now. He was a fine man with a good family, but then he became a religious fanatic. He had discovered how to fashion sharp knives, and began to believe zealously in animal sacrifice. I disagreed with his views but had to be dutiful. One morning Neal slit the throats of several sheep and hung them over rocks so their blood dripped into a pool below. He then ordered Cathy and me to bathe in that water. Meekly we obeyed, but I drowned. He let my body sink and made Cathy swear silence.

'Whew – well, Neal, that's the second murder you got away with, not counting Babylon. Somehow since then you must have learned a respect for life, because you are so compassionate and non-violent now. And I wonder if that life might explain my extreme aversion to murky water, hmm.'

'Maybe so, and I'm sure a lot of people think I'm a religious fanatic now.' Dr Gordon said one reason I'd come in with Neal this time was to show him I'd forgiven him … just as Neal had surmised when we first discussed our relationship after learning of reincarnation. 'Forgiveness' means giving good for evil. As long as I held a grudge, nothing he did would please me. I hadn't been totally successful yet, evidently. Yet again we were reminded of the futility of revenge. Retaliation brings no peace and no progress.

In the last life given, only one incident was revealed, but it was more than enough. Johnny was his son in Assyria and a champion chariot racer. Neal raced, too, and would drive right behind Johnny, knowing he was the fastest. Neal had invented the curved knives attached to the hubs of the chariot wheels, intended only for use in battle, but Neal left them on when racing. During a race one day, Johnny glanced back to see Neal losing his balance, and with a mighty lurch he leaned backwards to shove Neal clear of the blades. In so doing, Johnny lost his own balance and also fell. As Neal lay in the sand, he watched his son being chopped to death by the weapon he himself had provided. We were silent again for a time. Then I said, 'I've noticed you aren't interested in any knives now. That was the second time you misused them.'

'Yeah; I never wanted anything to do with them – not even a Boy Scout knife or jack knives like all the other boys.'

'And could that be why you only watch auto races and have no ambition to drive in them? How many times have I asked you why you don't do your expert driving on a track not on the highway?'

'Actually, racing has always scared me, even though I knew I could drive as well or better. And how about Johnny – the only times he's been hurt was when he was on wheels of one kind or another.'

'Yes, well. Maybe we are assuming too much, who knows. But at least these stories don't sound like anything anyone could just make up – that would be more amazing than as they are.'

At the end of this string of depressing lives, Dr Gordon left Neal with a ray of hope that in this lifetime he was already overcoming much of the bad karma and, as Hugh Lynn and Starr Daily had also said, if he made up his mind to it, he could do a great deal more.

We, the Master Teachers, or even the God within cannot
do this for you; you have to do it yourself, but They can
help if you will ask! Strange, it makes it very difficult for
those who come after...but they knew what they were
reaching toward when they chose you as their father...In
this lifetime you will have to watch very closely the intake
of your body, because the chemistry is now becoming
acclimatised to such a degree that soon what you put in
it...the body won't respond to any more.

There is no concrete evidence I can point to proving what benefit,
if any, Neal derived from this list of possible past experiences, but I
do know they meant a great deal to him. When he insisted on carrying
the tapes with him everywhere, I quickly had copies made, so afraid
was I he'd lose them – and so he did when his car was stolen many
years later.

Neva Dell was unable to remember anything Dr Gorden said while
using her physical faculties, but once in a while he would instruct
her to listen to a tape he had dictated. Such was the case when Neal
had his 'spiritual' reading a year later, quite the antithesis of the first
one. When Neva Dell played it back at Dr Gordon's insistence, she
said he performed in a way as never before. She had never heard him
sound so moved, so lyrical, so concise. It was also one of the shortest
readings, only about a third as long as the usual. 'There is very little
we can tell you you do not already know.' In the over 5000 readings
he had given, never before had he given one like that, and she couldn't
help the tears brought on by the beauty of it.

It made me say to Neal, 'See? I told you so,' pleased that my faith
in his inherent goodness had been so dramatically upheld, and that
the intuitions of the men who had seen his aura had been vindicated.
'No one knows what your light will do for man's future... You want
your family to know you think of them first...you have given them
a light few parents could have shared with their children...how
difficult freedom is to perform'...etc.

In a life in Egypt he was passionate to go on a spiritual mission,
like Buddha, but he was defeated at every turn. He became silent and
remained in a morbid state, with irrational mental outpourings.
'You were disgusted with the hypocrisy of the religious system, the
priests and their dancing girls...you felt it unfair...and it is hampering
you now.' Then he was a light bearer with the druids and learned

(through events) that only from the close cooperation of every human soul would the earth be lifted. Neal, however, seemed somewhere in space when he heard it again with me, and made no comment at all, scarcely able to credit it, I supposed.

I had been given two sessions of readings too – although not nearly as dramatic, tragic or sensational as Neal's. But an everlasting benefit came from my first one, true or not – it changed my life. Something like it must be true if it isn't. It had to do with a life in Egypt with Cathy. I won't detail mine, but the crux of this one was that she had been so awful to me in that life that she was eager to return to make it up to me. Alas, she came back too soon and brought the strong resentment with her. Everything the tape revealed was re-enacted in this life. I had been tortured with guilt that it was all my fault, and this explanation lifted that huge burden and helped me find a better way of relating to her from then on.

In subsequent lives, one was with Neal, in which he had seduced me into abandoning a noble mission to join him in the black arts. This one had other ghostly revelations later: Anne Murphy and Billy Craddock were both present with Neal and me in prison, awaiting our execution by guillotine. This was not in my reading, but Anne 'remembered' the scene. She had been begging for Neal's release without success. I was resigned to our fate. Billy told me of a dream or 'vision' he'd had of the exact same scene – I dunno.

I was told of another life with Neal. I collected poems and songs for King David, but I was not allowed to live in the court, because I was not pure Hebrew. My mother had been raped by an Assyrian soldier, my father. Jack was David's son, and we fell in love. Of course, David was opposed to our marriage, but we cut our hands and joined our blood, marrying each other in our own way secretly. I had a child by Jack – Neal. David then allowed me to live with his son. Neal was a sickly kid and brutal. He was killed by a horse he was abusing. (I couldn't get Neal interested in our horses on the farm, which surprised me, but I have a photo of him on a great white one from when Neal worked on Ed Uhl's ranch. He said Neal rode a horse the way he drove a car.)

Then Jack went to war and came back paralysed from the waist down. He became very bitter and abusive, and David made me leave. I ended up making and selling baskets into old age. I died when a big jug above me fell on me when I reached for it.

Dr Gordon said I needn't have died, but I wanted to. I can relate to that.

My second year 'spiritual' lives were also pale compared to Neal. They just told how I first gained my artistic talent. Then there were several lives with John and Jami – both Jami and I had been married to John in separate Egyptian lives, and they were my children in others. Great stuff, and all of these do explain so much. Even if all make believe, it sure makes life a lot more fun – mysteries to unravel and investigate. Nothing, again I say, have I 'carved in stone'.

After our readings, of course, we wrote to Jack, although we didn't tell him any details of our past lives. We urged him to find Neva Dell when she was back East, and get readings himself. He answered as expected, flippantly and with imaginative stories, but often before and after he would recite past lives he declared he remembered.

By this time Jack had taken to telephoning more often than writing. I was excited to tell him about our life when he was a son of David, which I thought would please him. He interrupted there and bellowed, 'I WAS JESUS CHRIST!' I gave up. He went on, 'Jesus was really a Frenchman, you know – a Norman! You know how the twelve tribes of Israel scattered throughout Northern Europe and all that – even Cayce said one of 'em built Stonehenge – Neal told me – well, Jesus was a Gaul, see? But the Church changed all that, kept it a big secret, and I come from the same place – Brittany, so you see...' I let him rave on.

| SEVENTY-THREE |

Neal had moved out piecemeal before he took his Eastern trip, and although he and I went through a certain number of emotional scenes, I hoped they were not noticed by the children. Only once they were shocked to see me break down in tears. Neal had hesitated at the door on his way out and once more begged me to let him stay. I said, 'Neal, Neal, please don't make me keep turning you away when all I've ever wanted is for you to stay. You know the only way that can be...' and I couldn't help the tears. He nodded and left. The children had come into the room just before, but now retreated.

The greatest relief for me, and certainly for the neighbours, was the disappearance of five broken-down cars from the driveway. All of them were dearly beloved, and even though none ran, Neal was ever confident he'd meet a mechanic to con into fixing them. Many people have supposed Neal repaired his cars, but that is another myth. He sometimes knew the cause but not the cure.

Instead, one of the city fathers of our new 'city', Monte Sereno, called on me and tactfully asked if we were running a repair service, in which case we would need a licence. When I told Neal, I expected him to damn authority again, but he said, 'Good. Just what I needed. Glad he came – just the impetus I need to get rid of them.' A good example, I thought, of the effectiveness of a wife's constant nagging. Neal called the wreckers, and even made ten or fifteen dollars out of each of them.

In adding up, we discovered Neal had gone through 18 cars in less than two years – we didn't add up the incalculable amount of money. I still drove the Jeep. It had been a real boon during my costume career in that the open space in the back allowed me to hang so many costumes. But when Neal left, I traded it in for a brand new Mercury sedan and bade a jolly farewell to battered and unreliable transport. The only other change was that Neal was around more often than before. Typical perversity. Just like a shadow, I figured; chase it, and it runs away; turn your back and you can't get rid of it. He never quite relinquished the idea that this was his home. Nor did I.

I had left the newspaper a month after the interlocutory decree, and took a job 'for a year' in a doctor's office until I could marry Bernie. The job lasted for seven more years.

Then one day Bernie vanished. He left the store, the town and… me. I was more relieved than I could admit, and more than ever felt sure Bernie had been 'sent' to serve only as an escape from Neal. When Neal learned of it, he said, 'Great! Now I can move back in.' But I held my ground, so hard won.

'Look Neal, all you do is come here to rest and regain your strength. It's my strength you sap, leaving me nowhere, neither fish nor fowl, neither married nor single. Please, Neal, no more. Go live the life you love.'

My hope was that once away from a solid home life he would come to respect it more, but that didn't happen. His job lost its purpose, and he quit, thereby cutting his only other lifeline.

For a time he was determined to pull himself together according to Dr Gordon's suggestions. Allen was in San Francisco again, and

Neal went to stay with him, vowing to set up a daily schedule of writing, 'if I don't go to Mexico,' he wrote in a note to Allen. I encouraged him all I could, holding out the promise that if he could just show me he was capable of self-control, how gladly I would welcome him back.

It was far too late. He increased his use of pot and now 'speed', as well as anything else available. In horror I'd watch him swallow pills he'd 'found', with no idea what was in them, and in the next four years I saw he was pursuing death with every breath of life. I wondered if I were to blame; if I should have kept up what little support I offered, but I knew I couldn't cope with teenagers and Neal too.

He had already expanded his circle of friends and admirers by the spring of 1961, and made up for lost prison time by seducing a number of girls simultaneously. I knew of some, and one in Salt Lake City he told me he always visited to and from his east–west trips. She had been a tough task, had been super-conventional, but in the end she had totally capitulated to Neal's charms, and eventually she became proud of the fact she had managed apparently to corrupt the whole city with drugs and free love. I have a batch of her letters that are testimony like no others of Neal's power.

In 1962 Neal met Anne Murphy, the woman of The Weekend. Anne had been married when she and her husband were students at Berkeley, and they had a son, Grant. Anne then ran off with another man, taking the child, but when she met Neal, the man had fled, and she was ill. She was also engaged in a bitter custody battle with her ex-husband over the child.

My first encounter with her was on the phone, when one day a tearful voice asked if I knew where Neal was. In trying to get to him in Los Gatos she had become confused, and took a number of wrong buses. Then she fell asleep and now didn't know where she was. I didn't ask her name, just told her to inquire for the name of the street, stay where she was, and I'd find Neal. Fortunately, I was successful, and he found her. Anne later told him and me she was so dumb-founded I not only wasn't angry with her but even did her an act of kindness, she was devoted to me from that day on. Ever after, she apologized for the weekend. She said she was so jealous I was Neal's wife, not she, she wanted to hurt me. Of course, that confession did nothing to excuse Neal, where the real blame lay.

Before and after that incident Neal had come home several times, always now sleeping on the couch. At which times I learned Anne was left in the car parked at the cul-de-sac at the end of the street. He was still trying to make me believe there were no other women in his life. When I learned of this I felt as I had about Jackie, but Anne wouldn't have it any other way. I told him not to come again if that was the case, or bring her inside, so at last she agreed.

At that time her hair was reddish blond and stringy, and she looked thin and unhealthy. I thought she could have been quite pretty, and I found she was intelligent and a talented artist as well. With me she was always meek and sweet, if a little too humble. Never could I picture the banshee Neal sometimes made her out to be. She proved to be a measure of my own progress as well. Gradually it dawned on me I had passed some exams; I had vanquished the green-eyed monster. It was a triumphant revelation.

Anne was to become Neal's slave and tormentor for the next eight years, and was ever-present in the foreground or background, always expecting to marry Neal when our divorce was final. Like LuAnne, she and Neal were too much alike; she couldn't leave men alone, nor he women, yet both felt bitter jealousy, and the emotional battles that ensued would have split most people much earlier on. I had to referee for each of them from time to time as each vented their anger and retaliatory designs on the other. I could see lessons I'd learned that they had not as yet, like letting another person tell you how to think or feel. Would they never tire of these feelings, as I had?

I was surprised to learn Neal was in and out of jail at this time. His driver's licence had been revoked again soon after his parole ended because of his everlasting citations, and when his friends were unable to pay his fines he'd spend a week or so in one or another county jail. He no longer seemed to care, and the time spent in jail was time he was away from drugs and other temptations. It made me so sad for him to end up a real 'jail kid' after all.

| SEVENTY-FOUR |

When Allen returned from India, Gavin had a party for him and invited me. Among the guests was Alan Watts, who had married Gavin's niece. I knew none of the other guests except Allen and Peter

Orlovsky, Gavin's nephew, and Joel Andrews and his wife, and since the rooms were lighted only by candles, I could barely distinguish features, only groups of bodies.

Allen called me over to where he was seated with Alan Watts, both of them in lotus positions on the floor. They invited me to sit between them, a wine jug making a fourth. Allen was wearing his Indian apparel of white loose trousers and tunic, and I thought they suited him perfectly, his lengthening hair and beard consistent with this mode of dress. He and Watts compared notes on their trips to India, sages and ashrams they knew and loved, and the various Eastern teachings they enjoyed. My head swung back and forth as if watching a tennis match – hardly one word connecting with my brain. This was partly due, I supposed, to the fact that I'd only ever seen these words written, never heard.

Neal didn't appear that evening, and Peter Orlovsky only bolted in and out with girls, so I didn't get to talk to him. On a weekend soon after, however, Allen, Peter and another brother of Peter's, Julius, came to the house. Neal and Anne also managed to join us. Allen had bought a Volkswagen van, and they were excited showing us how well it served as a home. They brought groceries, and Allen cooked another of his gourmet dinners, while Peter insisted on doing the dishes afterwards. I asked Neal about Julius. He sat wherever Peter told him to, gazed into space, and never spoke. Neal explained he had entered a catatonic state when around nineteen; he must be about thirty by now. He had to be told to do everything, like 'sit down, Julie. Pick up your cup, put your cup down, etc.' He wasn't dangerous to others, but he had to be watched constantly. One night, they told me, he had started out the door in San Francisco and just kept walking. Peter found him nearly thirty miles away, doggedly plodding on. Neal claimed he himself had given Julie some LSD, whereupon he talked and behaved normally. That story was not confirmed, and I just let it go by.

We had thought Allen's hair was pretty long for a man, but Peter enthralled our youngsters when he removed his stocking cap, and thick waves of dark red hair spilled down between his shoulders. Poor Johnny had been gamely trying to grow his straight white hair out of the detested crew-cut he had endured until junior highschool, but as soon as the sides grew long enough to tuck behind his ears, the school would suspend him until he cut it. I didn't like the longer hair, but I agreed with him the school was overstepping its rights. From then on, all his friends would come to me when they were sent home, and I would cut off a quarter-inch, put it in an envelope and send it back to the Dean. That didn't work, but we tried.

Allen, Peter and Julius spent the night in the van, and Neal made Anne happy by sharing a bed with her at last. I thought he'd come a long way from denying her existence, and I felt he must have at last acknowledged our divorce. I forgot legal manoeuvres were meaningless to Neal. The next afternoon Allen, Peter and Julius all went back to the City, backing out of the drive to the chimes of finger cymbals and with voices raised in Hari to Lord Krishna, while I filmed the departure with the super-8 camera I'd gotten free with my new car. We had endured a good deal of chanting the previous evening, since it was Allen's passion now, but Peter had livened things up with his improvisations.

The next evening Jack telephoned, well on his way to oblivion, but I was still excited. 'Oh, Jack! How I wish you had been here last night! We could have had such a reunion – even Neal was here.'

Jack had asked for Neal, as he always did, no matter how many times I'd told him Neal did not live with me any more. Now he yelled, 'Who was that answered the phone? By God, I'll *kill* him – got my machete right here!'

'Jack, *Jack* – wait!' I tried to yell louder. 'That was John – John!'

'John? John who? Who the hell does he think – comin' into Neal's home – I'm gonna come out there and ...'

'Jack, stop it! It's Johnny, you know – our son.'

'The hell it is – Johnny's a kid – I know Johnny's voice, that warn't no kid ...'

'No, of course not – not any more. He's fourteen now, and five feet eight.'

Jack was silent a minute, then said more quietly, 'Yeah?' Another silence. It had indeed been a long time. Jack still sounded a bit dubious. 'Yeah? You sure?'

'Come on, Jack, you know there wouldn't be anybody else here; I'd tell you if I planned to marry again – that's out.'

'Listen – wait – gotta get another drink – just wait right there – don't go 'way.' I could hear him rustling about and a refrigerator door open, then a howl. He grabbed the phone again. 'God damn it – somebody's stole my whiskey – 'sgone!'

'Oh? Who could have done that?' I hated having to play up to these drunken conversations.

'My Maw! – damned ole alcoholic!'

'Jack! Shame – now cut that out.'

'Saaay – lissen you … d'ya know what I'd do to you if I were there right now? Hunh? I'd grab you an'…' I stopped my ears; I'd heard it all before, and coming from Jack it made me sicker than it would otherwise. He was yelling again. When I dared to listen, he'd begun to wind down. 'An' marriage, hunh? I won't marry you as long as Neal's alive. We gotta wait till the halls of Nirvana, like I said in *Big Sur*. You're Neal's wife, an' you better not come aknockin' on ma doh lessen yo got that death certificate in you han', y'heah?' He'd fall back on a Southern accent only at such times. Later I was unable to read *Pic*, remembering.

Before he called again, I had received the copy of *Big Sur* he'd promised, and this time he was almost sober. I thanked him for the book, 'and I really like it, Jack; seems to me you wrote more honestly this time…'

'Yeah, I guess – but listen, I've been to Paris since I last talked to you – to Brittany, looking up my family name and all. Then I got drunk and messed up again and just came home.' He sounded completely defeated, then he brightened. 'But listen, Carolyn, I went to the little church of St Louis de France en l'Isle – the church that is the sister of the one in Lowell where I was baptised, remember? And I've always wanted to see the original, like I used to tell you when we sat in Washington Square. Anyway, it was – well, wonderful – a rainy, misty night, see? And I came in out of the rain to the warm glowing candlelit chapel with its ancient statues and stained glass, and there'r these guys in red coats blowing long brass horns and an organ playing softly. I sat down in a pew and took off my old battered hat that I wear in the rain, and I was holding it in my lap, upside down, you know – so the rain would drip off – an' I'm sitting there spellbound, when a family comes up the aisle and the woman leans over and drops twenty centimes – four cents! – into my hat!' He stopped.

I didn't know what to say. A stab of pity shot through me; his voice was close to breaking. Then he said softly, 'Think of that.' He was quiet, thinking of that. The mood passed. 'My Maw said I should put the money in the poor box, and I should; I didn't think of it, I was so stricken.'

That was our last sober conversation, and soon after I received the last serious letter as well: he wrote that he didn't feel capable of living up to my knowledge (whatever that meant) but he understood me perfectly. He said he had always known nothing stood between him and me but my husband, his friend. He knew I had faith in him for that. He said it was true that he had turned into a drunk, an 'orating author', but he was fighting against it. It was all managed blindly by hundreds of people who were not ill-intended but who would not allow him to sit with me by the fire or have a day with Neal alone, and we had to and would stop it. He said I was the only woman in the world he could talk to without the subject being changed, or love with. He told me not to worry, he'd do his best by me and called me 'dear heart, sweet lady, lover'. He was going to Mexico to think alone, then come to California in the fall – or winter. He signed it with kisses.

Although he telephoned frequently after that, and wrote a few postcards, he was never really 'with' me again. As he called more and wrote less, I began to see it was a voluntary plunge into the void. Earlier I had not taken seriously his pronouncement that he intended to drink himself to death – the only escape.

| SEVENTY-FIVE |

There were periods now when Neal wouldn't turn up for a month or two, and I'd be vaguely worried about him. After one of these long absences when I was about to leave for work, a car swerved into the driveway with two Highway Patrol cars screaming in hot pursuit, lights flashing, sirens blaring. They parked their cars so as to completely block the drive. The sickening sensation surged through me I thought I was free from forever. I was shaking, but I mustered all the grit I could to walk calmly out of the house, locking the door for the first time since we'd bought it. As I approached the melee, Neal was emerging from the driver's seat of his car, and I could see within it several shaggy heads. A couple of the officers closed in on Neal. I didn't want to find out what it was about. With impatience I accosted one of the officers: 'Could someone move one of those cars; I have to go to work.' He replied courteously and swiftly backed a patrol car out of my way. To the other officer I said, 'I would appreciate any speed you can manage in dispatching your duty; it doesn't make me too popular with my neighbours'. He couldn't have been more polite. To Neal I said, 'I'll be home for lunch.'

As I typed out routine x-ray reports I became calmer, but wondered what was happening in my front yard. An odd idea flashed across my mind: Neal was in a big hurry to out-distance the police – was it possible he had planned to arrive after I had gone to work? Did he do this often when he knew neither I nor the children would be home? No, surely I'd have found evidence. Still, I felt a chill. Well, thank God, this time I'd locked the door.

My lunch hour arrived, and I rushed home, braced. Neal's car was still in the driveway. At the door I fumbled with the key; it wouldn't turn. I heard voices and found the door unlocked.

I hardly recognized my own living room; it was rearranged and disarranged, and four or five scruffy, hairy, black-dressed creatures sat on the floor or were draped over the furniture. I turned away to close the door and stifle my rising indignation. When I could, I asked for Neal. One of them said, 'The cops took him with them; he told us to wait here.'

'How did you get in?'

'We found a window we could open.' So much for my locked door. I went into my bedroom to think. It, too, was a shambles; bedclothes and pillows strewn about. I retreated to the kitchen while my anger rose like mercury in a thermometer as I picked up remnants of an uninvited feast, returned milk, cheese and eggs to the refrigerator, crumbled empty cracker and bread wrappings, put pans, glasses and dishes to soak in the sink. Had they left anything? By now I was so furious I had to make another dash for the bathroom and hold my head, trying desperately to remember some useful affirmations. In cases like this Neal would say, 'What would Jesus do?' He had said if anyone took your shirt, give him your coat, too. But *Jesus*, dear Jesus, give 'em an inch, and they take a mile! Go the extra mile? How about not casting pearls before swine? That's the one! Besides, my lunch hour was fast disappearing, along with my spiritual progress.

Still making a superhuman effort to remain serene, I went back to the kitchen and sat on the stool behind the counter that opened into the living room. Keeping my tone even, I said, 'I'm sorry, but I have to ask you all to go. This is my home, not Neal's.' My ire began to simmer again, and I had to measure my words. 'I have a job and go to work every day, not because I like it, but because I want what it provides, like this house, a car and food. I don't expect anyone else's labour to furnish these things for me. If you are genuinely in need, or if you allow me the opportunity to *give* to you, I might give you all I have, but if you simply take what I've worked for without asking and take me for granted as well…' I had to stop, and I felt rotten, making me resent Neal and them all the more.

Sheepishly, they began to collect their scattered goods. One girl came over to me and said reverently, 'May I shake your hand?' I wanted to belt her, but I couldn't tell if she were mocking me or sincere. At least she surprised me, so I couldn't reply. When I closed the door behind them, I released my pent-up anger putting the house back in order. When next I saw Neal I insisted such an episode would never be repeated.

'Don't make *me* call the police, Neal,' I threatened, knowing I never could, but did he?

Gavin was having his problems with Neal at the other end of the line. Gavin had hoped to be a magus to Neal on his release from prison, and offered Neal the use of his home in return. Instead, Neal took advantage of the home but ignored the counsel. After one of Neal's visits, Gavin wrote him:

> Dear Neal – (No longer Saint Neal!)… you see, the ruthless way you carry out whatever impulse your *desire body* may have makes one realize what a complete slave you really are. You talk glibly about Cayce and all that spiritual stuff, but make no effort to become master of yourself. You and I had an agreement, and about half the time you lived up to it. I very much wanted to rescue you from that shadow underworld of racing touts and junkies – & loved you so much that I was willing to go far out on a limb to do so. Love to all from your very sad friend and would-be comrade, Gavin.

By Christmas things were getting worse, and Gavin's card to me bore a dismal message: 'Neal was here for a week, but I finally had to ask them to leave, as chaos was taking over. Do drop in for any meal you like at any time. Love to you & the kids, Gavin.'

Neal may have been wearing out his welcome with his old friends, but he was still capable of making new ones. One of them was a writer and publisher of a literary magazine in Palo Alto, Gordon Lish. Neal often visited his home, alone or with Anne, and in exchange for their hospitality gave of himself, charming Gordon's wife and children and endearing himself to them forever.

| SEVENTY-SIX |

Also in Palo Alto, Neal became friends with Ken Kesey, whose book *One Flew Over the Cuckoo's Nest* had just been published. As Neal now added LSD and other new drugs to his diet, I discouraged visits even more. I had no desire to meet these new friends, nor have them influence the children. So far, I had seen nothing of merit in the lifestyle these rebels promoted, and I was having enough trouble with adolescents, the school and my feelings of inadequacy. So I told Neal to come alone or not at all. He did so until my fears diminished.

The group that collected around Kesey called themselves 'the Merry Pranksters', and occasionally one or other of them were permitted to come with Neal, since he sometimes needed a ride. The one considered the most acceptable to me, and who came most often, was Ron Bivert, who owned a bookshop in Santa Cruz and had quiet good manners and clean clothes, even if his hair was cut in the style of Prince Valiant of comic-book fame. All of the Pranksters had nicknames, and Ron's was 'Hassler'. Of course the children got a big kick out of the names, as well as the escapades Neal recited. No wonder, I thought, since most of them sounded on a junior-high level.

One day Neal told us about a proposed trip they all wanted to take around the country in Kesey's new wildly painted ex-school bus. It was not to be simply a prank, but a very serious mission to enlighten the rest of the USA in new-age thinking, and they planned to film the whole trip for a socially significant movie. The destination printed on the front of the bus was 'FURTHER'.

The plan actually materialized, and we had some peace during their absence, but in far less time than I expected Neal was back. He had started out as the driver of the bus ('Speed Limit' his nickname) but had left early to return to California. Hassler came with Neal to see me and tell us about the great success of their endeavour. He had taken a shoe box full of photos, which we all poured over. Not too surprisingly, they encountered a good deal of red-neck resistance, and I found myself recognizing some of my own attitudes mirrored in the faces that lined the streets of cities they passed through.

Weeks extended into months, and the reports were that the movie was to be professionally edited. Ken came with Neal once, and assured me it would be a great film, and Neal would make a lot of money. In the end, however, fun and games were more important. The editor was turned on to LSD, and along with wanton destruction of film and equipment, lack of purpose and persistence, the movie was abandoned as a serious effort.

Ken was now living in a cabin in the woods in La Honda, a place down the coast from San Francisco. Great floodlights were installed in the trees, along with amplifiers, and much of the film ended up draped among the branches. Most of the Pranksters and assorted hangers-on shared the premises, among them Neal and Anne. As far as I could see they all thought the purpose of life was spontaneous 'experience', so at least they had that.

The children revelled in Neal's visits and his tales. He'd tell us of his encounters with the police while driving the bus, such as the time the bus stalled in the middle of the thoroughfare. Neal got the policemen to push the bus to one side while he directed traffic at the intersection. If Neal got carried away and began salting his stories with descriptions a bit too 'adult' in my view, or too much about drugs, I would nudge him or kick him under the table, which only brought on a chorus of 'Oh, Mom'. My influence was weakening even more as they entered their teens, and the school system was more an adversary than an ally. John was not performing well, in spite of testing as high as tests go. I suppose he was bored, but he was branded a 'poor achiever', and the school's idiotic cure for this was punishment, sentencing him to classes with even less stimulation rather than more. Instead of Chaucer and Shakespeare, they gave him Tarzan. He had a looney counsellor who demanded I read the book by her psychiatrist to understand my weird son. *Alice in Wonderland* again. In spite of her I tried every way I could to motivate John, without success. So I tried passing the buck to Neal, hoping he might help. I sent a letter to him at La Honda full of all my insecurity and anger.

> Now I believe a possible explanation for John's trouble
> has come to me, but so far no answers as to what to do
> about it. Here's the picture as I see it: Could it be that

John's father, whom he loved more than anyone, has rejected all the values I try to inspire in him and has chosen a way of life in which none of these values are important or needed? John has been told repeatedly his father, too, has a brilliant mind, and I can tell him you are the most miserable of man, but is he going to believe that? Why should he, when all he ever sees or hears is that you lead the most carefree hilariously delightful existence – no dull books, no rules, no responsibilities, no respect for law – free to do just as you please in a perpetual pre-school level...You didn't even lose the love of your family and can see them whenever you've nothing better you want to do. When you're through telling them how great you are and how fun your activities are, you can just eat, sleep or watch TV. Now, how can anything top that?...I tell you all this because, though I doubt it will help now, I want you to stop building the big glorious pictures of life. I told you not to 'drop in' but that, too, you ignore. John *loved* the bus tour, naturally. No doubt he can't wait to join the happy band – and his books are less and less appealing. So, here we go again. If you can't contribute something of value, don't come at all.

I can't say what the effect on him would be if you vanish, should you choose to, but I do know what is resulting from the present visits, and that, at least, must stop. Naturally, I'd prefer your cooperation, but I don't know if you're able to. Any comments would be appreciated. Love always.

No answer was forthcoming, but Neal stopped coming so often, and even took up the considerate habit of calling me first. This was during the time he was in and out of jail, also, so there were longer periods without any communication, let alone support, moral or otherwise. I had carefully explained to Neal that the $200-per-month child support awarded by the divorce settlement was merely a figure my lawyer had suggested only in order to preclude any argument from the judge, but he was not bound by it. Still, Neal harped on it constantly, adding it up and keeping track to the penny how much he owed me. All he actually *did* about it was bother other people asking them for money for us. I cringed to see him go from con man to beggar. And, I figured, it was the one last thin thread he held to for any self-esteem and connection with 'respectability'.

One of the strange communications the likes of which were to arrive frequently in the future was written by him and Anne 'in the corridors of the S.F. Hosp'.

> Dear Carolyn; Dearest: This $15 will be for kick-off on my beginning to send you money regularly again; no job yet…(Note from Ann) Dear Carolyn…Neal & Sharon & her brother and me (again) are all sitting here…I started to write you but couldn't because I promised Neal not to. Hope you are OK & that the money Neal (& Sharon) sends helps. Still trying (to get him) Love him still. I've been reading desolation angels and the Dream Book – all about Evelyn & Cody. Neal's reading Big Sur now…I wanted to tell you just simply how devastating it was to know beyond all doubt what if you don't mind being called 'sweet,' what a sweet woman you are. Because secretly I thought the opposite, just because I wanted to, I guess (a long time ago) I just wanted to tell you…

Neal took it up again: 'Dear Jami (stage name, natch) & Cathy: Well I hear your Sunday School's slipped some. Gee, I'd like to conduct some more soon; help your mother by being less nervous, OK?'

Then to me again: 'If don't get strictly business trip to Idaho underway tomorrow or so, may not go, so hip hip hooray! P.S. WORK WORK – if we, my soul and me, can have lasted till today in the hell of 365 times not going to unemployment for your $200 a month (see you if got car). We can also reverse. Love, N.'

On an early trip East Neal had written postcards to me, and he had expected Jack to give him a sizeable sum. What he had received was $10, Jack using the size of his phone bill as an excuse for giving no more. With Allen, Neal fared better as a rule – for a while. From Seattle now, however, a postcard came from Allen:

> Dear Carolyn: Up here on camping trip with Gary Snyder. I'll be back in S.F. in a month, hope to see you then. Neal asked me to send you some $ which I said I would, but then I bought a car and used up all my bank reserves, so was not able to, I'm sorry. Neal seemed in good shape when I saw him in SF – Few or no chemicals & mostly natural energy, more lucid than of recent yore…

Neal covered a lot of ground in these last four years, going East again in the summer of 1965, and this time he did not write to me; I supposed he'd run out of excuses. He was still guilt-ridden about us, and even considered taking a job driving a truck for a few weeks in Chicago.

Anne was living with the Keseys at La Honda, and wrote to Neal to keep him posted on his friends as well as her own lonely vigil. She summed up their lifestyle quite clearly:

> I didn't think you'd really gone, and now I'll just wait and see what happens. I'm glad you didn't take me with you, as I am having a great time here, trying to seduce, unsuccessfully, every male member of the gang. Everyone misses you especially me... And I never had such a gorgeous time as we spent together at the Lish's. There's lots of things I want to say like if you love me why did you leave, etç.... I'm helping paint the bus, washing and cleaning for Faye. It's a beautiful morning; the Hermit gave me some white powder he thinks is ground up aspirin, in your spirit (and mine) I gobbled it up, and I must admit I haven't got a headache, it might have been a little LSD, whoopee... Ken wrote a story about you before the bus trip, which I typed, and June helped, too. It's good. The part about you was very revealing and showed how others look at you, again, which is not at all the way I see you, for I see you as my love not as a character, running wild. I'll copy it out for you:

> 'Cassady and crew have arrived, banging on the gate, and he didn't go to sleep last night with his mind on freedom. "Been up for days, Chief, since we were out here last. In fact in great shape, and look here, *three* to bring, now what do you think of that?" Anne and Sharon on each side, and to this usual twosome he indicates that he may have added the blonde Swede, trying burlesquely to put his arms around all three. "Oh, no, no, no!" admonishing himself, breaking away becoming confidential about a score, or two bucks for some minor repair on some ailing vehicle somewhere, making my refusal somehow inevitable by the tone of his asking, always skilled at wheedling a "no" from me, as one of the orneriest old farts to ever draw breath, as well as being one of the most phenomenal testimonies of the hidden human potential, talking and

moving while doom cracks under his feet, a ball of burning time.'

This view Ken had of Neal reminded me of a part of Neal's last reading, in which Dr Gordon had said, 'Strange, you have always led, but you have always felt you followed – but they wrote about you…you program yourself, as you know…you are standing on a precipice…do not be frightened – you are in the NOW – and – tomorrow – may not – be – your – gift. When you see the greatness of the inner you – you will walk a different path.'

Anne continued:

> My, my, shame and a pox on your harem. I wish we were married, the ring is on my right hand now. This typewriter is labelled 'Neal's Printing Co.,' and they're playing 'I can't get no satisfaction.' That's true all right! They just hid the last of the IT290 and I tried to follow Babbs & the Hermit to see if I could get any, but was sidetracked by the foxy Mt. Girl, and Sandy sends his love, as he eats a sandwich made of Jewish rye bread and guess what, peanut butter and jelly. I made some cookies yesterday, and put Scotch lemon curd on the top, and we had venison one night, they just played 'I got you, Babe.' We should stop believing all the unhealthy things that seem to be. After all we're still alive…Please come back and tell me to come to you and how…Forgive and forget? and the casual attitude to Sharon…I still can't believe it, my love…Love to my Cassady and everybody's Cassady.

Neal wrote Kesey a 22-page, play-by-play description of his trip, and inserted an answer to Anne, commenting on every thought she'd expressed, and ending with:

> your love is the nourishment of my life – would that my life were the nourishment of your love, or at least more so. Thanks for the little quote from Ken. I don't think it will ever be that way again (all those girls, I mean) '…after all we're still alive' – that's right! & you damn well better keep it that way, or I'll spank your bottom good in the Astral plane too. Hoping to see you again. Love always, Neal.

Neal often spoke to me of getting away from Anne (as he did all of us), yet in his expression of sentiments like these he held out the lifeline of hope, and none of us could let go. The same names kept coming up in his correspondence, others were added, but none subtracted. The girl in Salt Lake City was still on the list, and he still visited her each time he travelled, once even taking Anne with him, so the two Annes became friends. The Utah Anne made our Anne look extremely conventional by comparison. Our Anne told me they went to the races, and while she was seated Neal and the girl held up a betting window at gunpoint. I couldn't believe that of Neal, but I could believe that afterwards they drag-raced each other in two cars down the main street of the city.

Sharon's family moved to Los Angeles, but she was not about to give up Neal, and waited for him to rescue her. 'I love you and am still waiting for you. Hope you get your car running soon…If you want to get ahold of me here, you'll have to phone when my parents aren't home…I miss you…I can't even see or talk to…anyone I knew in Palo Alto as long as I live here. But I trust when you get here you'll find a way…'

Sharon was a mousy girl in glasses and Buster Brown shoes, but like Anne and Natalie, Neal often attached these women hoping to help them. Compassionate though he was, few were saved, all enslaved, and this fact became another guilty burden on his suffering soul.

| SEVENTY-SEVEN |

The Pranksters were now engaged in running up and down the coast going to colleges or other gatherings and giving shows they called 'acid tests'. Refreshment was Kool-Aid spiked with LSD, loud rock music, lots of Day-Glo paint and splashing coloured lights. From all I could glean from Neal's efforts to make some sense of them to me, they consisted largely of a lot of sensory self-indulgence and pointless nonsense, not to mention danger.

Tough bikers, like the Hell's Angels, were attracted to these events, and although their lifestyle shared common interests, there were wide differences as well, violence the chief among them. For instance, once in San Francisco a biker made a rude remark to Anne and Neal objected. The biker went for Neal, who dashed away from him until he'd outrun him. Some would say this was cowardice, but Neal didn't know the meaning of that word. To him (and to me) it was just common sense: he didn't want to get hurt, and he didn't want to hurt anyone else.

I thought the Pranksters just wasted a lot of time and energy, when they could have used both to create something to benefit mankind, such as Ken's book. It was not only proving to be of great value to psychologists, but was also beginning to carry weight towards a reform of the disgraceful mental health system. I believed *that* was the way to change objectionable factions in society, surely, rather than the kind of influence he was exerting over young minds now.

Perhaps Neal's sojourns in jails were a welcome escape from the devotees who yearned for him in so many near and far places. Could it be, I wondered, that he had accomplished at least one overcoming? Had he let go all fear of police and prison? Or was the fearlessness part of a total surrender of his will to live? I heard he was taking more chances in cars and vans – rolling them purposely, and driving more carelessly.

There was one incident told me by my writer friend Billy Craddock, of volunteering to join Neal, who had asked if anyone wanted to watch him roll a VW end-over-end. This he did, said Billy, never stopping talking, and returned the car, now resembling crushed tinfoil. Billy did not volunteer again.

Anne was always ready and waiting for Neal to get out of jail, and often wrote me long letters of her hopeless love.

> He'll never love & respect me like he does you, but if only he'd not hate me…I'd like to see you…and you are my only friend, really if I may so presume…Last night I turned down my landlord, trying to become a lady – (like Neal tells me you are) waiting for him to return at midnight, he didn't, of course, and the rent's not paid, so I did get f___ed in another sense. Neal says, 'just try to be true' then goes off assuming I'm not and leaves me holding an ideal in my empty arms & my empty stomach & my empty head – Oh, empty bed! I told him to listen to you…

I'd answer with motherly advice and sympathy.

> The very fact he returns to you so often – even if you are but a lighthouse in the dark…still I'm sure there's a strong bond…His jail tours are a shame, but I can't bring myself to any emotion about it. All his recent escapades

are so senseless...death would appear to be a blessing to him so many times. I do so wish I could help you...you are very wise and very sweet and must be awfully strong to have this struggle...

Be patient with yourself. Keep writing and much love...

When Neal was in jail, Anne probably enjoyed the short time she could be sure where he was, and how well I knew that his drugless letters were all any girl could wish for. He wrote them to me, too, filled with the old brilliance, zeal, metaphysical quotes, reassurances, vows: for pages he wove the pattern of another dreamy future, 'knowing, as we do, when all is said, that what I truly want is only to succeed as husband and father...' Or,

> I pray each nite that *we* might find our way clear to remarry & still live up to our missions – mutual and otherwise. I'm just about ready to go forth as a real man; not thinking of self first any more ...but truly inspiring & helping as I know I can – and must! Have so much to tell you...P.S. Please, love, search your heart; is there still room for me? *Love*, Neal.

While Neal was in jail in San Mateo, Ken was arrested for possessing marijuana, a previous 'bust' still pending in Palo Alto, so he staged a suicide and fled to Mexico. What next? I wondered. The careless performance was soon unmasked by the police. Now Ken added an automatic felony to his blooming record. That summer the group went to Mexico to find him, Neal and Anne included. From Neal I received strange wobbly notes on any kind of scrap paper or obscure postcards, but sometimes small amounts of money, either US or Mexican. In one letter, more lucid than most, he did inform me he had sent Anne back to the States soon after their arrival in Mexico. I could not tell what magic had made it possible this time, and Anne's letter a few weeks later gave no clue. She was braving it alone in Venice, California, a seaside town I'd been told was rapidly degenerating into a hippy haven.

> Dear Carolyn, I held off writing as long as possible, due to the fact that our friendship is a fluke, so it isn't easy to disregard the implications. But I do miss you, and I've been playing the races again (and losing) and going to sex orgies (imagine – 30 people all copulating in plush

Hollywood pads) and painting (one painting – all breasts, beads and eyelashes) and water skiing and swimming – and going out with handsome bachelors, movie actors, & a bank robber! in Cadillacs and Mercedes, and I can't complain except I'm trying to catch a man of my very own, and, to that end, it's not very wise to contact Neal, by proxy or otherwise. (I wonder if I deserve my very own man?) My horoscope today said to take any advice, but since I lost my last $ at the racetrack yesterday, and the rent isn't paid, nobody has offered any advice! (I live on the ocean and its effect is good for peace and calamity.) I'm afraid my luck may have changed and if so, I have enough sleeping pills to leave this life. So I'm for accepting a 'no' or a beating & my heart is pure, and the next time you hear of me, let's hope it's my funeral or wedding and put an end to this disgrace.

PS: I've been invited to the bull-fights in Mexico with a real, blue-eyed darling Mexican bull fighter.

I figured she'd postpone her suicide until after the bullfight, but mad as this girl seemed, it was impossible for me to censure her; there was something so real, so honest about her. A lack of phoney efforts to sell herself as anyone other than she was, and no excuses or apologies, and I loved her 'pure heart'.

Kesey wearied of exile, and the group sneaked him back into California 'to rub salt in the wounds of J. Edgar Hoover,' he said. A strange 'coincidence' occurred when Neal was on his way back with Ken. He had never ever telephoned me while away, but for some reason he made an expensive phone call, and with no apparent point. In the course of the conversation he told me he was going to be in San Antonio the next day. Our Cathy had married a boy who'd been drafted and was stationed there, and Cathy was due to have a baby at any time. I gave Neal her address, and he arrived at the hospital just after she had delivered his first grandson, both Cathy and Neal speechless at the apparently accidental nature of the reunion.

Neal came to see me on his return, and told me Kesey planned a big Halloween party, the last of the acid tests, and he'd wear a costume so as not to be recognized by the police. I seriously doubted that, but they all thought it terribly daring and exciting. It was to be a 'graduation' from LSD, Kesey planning some charade about reassuring the authorities that he would now inform young people it would be better not to take LSD after all. Neal urged me to come. I would never have considered it, especially alone, but when I told Helen about it, she was curious, and thought we should learn about these things, having gullible kids of our own. Neither of us had seen any of the psychedelic world first hand, only the descriptions in the media, which we knew often distorted things.

Gavin had visited me the previous week, and I had driven him to the home of Gina Cerminara (the author whose book had changed our lives), where he had been asked to speak to her psychology students. When he returned to San Francisco, he wrote me a note.

> Thanks for your hospitality – so simple & loving and fine. Came back to a shambles here – some of Neal's chelas had got Cappy high on acid – pot all over the floor – cigarette butts in half-glasses of good Red Mtn. I could have used. After listening to those tapes of his life readings, all my fury concentrated against Neal. I'm glad I have his address. He's going to get a blast... What a contrast to the beautiful, well-ordered life you have achieved! The more I live the more I realize that the object of evolution is to make order out of chaos. Neal & his followers reverse this process. They are sliding down the mountain – we are climbing up! I will always love Neal, but the way one loves a lost soul, hoping to redeem it. Love to all four of you, Gavin.

Cappy was a 40-year-old man 'going on 13', we used to say – maladjusted in an undefinable way and who lived with Gavin and served as general brownie and scapegoat. He was a lovable chap, a veteran of some war and as fond of Red Mountain wine as was Gavin. (His glass was always half empty, never half full.) Several years ago he had arrived one rainy night at Gavin's door. Gavin was reading *On the Road*, on the cover of which was a drawing of a man who looked just like Cappy, so Gavin invited him in, and he never left.

On the day of the party, Helen and I went to Gavin's to await directions from Neal. I had no desire to see or hear Neal 'perform'. I had seen enough photos and heard enough – more than enough, and I only wanted to cry at his humiliation. I couldn't help thinking of the tragic professor in the film *The Blue Angel*, whose obsession resulted in his degradation into the role of performing bear. Neal had now added sound to the non-stop sentences he once only wrote.

He exploited his brilliant mind by talking incessantly 'on three levels at once,' Gavin pointed out, and it was too much for me. When he and I were alone and he'd start talking, I'd attempt to stay with him and his lightning shifting thoughts until my mind would spin from the effort, and I'd have to beg him to stop. It took a great effort on his part. Whatever I could digest made good sense, but it took too much concentration too long to follow all the leads. I knew he was simply letting out all the thoughts he'd had most of his life that he couldn't write down – just 'getting them out' with no aim or purpose. That wasted mind.

Neal telephoned two or three times during the afternoon to keep us posted on the efforts to find a suitable location for the party, as one after the other failed. We heard on the radio that Ken had been apprehended already, but Neal said everyone had pitched in and bailed him out for the evening, so the excitement was at an even higher pitch.

Helen and I were far from bored while we awaited news. At Gavin's there was always a perpetual stream of visitors, and they were an assortment of individuals seldom encountered elsewhere. Today one was the 'champion swimmer of China', or so he said. A short thick man who jogged in wearing short shorts and had just ridden his bike the 82 miles to Santa Cruz and back asked us to guess his age. Wrong. And he jogged out again.

While he talked to us so briefly in the kitchen, in the living room Gavin was entertaining a pear-shaped large man, well dressed all in black – suit, shirt and tie – with a bald head and a Fu Manchu moustache, soft features and protruding large dark eyes. He waved a pudgy hand languidly as he spoke, and on his index finger shone a gigantic topaz ring.

After Gavin had escorted him to the door, Helen and I pounced:

'Who was *that* Queen, Gavin?' Helen asked. Gavin had one of his sputtering attacks.

'Queen? Queen? Why he is one of the *most* virile men I know – has a lovely wife and children – why, how could you think –?'

'I thought so, too, Gavin. Why the masquerade, then – and that obscene rock on his finger?' It was irresistible not to keep kidding Gavin; his responses were so delicious.

'Oh my,' Gavin sighed and sat back in his chair. 'That was Anton LeVey, the famous leader of the Satanist Church. You remember,

Carolyn, we stopped by his house on our way back from the Highland Games last summer. He wasn't home, so I couldn't show you the occult furnishings and booby-traps in his house – nor his pet lion.'

'Oh yes, I remember – the house with the peeling black paint – very spooky.'

'Pet lion??' Helen looked blankly at Gavin.

'Yes. He has this huge pet lion, a male,' explained Gavin. 'Now, however, the neighbours are objecting to his roars, so he may have to put him in a zoo. I never heard him roar, but I do remember sitting next to him at the dinner table one night, and the thing began licking the side of my head. Well, you know their tongues are so *rough* – like a metal file – I thought my ear would come right off. So I asked Anton if he could stop him from doing that, and Anton said, "Oh just hit him in the mouth and he'll stop." Well – I wasn't about to hit this five-hundred-pound beast in the mouth!'

Neal called again, and now informed us a warehouse had been found in the Mission district where the party could be held, and he'd call again and tell us how to find it. I suddenly thought it odd Neal had not come up to Gavin's to see us. Gavin explained, 'He knows I'm angry with him, that's why. The last time he was here, he picked up the phone and began calling long-distance. I told him he was welcome to use the phone any time he liked, but I'd appreciate it if he wouldn't make toll calls on it – you wouldn't *believe* my phone bill; it's astronomical! And, do you know, he got so mad, he *threw* the telephone at me? Look at it, see? There's a chip out of the base. Why, I've never known Neal to do a thing like that before.' Gavin was right. Neal's temper was getting shorter, and it frightened me to think what he might do next.

Cappy came in to tell me a friend had arrived who was in 'Q' with Neal, and could he bring him in to meet me. I said, 'Well, yes, I guess so,' and Cappy ushered in a short swarthy muscular man. This one had thin greying black hair brushed back from his face and hanging in wisps to his shoulders. Around his brow was a thick braided leather band. He had a short grizzled beard and moustache, and no upper teeth. He was wearing nondescript trousers and boots, and his coat was a naval officer's summer khaki. It was too small, and tightly buttoned. Discoloured oblong patches bore evidence of the removal of insignia and 'fruit salad'. 'You knew Neal?' I opened.

He nodded. 'I've just recently been released. This last time I was in for eight years.'

'What for?' I asked sociably.

'Murder.' His tone was equally sociable. I couldn't go on this way, but he could. 'I live on Alcatraz now. I'm an Apache medicine man.' I was trying to remember if Indians had beards. Helen took over:

'How do you treat illnesses?'

'Oh, well, with herbs mostly – and ceremonies, you know.' We didn't, but now Cappy reminded him of the time, and after asking us to guess his age, and after happily informing us we were seventeen years off, he followed Cappy to the front door, grinning edentulously. Helen and I wondered what this age thing was today.

It was getting late. We discussed whether or not we felt up to acid test graduations to be followed by the long drive on the freeway after dark.

'Why don't you come with me, instead?' Gavin piped up. 'Anton came to invite me to a black mass he's conducting tonight – it is Halloween, after all, and the mass is being held in the Wax Museum.'

'What's a "black mass"?' Helen and I chorused, but Gavin had gone over to his desk to find the invitation and didn't hear.

'Let's see, I don't know if I can bring guests.' He studied the wildly decorated card. 'It doesn't say, but I'll call Anton.' When he'd hung up, 'No, Anton says one of you would be welcome as my guest, but guests must be restricted to pairs – absolutely.' So that settled that, and we didn't dare ask Gavin who his 'pair' would be. Later that night at home I looked up black mass in my occult encyclopedia and called Helen.

'It says here why only couples are allowed at these things,' and I read her the lurid description. We broke up in laughter, imagining what might have happened if we two dumb females had found ourselves trapped in such a ceremony.

Instead, hoping our guardian angels were in attendance, we headed for home and bid Gavin farewell. As it wasn't yet dark, we decided to detour and search for the warehouse. We followed Neal's instructions and found it easily. I would have liked to talk to Neal before going in, but he was nowhere to be seen. I did see Mountain Girl sitting on a car fender nursing her baby, and I asked her about Neal. She told me he had been there, but was gone again.

'He'll be back sometime, I'm sure.' So we entered a narrow dark hallway partitioned from the main warehouse room. In that vast space with no windows it was very dim. Only a few scattered hanging light bulbs furnished splotches of light wherever men were working. We made out the bandstand across a large open space, but beyond that there were only beams, posts and cave-like openings on the far side. A few rows of old theatre seats were arranged to our right near the entrance, so we sat down to await developments and Neal. As I'd noted often, Neal and friends had nothing if not time. We waited and waited for something to happen.

A few Pranksters ambled about, some setting up band equipment, others lolling on mattresses around the floor. We saw Kesey's cousin, who, like the other members of the inner circle, wore white coveralls with patches of American flags. We were surprised to see so many small children, and Helen made a face and shuddered.

'Poor kids.'

'Yeah,' I agreed. 'When they grow up they won't have a choice of a lifestyle their parents had.' By now teenage boys and girls began to swarm, all in bizarre outfits. We couldn't tell if they were Halloween costumes or their daily garb.

The sound system worked well as a band struck up. Ken had expected The Grateful Dead, but they had a previous engagement. Between the sets of shouted and blasted 'music' by the spontaneous replacement, someone did something of an electronic nature. I wondered if the point was to find out just how much the human ear and nerves could tolerate. I had read that the 'pulse' beat of rock music was the opposite of that of the earth's pulse rate, so creating an energy drain, necessitating even louder noise and more physical stimulants – like strobe lights and drugs or alcohol – to generate energy in the body.

No conversation was now possible; it was even difficult to think. The centre of the hall was crowded with squirming or wildly leaping bodies, and a few wiggled by the wings near us, their faces devoid of expression, their eyes glazed or closed. Behind us against the wall were more rows of seats, and through the smoke we could see some painted faces dully staring nowhere, and beneath these human masks catatonic bodies with drooping limbs.

Kesey strolled around the fringe in front of us. He had donned his white tights, red boots, a red and white satin cape, and across his bare chest a red, white and blue sash – his Superman outfit. He didn't see us, or at least gave no sign of recognition, and he was evidently in no hurry to get on with the graduation ceremonies. The sutures of my skull began to stretch. We then had to move aside for an invasion by TV cameramen, who climbed around and over us. In their wake a half dozen elegantly dressed men and women craned their necks to view the scene. When I could stand the pain no longer, I looked at Helen, and she reached for her bag. Neal had not returned, and I suspected he'd not miss us. It took the entire ride home with the car windows open to shrink my head and restore my ears and nerves to normal. Helen was silent, too, until we were nearly home. 'God – that's a far cry from our idea of fun when we were that age.'

We watched the late news and, needless to say, the film was edited in such a way that the whole impression was of a wild bacchanalian rite with much greater depravity than even we had thought. It angered us considerably; there were enough serious implications in the real scene not to make it appear worse than it already was. Evidently the newsmen got tired of waiting too, because the graduation ceremonies were not shown. Later we learned Neal had shown up to add his bit, and I'm glad I missed that.

Ken had made little ID cards with a picture of Uncle Sam pointing his finger and saying 'Can YOU pass the Acid Test?' On the back was a photo of the recipient with the personal data, then 'I am a member of INTREPID TRIPS, INC. and am doing nothing,' signed. Neal gave me one of these, but mine was stolen when my wallet was; I still have his.

| SEVENTY-EIGHT |

Neal's entanglements with the law had become just plain sloppy. There were no longer issues involved; he simply indulged himself at will, paid the minimum penalty and continued his disregard for restrictions. Apparently, early Sunday mornings were the times the authorities thought best for trapping, because we were now periodically aroused by the two clean-cut, overcoated gentlemen inquiring for Neal at that time – a routine that continued long after his death. I began to get a 'Big brother is watching you' paranoia, and I from then on refused Neal asylum at home except in extreme need, although it made me sad to see more bridges burned.

He seldom called me any more just for news or a chat, and when he asked to see me, I'd agree only if we could meet at a friend's. Above all, I never wanted to witness his arrest, nor to subject our home to further suspicion and surveillance.

One day in the spring of 1966 he called me at work and asked to see me. I told him I was planning to attend a lecture in San Jose by Hugh Lynn, and wouldn't he like to meet me there and see Hugh Lynn as well. He was delighted. 'Great! I'll see you at 7:30 *sharp*.'

John was away for the night, so I asked Jami, now aged 16, if she'd like to come along. We arrived a little early, taking seats near the back of the hall so we could catch sight of Neal at either entrance. We sat through the inspiring lecture, but there was no sign of Neal. This wasn't too surprising, but we were disappointed.

On the way out we waited to speak to Hugh Lynn, and here came Neal striding towards us. He was wearing Kesey's red cowboy boots, tan jeans and a light blue velour shirt. It was fun to see him dressed in something other than old work clothes, and he was quite tanned – something he had always insisted was impossible for his sensitive skin. He looked better and younger than I'd seen him in years. My heart skipped a beat.

Jami and I broke into welcoming smiles, and he hugged us both. Then I saw Ken and a few of his friends standing by. I turned to Neal: 'There's Hugh Lynn; do go say hello; he's been asking for you, and it's been such a long time…'

Neal went to him, but to my sorrow and chagrin for them both Neal affected a phoney bravado that Hugh Lynn was unable to penetrate with sincere inquiries. I knew it meant Neal felt guilty for having failed this man who had tried so hard to help him. I said nothing.

Neal rejoined us and asked if we'd like to go with him to a friend's house for a while and chat. Jami was eager to go, and I thought it might be a good idea for her to see some of this group while I was along.

We drove to the address Neal had given us. Whoever lived there wasn't home, and a young girl was babysitting. Jami and I sat in the living room, Neal paced about or stood on the hearth, shifting from one foot to the other, preoccupied. Some friends were in the kitchen, others came and went, one busied himself flirting with the babysitter. All I could make of it was that someone was telephoning to find the host, and probably whatever else they lacked. It was approaching midnight when Jami whispered to me, 'What's happening?'

'What always happens, honey, as far as I know. Nothing. Waiting, hunting for someone or something and more waiting. It seems to be what Neal and his friends do best. You had enough?'

'Yes; let's go home,' she replied and sighed. I'd no idea why Neal asked to see me or asked us there.

The next day around noon Neal called again. He and Kesey were going to a concert by The Grateful Dead, and he wanted to take John along to meet them. It was the last thing I wanted, but I knew John would be furious if he learned I'd denied him this thrill. Neal promised not to drive, not to smoke pot, etc. etc., and they'd get him home in time for dinner.

They collected John from school, and I spent the afternoon positive-thinking. About 5.30 Kesey called me at work telling me they were home safe and sound, and if I approved they'd like to stay for dinner.

'Uh – well, sure, Ken; I'll stop by the store on my way home. What would you like?'

'Now just never you mind. You forget all about it and come straight home; I'll take care of everything.'

When I arrived home, I was handed a beer and told to stay out of the kitchen. While Ken's masterpiece was cooking, I filmed John, Ken and Neal playing catch on the front lawn. John had had a memorable afternoon, and Neal had kept his promises, 'Zonkers' having done all the driving. What a blessed relief not to have to scold! Topping it all was a dinner as delicious as any I'd had. And I liked Ken a lot. He kept saying to Neal, 'She's just like Faye! She's just like Faye!' His wife was a homemaker and mother from the old school like me – with some variations.

The week following, Allen called from San Francisco and asked if he could come for the weekend. It was his birthday.

'Is there a chance Neal can be found and persuaded to join us?'

I urged Allen to come, and promised to do my best to find Neal. The Pranksters were between pranks, recuperating from their second Mexican trip or searching for new fields to conquer. So many of them in the area made me nervous; I hoped Neal's efforts to include the children in their activities would not become a habit, although the children naturally wished otherwise.

Their friends at school had become increasingly aware of Neal's identity, and they were all so struck with hero-worship of the whole gang; I was receiving less support for my uncordial attitude. In spite of Neal's good performance on the day of the concert, I knew better than to count on him every time. At the same time, I was ashamed of my former hostility towards Ken, who impressed me greatly with his warm empathy and kindness, and I wished to make it up to him. I'm sure he understood. Allen's request gave me an idea.

It was a bit frightening, but after much pro and con ruminating I felt it a unique opportunity to accomplish several goals at once. I would invite the lot, not only Neal, and perhaps if the children and their friends were in the midst of these people *en masse* and at ease, they might see them in a more realistic light, and even gain some insights into the reasons for my restraint – I did hope not too dramatically. I told John and Jami to invite anyone they wished, and I asked old friends of mine and Neal's who had not seen him for a long time and who would be interested in meeting Allen and Ken as well – and someone in my camp?

Saturday morning I ordered a cake with 'Happy Birthday Allen' on it, stocked in hamburger, hot dogs, beer, chips and wine, and turned my eyes heavenwards.

Early in the afternoon Ken was the first to arrive. He was accompanied by a dark-haired girl named Paula and an eight-year-old long-haired boy named Jason. Misgivings set in already; I had not expected to have to cope with a wild child. Paula explained why they had brought him: that morning they had gone to the apartment of The Grateful Dead and found Jason alone there. The band was in New York for a recording session. I broke in with, 'He was living there *alone*?' I made an effort not to show my un-hip outlook. 'Don't you know who his parents are?'

'We know *who* they are but not *where* they are,' Paula replied. 'So I thought he'd like to come with us.'

Jason meantime had taken a lightning tour of the house and grounds, and apparently it would do. Ken asked, 'Where's Neal?'

'Haven't a clue; don't you know?'

'No. Guess I'll go look for him. Mind if I take Jami and John with us?'

Both were tired of waiting for something to happen, and leaped at this suggestion. In about another hour Ken, Paula and Jason returned. Ken slumped into a chair.

'Well,' he said, 'I've not only not found Neal, I managed to lose John and Jami, too.' I had to smile, and I was glad I could.

In a few more minutes Ken's friend George Walker drove up in his convertible, Jami and John triumphantly seated up on the back of the rear car seat, colourful scarves flying from their heads. George was wearing an outfit I assumed he'd acquired in Mexico: the pants were a bright pink woven material with a jagged pinstripe of alternating purple and yellow. A bright green satin shirt and a bright yellow scarf around his neck added more colour. His hair was kept from his eyes by a flowered dayglo orange and yellow scarf, but he took it off when he came into the house, releasing not very long blond hair. He was of medium height, very slim, attractive, quiet, sweet to the kids, and he gave Jami a carved wooden comb as a souvenir of Mexico.

Not long after, Neal wheeled in, driving the 'Dead's' van covered with stickers advertising the band. Allen was with him. Some of John's friends began to straggle in, wide-eyed in awe, and Jami drove my car to get her friend Kym. Everyone was excited but restless, waiting for things to fall into a 'happening'. Allen and Ken's group had never really been close, and I half expected a conflict of egos.

Neal behaved in a nervous and erratic manner, and was in a foul mood, perhaps because I'd forbidden drugs on the premises and he was in need. I casually made one of my thoughtless wifely remarks that was intended to be jocular, and Neal's temper exploded. He burst forth in an angry stream, the reaction I had gone to such lengths to avoid in the past. Oh no, we could not have it now – the whole day would be ruined! I feared his anger, but I braved going to him, and hugged him, muttering shushing noises. I could feel the wrench it took for him to surrender, but in a minute his stiffness relaxed, his arms went around me, and he dropped his head on my shoulder. 'Thank you, God,' I breathed.

Ken, Neal and the highschool boys retired to John's room and gathered together whatever instruments were at hand: guitars, harmonicas, recorders, maracas and drumsticks were the lot, and someone produced a flute. I knew this supply would be more than adequate for plenty of sound, but John and friends scurried around in search of amplifiers.

In the living room, Allen graciously read Kym's poems, wrote comments and suggested books for her to read; Kym was floating on air. Then Allen and I sat on the floor while he unpacked a case of relics he had brought back from India and Tibet. With his usual generosity he asked me to pick out anything I'd like. There were ancient and varied prayer beads and a collection of brass and carved objects used in religious ceremonies, each of which he explained and demonstrated. For his namesake, John Allen, he relinquished one of his own sets of finger cymbals.

My friends arrived, among them George and Berylann Nelson, who also brought her mother ('Grandma A-Go-Go'), her brother and sister-in-law with their two baby girls. All three women were psychic, and their talents were soon being put to use. Berylann 'amortized' one of Allen's relics, which impressed him, then her mother read Kym's palm. She asked to see Allen's. I tried to discourage this 'entertainment', since these friends had come to see and talk with us and Allen, not to furnish a side-show, but Allen didn't understand Grandma's reading anyway, thoroughly earth-bound in spite of his Eastern studies.

Jason burst in from some door and asked if he could go swimming. He asked very politely, and my fears were checked. George Walker offered to life-guard. Paula was not available now to care for Jason; she had been telephoning Santa Cruz every few minutes, telling me she simply *had* to find Hassler; she was crazy about him. In an hour or so she was successful, but how to get to him? Neal, always the answer to a maiden's prayer, especially when she's in need of a ride, volunteered to drive her the 22 miles over the mountains, and off they sped in the van.

Allen had retreated to the patio, where a group of highschool boys were standing around talking. Allen seated himself in a canvas chair, and all the boys stopped talking and turned to stare at him, at a loss for words. It looked a bit sticky, but I figured Allen asked for it, and could break the stalemate.

Al and Helen Hinkle came with their two teenagers, and I felt better having Helen there. She joined the women in the living room after greeting Allen, and by now that room was solid bodies, with the squirming babies in the centre. The patio was filling up as well. I looked up once to see a tall, distinguished-looking gentleman with a goatee come through the front door, proceed to the patio, sit on the sidelines for about ten minutes, then as quietly walk back into the house and out the front door. Who could it have been? He didn't look like a cop. I learned later he was the professor father of one of the boys who'd come to check out Allen Ginsberg.

The musical din was pretty constant from the back room in spite of changes in personnel and instruments, and the conversations everywhere were increasing in volume to surmount it. Neal returned in a cloud of dust, and the tempo rose more sharply. At first sight I could see he had not wasted the opportunity to get thoroughly stoned. He had stood it as long as he could, and technically he wasn't breaking my rule; he hadn't taken it here. Seeing his strung-out condition, I took a moment to recharge my firm resolve to remain 'lovingly indifferent' throughout this day.

Everyone welcomed Neal joyfully, as always, and he went into the kitchen, yelling back at them all the while, then reappeared with a half-gallon of ice cream and a large plastic mixing spoon. With no break in his monologue, he stood on the raised hearth, slopping ice cream into his mouth, dripping it down his front and waving the spoon about to emphasize his words, melting ice cream flying about in all directions. It was another funny act they would all recall, but it sickened me to see him like that.

Allen was called to the telephone. An old friend, Alan Ansen, who had lived in Italy for some time, had come to San Francisco purposely to see Allen. I would have expected Allen to return to the City, but instead he invited Alan to join him here in Los Gatos. An hour later this new element extended the already widely diverse group. Ansen was in his sixties and obviously homosexual, as was the man who accompanied him. I don't know where I was when they arrived, but someone cleared a space on the couch for them to sit. When I entered the living room, I noticed that any chinks between the wall-to-wall bodies were now filled in with beer cans, wine bottles, glasses and ashtrays, and the babies lay asleep in the middle.

Then I saw on the couch the apparition of two elderly gentlemen straight out of Wodehouse, exquisitely attired from spats to gloves to walking sticks, with an expression on their faces of disdainful hauteur. I scrambled to hail Allen, who came swiftly to the rescue and escorted the two out to the patio and fresh air. I got a definite impression of skirts being pulled aside as they stepped gingerly over and around the pulsating floor. Helen was watching this too, and when our eyes met we exploded in our usual private laughter.

The crowd began to thin out as the dinner hour arrived. Paul Robertson, a lawyer friend of Kesey's, told me he must take his wife and child home, since he was scheduled to perform at a Palo Alto nightclub later that evening. Ken and his other friends were preparing to leave too, but Ken urged me to come to the performance. He was very kind, and made me think he really wanted me to be there, and for a minute I hesitated, thinking it might be fun. Then I knew it was useless to kid myself; I'd be a wet blanket all the way and never be able to hide my feelings if I saw Neal perform as I had heard he did.

Those of us remaining had a picnic sort of dinner, followed by Allen's cake. John and his friends wanted to go with Neal and Allen to the nightclub. Since most of the boys were planning to spend the night at our house, they felt free of the need for parental approval, so they ganged up to persuade me to let John go. I didn't care for this multiple responsibility, and I told John I'd really rather he didn't go, but I could give them no sensible-sounding reasons without exposing my fears and lack of faith, all based on supposition. They finally wore me down when I remembered the reason I'd started this but had proved nothing yet. May as well go for broke. Reluctantly I gave in.

Neal, in no condition to, promised not to drive and to be careful of the boys and the law. Allen, Neal, John and his friends ran out to the van and piled in, Neal immediately jumping into the driver's seat, and Allen in the back, dispensing the pot. My carefully tended benevolent attitude of trust bit the dust, my fears emerged triumphant, and I was disgusted with Allen.

There was no longer anyone around to witness my defeat or offer solace, but there were plenty of glasses and ashtrays to keep me busy. Around midnight I went to bed, knowing sleep was out of the question. I tried not to listen for every car, and turned the dial of my thoughts to positive – if somewhat rote-like – prayer. As the night wore on, my imagination revealed an unsuspected range of invention. Two o'clock came and went. They'd be home soon; nightclubs closed at two. Three o'clock. Had they gone on to San Francisco for more? Or out for a meal? Or worse? Places like Little Harlem reincarnated in my mind. The boys were under age. Were they all in jail? In hospital? Four o'clock. How could I possibly have allowed this, risked this? What a fool I'd been! Now what to do? By five-thirty I was a shivering wrung-out rag, but John was home and his friends too. Whatever horrors they'd been exposed to I'd deal with later; I pushed those new anxieties away, gradually uncoiled and slept.

Peace and order returned, but what had I gained? At dinner the following evening I asked John and Jami for their impressions. Both of them admitted to some disillusionment now that they had seen these men as ordinary people, no longer symbolic idols. My sacrifice had not all been in vain. John and the other boys had told me they'd enjoyed the evening. The band in which Paul played they thought great, and Paul could play two saxophones at once. During the break the Pranksters took over the stand with their mind-blowing noise and nonsense, thrashing away on instruments none of them could play. Neal took the mike and darted among the tables talking on his three levels in a steady stream. I shuddered and asked no more.

Some weeks later I felt strong enough to ask John what they had done from two to five-thirty.

'Oh, was it that late? Well, we went to some house – I think it was in Palo Alto. Dad and Ken disappeared, though I do remember Dad and Allen sitting in the kitchen part of the time. Dave and I and Steve just sat and looked at magazines; we didn't dare say anything or ask questions. When Dad and Ken came back, we split and got in the van to come home. Allen insisted Steve drive home...'

'Really?' I was surprised and pleased.

'Yeah, he was terrified of Dad's driving.' John laughed. 'Poor Steve – just 16 – brand new licence. But the van was stuck in a ditch, see? and Steve kept stalling it and spinning the wheels and saying, "I don't want to drive," so Dad took over "to get us out only".' John giggled again. 'I was sitting next to him in the front seat with Steve, and everyone else was in back where you can't see out too well. Dad would come to a stop light and pretend he wasn't going to stop, but he winked and grinned at us. Allen and the others would scream, '*Neal*! – it's a *red light*!' Dad would roll back a little but keep on sneaking out, just enjoying getting everyone frantic – nothing coming the other way, of course, and I knew he knew what he was doing – but –' John hesitated, casting a sheepish look at me, 'I suppose my laughing only encouraged him.' I had to laugh, too.

'No doubt,' I agreed, 'but Steve told me Dad never looked at the road, just kept turning around to talk to Allen, and half the time with his hands off the wheel.'

'Yeah, oh, well, yeah, but he *always* does that – pounding on the wheel to the music – you know how he is.'

'Yes,' I sighed. 'I do.'

Recently, someone asked John to appraise his feelings for Neal, and he said, 'Well, all I know is I'd rather have had him for a father than anyone else I've ever met.' By then, too, it was safe for John to tell me some of the times they'd shared together when he was a child. One of these was a day when Neal was home and joined John and his neighbourhood friends in their games. They 'borrowed' a friend's go-cart, even though he wasn't home to ask. They would ride down the steep driveway of his house. Neal, arms and legs akimbo, was having his turn when the family returned. The boys still howl remembering Neal looking at the ground penitently as the mother soundly denounced his behaviour. 'I can understand the boys – but a *grown man* – a *grown man*!'

| SEVENTY-NINE |

When Neal had returned from Mexico he had collected another girl, whom I didn't meet then, but I heard from Gavin that she had much in common with her predecessors.

'They have such *terrible* fights; I can't see how they *survive*!' This girl went by her initials, J.B., and was the daughter of a wealthy family in Erie, Pennsylvania, but, like many of her peers, did not see eye to eye with them in manner or mode of living, although their money was acceptable. She had left the group for a visit home at the time of our party, but she telephoned me frequently to discuss Neal. Like Diana, when she spoke of Neal it was with a proprietorial tone, one of ownership and authority, yet I could tell she knew Neal even less than had Diana. Like Anne she talked a lot of astrology, but she had an additional talent: she heard voices. She called from her parents' home and talked for as many hours as I could stand, telling me what Neal needed and how she was going to straighten him out.

'Good,' I'd respond, 'I certainly hope so; I'm all for it. Good luck.'

The few times I saw Neal after the party made me wonder if she'd been giving him some kind of 'treatment' already. His mind had taken a definite turn for the worse. He would be perfectly lucid and logical one minute, then in all seriousness say things like, 'I've been getting acquainted with the devil, you know. Oh, I know you don't believe in him, but there really is one, and I talk to him frequently. I told you, remember, that "666" lives in the hills above Redwood City.'

'What? Who? "666"? What are you talking about?'

'The reference to Lucifer in Revelations, you remember.' I didn't, and I still didn't know what he was on about. He had a strange look on his face, too.

'Neal – you can't be serious – you believe that?'

'I have my reasons.' He was serious. I was so baffled I didn't know where to attack, and I didn't understand well enough, and something told me I didn't want to.

Then there was the time I was driving him to the highway to hitchhike, and when we turned onto the main road, he said, 'I can influence people with my mind now. Honest; I've really got it perfected. Watch, I'll show you. See that woman who just passed us? She's going to turn on her lights – *now*. See?' He smiled in triumph. The woman was descending the hill in front of us and had hit her brakes, and sure enough, her tail lights went on. I sneaked a glance at Neal; he had to be putting me on – I hoped. Dead serious, he was, and I became even more wary.

I also discovered he was keeping a short hop ahead of the law again. I thought something was wrong when he was hitchhiking so often; he rarely needed to in the past because he could always find a car somehow. More often we had visits on Sunday mornings from the two gentlemen as the warrants and fines increased. My fears for him rose with them. Surely, if they apprehended him now, he could be sent back to San Quentin, as Gavin had feared, but I wasn't sure just how it worked. I had to be more careful not to meet him at home.

One day Neal opened up to me and reviewed his lamentable condition. I asked, 'Then why do you hang around with those people?'

'That's just it. I can't help it any more. I don't know where else to go. I'm a danger to everyone – ha – to myself most of all. I keep swearing I'm going to stop making an ass of myself, but then I get in a group, and everyone stares at me, waiting for me to perform – and my nerves are so shot, I get high – and there I go again. I don't know what else to do. It's horrible.' His voice broke and with it my heart. I was as helpless to help as he. He had dodged his own 'about-face' for so long, had gotten no closer to his source of strength, and I felt sure it was too late. When he was away I had to try and keep him out of my mind. 'Let others do as they may, as for me…' is the way it had to be. The more he demonstrated the ravages he had created in his life, the more determined I was to find a way for myself. I needed no other inducement.

One Sunday morning some months later, Neal telephoned, his voice weak and trembling. 'Carolyn – I'm sick –'

'Do you want to come home?' Now what had happened?

'Could I? Please?'

'Yes, of course, Neal, if you're sick you should. Where are you?'

He said he was in the home of a lawyer friend in Larkspur, a small town in Marin County north of San Francisco.

'I'll call Al Hinkle and see if he'll drive me, all right?'

'Yes, darling – hurry, please.'

Reliable Al came right over and picked me up. It was early afternoon when we found the house. The wife told us Neal was asleep upstairs, and her husband had gone to wake him when they saw us arrive. I tried to find out from her what was wrong with Neal, but apparently he had concealed his problem, for she said, 'Just tired out, I guess. He has been asleep since he arrived last night.'

After a long enough time to make me impatient, Neal appeared, a little drawn but otherwise looking normal. He was, however, very nervous and eager to get away. When we got to the car, he climbed into the back seat and lay down. He reached for my hand. I could see he was controlling himself with great difficulty. He closed his eyes and clenched his teeth, his forehead perspiring. Al chatted genially as though everything was like old times, and I knew Neal appreciated his homey strength as much as I. Occasionally, Neal would try to answer or comment, but though he smiled, his teeth would chatter if he unclenched them, and he was shivering in spite of the heat.

When we arrived at home Neal appeared to relax much more. He sank down on the couch and could now talk, persuading Al to stay for a cup of coffee. Neal said he'd been at Ken's farm in Oregon the night before, and the constant party was in progress. Suddenly, he became unbearably overwhelmed by revulsion of the whole scene, and had run out of the house straight to the highway to hitchhike to Larkspur, not stopping for his jacket, his cigarettes – anything.

'I simply could not stand it another second.' Timid flickers of hope stirred in me whenever there was a major upheaval such as this, for it seemed to me the only rescue left for Neal would have to be a sudden illumination, like that of St Paul or Starr Daily.

Al offered a practical suggestion. He told Neal that personnel had changed at the top echelon of the railroad, and perhaps now Neal could get his job back. They had been desperate for men, and one with as much experience as Neal would be really valuable. Neal accepted the challenge and was enthusiastic, if not overly excited.

'Yes – that's it! Go back to the world of peace and sanity and regular work. Ah, yes.' Then and there Al telephoned a conductor friend who knew Neal and who worked an early morning commute train from San Jose. The conductor agreed to come by for Neal, drive him to the depot and let him ride his train. In the City he would steer him to the proper authority. Perfect.

Neal removed his shirt, shoes and socks, his high spirits returned. When Al left and Neal stood at the door rubbing his bare tummy and smiling good bye, it was as though I'd been plummeted back fifteen years. Neal took his clothes back to John's room where he would sleep, and I sat on the couch gazing at my hill and mused, 'Could this really be? Was it possible it could all drop away?' My old dream didn't really surface, however; it had been too long buried.

Suddenly, Neal was standing over me.

'Where's John? Where's John?' his voice echoing alarm, his eyes wide and dark.

'Why, Neal – I told you – John's spending the night with Jim, and Jami's at Kym's.'

Neal clutched his temples, wheeled around and swiftly walked to the back of the house, moaning, 'Oh my *God* – I've killed my son! I've killed my son!' A sob caught in his hoarse throat. I jumped up and followed him, my heart racing. In John's room he had thrown himself on his knees beside the bed, his elbows propped on it, while he held his head in both hands and rocked back and forth, sobbing. I put my hand tentatively on his shoulder, but he recoiled, saying in a normal voice and gently, 'No, please, please – just leave me alone. I know – there's nothing you – I'm all right, really –'

I couldn't sit still anywhere, so I fussed about in the kitchen, the bedroom, praying to myself and listening. Once again, Neal strode down the hall to the living room, grabbed his head, crossed his arms and bent over, straightened, flung back his head and continued to repeat, 'I've killed my son, I've killed my son!' What could he mean? What was he thinking? I had a flash of John being chopped to death by the blades on a chariot wheel. Could that be what Neal was remembering? I wished I could question him. He went back to leaning on John's bed, rocking himself and muttering unintelligibly through sobs. Why was there nothing I could *do*?

Then I heard the front door open, and John and Jim ran in and made straight for John's room. I gasped and ran to intervene, but as I reached the hall I saw Neal emerge from the room as the boys approached. He smiled, ambled out and greeted them warmly. Then he turned to me. 'Say, I'd better polish my black shoes for tomorrow – they're still here?'

'Yes, dear, but I'll polish them, as I always did.' Neal stood leaning against the kitchen door frame, as cool and charming as he once was while I placed newspapers on the stool and polished his shoes. I experienced another of those time lapses or relapses. John was lugging his guitar in its case, chattering to Jim, and then paused to say good bye and tell me their plans for the morrow.

'Good bye, son,' Neal called after them, 'I'll see you tomorrow night after work.' I put the polish away and began to prepare a dinner for the two of us. I thought it an odd coincidence that both Jami and John were away for the night; they didn't stay overnight very often, and hardly ever at the same time.

Now Neal was staring out the front window, and I could sense his nervousness returning. At dinner he picked at his food, something I'd never seen him do before, and he didn't seem aware of my presence but was deep into his own thoughts. Then abruptly he stood up, pushing back his chair. 'I've got to wash my hair,' he said flatly, bolted into the shower room and turned the shower on hard.

My apprehension increased as I cleared the table and listened. Neal was in the shower, but he wasn't washing his hair. Instead he was yelling and pounding on the walls, audible over the sound of the water. I wasn't exactly panicky, a fact that surprised me, but I was certainly frightened. I went to the phone and dialled Silent Unity in Missouri, something I'd never done before or since, but I had to turn to *something*. A degree of calm returned when I had to give them some sort of request, and then heard the soothing voice say, 'We will pray, knowing that your husband is surrounded by the protection of God and enfolded in His love; his mind is healed.' I sat at the table again, my eyes on the bathroom door, and repeated over and over the affirmation, blotting out all other thoughts and holding my fears at bay.

In a minute or two the shower stopped. Now I could hear Neal pacing back and forth in the bathroom, continuing his one-sided conversation with the devil but more quietly now. In another few minutes he came out, his face pale but composed. He sat down at the table beside me and reached for his shirt to extract the tiny New Testament he always carried in his pocket. He closed his eyes, opened the book at random and then began to read. 'Be not thou envious against evil men, neither desire to be with them. For their heart studieth destruction, and their lips talk of mischief.' Neal stopped reading and gazed at me open-mouthed, looking stricken, then nodded and continued: 'Whoso keepeth the law is a wise son; but he that is a companion of riotous men shameth his Father. He that turneth away his ear from hearing the law, even his prayer shall be abomination...' Neal slowly closed the book, nodding his head, and whispered, 'You see? I want to go to bed; don't leave me.'

I turned down one of the twin beds in John's room while Neal took off his jeans then climbed in.

'Please stay with me, darling,' he said sadly, looking at me wistfully. The twin beds were in the corner head-to-head, so I lay on the other one on my stomach, my arm outstretched. He grasped it with both hands, laid his cheek against it and was asleep. I stayed in that position until my arm was numb, and I had to extricate it from his grip. Never had I seen Neal in such a deep sleep. There was no sign of breathing, unusual with his troublesome nose, and if I hadn't felt some warmth, I'd have thought him dead.

Thus he remained all night, and at six o'clock the next morning I woke him as he had requested, even though I was doubtful he could go through with his work plan. But he jumped up, alert and agreeable. He dressed carefully, shaved and fussed with his hair, as of old, while I made a big breakfast. By all appearances, he was perfectly normal and ready for a day in the life of the average conductor. I didn't dare mention the night before. Slurping the last of his coffee, he saw his ride turning into the drive, kissed me wetly and ran out, yelling back, 'Remember – I'll be back tonight, darling, after I get hired.'

I closed the door and sat down to think. Did I want to start this all over again? Could he possibly get hired, and if he did, would his conversations with devils or whatever continue? I felt it quite a remote possibility that he could return to the railroad so simply, or that he could stay with it if he did, but sometimes I hated to be right.

| EIGHTY |

Two weeks later John and Jami spent a day in San Francisco with some of their friends, one of them Kym. They came home in the early evening and ran to me excitedly to tell me they had accidentally run into Neal. They had been walking along a Haight-Ashbury street when they saw Ken's bus park and the Pranksters get out. Neal was behind the wheel.

Both John and Jami greeted him gladly, but they said he was casual and off-hand, showing no surprise to see them. They asked him where he'd been, why he hadn't returned home that night, and if he hadn't been rehired. Neal paused to think, then said, 'Oh, yeah, that. No, I didn't go; the cops arrested me – just got out.' He went on fiddling with something on the dashboard.

Ken called to them, 'Come on – you want to come with us?' The merry band was walking towards a building that looked like an old church. All but John joined them, as did Neal, but John said he preferred to 'guard the bus'. It was the collection of sound equipment that fascinated him.

Inside the barren hall, decorated with current fads, posters and dayglo paint, mattresses were strewn around the floor. The main attraction was tanks of nitrous oxide, or 'laughing gas' as they called it. To spare me, and perhaps herself, Jami was afraid to say she'd tried it, but later she confessed she had. 'I only took a couple of whiffs, but I didn't like it, and nothing seemed to happen.' Kym, however, was working on getting results, and Ken was urging her on. Jami said she, herself, was reticent anyway because whenever she and John had been with Neal and were offered pot, they sensed he would prefer they didn't indulge, and, wanting to please him, they had always refused. This was surprising but welcome news to me.

Today, however, Jami, close to tears, said Neal hadn't recognized her. He kept talking affectionately to Kym and calling her 'Jami'. It hurt her deeply, not so much for herself, but from the knowledge of how Neal would feel if or when he realized his mistake. Poor Neal. I hoped he never would.

The next afternoon I was sitting in the living room reading, when I noticed a car had passed the house two or three times. Getting up to look more closely, I saw it was Neal driving with a girl sitting next to him. What on earth? I walked out to the road. Neal backed the car at my approach but made no sign of parking. His chest and feet were bare; he wore nothing but jeans. When I reached the hovering car he leaned forward past the girl, who looked about eighteen, had long blonde hair, and wore the white Prankster coveralls. I said, 'What are you doing, Neal? Why don't you come in?'

'Get in, and we'll talk.' He looked so strange – grim, yet as though he had a secret to impart, and he was angry. The girl stared at me accusingly. I tried to act chummy and casual, but grave forbodings quickened my heartbeat.

'No thanks, I'll stay here. What's up? What is it you want?'

Neal's face became rigid, he clenched his jaw and spat out, 'What about your *daughter*, eh? Taking *drugs*! Yes – in the City yesterday.'

'What? What do you mean?' Neal churned the car back and forth, swaying me with it.

'Get in.'

'I don't want to get in. If you've something you want to tell me, park the car and get out. I don't understand.'

The girl now came to the rescue. 'Jami, your daughter, was taking drugs. How come you let her? She really shouldn't, you know; she's too young.' She flipped her cigarette ash while I gaped at her. It was all so nutty, especially since I realized they were talking about Kym.

'Look Neal, I know all about it; it wasn't Jami, it was Kym. I wasn't there, but *you*, her father, was. So?' I did my best to ignore the adolescent and her supercilious gaze. Neal didn't answer. He still looked angry, but now also confused. I was growing frightened. By the look of the two of them I could only guess they must have dashed compulsively all the way from San Francisco or maybe Palo Alto to tell me this urgent news. What sort of torture was Neal going through now?

'Is that all you've come for?' I tried to sound gentle, reach him somehow. 'It's *all right*, Neal – Jami's all right. Thank you for your concern, but don't worry. I must go in now, good bye.' I turned and ran back to the house, and thank God Neal gunned the car and sped away.

In 1967 we no longer received special messages or contributions from Neal on holidays and birthdays, but I knew, if he were able, he was thinking of us, and we included him in our thoughts and prayers even more. For several months I had been urging him to go to Mexico and be free of the danger of being hunted down. I figured the net was closing in, and J.B. had called to say she had a house rented in San Miguel de Allende he was welcome to use. It had a typewriter and everything he'd need. She, herself, wouldn't be able to get there until the first of the year. When we didn't hear from Neal at Christmas, I thought perhaps he'd gone, and I felt relieved. I was wrong. He telephoned the last week in December and asked if I would see him on new year's eve. This wasn't one of our special dates, and I wondered why he wouldn't be spending it with his friends. Could he be contemplating another go at 'new beginnings'? Whatever his purpose, I agreed to meet him at a friend's, not at all counting on his turning up.

As I prepared to go, I thought it curious that I still felt a rise in excitement at the thought of seeing Neal alone, although I held out no particular preconceptions. Since he had chosen the date, perhaps he would be romantically nostalgic. By the time I arrived I had worked myself into a sentimental and expectant state.

There was another couple already there, with whom our friend and his wife planned to go out to celebrate. As I was introduced, I surmised by their appearance and dazed expressions they had all jumped the gun somewhat. Neal was there too, seated in a chair opposite the couch across the room where I went to sit, smiling my most welcoming smile. He greeted me so casually, I peered at him, afraid he hadn't recognized me after so long.

Yes, I could see he had, but he was little moved. He was listening to the stereo, gazing into space, and now and then made a remark that could be aimed at anyone or no one. He then started humming, his glances occasionally falling on me as though I were a passing pedestrian. I made a few efforts at establishing a closer connection, but failed.

I wished everyone would leave us alone – go out as they'd said they had planned. There was nothing for me to do but sit and wait, and since I wasn't in whatever world they were, repartee was limited. I was coming down rapidly. My romantic expectations were turning into equally romantic feelings of rejection, even though I knew them to be unjustified.

Then, to my dismay, it appeared none of them had yet had dinner, even though it was now after nine o'clock. The wife brought Neal and the others plates of food, and they leisurely began to eat. Neal waved his fork to the music, hummed between mouthfuls, and continued to gaze over my head. To muster a measure more patience, I tried looking at a magazine, but the lighting was too dim, and I didn't want to look at a magazine!

At long last the dishes were collected and the assemblage departed. I looked to Neal now to divulge the urgent reason for this tête-à-tête, but I was still not included in his field of vision. After a minute or so more, I said, 'Well, if this is all you wanted to see me for, I have other things to do at home,' and I rose from the couch.

Neal didn't speak, but he got up and gently pulled me back on the couch, then stretched out with his head in my lap. Closing his eyes, he clasped my hand on his chest and said, 'Please – please tell me about the children – about yourself – everything you've been doing.' His voice sounded weary. To oblige him I dredged up all the trivia that makes up the daily lives of a growing family, Although his eyes remained closed, he was more responsive now, and if I paused or sounded as though he couldn't possibly care, he'd prod me by repeating my last two words or ask a question. For a time I felt compensated, but soon I wore down and became bored, and I didn't want to get too deeply involved in the problems with the children, most of them the result of my coping alone. I tried to shift the subject to him, but he was evasive or answered in monosyllables.

'Neal, darling, aren't you going to go to Mexico? Really, you *must*!'

'Yeah, yeah,' he sighed. 'But I have to go to the City first and get money.' Another delay? Money now? Why was he dragging his feet?

'Oh, Neal,' I wailed, 'every day and every trip to the City increases your chances of arrest. Surely you know that?'

Instead of answering, he said matter-of-factly, 'I have to take a bath.' He got up and went into the adjacent bathroom. Not knowing quite what to make of this move, I followed along. He said no more, started filling the tub, undressed and climbed in. I sat on the edge a minute in case there was anything else on his mind. He leaned his head back against the wall, folded his hands across his chest, gazed into space a minute, then closed his eyes and resumed humming. I concluded the audience was at an end.

'Well, Neal, I guess I'll be going.'

'Ah, yes – thank you, dear –' His eyes were still closed, but he patted my arm.

'Good bye, Neal. Hap – happy new year.'

'Mmmm.'

Three weeks went by, and I heard no more. I did hope no news was good news. Then Neal telephoned; he was in Los Angeles at the home of a couple who, like countless others, had met and responded to his charm but little understood his nature. That is, they published a vulgar underground paper like so many becoming popular at this time and offered him a job, never knowing his disgust for these papers. He had only just said where he was when I pleaded, 'Oh Neal! Still not out of the country? Poor dear – please stop tempting the law. Do you want to get caught? Go to Mexico. Stay at J.B.'s house, relax in the sun and get healthy. Then you'll be able to write again. You can do it, honey, do it for us if not for yourself.'

Was he listening? There was a long pause, then in a tone of finality he said, 'I'm coming home.' Oh, God, what now? I swallowed the lump in my throat and tried to be normally casual.

'Now, Neal, darling, you know all about that…'

'I'm coming *home*!' More determined. More final, yet only a hair away from a scream. Don't say that, stop saying that, what was he doing, making me say no again. He'd witnessed before what that did to me. So now he was asking again, and in such despair. What could I say? There was nothing I could do to soothe his torment.

'No, Neal, dearest. Please go to Mexico first and get well. *Then* come home; you know we'll be waiting.'

'I've got to come home *now*.' I could hear the effort he was making towards control, and my hands were shaking.

'Neal – please, please…' There was a long pause.

'Well – maybe – maybe by my birthday –' He mumbled the rest, but there was a trace of defiance in his tone.

'Yes, yes, Neal – God be with you!' He hung up sharply.

Later I heard he was refused entry at the border because of his appearance, but he had managed to connect with a film crew, who took him in with them.

He had delayed so long when he arrived in San Miguel that J.B. was already there, and she had called me to find out where he was. I told her what little I knew, but I could not explain his reluctance to get there.

'Well, anyway,' she said cheerfully, 'my voices tell me he is going to be all right.'

'Oh? That's good news. The last times I've seen him, his mind has been pretty well muddled; I'm afraid the drugs have taken their toll.'

'Not at all. He's going to be completely cured; he'll write again and get steadily better. Within the next six months, they say.' She was confident.

The next time J.B. called it was less than two weeks later. It was a Sunday morning, February 4, four days before Neal's forty-third birthday. In semi-shock she said, 'Carolyn – Neal is dead.'

'Thank God!' I breathed. 'Released at last. God is merciful.' J.B.'s voices could have spoken the truth, after all. He was cured, and he was truly 'home' – and by his birthday.

| EIGHTY-ONE |

Jami, John and I were finishing breakfast when J.B.'s call came. I told them softly, although they had guessed, and we sat a few moments in silence of one mind and prayer. Sweet Jami's face was wet; her warm heart ever overflowed. John stared into space. Of course, it didn't sink in all at once; it took months to become a fact. Neal had been absent so much of our life, thankfully there was no sudden change in our routines. Only as time passed did we miss him and remember how much he had been a part of our lives. Whenever I'd occasionally be overtaken with weeping, I knew it wasn't for him but for the golden light that had been his gift, and for the dream I never got to hold.

The same afternoon, J.B. called again, bless her. I had completely forgotten about the mechanics of death, and I knew nothing about them, not even in this country, let alone a foreign one.

'What shall I do?' She's asking *me*? But she sounded much more sensible and efficient now, and said she'd take care of the arrangements; there would be no need for me to take the trip there.

'Oh good, J.B. You do know he has to be cremated. Can you arrange that?'

'Cremated? Why cremated?'

'Never mind. He made me promise. Just find out how to go about that, okay? And, my dear, I can't thank you enough. What would I have done without you?' She could speak Spanish, and knew the town, so if she could function normally I knew she'd be more useful than I. Ken's lawyer friend, Paul Robertson, graciously came up with the necessary financial aid.

For my part, I had to think about whom to inform. First, the Hinkles, who felt much as I did, and then Allen and Jack. The last phone number Allen had given me had been changed. Being unlisted, there was no way for me to reach him. The New York operators and their supervisors were admirably adamant in protecting his privacy. By great lamentations, I finally got an operator with a Spanish accent to agree to call him, give him my message and ask him to call me back. This she did. Allen was subdued, fatalistic, sad. He'd known death before.

Next I called Jack. He wasn't home, but the operator left a message to call back with Stella, his wife. A few years previously, Memere had had a stroke, and to care for her Jack had married a member of the Sampas family with whom he had grown up in Lowell. Monday rolled around and still no call from Jack. I wondered why all day, finally deciding to try again; I couldn't have him hearing about Neal's death any other way.

This time Jack answered the phone. I had only just blurted out the news when Stella began yelling behind him, 'Jacky, Jacky, stop it…'

He shouted at her, 'Shut up – Neal is dead!' There was a scuffle and she came on the phone, overwhelmed with apologies for not having given him my message.

'But you see, if I don't do something, he'd spend all our money on telephone bills – I had no idea –' I sympathized with her, and told her I was glad Jack had someone protecting him from himself. Jack came back on the phone, sobered considerably, and said all the beautiful things I wanted to hear about Neal – but he wouldn't believe Neal was really gone.

'It's just a trick – he's hiding out someplace, like Tangier.' Each time I'd try and get him to see it was for the best, he'd cut me off and rhapsodize some more.

For days and weeks J.B.'s calls and confusion mounted. She gave me three different versions of the cause of Neal's death and the circumstances preceding it, the one constant being that she and Neal had fought the evening before, soon after his arrival, and he had left the house angry.

'You see,' she often repeated, 'whenever he got mad at me, he identified me with you.' I let it pass, but she was having other hallucinations that bothered me more. She could 'see' Neal and hear him. When she looked in her mirror she saw his face instead of her own.

My anxieties increased; maybe I should go tend to it myself. But I couldn't leave work that long, and I had no money. I had to trust her.

Her final version was that Neal had swallowed a lot of 'reds' and had stormed out to go get his luggage, left at the next station, Celaya. On the way he'd been hauled into a wedding ceremony, where he drank alcohol. I doubted that, knowing how sick spirits made him, although he would have had some wine if he had been asked to toast the bride, even if he knew the combination of Seconal and alcohol was lethal. Could he have done it on purpose? I didn't think that likely, knowing his beliefs on suicide.

The autopsy report said only that every system was 'congested', which could have been caused by a number of things, like renal failure. They did not report the laboratory findings, because, they said, there were drugs involved, and he was a foreigner. So no one will ever know the exact cause. He had been found the next morning still alive a few yards out of town by the railroad tracks, but he died soon after in the hospital.

J.B. called a few days later.

'Are you sure I should have him cremated? He'll have to be shipped to Mexico City for that.'

I sympathized with her hassle, but, 'Yes, J.B. It is imperative, I'm sorry. The theory, you see, which Neal believed to be true, is that fire purifies the body cells and makes the transition faster and easier for the soul's release from matter. Since we can't prove it, I'll have to take it on faith, like the Hindus, and do what Neal was so adamant to have done.' She sighed but said she'd try some more.

Not being familiar with anything J.B. was having to contend with, yet being too familiar with her mental quirks and her great attachment to Neal, I became more convinced I'd never see those ashes. More than two months had passed.

Living with me during this time was a writer friend, Florence. She remembered she knew a man in the U.S. embassy in Mexico City. She telephoned him and asked if there was some way he could intercept the process, and instead of shipping the ashes back to San Miguel, have them shipped directly to me. Surprisingly, he said, 'No problem at all; I ll be happy to attend to it.' We never heard from him again, and I never received a parcel. What was happening down there?

After several weeks of my agonizing, J.B. telephoned from Los Angeles. She and the ashes were safely within U.S. boundaries, and she would fly to San Jose. I agreed to meet her at the airport. One more leg of the journey to go. Would she change her mind?

On the evening of her arrival, Flo came with me to pick her up. J.B. had said she'd be wearing jeans, but that was all the identification she offered. It was now dark, and we turned into the terminal drive, where I had to swerve to avoid a mound of rags and hair, cacophonically blowing on a harmonica. Flo observed, 'Hunh, you don't usually see hippies here.' I cruised slowly past all the exits from the lighted terminal, and we both scanned the few passengers to find a girl in jeans. There were none. At the same instant and with the same thought, Flo and I turned to look at each other, and I drove back to the entrance and pulled up beside the huddled figure sitting on the curb. It pocketed the harmonica in a large loose poncho and turned to pick up a woven satchel and a shoulder bag, all the while never letting go of a large wooden box cradled in one arm. She managed to climb into the car without dislodging it, and all the way home she hugged it to her. There was no doubt in my mind what that box contained.

We chatted amiably and generally coherently on the drive home, with the emphasis on my thanks to her, which were sincere indeed, and I did so hope justified. At the house, I ushered J.B. in, closed the door, smiled at her, 'Here, let me take your burden from you now. You've been simply wonderful; I'll never be able to thank you enough.' I held out my hands, but she hesitated, looking from Flo to me and back, weighing. I thanked God there were two of us. With some resistance, she slowly handed over the polished wooden box. Not wishing to advertise my suspicions, I put it down on the table in plain sight, and invited her to sit on the couch.

'Let's have a glass of wine to celebrate, shall we? And to give you a lift after your tiring trip.' I went to the kitchen, Flo settled herself and lit a cigarette, and J.B. sat cautiously on the edge of the couch.

Neal and I had come to believe firmly that there is no death except for the flesh, and that the person's soul is being cared for mercifully in the transition to the new state of consciousness. We also concurred that grief and mourning only slowed down the progress onwards of the soul, and strengthened whatever bind there had been to earth, which needed to be broken quickly. No doubt it was easier for us than others to embrace this idea, since neither of us had experienced a traumatic loss through death, and it was a great comfort for me now. J.B., on the other hand, was inclined to the view that the box on the table contained the Neal she had known.

We did our best to discourage her in this, but also to probe her plans. Gavin had offered to put her up temporarily – three months ago – but it was too late to get her to San Francisco that night, and I kept getting the disquieting impression from J.B. that she, along with the ashes, was home and intended to stay. I tried to counter-mand that idea too: 'Well, J.B., I'm afraid you'll have to stay here tonight; I'll get out the sleeping bag. The couch, I've been told, is really very comfortable.' I suited my actions to my words, and Flo went to fetch a pillow. When I had spread out the sleeping bag for her, I picked up the wooden box.

'I'll put this away now,' I said as off-handedly as I could. 'I don't think we want it in the middle of the living room, especially when the kids come home tomorrow. It's a bit morbid to be faced with right now, don't you think?' I smiled at J.B. as I started for the back of the house. She half rose from the couch, but sank back without answering. Was she going to fight me for it? Not yet. I put the box in a metal filing cabinet in the family room, and locked it.

Again, I thanked heaven Flo was in the house and the children were not, but nonetheless I spent a restless night and got up early the next morning. J.B. seemed eager to rise as well, and strode briskly about the house while I cooked breakfast. She was cheerful, and made an effort to be more friendly.

'Say,' she accosted me in the kitchen, 'did you jump into my body last night?' I dropped a spoon. And that was only the beginning. By the time we'd finished eating, I was beginning to twitch. She had sounded at least capable of sensible communication with me in most of the telephone calls. Now I was having difficulty connecting one of her sentences with the last. She began suddenly bursting into convulsions of laughter or song with no discernable motivation. I recognized a few references to astrology or other occult phenomena, but what was she *saying*? My head swam in my efforts to respond. Flo and I sent each other baleful looks, and she was only too happy she had appointments most of that day.

I had the day off, and I tried to think what I could do while J.B. was in residence, and at the same time encourage her to move on. Several times I had brought up the subject of her immediate and future plans, offering to drive her to buses or trains or planes, but she skillfully sidestepped the issue every time. I couldn't bring myself to be rude; I owed her too much.

The previous week I had begun work on a large painting. Now seemed a good time to get it out and continue. She genially pulled up a chair alongside, and didn't seem to mind that I added nothing to her conversation, which she continued in her erratic, senseless manner, interspersed with wild laughter and song. I minded terribly, and the strain was tying my stomach in knots. About once an hour, she'd knock it off and say, 'Where are the ashes?'

Each time I'd respond like a parrot: 'They're put away now, J.B., let's forget about them and not be morbid.'

She'd say, 'What will you do with them?' and I'd say, 'I don't know yet; I'll have to think about it and consult the kids. These ashes are not Neal, J.B., but let's say symbolically he is home now as he asked to be – and loved.' Nausea threatened each time I had to repeat this script. Later she tried a different tack, but I held firm to, 'They're put away, and there they will stay.'

This was possibly the longest day I can ever remember. When Flo came home, I had dinner ready, and I followed her into the bedroom to consult. I knew I could not stand another night with J.B.

'I think she's planning on moving in and living here next to those ashes, but, believe me, another few hours of her and I'll be the one you'll have to cart off to the looney bin.' Flo was sympathetic, and agreed to do whatever had to be done, but she was not enthusiastic about an adventure at night when she had obligations first thing in the morning. The only solution I had thought of was to pack up J.B. and head for San Francisco.

Providence intervened in the form of an old friend and lover, Paul. He was a large, strong man, although not at all aggressive, but J.B. didn't know that. She would have recognized him as a Leo of the pussycat variety had she known him. He stopped by to return a book he had borrowed, and I immediately pressed him into service. He agreed to drive me and J.B. to Gavin's. I put the dishes in the sink and said cheerily, 'Come along, J.B. – I know you're anxious to get moving on: Gavin has told me he hopes you'll visit him, and Paul here has offered to drive you there – isn't that great? What a coincidence! And save you any fare.' I was struggling into my coat, and Paul and I headed for the door, holding it for her. Slowly, she gathered her things together, the mind at work, I could tell.

'May I see the ashes one more time?'

'No, J.B., I'm sorry. I have told you again and again – please, do try to transfer your thoughts of Neal from the ashes of his body to his living spirit – still with us. I'm sure he'd prefer that, and you'd be much happier, too. Ready?' I went out the door and Paul waited for her to precede him.

On the way to the City she entertained us with her harmonica, obviously having had lessons from the Pranksters. I tried to help her build up some identity of her own, independent of Neal, and point her thoughts forward. I doubt I had much effect, but I did wish I could do something to compensate her for her service to me.

At Gavin's I ran into another brief setback. He said, in front of J.B. and several dinner guests, that he no longer had any spare bed available. Oh, no, I gasped – I couldn't take her back! Then a young man, to whom I shall be forever grateful, spoke up with extra-ordinary chivalry and offered his room to her for the night. Gavin's impeccable manners would not allow him to protest, and pressing my advantage, I said Paul and I must hurry home – 'Work day tomorrow, you know.'

Gavin walked to the door with us, and I gave him a brief summary of the tribulations I'd just experienced with J.B. and the ashes. He understood, and forgave my rude haste in dumping her on him without warning. He smiled wryly, 'The whole thing reminds me of the battle over D.H. Lawrence's ashes in New Mexico. Frieda mobilized a bunch of Navajos to see that Mabel's Pueblo Indians didn't waylay the ashes on their way from Taos to the Lawrence ranch near the Colorado border. I heard the story from both sides.' Our drive home was one long sigh of relief; it was over.

Two weeks later the doorbell rang, and opening the door I faced J.B. standing on the stoop. 'I want to say "good bye" to Neal. I want to see the ashes once more. I'm going to tour the country tomorrow.' She had hitchhiked all the way to see the ashes. See them – or collect them? In one sense I felt she had some right, considering her part in obtaining them, but I was still afraid of a battle I could not stomach. My puny defences rose. I stood in the doorway. She pushed past me, but I didn't move, and held open the door.

'No, J.B., I'm very sorry, really, but I've told you again and again how I feel. It is your prerogative to treat death any way you wish, but since you knew Neal such a very short time, I feel I have a better idea of how he'd feel about this. Honour Neal some other way, if you like, but leave his ashes out.'

I was quite frightened of her now. If she'd go this far, how much further? I still believed she wanted to get the ashes for herself. We stood eyeing each other. It came into my mind I should ask her what Neal was telling her. Many times she had written that he communicated with her, and had been responsible for the long delay in her leaving Mexico. Did she think he was 'guiding' her now? She leaned back against the door frame. 'How well you must have known him. How fortunate all your years together. You know what a fine man he was and how he loved his children.'

'Yes, J.B., I do. And I think it would grieve him for us to contend in any way – especially over this.' She accepted defeat, and walked away down the drive and up the road to the highway.

She did not tour the country, but went straight to New York, where she remained, as far as I know. I'd have been willing to answer her spasmodic poetic notes could I have found a subject of rapport.

| EIGHTY-TWO |

Day after day came condolences from many varied sources, all emphasizing the tremendous effect Neal had had on their lives. Some were from people I'd never met, and I was doubly touched by these, because Neal had made so many friends in his last years who were unaware of his family's existence. There were inspired poems from young people, a sweet one from Kym, and a moving long letter from Gordon Lish, as well as from his former wife.

The national press took little notice of his passing, and I expected nothing more, if even this:

> SAN MIGUEL de ALLENDE, Mexico; February 4, 1968
> (AP) Neal Cassady, 43, of San Francisco, a former railroad
> conductor and long associate of prominent members of the
> beatnik and hippie generations, has died here. Police
> reports said Cassady was found unconscious but still alive
> early in the morning along the railroad tracks. Cassady
> was a friend of novelist Jack Kerouac and the poet, Allen
> Ginsberg.

But the underground press and local papers were exceptionally fervent in their eulogies. Without judging Neal's personal merit, Ralph Gleason, in the *San Francisco Chronicle*, commented briefly, 'only the underground press mourned this remarkable man, who was intimately involved with two major novelists and a major poet.'

From the time of Neal's death, Jack telephoned more frequently, but he was rarely sober, and it was always in the wee hours. One time he'd say, 'Neal's not dead, you know – he couldn't be! Naw, he just wanted to get away.' Then another time he'd say, 'Ah, Neal – I'll be joining you soon.'

'Jack, don't.'

'Yes, I will. It won't be long. I'm gonna join him.'

'Please, Jack, don't talk like that. Why don't you come visit me?'

'Can't. Can't hardly get myself to the bathroom for a leak.'

'You seem to be able to make it to the refrigerator okay.'

'Yeaaah,' he'd laugh. 'You know what I drink now? Boilermakers. The best whiskey an' the best beer for a chaser – I have my little glass here now, m'dear – yep, really grrrrreeeaat – but – ah – yes – if I were with you now, we'd sit by the fire – you'n me, eh? An' we'd talk again like we usta –' He'd be silent until I'd think he'd fallen asleep.

'Well, Jack, in that case, you'll have to go back to wine. I don't like whiskey.'

'Mmmmm. Yeah – well – I ain't goin' nowhere – 'cept with Neal.'

'Have you been writing?' Again I'd try to change the subject.

'Hmm – yeah –' he brightened, 'just finished one. It's about two little boys hitchhiking through the South.'

'Really, Jack? Not autobiographical?'

'Nope. Just – fict-shon.'

'Well, Jack, that's really fine!' (How phoney could I be!) 'Now, see? You've got all that self-analysis out of your system – you can now start a whole new career. I'm so glad. I've always thought you could write beautiful imaginative fiction – like *Dr Sax*.'

In my heart I wondered if he could still do it. I doubted it very much in his condition. Neal and I had wept watching the awful exhibition Jack had made of himself on the Buckley TV show, even though some of his remarks were fine – like telling Ed Sanders he had nothing to do with 'all that Beat stuff. All you guys want to do is tear things down – I want to raise them up.' And saying he was arrested for decay – sad, but funny.

On the following Easter eve in 1969 I was invited to a dinner party by some prominent people who were interested in many fields and acquainted with many creative artists. I knew them from having painted a portrait of their son. I had a thoroughly good time, and I usually hate parties – especially when I know almost no one else. So for me it was a rare treat to meet a group of people all of whom were active, optimistic and uncritical – no chips on shoulders, no axes to grind. Maybe, just maybe, a new life might open up for me. The guests of honour were well into their seventies and still leading a stimulating life. All the *joie de vivre* that evening was an exhilarating tonic for me, but I rather overdid the wine.

When I ran into my house at two-thirty the next morning, I was more than ready for bed, my head not quite attached. Gratefully, I lowered the throbbing temples to the cool pillow. It took a few minutes for the whirring to stop and the giddy stimulation to subside, but when it did I was totally limp, over and out.

The telephone ring came from a long way off, or had it rung only in my head? I started climbing towards the hallway when another ring lifted me up by my ears. I dashed, stumbling to the counter in the kitchen on which the phone sat and grabbed it, but my head descended and sank on my elbow. 'H'lo,' I whispered.

'Go pour yourself a glass of wine and talk to me.' Jack's voice was mellow, slurred and cosy, ready for a nice long chat. Oh, where was his wife when I needed her?

'Jack – please – not tonight; I've just crawled into bed with a terrible headache – it's three o'clock in the morning here. I've been at a party and had way too much wine already – I simply can't –'

'Aw, come on – I wanna talk to you.'

'No, please Jack, I mean it – I really can't – have a heart!' I shook with the cold, and my teeth were chattering. 'Call me tomorrow – in the daytime, please, please –' I hung up and scurried back to my warm bed.

The phone pealed again. 'Hey – you can talk to me – go get a drink.'

'No, Jack, please – I really can't. Tomorrow, yes? I'd love to talk to you, you know that, but this is the wrong time – honest – please think of *me* this time, this once? Couldn't you do that for me?' I felt my indignation rising, and I hung up. Good grief, it must be six or seven in the morning in Florida; had he been at it all night? Well, hell, *one* time he could consider me.

The telephone screamed again. I pulled the pillow over my ears and gritted my teeth, adamant to stick to my guns. Oh, Jack, dear Jack, have mercy – *please* understand!

He never called again, and seven months later he did join Neal, just as he'd said he would.

> ST. PETERSBURG, FLA. October 31, 1969 (UPI). Novelist, Jack Kerouac, 47, father of the literary 'Beat Generation' in the 1950s and reluctant godfather of today's hippie movement, died today of a massive abdominal haemorrhage. Kerouac, of French-Canadian extraction soared to fame after publication of his novel *On the Road* in 1957. He wrote 18 books which sold several million copies and were translated into 18 languages. Kerouac and poet, Allen Ginsberg were the prophets of the beat movement which flowered in San Francisco & New York.

I felt strangely lonely and remote from his death at first. A trifle resentful, even. Then I realized I'd not been near either man when he'd died – other women had tended to the business of their passing – yet I'd been closer to those two in life than anyone. Good. It was right. Alive I knew them, and alive they would always be to me. 'Let the dead bury the dead; our concern is with the living.' And I could never imagine Neal elderly – he epitomized youth.

Although I felt angry, I was grateful to Allen for writing me after he had attended Jack's funeral, and I felt somebody recognized I'd been a part of his life.

> How are you and yr children tonight? Jack's funeral very solemn. I went with Peter & Gregory & John Holmes in Holmes's car, saw Jack in coffin in Archambault funeral home on Pawtucketville St. Lowell, some name and funerary home from Jack's own memory – & pall bore thru high mass at St. Jean Baptiste Cemetery – Jack in coffin looked large-headed, grim-lipped, tiny bald spot top of skull to finger touch on his brow, fingers wrinkled, hairy hands protruding from sports jacket holding rosary, flower masses around coffin, U-shaped wrinkle-furrow familiar at his brow, eyes closed, mid-aged heavy looked like his father had become from earlier dream decades…shock first seeing him there in theatric-lit coffin room as if a Buddha in Pari-nirvana pose, come here left his message of Illusion – wink & left the body behind.

And I didn't call you before, but too much woe, life &
business on my desk till this dusk. Take care of yourself...

Every word shook me, so unaccustomed to these death customs, and
I was wracked with spasms of horror and pain, Allen's description
more detailed than even I would have noted had I been there. I knew
Jack had emphatically asked not to be buried in Catholic fashion, and
to be laid to rest beside his father and mother – later his daughter – in
Nashua, New Hampshire. Instead, the Sampas family had done it their
way and made a tourist attraction out of his simple grave with no head-
stone. Poor Jack, still a victim of other people's manipulation of him.

There was naturally more public notice of Jack's passing than of
Neal's, but not all of it was kind. The media praised Jack mildly for
his work, but condemned his life. Neal had produced no 'work' and
led a life opposed to every social decree. True, the underground press
was kinder to Jack than the majors, and the *Village Voice* of New
York carried a beautiful tribute, but they also published a ruthless
and scathing denouncement of him. Why was there this need in people
to tear down the heroes they had created?

Back in my own backyard, no sooner had I shuddered and dismissed
J.B.'s morbidity than Diana's took over. She called and called from
New York, at first telling me all the things I should do about a
funeral for Neal, the children, myself, etc. etc., like the Mother
Superior – or maybe the Super Mother? Besides, she said I should
split the ashes with her.

My blood boiled even more than it usually did when I was forced
to be in contact with this female, and I had no difficulty understanding *her*.

'Dammit, Diana, won't you ever quit? Who do you think you are?
You knew Neal only one out of his 43 years; your marriage was
void, Neal had never seen your son since he was born, and all of
that happened *twenty years* ago. Where do you get off advising *me*
anything? And now wanting part of his ashes is sickeningly morbid
and disgusting. Good God, woman! I shouldn't have had him cremated; I should have chopped him up in little pieces and passed him
around to all his women like relics – YUK; it is *revolting*!' and I hung
up the phone.

I was ashamed of my outburst afterwards, it's true, and when she
called right back, I said more calmly, 'Diana, listen once and for all

– get this through your head: I do not want to discuss Neal's ashes – ever! Now look, I don't like yelling at you; I don't want to be angry. Just be a good girl and *leave me alone*! I will not talk to you, and I'm going to hang up now.' She wasn't listening, just barrelled on. 'Diana – I'm going to hang up *now*.' And I did. She called back. This time Flo answered, and she was too nice to hang up on anyone, so she let Diana rant and rave for over an hour, giving out all sorts of fantasies, like how Neal owed her $80,000 and my children weren't his – *everybody* knew *that*. Dear Lord, would she never get off my back? What an albatross.

How much I admired Anne during all this – her selfless dignified adjustment to the death of someone at the very core of her being. When she wrote, she was still in bandages from having succumbed to silicone breast transplants, hoping to re-entice Neal. In spite of her sacrifice, her initial reaction to my telling her of his death was brief: 'I almost killed myself,' she wrote, 'but, well, it's not right to do that. I'm going home for a visit, and I'll be at my mother's. If there's anything I can do, let me know. I am so sorry. I hope you're ok. Thanks for the note...'

When she was settled at her mother's, she wrote again, still thinking more of me than of herself:

> I'm at my mother's now and wouldn't want to go to any funeral or wake. He told me to try to be a perfect human being. That means paying bills, debts, and so I've got to earn some money. I still think he's alive sometimes. So grieving is destructive. And it's difficult to see people or places which confirm the negative. Then there's joy – thinking it's all a lie because he'll really be back, just teaching us or me a lesson. I can't go on any other way. I think you must be very sad and I wish there was something I could do; I'd do anything to have him alive again. Please try to find some happiness for yourself – you've lived for him so long, and you'll get and deserve such pleasure if you'd love someone else. I love you, Carolyn. And I wish you all the tolerance, patience and devotion you've shown, and love. Anne.

In another week Anne went back to Seattle, where she had been living since Neal sent her away and she set out to carve a new life for herself. She never forgot Neal; he was still her inspiration, but when she felt insecure, she took trips to Mexico to find him. Needing him, she let herself believe he wasn't dead. Little by little over the years she accepted what was, continuing to draw sustenance from what she'd received from him, and was determined to keep on trying to be worthy of the ideal he had sowed in her consciousness.

When we first met, Anne had told me the purpose of women's existence was to make men happy. This she did liberally. She moved to the clean air of Santa Cruz, California, is a feminist, a celibate vegetarian and works on a brilliant history of female sovereignty around the world. We are still very close, and see each other once a year and correspond.

In contrast, I spent another six months fending Diana's incessant requests for ashes, until I had to succumb or go mad. I agreed to send her some if she would stop calling me. 'Yes,' she said, 'of course.' Then she said, 'You have my address?'

'Yes, Diana, I have your address.' I let her go on and on reviewing everything she'd told me a hundred times before that I'd not wanted to hear in the first place. I finally reached the point I'd do anything to turn her off.

With the utmost revulsion, I opened the silver silken bag for the first and only time and spooned a tablespoon full of ashes into a little box, feeling any minute I would faint. As rapidly as possible I expedited the wrapping and mailing and sighed, 'There now.' Again, it was an idle dream.

Every other day or so she would call with a new idea of what she would do with the ashes when they arrived. First it was to be in Jack's ancestral plot in New Hampshire.

'Great,' I said. 'Do that. Good bye.'

In another day or two: 'Do you think maybe I should buy a tree in Washington Square and bury Neal under it?'

'Oh, good grief, Diana – I've told you how I feel; do anything you want, but stop telling me about it. You're only getting a tiny spoonful.'

'Yes, I know. It's all I deserve.' Now that surprised me, coming from her. 'You know what I think I'll do?' Here we go again. 'I'm going to bury an old-fashioned quarter with him.'

'A what? Why?'

'You know – those old quarters that had an eagle on the back? Well, when you look at it one way it looks like an eagle, but going the other way it looks like a cowboy with a hard-on. Don't you think that is terribly appropriate for Neal? Really, Carolyn, isn't that a great idea?'

'Oh my God,' I groaned.

Soon after Jack's death Diana called again, just as I was settling down to watch an episode of *The Forsyte Saga* – my one sacred television indulgence. After repeated efforts to persuade her to call some other time had failed, and I was missing great gobs of important dialogue, I let fly – stamped down ruthlessly all my carefully constructed fences of redemptive behaviour. Blast the woman! 'Will you shut up a minute? Don't you ever think of anything except what happened twenty years ago? *Twenty years*, Diana, my God, woman, what are you doing with your life? And on and on condemning.

And then a strange thing happened to me. Right in the heat of my rage, it was as though I heard a click somewhere inside me, and with no pause or change in my angry tone, I went right on yelling at her, but now – I suddenly *loved* her! I began to feel warm, melting and joyous, and I listened to my words in awe. 'Now, lookit, Diana – life is to *live* – you're a young woman still – yes you are,' as she started to object. 'God gave you *life*, not age, and you're attractive – you used to be a model, remember? Well, remember things like that – let the dead past die. Life can be so great, Diana – come on, now, quit all your moaning, complaining and looking back – get out there and use your brain and good looks. You've been blessed by knowing Neal – use the gift he gave you – for good! For living!'

Now I couldn't think of enough hopeful, positive things to say to her. She had mumbled a time or two, but mainly she'd been quiet. Never before! She had always talked right through me. Could I possibly have reached her at last?

'Do it for Neal, Diana, it's what he would want you to do, don't you agree?'

'Yes – I think so. Would you send me something? Some literature?' I could hardly believe my ears. She was as excited as I was, and it felt good. I hoped a seed had been planted, and I vaguely wondered if Neal had anything to do with this.

We ended the conversation dripping with compliments, sweetness and light. Love conquers all. And I was ecstatic – by golly – I bet I was free of her at last! How funny, me who was forever preaching you can only change your environment by changing your own mind, and I'd never thought to apply that to Diana.

She soon gave me the chance to test this theory. In a few more days she called again to tell me she had received the ashes.

'Thank you very much!' she said warmly, sincerely. 'You know they arrived on my husband's birthday, and my daughter put them beside his plate with his other gifts!' She squealed with delight, while I held my breath. 'But I rescued them just in time; he didn't see them – ha ha ha – and now I've finally decided what to do with them. I want your approval.' I sighed. I hadn't made a dent in her understanding of my views. But now I only felt amused, not defiant or angry, that in itself a relief.

'Okay, Diana, let's have it; what now?'

'Well, I telephoned Jack's wife in Florida. Of course, she doesn't know who I am, but I asked her if I could bury Neal's ashes in Jack's grave.' I couldn't help an involuntary spasm.

'And what did Stella say?'

'Actually, she sounded pleased. She said she hadn't been able to afford a proper tombstone yet, but when she sells the house in Florida she'll be coming back to Lowell, and she wants to do it then. She said I could meet her there. Isn't that just wonderful?'

'Wonderful, honey.'

'We'll have a nice little ceremony, you know, something simple, and maybe I'll get a plaque – something about Neal being buried in Jack's heart. Don't you think that would be fitting?'

'Anything you say. Do it any way you like; you have my blessing.'

'Yes – I think it will be nice. Now – I'd like to do something for you. I'll place a bet for you on the Derby – I've really gotten into it! Which horse do you want to win? Pick any one you like. Two dollars, okay?'

'Lovely. Put it on the third choice, Di, in memory of Neal.'

— THE END —

Index

Gatos 255–64, 268–69, 272–76, 344–48, 356–59; seaman 211; ranger 271; in New York with AG 279–80; in Tangiers 280; publication of *On the Road* 282–85; in California, 1959 332–33; *Big Sur* 351–56; 1961 379, 384–85; at NC's death 425; after NC's death 432–34; Buddhism 209, 224–25, 229–30, 234, 270–71; death and funeral 434–35; obituaries 434; grave 439; relations with CC 28–30, 160–64, 190–95, 199–200, 273; letters to CC 200, 202, 204–5, 211–12, 237, 245, 255, 269, 324–25, 338, 359–60, 366, 370, 371, 386; relations with NC 14, 16–17, 181, 182–83, 183–84, 244–45; letters to NC 132, 183–84, 201, 202, 210–11, 219, 227, 229–40, 233, 244–45, 280, 281, 282, 366; NC's letters to 16–17, 43, 45–46, 49, 49–50, 55, 68, 70, 72, 94–95, 96, 97–98, 123, 125, 130–31, 138, 143, 144–45, 187, 220, 332; works: *Big Sur* 360, 366, 385; *Desolation Angels* 338, 366; *The Dharma Bums* 329; *Doctor Sax* 184, 185, 193, 432; *On the Road* 142–43,

157, 181, 184, 203, 216, 237, 269, 275; (after publication) 281, 282–83, 310; *Pull My Daisy* (film) 283, 333; *The Town and the City* 50, 95, 155, 190, 212; *The Subterraneans* 239; *Visions of Gerard* 366

Kerouac, Joan (second wife of JK) 134, 144, 149, 175

Kerouac, 'Memere' (mother of JK) 87, 173, 194, 200, 229, 271, 281, 282, 385, 425

Kerouac, Stella (third wife of JK) 425, 439

Kesey, Faye 393

Kesey, Ken 389, 390, 394, 396, 403, 406, 408, 410, 419

La Honda, CA 390, 393

Langley-Porter Clinic 138–39

Larkspur, CA 415

LaVigne, Bob 243

Lawrence, D.H. 430

LeVey, Anton 400, 402

Life 332, 338, 343

Lish, Gordon 388–89, 393, 431

Los Angeles 25, 32, 35, 176, 423, 426

Los Gatos, CA 238–439; ballet school 240;

Los Gatos Times Observer 293

Los Gatos Tire Company 350

Lowell, MA 325, 385, 425

Overlook Illustrated Lives

Samuel Beckett
978-1-58567-266-0

William Faulkner
978-1-58567-542-5

F. Scott Fitzgerald
978-1-58567-265-3

Henry James
978-1-58567-543-2

Franz Kafka
978-1-58567-267-7

Vladimir Nabokov
978-1-58567-263-9

Marcel Proust
978-1-58567-405-3

Ayn Rand
978-1-58567-406-0

Virginia Woolf
978-1-58567-264-6

The Overlook Press • Woodstock & New York • www.overlookpress.com